EVALUATION and POVERTY REDUCTION

World Bank Series on Evaluation and Development
Robert Picciotto, Series Editor

Evaluation and Development:
The Institutional Dimension
edited by Robert Picciotto and Eduardo Wiesner

Involuntary Resettlement:
Comparative Perspectives
edited by Robert Picciotto, Warren van Wicklin,
and Edward Rice

Evaluation and Poverty Reduction
edited by Osvaldo N. Feinstein and Robert Picciotto

EVALUATION and POVERTY REDUCTION

World Bank Series on
Evaluation and Development
Volume 3

Edited by Osvaldo N. Feinstein
and Robert Picciotto

Foreword by James D. Wolfensohn

Transaction Publishers
New Brunswick (U.S.A.) and London (U.K.)

Copyright © 2001 by The World Bank. Published by Transaction Publishers, New Brunswick, New Jersey.

All rights reserved under International and Pan-American Copyright Conventions. No part of this book may be reproduced or transmitted in any form or by any means, electronic or mechanical, including photocopy, recording, or any information storage and retrieval system, without prior permission in writing from the publisher. All inquiries should be addressed to Transaction Publishers, Rutgers—The State University, 35 Berrue Circle, Piscataway, New Jersey 08854-8042.

This book is printed on acid-free paper that meets the American National Standard for Permanence of Paper for Printed Library Materials.

Library of Congress Catalog Number: 00-067305
ISBN: 0-7658-0092-6 (cloth); 0-7658-0876-5 (paper)
Printed in Canada

Library of Congress Cataloging-in-Publication Data

Evaluation and poverty reduction / edited by Osvaldo Feinstein and Robert Picciotto; foreword by James D. Wolfensohn.
    p. cm.—(World Bank series on evaluation and development ; 3)
    Includes bibliographical references and index.
    ISBN 0-7658-0092-6 (cloth : alk. paper)—ISBN 0-7658-0876-5 (paper : alk. paper)
    1. Poverty—Evaluation—Methodology. I. Feinstein, Osvaldo Néstor. II. Picciotto, Robert. III. Series.

HC79 .P6 E9 2001
339. 4'6—dc21   00-067305

Contents

ACKNOWLEDGMENTS		vii
FOREWORD		ix
James D. Wolfensohn		
WELCOME ADDRESSES		xiii
Jan Piercy and Elizabeth McAllister		

PART I: INTRODUCTION: IDENTIFYING THE CHALLENGES

Synthesis and Overview *Osvaldo Feinstein and Detlev Puetz* ... 3

PART II: EVALUATION: A MACRO PERSPECTIVE

1. **Valuation and Evaluation** ... 19
   Partha Dasgupta
   Floor Discussion ... 36
2. **Evaluation in a World of Complexity and Information Failures** ... 39
   Joseph Stiglitz
   Floor Discussion ... 49
3. **Panel Discussion: Evaluation Perspectives on Poverty Reduction** ... 51
   Vinod Thomas, Alison Evans, Moise Mensah, Niels Dabelstein
   Floor Discussion ... 58

PART III: METHODOLOGICAL ISSUES IN EVALUATION

4. **Impact Evaluation: Concepts and Methods** ... 65
   Kene Ezemenari, Anders Rudqvist, Kalanidhi Subbarao
   Comments *Thomas Cook, James Heckman* ... 76
   Floor Discussion ... 85
5. **Panel Discussion: Quantitative and Qualitative Methods in Evaluation** ... 89
   Timothy Marchant, Sarah Gavian, John Eriksson
   Floor Discussion ... 101
6. **Theory-Based Evaluation: Theories of Change for Poverty Reduction Programs** ... 103
   Carol H. Weiss

PART IV: PARTICIPATORY EVALUATION: COSTS AND BENEFITS

7. **The Front-End Costs and Downstream Benefits of Participatory Evaluation** — 115
   Edward T. Jackson
   Comments *Nicoletta Stame* — 127
   Floor Discussion — 131

8. **Building Local Capacity for Participatory Monitoring and Evaluation** — 133
   Rolf Sartorius
   Comments *David Marsden* — 144
   Floor Discussion — 147

PART V: POVERTY-REDUCING GROWTH

9. **Africa and Asia: Evaluation of the Poverty Alleviation Impact of Alternative Development Strategies and Adjustment Responses** — 151
   Erik Thorbecke
   Comments *Richard Gerster* — 163
   Floor discussion — 166

10. **Lessons Learned from Evaluation of DFID's Aid Program** — 171
    Andrew Shepherd
    Comments *Octavio Damiani* — 184
    Floor Discussion — 187

PART VI: SECTORAL AND MICROLEVEL INTERVENTIONS

11. **Evaluating Microfinance's Impact: Going Down Market** — 193
    Monique Cohen
    Comments *Mohini Malhotra* — 204

12. **Evaluating Targeted Versus Nontargeted Approaches to Poverty Reduction** — 209
    Joachim von Braun, Mona Bishay, Sohail J. Malik
    Floor Discussion — 218

PART VII: SOCIAL FUNDS AND SAFETY NETS

13. **What Are Social Funds Really Telling Us?** — 223
    Judith Tendler
    Comments *Soniya Carvalho* — 228
    Floor Discussion — 231

14. **Economic Crises and Social Protection for the Poor: The Latin American Experience** — 235
    Nora Lustig, Arianna Legovini
    Comments *Raghav Gaiha* — 246
    Floor Discussion — 248

PART VIII: DEVELOPMENT EFFECTIVENESS IN HEALTH, NUTRITION, AND POPULATION SERVICES

15. Delivering Social Services: Lessons on Health, Nutrition, and Population — 253
    Susan Stout
    Comments Margaret Goodman — 264
    Floor Discussion — 266

PART IX: CRISIS PREVENTION

16. Tackling Horizontal Inequalities — 271
    Frances Stewart
    Comments Lawrence Haddad — 284
    Floor Discussion — 288
17. Governance and Anticorruption: New Insights and Challenges — 289
    Daniel Kaufmann
    Comments Anwar Shah — 295
    Floor Discussion — 299
18. Panel Discussion: Combating Public Corruption
    Jack Titsworth, Navin Girishankar, El Sayed Zaki — 301

PART X: SOCIAL INCLUSION AND CIVIL SOCIETY

19. Nongovernmental Organizations and Evaluation: The BRAC Experience — 311
    Salehuddin Ahmed, Mohammad Rafi
    Comments Ariel Fiszbein — 322
    Floor Discussion — 325
20. Social Exclusion and Rural Underdevelopment — 329
    Adolfo Figueroa
    Comments Aloysius Fernandes — 338
    Floor Discussion — 340

PART XI: CONCLUSIONS

21. Panel Discussion: Final Roundtable — 345
    Frances Stewart, Ravi Kanbur, Joachim von Braun, Nora Lustig
    Floor Discussion — 352
22. Concluding Remarks — 355
    Robert Picciotto

LIST OF AUTHORS AND DISCUSSANTS — 363

INDEX — 367

Acknowledgments

The Swiss Agency for Development Cooperation (SDC) provided important support for the organization of the workshop and the publication of this proceedings volume. SDC's cooperation is gratefully acknowledged.

The Royal Norwegian Ministry of Foreign Affairs and the United Kingdom's Department for International Development enabled the participation of developing country evaluators and policy makers.

Detlev Puetz made a distinguished contribution to the organization of the 1999 conference and supported the initial editorial work. OED's Outreach and Dissemination team, led by Elizabeth Campbell-Pagé, played a key role during the editing and production of this book.

The Conference was jointly organized by the Operations Evaluation Department (OED) and the World Bank Institute (WBI).

Foreword

James D. Wolfensohn

I am delighted that this conference is a joint effort of the World Bank's Operations Evaluation Department (OED) and the World Bank Institute (WBI). I am also grateful to our guests for coming here to participate in our ongoing search for knowledge and evaluation.

Evaluation is a central aspect of any poverty reduction endeavor. Evaluation implies that we have adopted a methodology that allows us to look in an effective way at the results of what we are doing so that we can, in turn, adapt our future actions toward the effective achievement of our goals.

Evaluation adds value if we can learn something useful from it. It is not just a scorecard. It is something that helps us change our behavior or influence the behavior of others. When we do not do that, we lose a tremendous advantage of the evaluative process.

I am committed to evaluation—to having the results of the evaluative process incorporated in the learning agenda of the World Bank. Evaluation is needed not because what we are doing so far is not right, but because we do not yet have the answers to some fundamental issues.

Setting Goals Broader Than Individual Projects

I have been at the Bank for four years. I come from a discipline where results become clear fairly quickly so that managers know whether they have achieved their goals or not. In the development business, however, we work with a range of goals in trying to confront poverty in a sustainable way. For instance, targets such as those formulated by the Development Assistance Committee of the Organization for Economic

Cooperation and Development (OECD) call for halving the percentage of poverty over a predetermined period, for raising school enrollments, and for enhancing gender equality. Can these targets be achieved? While the percentage of poor people is diminishing in some countries, the absolute number is increasing. Over the last five years, we have moved from a world total of 1.3 billion people who live on less than US$1 a day to more than 1.4 billion people. Three billion people live on less than US$2 a day. At the same time, the absolute numbers of people without access to clean water, health care, and sewerage systems are moving in the same direction.

Evaluators should look closely at the interdependencies and synergies among the different targets. For instance, what are the implications of making health care accessible where there are no sewerage systems? What happens if education but not health care is brought to communities? How effective is a school built with communal help that only serves a third or a half of the number of school-age children because there are no roads? And if the school situation is dire and teachers have not been paid for months what is the likely quality of education?

If you want to evaluate the effect of projects by international donors to improve road infrastructure, you have to see whether the roads were built to the ministers' houses or to the markets. Roads built to the markets help the poor people market their chickens or eggs. So continuous evaluation is needed, not only at the end when the road is already built, but also prior to project implementation. We need to measure quality in terms of poverty impact at entry. Bad quality at entry leads to poor results.

People tell me that we should be doing more poverty projects. But what is a poverty project? Quite apart from macroeconomic and financial policy, a functioning legal system and a functioning justice system that work are poverty projects, as are good governance and fighting corruption. We have just seen in Indonesia, the Republic of Korea, and Thailand that those hit hardest by an economic crisis are the poor. The poor benefit from proper financial supervision and control, an independent central bank, well functioning capital markets, and social safety nets. Can one distinguish building roads, or a power grid, or a water supply system, or a judicial system, or good governance from poverty reduction? These are the questions which evaluators need to address.

The Comprehensive Development Framework as a Multidisciplinary Approach for Poverty Alleviation, Partnerships, and Evaluation

In the Comprehensive Development Framework (CDF), there is a list of sectors that must be developed to alleviate poverty: education, knowledge, health care, water, sanitation, roads, and power. Where basic infrastructure is lacking, carrying water and gathering fuel are time-consuming activities that hold women back.

How can the effectiveness of these activities be evaluated? This cannot be done accurately in terms of a singular project but in the broader context of measuring the interdisciplinary impact of what we are doing. How do we measure the impact of judicial reform on poverty? How do we measure the impact of rural roads on poverty? How do we prioritize our efforts in water and power? I do not know the answers, but I do know that we have to bring together a whole sequence of issues if an economy is to develop in an equitable way. I know that this is hard to do.

I support the evaluative work being done on individual projects, but what about those at the national level? When is scaling up feasible? How do we move from project to nation?

The CDF tries to establish priorities with governments, with nongovernmental organizations (NGOs), and with the private sector, not by imposing the Bank's leadership, but by encouraging debate and promoting participation. We also want better information and better ways of assessing the results of what we are doing in this broader context. This is why I look forward eagerly to the results of this conference.

Welcome Addresses

Jan Piercy, Elizabeth McAllister

Jan Piercy

It is a privilege to be invited to welcome you here and to open the conference on behalf of the Bank's executive directors. We represent the 180 shareholders of the Bank. We are a full-time, resident Board of 24 here in Washington. Through a system of Board committees, we provide direction to, oversight of, and accountability for, the Bank's work.

One of the committees that was created only a few years ago was the Committee on Development Effectiveness, of which I am the chair. It became the committee through which OED reports to the Board—it is the only part of the Bank that does report directly to the Board, in order to provide for independence and objectivity in the evaluation function. Until we had the committee, there was no real nexus where we came together, so it has been an exciting, at times very controversial, committee. Our discussions and the OED reports have often elicited management responses that have led us to grapple not so much with the legitimacy of the findings but with their realism in terms of the capacity of the Bank and its partners to implement the findings. We wrestle with the implications of OED's findings for the design of new programs and how we do our work, which is fundamentally the critical question for our going forward.

When James Wolfensohn became president of the Bank, he was impatient with our evaluation function. He did not dispute its caliber or its importance, but he wanted it to work faster, sooner, and in real time. If it is going to have an impact on what we do and how we do it, then we need to know closer to the inception and operation of actual programs whether they are the right interventions and whether they work. If some programs did not work, why not? What should we take from them to better influence what we do in the future?

His impatience led him to endorse a recommendation of the Director-General, Operations Evalaution, and create the Quality Assurance Group to work with OED to try to begin earlier in the project cycle to embed in the design of programs the kinds of indicators and monitoring systems that would ensure greater effectiveness. You can tell me better than I can tell you that this is not easy. Knowing the right questions to ask and how to design evaluation in a way that ensures the integrity and usability of its results is not straightforward, but the pressure for results has strengthened the importance of evaluation within the Bank's operations.

> The pressure for results has strengthened the importance of evaluation within the Bank's operations.

That said, this meeting is important to all of us. I stand here today as a consumer of evaluation. Development policy makers depend on your thinking, so your coming together—from across organizations, across institutions, across academia, to development organizations and multilaterals like the Bank—helps us agree better than we have in the past on ways in which we can measure our effectiveness and feed the results directly into what we do.

We should all share a sense of urgency at the current statistics on poverty. I feel tremendous frustration that in the nearly five years in which I have had the privilege of representing the United States on the Board of the Bank we have seen poverty reduction numbers going in the wrong direction. Certainly we have seen the inequities and a widening divide within societies between those who have economic mobility and are benefiting from a global economy and others who seem to be locked out. This extends even to my own society: we in the United States know that we do not have all the answers. The kind of research that is under way in the United States on the results of poverty reduction interventions is not yet conclusive.

How can we best evaluate and measure our impact on poverty reduction? What have we learned from experience? What can we do better? How can we begin to tell a better story about what works and what does not work in reducing poverty?

Let me dwell on this one as someone who is in the position of representing a shareholder of the World Bank. In recent years our work has expanded to include a focus on how we tell the story, because unless we are successful in demonstrating that development interventions work, we will not be successful in securing public support for the financing that is necessary for bilateral and multilateral development assistance. A recent Bank report, *Reassessing Aid*, looked at the environment needed for development interventions to succeed. In some quarters, that has been interpreted to be a good policy environment, because if you do not have a government that is receptive to reforms, we do not belong there at all. Does this mean that we are going to walk away from the millions of people in poverty in less than perfect economies? Or are we going to be led by the implications of our research to ask how we can design appropriate interventions with appropriate partners?

In recent years the Bank has come to know that some of the most effective work is being done in civil society, and in some cases in civil society where governments are not as committed to reducing poverty. How does an organization like the Bank partner effectively interact with civil society organizations? We still have a lot to learn, and we are, after all, owned by our member governments.

So you can see that my colleagues on the Board and I are keen to learn about what works and for findings by researchers such as yourselves that we can use to make the case for continued engagement in international development assistance. Unfortunately, what is most likely to be publicized are the interventions that are ineffective. However, I have been encouraged by much that I have been seeing recently, and I think we now have better tools to evaluate our projects and ourselves. It is up to me and others of us who are committed to securing public funds to use your findings to make a constructive case for staying with this international commitment, which is important to sustain.

I alluded earlier to the question of how we can balance the inherently long-term nature of achieving results in a development program with the demand for quicker insights as to whether we are on the right track. How can you do short-term work along a long-term horizon? We are challenged by the tension between knowing that in reality it will take a long time, which cannot be abbreviated, to know the effects of our work and knowing that public policymakers must have some early indicators of the effects of our work to sustain their commitment to financing it. I expect that managing this tension will be one topic of your discussions.

Let me go through a few other questions on our mind at the Board that might inform individual research and the collective discussions of the conference.

First, questions that have assumed greater prominence in the past few years in the multilateral arena: What is the role of good governance and anticorruption in the fight against poverty? How do we diagnose the problem, and how do we evaluate the correlations with poverty?

Second, have rural and urban growth strategies reduced or exacerbated poverty? Which interventions have been most positive? Which have been negative? What shall we take from this for our future directions? The Bank has recently entered into a partnership with Habitat, for example, in recognition of the need to look beyond our individual work in infrastructure on the one hand and education on the other, to ask what strategies for an urban area will maximize the effectiveness of a focus on education, on health, and on infrastructure, and to ask about the interactivity of individual interventions. We very much need your help in this arena.

Third, how has the recent financial crisis affected the poor? What are we learning about the efficacy and limitations of social safety nets and social funds in protecting the poor? How can we prevent future crises or mitigate their impact on the poor?

Fourth, what about the methodological issues of impact evaluation? Building on our experience using participatory approaches, holding stakeholder consultations, and combining quantitative and qualitative methods has assumed a new urgency since January, when James Wolfensohn talked about the CDF, a vision for bringing together all the actors in a society's development and working on all the areas that need strengthening to produce sustainable economic development.

This is conceptually compelling, but actually doing it is challenging, given individual, bilateral, and multilateral priorities; the increasing role of the private sector; and the civil societies that are still in formation or changing governance. The call for participatory evaluation is something no one can fault, but it also alters the budget and the timeline within which this is all taking place. So there are many different considerations to reconcile.

Fifth, how do we evaluate the extent of social exclusion and inclusion and the critical role of civil society? Sometimes I feel here at the Bank Board a little like David, the Bank being Goliath. The Bank is so large that it does not yet know how to partner effectively with smaller organizations in civil society. Yet when I look at individual case studies, I am convinced that the most cost-effective and sustainable interventions are the ones carried out on a small scale that is difficult for the Bank to reach.

During the recent financial crisis, a great deal of pressure was exerted on the Bank to conduct rapidly disbursing operations with few conditions or little specificity about what program results we were seeking in return for the financing. Indeed, some external critics might say that we had begun to look a lot like the International Monetary Fund, providing liquidity rather than development finance. So I am not sure that the recent financial crisis did not take us in some respects off course from our focus on forming long-term partnerships with our borrowing member governments through operations that will reduce poverty and make for sustainable development and growth.

Sixth, what is our experience with so-called pro-poor growth and what does that mean? Different organizations use it almost as a rallying cry but without sufficient intellectual underpinnings to support one set of interventions over another. I am particularly interested in what you will have to say about the impact evaluation of microfinance interventions. In my own experience with microfinance, both in Bangladesh and the United States, I have seen some powerful consequences that extend well beyond financial transactions into increasing demand for education and better standards of health. In other words, I see microfinance to be much more holistic than one might assume from just looking at a free-standing operation.

Finally, what lessons are we learning about the delivery of social services? An active debate is under way in the Bank and elsewhere on the relative (and appropriate) roles in the delivery of social services of government versus the private and not-for-profit sectors. Recently, for example, the International Finance Corporation (IFC), our private sector arm, has been looking hard at whether it should have a significantly expanded role in financing health and education. This, of course, immediately raises a host of questions. For example, does financing the private delivery of education in developing countries simply siphon off some of the financially better-off students from the public system into a private system? Or does it reduce pressure on governments so that they can better focus on people who cannot afford education? It is probably some of both, but there is a whole range of questions here. I certainly will be calling for financing in education at the Board level as we discuss the IFC's strategy in the next few weeks. I will be calling from the outset for embedding the kind of evaluative questions that will enable us along the way to assess whether we are on the right course and what some of the consequences of our actions might be.

This is by necessity a full and comprehensive agenda, and I have by no means exhausted the list of questions. Easy, quick-fix answers are not available. Poverty is a complex issue. It relates to social will and values even beyond economics. Multidimensional in nature, it is going to require a multisectoral response, and that is why I am so pleased to see so many disciplines and organizations represented here today. With the caliber of expertise here for this meeting, I am sure you are going to learn some new lessons and send some new challenges back to the Bank Group. So as a consumer of evaluation I thank you for assembling, and I look forward to the outcome of your deliberations.

Elizabeth McAllister

I am pleased to welcome you to the third biennial evaluation conference, sponsored jointly by WBI and OED. Before we start, I would like to thank some of OED's important partners: the Swiss Agency for Development Cooperation, which has supported the conference financially and in spirit, and the Royal Ministry of Foreign Affairs of Norway and the United Kingdom's Department for International Development (DFID), for supporting the attendance of our developing country participants.

A recent Bank report on poverty told us that the global picture that emerged in the 1990s was one of stalled progress, with the exception of China. We see rising numbers of poor people in India, continued rises in Sub-Saharan Africa, and a sharp worsening in Eastern Europe and Central Asia. By the end of 1999 we could see 1.5 billion people living on less than US$1 a day, and if the proportion—which is about 30 percent of the world's population—remains the same, the absolute number of poor people could grow to 1.8 billion by 2015. We are also seeing that some countries are losing ground in the critical areas of education and health, and in many countries few people have access to safe water. In Cambodia, for example, only 13 percent of people have access to safe water, and in Mozambique, 24 percent. At the present rate of progress, one-third of all low-income people—more than 900 million—will still lack adequate sanitation in 2015.

OED's 1998 *Annual Review of Development Effectiveness* predicted that the Asian crisis could delay the achievement of the Development Assistance Committee's 21st century goals by five years. Our goal over the next two days is to explore ways to contribute to poverty reduction as an evaluation community.

Our three objectives are to identify lessons learned from our past efforts to evaluate poverty reduction programs; to search for the new evaluation frontier in methodology for future poverty reduction programs; and to discuss how partnerships in evaluation can be promoted and how evaluation results can be used more effectively.

The CDF that the Bank has put forward is based on a more holistic approach to development: breaking the barriers that separate economics, the social sciences, and the biological sciences and looking for ways to sustain economic and social development and encourage growth. Also important in the CDF, and guiding us all, is an increased emphasis on partnership. We know that none of us can do it alone. Resources are being reduced, and we need to work more effectively as a community with the resources we have to meet the increasing challenges ahead.

As Pascal once said, "In order to discover hope, we need to lift our gaze on high." We hope that the next two days will help us all lift our gaze as we learn from one another.

Introduction:
Identifying the Challenges

Synthesis and Overview

Osvaldo Feinstein and Detlev Puetz

Poverty reduction was the theme of the third Biennial World Bank Conference on Evaluation and Development, held in Washington, D.C., in June 1999. The conference was sponsored jointly by two World Bank departments, the Operations Evaluation Department (OED) and the World Bank Institute (WBI). It brought together more than 250 representatives of the international development evaluation community, including bilateral and multilateral donor agencies and civil society.

In plenary sessions and break-out groups, conference participants discussed lessons learned from evaluations of poverty reduction programs; ways to advance the methodological frontier; partnerships, ownership, and participation in evaluation. The participants also explored challenges for the evaluation of poverty reduction programs, both in methodology and in setting substantive priorities.

The conference provided ample opportunity for debate through parallel group sessions, audience questions and comments, and electronic messaging.

The addresses of the plenary sessions are presented, as well as papers, comments, and excerpts from floor discussions. Conference topics include the role of targeted and pro-poor growth policies and programs for poverty reduction; the design of social funds, safety nets, crisis prevention, and social service delivery mechanisms; and ways to include civil society and private sector institutions more effectively in development.

Evaluation methodologies figured prominently in the conference discussions, not only in the discussion group devoted to methodological issues, but also in plenary and thematic break-out sessions. Methodological discussions centered on measuring development impact, with special emphasis on factoring in externalities, choosing appropriate counterfactuals, and including randomization in evaluation design. Mechanisms, benefits, and costs of participatory evaluations were also discussed extensively.

The variety of papers and panel presentations and the intensity of floor discussions and web site interactions valuable lessons for designing and implementing evaluations and poverty reduction interventions.

From a "Bustling Marketplace of Ideas" to Lasting Lessons

The conference was a "bustling marketplace of ideas" (Robert Picciotto). Hence, these proceedings include a variety of views and approaches to addressing and evaluating poverty reduction. This overview chapter highlights the main areas of consensus, emerging agreement, and continuing debate. The focus is on lessons learned from evaluations of poverty reduction, challenges the evaluation community faces in designing and prioritizing future evaluations of poverty reduction programs, and ways to maximize the utility and impact of future evaluation efforts. As Vinod Thomas stated, improved interactions and complementarities among the various actors may help us to address poverty reduction more effectively.

Conference participants were interested in learning from the past and in learning if, and under what conditions, successful and exemplary interventions could be scaled up and replicated. In the words of Jan Piercy, "Unless we are successful in demonstrating that development interventions work, we will not be successful in securing public support for the financing that is necessary for bilateral and multilateral development assistance."

Lessons Learned from Evaluations

Poverty Reduction: What Works?

What major lessons have we learned from evaluations of poverty-reducing growth strategies, social development and crisis management, and institutional development? The following describe successful approaches to reducing poverty:

- **Make development interventions context-specific.** Above all, the development community must acknowledge the diversity and context-specificity of the poverty problem. Although Erik Thorbecke reports an emerging consensus regarding the major strategic elements that have caused poverty to retreat more quickly in some regions than in others, no blueprint exists on the specifics of such factors. Optimal solutions differ by region and target group. Although basic values may be similar across the development community (Partha Dasgupta), diversity of opinion and development priorities, as well as political will and political economy factors,

should be recognized (Raghav Gaiha, Andrew Shepherd). The question is how best to deal with and address such differences in evaluation.
- **Take a holistic view.** Poverty is a complex and multifaceted issue that relates to values and goes far beyond economics. Such complexity precludes quick-fix answers. The multidimensional nature of poverty requires a multisectoral response (James Wolfensohn, Jan Piercy, Joseph Stiglitz). Development agencies and governments will have to work together to deal with the holistic and complementary nature of poverty-reducing interventions. Thinking broadly to achieve coherent results may be a precondition for coordinating programs and service delivery more effectively and evaluating the benefits and costs of specialization, joint planning, and partnerships. Yet, from a practical perspective, Tim Frankenberger suggests that a clear distinction is needed between the holistic *programming* and the holistic *analysis* of poverty reduction.
- **Broaden the poverty concept.** Poverty is location specific. The perceptions of the poor themselves are of paramount importance, and cultural differences must be considered. For example, while Indian development practitioners focus on income poverty reduction, Mozambique policy makers frame an attack on structural poverty, and a participatory poverty assessment in Zambia saw widows' lack of access to land and other assets as the key obstacle to poverty reduction (Sheperd). Defining deprivation in terms of needs and rights and moving beyond drawing the line at a predetermined income cut-off are important. Operationalizing the poverty concept in broad terms is a major challenge. We will have to identify indicators for all the components that make up poverty, such as livelihood, access to resources, knowledge, and rights, to identify the optimal point for policy and program interventions.

Pro-Poor Growth and Targeting

Conference participants extensively debated the merits of broad-based growth, or universal provisioning, versus targeted policies and programs.

Results from a recent OED evaluation of the World Bank's 1990 strategy on poverty reduction (*World Development Report 1990*), presented by Alison Evans and Sohail Malik, show that even projects without explicit poverty reduction objectives can have a significant impact on poverty. For instance, World Bank general water infrastructure projects yield major health benefits for the poor. The OED poverty study also points out that the success of targeted poverty programs depends on the presence of broad-based, complementary activities and favorable socioeconomic environments. For example, microfinance projects for the poor rarely achieve the expected increase in income without parallel investments in communication, infrastructure, and information dissemination.

Yet, Malik reports that Bank projects that were designed as targeted interventions usually had better overall outcomes and similar sustainability ratings, but generally fared less well in institutional development impact.

Joachim von Braun argues that policymakers should not get carried away by focussing too narrowly on targeting or by assuming that all infrastructure investments or improvements in governance will automatically alleviate poverty. Programs and interventions that target the poor should be embedded in broad-based programs, such as public health services, which often indirectly—or even directly—benefit the poor. Potentially high administrative and opportunity costs of operational targeting have to be carefully assessed in view of the expected benefits. Referring to examples of the widespread gains brought about by the green revolution, the recent allocation of mobile phones to poor women in Bangladesh, the identification of malnourished children through universal anthropometric screening, and the collateral benefits of self-targeted public work programs for general infrastructure development, von Braun's basic policy prescription is not just to design and develop public goods for economic growth and social development broadly, but also to ensure access by the poor.

Mona Bishay further examines the important elements of well-designed targeting and of increasing the engagement of the poor in program design and implementation. Bishay notes that more needs to be learned about how to shift targeting costs from design to implementation and how to target the poor in areas with higher potential.

What have we learned about the efficacy, scope, and limitations of social funds and safety nets in protecting the poor, particularly during times of economic and political crises? How can we improve the effectiveness and efficiency of social services that target the poor? How can we better prevent future crises and mitigate the impact of unavoidable crises on the poor? These were some of the major questions considered in the break-out discussion group on social development.

Social Funds and Safety Nets

Judith Tendler challenged some of the key assumptions about the performance of social funds as a major instrument for mitigating the social costs of structural adjustment and macroeconomic turbulence. She posed several questions. Are social funds truly participatory and demand driven, or are they becoming increasingly politicized and bureaucratic, possibly depriving line ministries of valuable resources and incentives for reorganization? Are social funds sustainable? Above all, does their often limited coverage justify the costs incurred? She advocated more careful evaluation of funds that have been successful.

In response, Soniya Carvalho called for an understanding of effective service delivery that encompasses the combination of supply and demand in varying proportions and intensities, depending on the country and sector context and the nature and scale of the services being provided She rejected the black and white notion that often sees social funds as demand driven and government programs as supply driven. Carvalho also offered a specific evaluative framework being used by OED to assess alternative service delivery instruments.

Arianna Legovini and Nora Lustig argued that countries exposed to shocks need to better understand the impact of macroeconomic policy reforms, the needs associated with poverty-sensitive fiscal adjustment, and the importance of preserving human capital to establish comprehensive social safety nets that can provide a quick response and are better targeted to those most hurt by an emergency. They noted that the evaluative tools currently available are insufficient to assess the effects of macroeconomic policies on the poor. Until such tools are available, they recommended linking the effects of economywide developments, especially on labor demand and relative price changes, to the profile of key socioeconomic groups, drawing on existing poverty profiles and survey information. The authors also called for the establishment of social monitoring and early response units that can track danger signals of crises and mobilize research on relevant issues by employing community monitoring and qualitative evaluation techniques for quick turnaround reports.

Raghav Gaiha drew attention to the political aspects of macroeconomic policy reforms, microlevel interventions, and poverty alleviation. For Gaiha, building coalitions—of political parties, unions, professional associations, and the like—is vital to initiate and sustain reforms. Generating lasting democratic institutions is necessary because the political will to alleviate poverty cannot be taken for granted. Drawing on some disappointing experience with India's *panchayats,* elected village bodies in charge of development and poverty alleviation, Gaiha pointed out that much more needs to be known about the conditions necessary for the effective functioning of coalitions for poverty alleviation and the political obstacles that stand in the way.

Social Services

In her presentation of a recent World Bank study of the development effectiveness of Bank work in the health, nutrition, and population sector, Susan Stout emphasized the need to focus on consumer-level accountability and to develop measures of outcome that both consumers and providers find easy to understand. This means enhancing quality assurance and results orientation, increasing learning from past and current programs, strengthening partnerships and the strategic selectivity and quality of interventions, giving voice to consumers, and avoiding complex project designs. More needs to be learned about the causes of poor health among the poor and how to target this population with appropriate information, education, and communication campaigns and how to craft the policy and regulatory changes needed. Margaret Goodman added that development banks often look at things from a technical point of view. In health, nutrition, and population programs, development does not happen that way. Past evaluations and experience have shown that where the disadvantaged finally have achieved better social services, they have also gained some political power.

Crisis Prevention and Management

Discussions under this theme, introduced by Frances Stewart, dealt mainly with conflict mitigation and early warning systems. Stewart identified horizontal inequities among ethnic, racial, and religious groups as a main contributing factor to conflict, and noted that conflict itself is one of the major sources of poverty around the world. She challenged the evaluation community to obtain better data on potential hot spots, horizontal inequity, and early warning systems. Tracking factors that predispose a country to conflict and introducing policies to offset excessive horizontal inequalities are important in this regard.

Lawrence Haddad suggested studying horizontal inequalities, particularly the reasons for governmental failure to adopt poverty-alleviating policies that could reduce the propensity for conflict and the high transaction costs of reaching disadvantaged groups. He also pointed to the rich gender literature.

Informal Social Security and Insurance Systems

Several contributions and discussion groups included in the volume call for a better understanding of, and stronger support for, traditional social security and insurance systems for the poor. We are challenged in our evaluations to better understand the functioning of informal systems, nonmarket mechanisms, and traditional group mechanisms, and how these systems respond and change in the face of dramatic economic and political changes, if we wish to identify entry points for policy, program, or project interventions.

Institutional Change

The participants agreed that bringing about institutional change and evaluating this change in the context of social capital and the impact generated is a major challenge for future poverty alleviation efforts. As Robert Picciotto notes, the new concept of social change promoted by the neoinstitutionalist school of thought has fundamental implications for development strategies in general and evaluation in particular. He further states that the focus must be on organizations, the players in the game that generate the policies and programs that transform society. Poverty reduction requires major changes in beliefs and values, as well as massive institutional adjustments of state, market, and voluntary sector organizations. Leadership is needed to bring about change and social learning and to improve our tools for measuring progress in building institutions, social capital, and governance.

Civil Society, Governance, and Anticorruption Programs

The role of civil society and the private sector in poverty reduction was extensively debated. The participants considered that one of the important contributions of these organizations is their ability to compensate for poor governance and combat widespread public corruption. When endemic corruption limits the capacity of the state to provide public goods, alternative mechanisms for service delivery are needed. Corruption inflates the cost and diminishes the quality of service provision. Most important, the poor often are charged a premium to obtain access to critical social services, such as health care, drugs, or education. The participants considered the inclusion of checklists, questions, and indicators on corruption in all program and project evaluations as a major starting point for improving institutional performance.

In his paper about governance, Daniel Kaufmann takes up the challenge of institutional failures and how to evaluate them. He suggests promoting civil society and participatory processes and rigorously collecting solid empirical data on governance, with particular attention to countries that have tackled public corruption relatively successfully, such as Poland. Anwar Shah advances a different strategy to curtail corruption. Rather than simply following the flow of money and striving for full transparency of public officials and indicators of corruption, he suggests that the onus be placed more strongly on accountability for results. Public trust can best be achieved through improved public performance, and this requires an incentive structure that transforms the culture and values of the civil service. Shah calls for citizens in developing countries to become more involved in providing the right perspective for the evaluation and monitoring of the causes and consequences of corruption.

> Improving public performance requires an incentive structure that transforms the culture and values of the civil service.

Mobilizing the Poor

Focussing on the role of evaluation in the attributes of NGOs, Salehuddin Ahmed describes ways to organize and mobilize the poor, alternative models for service delivery, and methods for evaluating these from the perspective of Bangladesh's largest nongovernmental organization, the Bangladesh Rural Advancement Committee (BRAC). Ahmed argues that the best way to reach the poor is by working directly with them to implement and evaluate programs, based on the belief that poverty is a complex syndrome that goes well beyond a lack of financial resources.

Reflecting on Ahmed's central message that poverty reduction is at least partly about power relationships, Ariel Fiszbein notes that BRAC's experience could help the international development community better understand the interactions and synergy between NGOs and other local institutions and partners in development, including grassroots organizations, labor unions, and political parties, and the links between economic and political empowerment and reforms. Fiszbein also sees BRAC as a model learning organization that has for some time been using evaluation to develop a businesslike approach to improving its products and client service.

Social Exclusion and Community-Based Organizations

How to reach and engage the poor institutionally, particularly in unfavorable natural, socioeconomic, or political environments, is a major concern of social exclusion theory. Focusing on rural areas, Adolfo Figueroa considers widespread poverty and backwardness more a result of social exclusion than of market exploitation. He argues that start-up costs—for example, the transaction costs of providing public and other services to many disadvantaged groups and areas—are high. This results in poor access to education, work, markets in general, technological innovations, and financing. Socially excluded groups will have to be included in the system, and services, technologies, and financing mechanisms adapted to their needs. Thus, "social exclusion" provides an additional perspective to evaluators.

Probing the role of the civil society, Aloysius Fernandes pointed to the diverse natures and objectives of NGOs and community-based organizations (CBOs), which have been only incompletely understood and evaluated. Fernandes classifies NGOs and CBOs into three groups: (1) those challenging the government or largely working outside the public system, (2) those working with the government, often as part of a delivery chain of services, and (3) those set up by the government or large donors. He sees particular potential for reaching the poor in traditional community-based groups, which are usually based on affinity rather than on formal membership. However, such groups often opt for exclusion, self-reliant strategies, and nonconforming behavior.

Donor Assistance

Kanbur sees revamping the institutional system of aid delivery as a major step toward coordinating donor assistance. Partner countries should come up with comprehensive and coherent national and sectoral programs that the donor community could jointly assess and evaluate. Each donor would then put money into a common pool. Sector investment programs and the Comprehensive Development Framework (CDF) are a step in this direction, refining comprehensive evaluations.

Evaluation Methodologies and Focus

The questions of what to evaluate and how to evaluate it—in other words, evaluating the right things and evaluating them right—dominated much of the conference. This was the case not only in the discussion group on methodology, but also in several plenary sessions and other break-out groups.

What to Evaluate

The development community has to be concerned about results, ways to achieve them, and methodologies to measure them. As James Wolfensohn points out, in some areas, results become clear pretty quickly. But in development, what we want to achieve, how to measure it, and how to relate it to specific interventions is more complex. Ultimately, we have to measure optimal well-being, which means looking at its constituents at the level of the individual: basic needs, health goods, pleasure goods, human rights, and so forth, as argued by Partha Dasgupta. Goods and services provided through informal institutions and nonmarket channels have so far been largely overlooked and should be added to the more routinely measured constituents of well-being. Similarly, it is important to develop indicators to track and measure future net capital formation in environmental, human, and social capital , rather than simply measuring current well-being. Based on examples from the health sector, Stiglitz calls upon the evaluation community to focus more on the outcome of an intervention—the results—rather than on mere outputs. This means, for instance, that the quality of health services is more important than the number of health centers, clinics, or doctors, the ultimate goal being better health outcomes for the poorest.

> The quality of health services is more important than the number of health centers, clinics, or doctors.

Evaluating Social Capital, Sustainability, and Governance

What are the implications of the emerging paradigm shift? In the past, evaluation focused on physical capital. The development community then shifted toward human capital and natural capital. With the recognition that inclusion was a key instrument of poverty reduction, social capital has become an important focus. And the emphasis on holistic development has brought a new architecture into the mix, led by governance. How then must we reorient our evaluations? As pointed out by Picciotto, we may need more analysis of the generation of sustainable institutions, with institutions defined not only as the organizations implementing policies, programs, and projects, but also as the rules of the game.

This means that although the major focus of development impact assessment should be on the ultimate constituents of well-being, we cannot afford to lose track of intermediate results, and basic assumptions about the interventions and policies that may lead to these outcomes. We still have to focus evaluation on illuminating the processes that will allow us to better reach the poor. Ahmed identifies the following issues as still largely overlooked in conventional evaluations: management processes, structures, values, and indicators of the interaction between implementers and beneficiaries.

Dasgupta, Picciotto, and Carol Weiss noted that to facilitate this task, our evaluations should be based more strongly on theories and concepts of social and economic change. In an expansion of the traditional logframe matrix, Weiss proposes theory-based evaluation as an approach that brings to the surface the underlying assumptions about why a program will work, and then tracks those assumptions through the collection and analysis of data at a series of stages along the way to final outcomes.

Measuring the Totality of Development Efforts

A tension exists between measuring the impact of a particular poverty program or project and the synergistic nature of development, or the totality of efforts that so often determine the overall success of individual interventions. Both keynote speakers, Dasgupta and Stiglitz, ask in their presentations how we might better capture spillover effects and externalities in evaluations. A related question is how to measure, ensure, and explain the impact of policy, program, and project interventions on a broader scale—for example, at the regional or national level. Scaling up evaluations and moving from localized projects and programs to the regional, country, and global levels is a major challenge. Kanbur expressed his hope that donors will develop a greater appreciation of the fungibility of funds. Donors should be less interested in where their tax dollars—or euros or yens—go. By focusing more on the totality of interventions and their impact, we also may reduce the temptation and fallacy of generating easy impacts, targeting groups that, while not the most vulnerable, may promise greater short-term impact.

Selecting Relevant Units of Analysis

Another methodological issue raised was the fact that evaluation and research may have focused too much on the individual unit—households and individuals—and not enough on groups, communities, neighborhoods, and national units and their interactions. Evaluating policy impact, necessities, and constraints at the level of groups defined by ethnicity, religion, or other distinctive characteristics is particularly important. Evans and Stewart call for appropriate models for such evaluation.

How to Evaluate Poverty Reduction

To measure the impact of our interventions, we have to better address the basic evaluation problem: disentangling policy, program, and project effects from intervening factors. Kalanidhi Subbarao emphasizes that the task of netting out the effect of interventions requires the use of control groups.

Thomas Cook, in his comment on Subbarao's paper, discusses the need for randomization when measuring development impact. Following methodological standards developed for social science programs in the United States, he argues that randomization may only be forfeited in cases where (a) it may simply not be feasible or may not work, despite repeated attempts (failed randomization); (b) crossovers from control groups may dilute the results; and/or (c) there are solid, in-depth studies on the interrelations between, and effects of, specific interventions on targeted outcomes. In sum, one needs a sound rationale *not* to employ randomization in impact measurement.

Jim Heckman notes that many of the questions addressed by programs and policies of the World Bank and other donors are of a large-scale equilibrium nature and do not lend themselves to randomization. He also mentions a number of problems with randomized experiments.

Based on long-term empirical work on country performance, Thorbecke claims that there appears to be no substitute for sound historical comparisons of the socioeconomic performance of groups of countries that have followed alternative strategies. The relevant counterfactual scenario in this case would be the growth or poverty outcomes achieved by countries with similar resource endowments but different strategies, such as Indonesia and Nigeria. This is the realm of "history-cum-political" economy, and quantitative and qualitative approaches would be needed to produce an overall assessment. When the set of policy measures is not too extensive, computerized general equilibrium models may provide an analytical methodology to simulate the impact of a counterfactual scenario.

Less May Be More—Adjusting to Operational Realities

Sarah Gavian, Timothy Marchant, and Erik Thorbecke advise evaluators to adopt methodologies that are appropriate and practicable in the field.

The complex nature of many of the objectives may require a carefully calibrated evaluation and research agenda. Yet less may be more. Given the complexity of the tasks at hand and the many operational constraints in developing countries, a less ambitious evaluation approach may sometimes yield better results. This may entail a combination of quantitative and qualitative evaluation and impact assessment methodologies. Quality and analytical soundness is more important than quantity. Poorly designed or implemented impact and evaluation studies do not serve anybody, and may do more harm than good. This may mean using second-best solutions in some settings to evaluate and measure poverty reduction and its underlying factors.

Involving the Poor—Participatory Evaluations

Community-based participatory evaluations, often using qualitative rather than quantitative indicators, can play an important role. And as one participant put it, they could help to "give the poor and the marginalized the voice and leverage that have the power to reorient public sector bureaucracy."

However, as Edward Jackson argues, both the benefits and costs of participatory evaluations, with special emphasis on costs incurred by the poor and other beneficiaries, have to be more carefully assessed. Given that they may significantly alter stakeholders' budgets and time lines. Rolf Sartorius asks what it takes to make participatory evaluations work and describes a number of elements to consider. As noted in the the floor discussions, problems in communicating and dealing with illiteracy among the poor deserve particular attention. Changing relationships between outsiders and insiders and the importance of building trust and mutual partnerships between unequal allies are among the most pressing challenges for participatory evaluations, as indicated by David Marsden.

> Problems in communicating and dealing with illiteracy among the poor may deserve particular attention.

Providing Real-Time Information and Results—Achieving Better Use of Evaluations

In her welcome address, Jan Piercy challenged the evaluation community to make its work and findings more useful to development operations by providing real-time information. Embedding monitoring, evaluation, and results dissemination in the design and implementation of programs and projects is important. It could reduce some of the tension between the inherently long-term nature of measuring impact and explaining causes and policymakers' demands for quicker insights. Although the concepts of evaluation are usually well understood, the links to project implementation often do not work as intended. A major impediment may be insufficient training of evaluators, not only in analytical and statistical skills, but also in communication. To get the right information and share it with potential users, evaluators must apply communication techniques, sometimes traditional approaches but also strategies specifically adapted for the purpose.

Doing It Together—Fostering Evaluation Partnerships and Ownership

Conference participants discussed the future direction of evaluation, with frequent mention of the importance of expanding joint partnerships in evaluation, capacity building, and evaluations led by demand of the poor.

Joint Evaluations

Individual evaluations—by donors, recipient country governments, or other institutions—of complex poverty-related issues have become increasingly difficult, and frequently futile, given attribution problems, fungibility of funds, the holistic nature of the process of poverty alleviation, and rising evaluation costs, as demand for timely information rises. Thus the strong plea for joint and participatory evaluations by Elizabeth McAllister during her opening remarks was echoed throughout the conference. In sum, as stated by Jan Piercy, "the goal must be to come together as partners across organizations, from academia to development organizations, from bilateral and multilateral agencies, to agree on ways in which we can measure, evaluate our effectiveness and the ways in which that can directly feed into and impact on what we do." Clearly the focus is on joint learning. The emphasis is moving away from evaluating others, and toward learning from and with others, and on new forms of partnerships that involve all stakeholders and utilize decentralized, community-based monitoring. As Moise Mensah explains, "Joint evaluations must include the poor. Poverty reduction is a complex process, and that process can be successful only if the poor have confidence in their own ability to move out of poverty."

> The emphasis is moving away from evaluating others, and toward learning from and with others.

Forging alliances may not always be easy. Dabelstein, Shepherd, and others point out that enhancing partnerships in evaluation may involve problems associated with differences in development, evaluation priorities and philosophies, methodological approaches, administrative and other system requirements, and vested interests. In this context, a major issue raised is how to address donor accountability and how to apportion credit and blame.

Political economy aspects have to be considered. While better coordination of all actors in evaluation and a more holistic view are important, we must take account of vested institutional interests. Priorities and strategies for the right policies and interventions may differ. Kanbur points out that donors have to recognize that money is fungible and pay more attention to the overall impact of development efforts rather than to individual contributions.

Establishing Regional Centers of Excellence for Evaluation

Increasing know-how and institutional capacity in developing countries for solid evaluations and poverty-related research, preferably with the assistance of international research institutions whose mandate is to look into these more broadly based development issues, was considered absolutely necessary by several conference participants. "What does not work is parachuting people in to do external evaluations of impact," as one participant said. During the conference several participants argued that establishing regional centers of excellence for evaluation may be one way to supply such capacity.

Demand-Led Evaluations—Letting the Poor Determine the Agenda

Several presentations and discussions centered on the concept of promoting demand-led evaluations. An organization that is determined to learn will balance these issues and will try to get to know the market for evaluations. The relationship between demand and supply for evaluations is at the crux of the dilemma. Most important, the central role of the poor must be more widely considered.

Importance of Advocacy

As advocacy develops into a major factor for changing policies, donors and other development institutions are becoming concerned about leveraging their assistance by promoting advocacy. How will advocacy affect or constrain development partnerships? How does one evaluate advocacy?

Challenges for Future Evaluations

In sum, we need to better understand and reconcile the different expectations and information needs of the players involved, particularly the poor themselves; respect and expand partners' skill levels; and expand evaluation capacities, possibly by creating centers of excellence to facilitate more effective, joint, and participatory evaluations. We need workable processes for deciding strategic evaluation priorities, given virtually unlimited information demands, and we need more synthesis products and links with research.

Evaluation:
A Macro Perspective

Valuation and Evaluation

Partha Dasgupta

Means and Ends

In common parlance, we use "valuation" when comparing objects and "evaluation" when comparing the relative merits of actions. Of course, the objects need not be concrete; they can be abstract, and evaluation is not restricted to a narrowly construed notion of action. For example, we evaluate strategies, which are conditional actions ("do this if that happens," "do that if he does this," and so forth) that can be personal or collective. We also evaluate policies, which can also be personal or collective. In this sense, valuation is passive, while evaluation signifies a more active engagement.

Here I shall be considering public policies, the sorts of policies governments are expected to ponder. They involve such matters as the character of public investment, the structure of taxes and transfers, and the nature of environmental legislation. To be sure, when speaking of the evaluation of public policies, I mean the evaluation of changes in public policies. Both valuation and evaluation involve comparisons. To evaluate a public policy, for example, we have to compare it with some other policy, which could be the status quo—that is, the outcome that would prevail if existing policies were kept in place. Evaluation involves the consideration of counterfactuals.

Public evaluation means two often-related things. First, the choice of one public policy rather than another implies one background environment rather than another, within which the various parties in society can act. The choice influences the constraints the various parties are subject to. So evaluating a public policy requires assessing the likely responses of the economic system to the policy. Second, the evaluation needs to be conducted on behalf of a large, possibly disparate group of people possessing different preferences, values, and needs. This calls for an acceptable procedure to aggregate the often conflicting claims of the body polity and to identify the features of the consequences of the choice that are to be used to conduct the evaluation.

In recent years, the latter exercise has received a great deal of attention in such publications as the annual Human Development Report of the United Nations Development Programme (UNDP), but the former is the inherently harder task. In this essay I begin with the latter and then move to the former. At the level of international discourse on development policies, however, disagreements stem largely from our common lack of understanding of the ways in which socioeconomic systems respond to policy changes—that is, disagreements about what one might call moral values.

Economists stress that people differ in their judgment of what are the appropriate rates of tradeoff between competing social goals. Political differences among people are to be traced to this, or so the assertion goes (among the most prominent expositions of this view are Graaff 1962, Robinson 1964, and Samuelson 1947). My own understanding is otherwise. Divergences in people's opinions about how the world works assume importance in political debates long before differences in ethical views become manifest. I have yet to meet anyone who does not wish to see unemployment reduced or destitution a thing of the past or the rain forests protected. I have also heard many disagreements on what are the most effective means of bringing them about. As the philosopher Hilary Putnam has put it: "It is all well and good to describe hypothetical cases in which two people agree on the facts and disagree about values, but when and where did a Nazi and an anti-Nazi, a communist and a social democrat, a fundamentalist and a liberal . . . agree on the facts?" (Putnam 1989, p. 7).

Indeed, we can plausibly argue that if development policies espoused by international bodies have failed not infrequently, they have failed because of our vastly imperfect knowledge and understanding of the way economic systems respond to policies. By this I mean, of course, the way people respond to policies and the way ecosystems respond to the treatment meted out to them. I do not know of much evidence that the failures were caused by a wrong view of what constitutes economic progress. In short, even though we generally agree about ends, we typically disagree about the right means to further those ends.

Measuring Social Well-Being: Constituents Versus Determinants

To evaluate policies we require a criterion by which to make the evaluation. This leads us directly to measures of social well-being. I will use the terms well-being, welfare, and quality of life interchangeably.

I take it as understood that we are to build a measure of social well-being from the ground up. Because the locus of perception, sensation, and feeling is at the individual level, it is appropriate to start there and then build up. It is the individual who matters. So even though I will be thinking in aggregate terms, I want to stress that the aggregate is composed of aspects of the lives of individual people. To the extent that people differ in their access to basic goods and services, we would wish to place greater weight on those who lack ready access. So the aggregate measure of social well-being incorporates an explicit weighting system.

We need aggregate measures of social well-being for at least three different purposes. First, we may wish to compare the state of affairs in different places (for example, different countries) or among different groups of people (for example, the poor versus the rich or men versus women) at a given point in time. This is something the Bank, for example, does in its annual *World Development Report*. Second, we may wish to make welfare comparisons over time of people in the same place (for example, the same country) or people constituting the same group (for example, the poor, suitably defined, or the rich or women). This too is something the Bank does in its annual *World Development Report*, when estimating changes in this or that welfare indicator for countries or groups over periods of time. Third, and this is what I am concerned about here, we need welfare indicators to evaluate alternative economic policies. Criterion functions for social cost-benefit analysis of investment projects, such as the present discounted value of the flow of accounting profits, are examples of such indicators (Dasgupta, Marglin, and Sen 1972; Little and Mirrlees 1974).

Before all else, however, we should make clear to ourselves what the purpose of the evaluation is before we undertake it, and we should be prepared to conduct the evaluation as dispassionately as possible. Making good points with bad arguments may disguise the fact that good arguments exist that would have served the purpose. Here is an example of the kind of mistake one makes when attempting overkill: in drawing attention to the enormous inequality in today's world, UNDP writes, "New estimates show that the world's 225 richest people have a combined wealth of over one trillion US dollars, equal to the annual income of the poorest 47 percent of the world's people (2.5 billion)" (UNDP 1998, p. 30).

> We should make clear to ourselves what the purpose of the evaluation is before we undertake it, and we should be prepared to conduct the evaluation as dispassionately as possible.

Wealth is a stock and income is a flow. Therefore, one should be converted into the other before the figures are compared. The standard practice would be to convert wealth into a figure for permanent income by using a 5 percent interest rate—that is, to divide wealth by a factor of 20. When this conversion is performed on the UNDP figures, my calculations, although crude, tell me that the world's 225 richest people, with a combined income of more than US$50 billion, earn more than the combined incomes of people in the world's 12 poorest countries, or about 7 percent of the world's population (385 million). This is still a sobering statistic.

One could argue that if we seek a welfare indicator, we should measure social well-being directly and not look for a surrogate and give it a different name—present discounted value of the flow of accounting profits, net national product (NNP), wealth, or whatever. There is something in this. However, there are several reasons for seeking a welfare measure, so for many purposes the most convenient index could be something other than the thing itself. For example, we could be interested in an object X, but X may prove especially hard to measure, for example, because it involves estimating nonlinear functions of observable quantities. Suppose that for some purposes X is known to correlate perfectly with Y and that Y is easier to measure than X, for example, because Y is a linear function of observable quantities. Then we would wish to rely on Y to measure X. NNP and wealth are linear quantities, with the weights being at least in part revealed by observable market prices. This is also the case with the present discounted value of the flow of accounting profits. Therein lies the attraction of these indexes.

The preceding observation suggests that two ways to measure social well-being are available. One is to study the constituents of well-being—that is, health, happiness, and freedom to be and do, or more broadly, basic liberties. The other is to value the commodity determinants of well-being—that is, goods and services, which are inputs into the production of well-being, such as food, clothing, potable water, shelter, and resources devoted to national security. The former procedure measures output—for instance, indexes of health—whereas the latter values and then aggregates the required inputs—for example, expenditure on health.[1] If undertaken with sufficient precision and care, either on its own would do the job: changes in a suitable aggregate measure of either the constituents or the determinants can be made to serve as a measure of changes in the quality of life in a society (Dasgupta 1993). Along the former route, we would measure the constituents directly and aggregate them in a suitable way. Along the latter route, we would need to estimate the social values, or accounting prices, of the determinants of well-being in order to arrive at an all-embracing measure of wealth (Dasgupta and Mäler forthcoming). However, as we have already observed, wealth is a linear function of the quantities of stocks of goods and services. This is why we frequently measure social well-being in terms of its determinants rather than try to measure it directly in terms of its constituents.

One may wonder where, if anywhere, gross national product (GNP) or NNP come in. GNP is an indicator of overall economic activity, including as it does gross, not net, capital formation. NNP is superior precisely on this count. For this reason, NNP is widely regarded as being a suitable index of social well-being (see, for example, Weitzman 1976 and the large body of literature that followed in its wake). But as there are several reasons why we would be interested in indexes of social well-being, so there is no *a priori* reason why the same index can serve all purposes. Dasgupta and Mäler (forthcoming) have shown that NNP, properly defined, can be used to evaluate economic policies but that it should not be used in any of its more customary roles, such as in making intertemporal or cross-country comparisons of social well-being. They have shown that for the latter types of comparison, the appropriate index is wealth.[2]

In practice, neither the constituents nor the determinants, on their own, capture what we wish to see captured in any reasoned conception of the quality of life. The problem is that we would have far too many person-specific accounting prices—for example, distributional weights—to contend with if we were to estimate an overarching measure by means of the determinants of social welfare. At the same time, disposable income as it is customarily measured does capture aspects of welfare and the extent of certain patterns of freedom—namely, the freedom to choose over commodity bundles—matters that are hard to come to grips with directly. For this reason, governments and international agencies pursue both avenues at once, and today it is commonplace to assess the quality of life by studying a heterodox collection of socioeconomic indicators (see, for example, the Bank's annual *World Development Report* and UNDP's annual Human Development Report).

The problem is to identify a minimal set of indexes that would span one's conception of social well-being. It is useful also to ensure that we avoid double-counting. Thus, for example, statistics on the proportion of populations that lack access to potable water are in frequent use in quality of life indexes, as are statistics on infant mortality rates. However, one would expect the two to be highly correlated; indeed, one is an important cause of the other. If we have the former (or latter) piece of information, we do not really need the latter (or former) to construct a quality of life measure.

In choosing welfare indicators, we have to strike a balance between the claims of completeness and costs. Leaving aside for the moment the extent of civil and political liberties a person enjoys, we can use at least three broad kinds of indexes in constructing a measure of a person's well-being: his or her current and prospective real income, including certain nonmarketed goods and services; his or her current and future states of health; and his or her educational attainments. These are different categories of goods. Health and education would seem to embody positive freedoms, whereas income contributes to the enjoyment of these freedoms. So why would we wish to mix them up? The reason is that a person's real income measures the extent to which he or she can obtain consumption goods like food and clothing, shelter, legal aid, and general amenities in the market, but primary health care and education are not this sort of good. Private markets do not provide an ideal resource allocation mechanism for their supply. Markets for these goods need to be allied to explicit support by the state in a way that assures citizens of their supply. Government involvement in the provision of primary health care and education varies enormously across poor countries. For this reason, the average person might enjoy a higher disposable income in one country, yet suffer from worse health care and education facilities than the average person in another. Stating matters in the reverse way, people in one country, on average, can be better educated and enjoy better health than in another, even while their access to material goods is more restricted. Real income, health, and education indexes capture in their various ways various aspects of the average person's well-being (Dasgupta 1993).

Valuing Goods and Evaluating Projects

Policy changes are perturbations in a prevailing state of affairs. A project consisting of a dam would be a perturbation in an economy without the dam. The economic forecast without the project can be thought of as the status quo. We could, of course, analyze the consequences of a policy change in terms of their impact on the constituents of social well-being, but as I have just argued, analyzing them in terms of their effect on the determinants of social well-being does have advantages. The linear indexes I have been alluding to, such as the present discounted value of the flow of accounting profits from a project, work most effectively if the perturbation being evaluated is small. What constitutes smallness is a delicate matter, to which the project evaluator has to be sensitive. An investment project can be small in terms of a country's NNP and yet have a major effect on the lives of some very poor people, in which case it would not be small for them. The way to proceed would be to estimate the net benefits the people in question would experience if the project were undertaken. The net benefits would typically be nonlinear functions of quantities.

In an evaluation of an investment project, the need for labor, intermediate products, and raw materials is estimated, and the project's output and effect on the ecological system are predicted, quantitatively, for each period. Most often, though, one does not have sufficient knowledge to make precise estimates of the consequences. One therefore needs quantitative estimates of the uncertainties, preferably in terms of probabilities. This means that, in general, one has to model the integrated ecological and economic system (see Daily et. al. 1999 for an elaboration of this step). The evaluation procedure involves estimating the effect of projects on human well-being now and in the future. To arrive at an estimate, the analyst has to value each and every commodity of the project in terms of some *numeraire*. The social value of a commodity or service is measured by its social opportunity cost in terms of the *numeraire*. These steps are common to all methods of evaluation.

Note that the criterion to be used for reaching a decision about whether to accept a proposed investment project depends on the economy's type of decentralization in decisionmaking. If we wish to assess the effect on social well-being of a brief policy change, then NNP (suitably defined) would be the appropriate index of evaluation. One can go further. In principle, it is possible to deconstruct policy changes—for instance, investment projects—that are long-lasting into an appropriate number of single-period changes and use NNP as the criterion function, period by period. The decentralization envisaged here is a sequence of project evaluations. It would be as though there were as many independent project evaluations as there were project periods, in which each would use the corresponding single-period project's contribution to NNP (suitably defined) as the criterion by which to judge whether it were socially worthy of acceptance (Dasgupta and Mäler forthcoming).

A more convenient decentralization is the one commonly assumed in project evaluation exercises. It assumes that there is a single project evaluator evaluating the project over its entire life. What I am referring to as a commodity's value is usually called its accounting price. The net social profit from a project in any given period of its life is obtained by multiplying the project's inputs and outputs in that period by their corresponding accounting prices and adding them (output of "goods" is taken to be positive; inputs and the output of "bads" are taken to be negative). Using a suitable discount rate, often called the "social rate of discount," the analysis adds the per period net social profits yielded by a project.[3] Projects that yield a positive present discounted value of net social profits are then recommended and those that yield a negative present discounted value of net social profits are rejected.

Procedures for estimating the accounting prices of goods and services were much discussed at the Bank in the 1970s (see, for example, Squire and Van der Taak 1975). The theory of accounting prices that existed then assumed, in effect, that the economy in which social cost-benefit analysis is conducted has an optimal economic policy, perhaps a second-best policy, but an optimal policy nonetheless. This was assumed explicitly in Little and Mirrlees (1974). In contrast, Dasgupta, Marglin, and Sen (1972) had developed prescriptions for project evaluation in economies in which projects could be thought of as policy reforms—that is, as perturbations in economic forecasts that might be riddled with inefficiencies and inequities. However, they offered no formal theory to justify their prescriptions. Dasgupta and Mäler (forthcoming) have since developed the theoretical foundations of social cost-benefit analysis when investment projects are policy reforms.

What would the valuation techniques developed in the 1970s instruct us to do if they were put to work on current concerns? In a recent lecture, the president of the Bank correctly observed that the success of most projects depends on many assumptions extraneous to the project itself. Building new schools is of no use without roads to get the children to the schools and without trained teachers, books, and equipment. Initiatives to help create equal opportunities for women make no sense if women have to spend many hours each day carrying clean water or finding and gathering fuel for cooking. Seeking universal primary education without providing prenatal and postnatal health care means that children get to school mentally and physically damaged. Establishing a health system but doing nothing about clean water and sewerage diminishes enormously the impact of any effort (Wolfensohn 1999, p. 8).

> Just as a shoe for the left foot is useless without a shoe for the right foot, establishing a health system but doing nothing about clean water would not amount to much.

James Wolfensohn was pointing to the need to understand an economic system's response to project selection. His examples were about complementarities. Just as a shoe for the left foot is useless without a shoe for the right foot, establishing a health system but doing nothing about clean water would not amount to much. The accounting price of an object whose complements are unavailable is nil. Projects that produced one without its complements would register a negative present discounted value of social profits. In short, an integrated project could pass the test even when each of its components, on its own, would not.

Environmental Resources

A significant weakness of the several manuals on social cost-benefit analysis that were written during the 1970s was their total neglect of the natural world around us.[4] They simply did not consider the environment. Because market failure abounds in our dealings with the environment, we cannot rely on markets to provide us with prices that would even approximately signal the social scarcities of environmental resources. A great deal of work in environmental and resource economics since the 1970s has been directed at discovering methods to estimate the accounting prices of various types of environmental resources. In large part, investigators have developed practical methods for estimating the accounting prices of amenities but have developed relatively few for the multitude of ecosystem services that constitute our life-support system, such as soils, pollination, forest cover, biodiversity, biomass recycling, and water purification (Mitchell and Carson 1989). Since the early 1990s, valuable work has been done on this by the Vice Presidency for Environmentally Sustainable Development of the World Bank (and continues to be done at the Bank), most recently by John Dixon and his colleagues. However, we still do not have a systematic body of work on evaluation techniques for different categories of resources in different institutional settings.

Nevertheless, even now the following is abundantly clear. Indicators of social well-being in frequent use—GNP per head, life expectancy at birth, and infant survival rate—do not reflect the effect of economic activities on the environment. Because such indexes of the standard of living as GNP per head pertain to commodity production, they do not fully take into account the use of natural capital in the production process. So statistics on past movements of gross product tell us nothing about the resource stocks that remain. They do not make clear, for example, whether increases in GNP per head are being realized by means of a depletion of the resource base—for example, whether increases in agricultural production are not being achieved by mining the soil. Over the years, environmental and resource economists have shown how national accounting systems need to be revised to include the value of the changes in the environmental resource base that stem each year from human activity (Dasgupta and Heal 1979, Dasgupta and Mäler forthcoming, Mäler 1974). We should be in a position to determine whether resource degradation in various parts of the world has yet to reach the stage at which their current economic activities are unsustainable. However, the practice of national income accounting has lagged so far behind its theory that we have little idea of the facts. It is, therefore, entirely possible that time trends in such commonly used socioeconomic indicators as GNP per head, life expectancy at birth, and infant survival rate give us a singularly misleading picture of movements of the true standard of living.

To state the matter another way, current estimates of socioeconomic indicators are biased because the accounting value of changes in the stocks of natural capital are not taken into account. Because their accounting prices are not available, environmental resources on site are frequently regarded as having no value. This amounts to regarding the depreciation of natural capital as being of no consequence, but as these resources are scarce goods, their accounting prices are positive, so if they depreciate, a social loss occurs. It means that profits attributed to projects that degrade the environment are frequently greater than the social profits they generate. Estimates of their rates of return are higher than their social rates of return. Wrong sets of investment projects therefore get selected in both the private and public sectors: Resource-intensive projects look better than they actually are. It should be no surprise, therefore, that installed technologies are often unfriendly toward the environment. This is likely to be especially true in poor countries, where environmental legislation is usually neither strong nor effectively enforced.

The extent of such bias in investment activities will obviously vary from case to case and from country to country, but it can be substantial. In their work on the depreciation of natural resources in Costa Rica,

Solorzano and others (1991) estimated that in 1989 the depreciation of three resources—forests, soil, and fisheries—amounted to about 10 percent of gross domestic product (GDP) and more than a third of gross capital accumulation.

One can go further: the bias extends to the early stage of research and development. When environmental resources are underpriced or, in the extreme, when they are not priced at all, there is little incentive on anyone's part to develop technologies that would economize on their use. So the direction of technological research and technological change is systematically directed against the environment. Consequently, environmental "cures" are sought once the perception surfaces that past choices have been damaging to the environment, whereas prevention, or input reduction, would have been the better choice. Consider the following example. Chichilnisky and Heal (1998) compared the costs of restoring the ecological functioning of the Catskill watershed ecosystem in New York State with the costs of replacing the natural water purification and filtration services the ecosystem had provided in the past by building a US$8 billion water purification plant. They showed the overwhelming economic advantages of preservation over construction. Independent of the other services the Catskill watershed provides, and ignoring the annual running costs of US$300 million for a filtration plant, the capital costs alone showed a more than sixfold advantage for investing in the natural capital base.

> When environmental resources are underpriced or not priced, there is little incentive to develop technologies to economize on their use.

Bad habits are slow to disappear, however. Even today the environment has not entered the common lexicon of economic discourse. Accounting for the environment, if it comes into the calculus at all, is an afterthought to the real business of "doing economics." Thus, a recent issue of *The Economist* carries a 38-page survey of the world economy in which the environmental resource base makes no appearance in the authors' assessment of what lies ahead, but our habits are all so deeply ingrained in us that I rather doubt many readers noticed.

The purpose of estimating environmental accounting prices is not to value the entire environment; rather, it is to evaluate the benefits and costs associated with changes made to the environment by human activity. Prices, whether actual or merely notional, have significance only when there are potential exchanges from which choices have to be made—for example, when one has to choose among alternative investment projects. Thus, the statement that a particular act of investment can be expected to degrade the environment by, say, US$1 million annually has meaning, because it says, among other things, that if the investment were not to be undertaken, humanity would enjoy an additional US$1 million of benefits in the form of environmental services. The statement also has operational significance: the estimate could (and should) be used to calculate the present discounted value of the flow of social profits attributable to the investment in question.

Contrast such an estimate of the value of an incremental change in the environmental resource base to the one that says that, worldwide, the flow of environmental services is currently worth a total of US$33 trillion annually (Costanza and others 1997). The former is meaningful because it presumes that humanity will survive the incremental change and be there to experience and assess the change. The reason the latter should cause us to balk is that if environmental services were to cease, life would not exist. Who would then be present to receive US$33 trillion of annual benefits if humanity were to exchange its very existence for them? This is a case in which, paradoxically, the value of an entire something has no meaning, and is therefore of no use, even though the value of incremental changes to that same something has not only meaning but also use.

An approach similar to that of Costanza and others (1997) appeared in a recent article in another issue of *The Economist*. In observing the disturbing tendency of compound interest to make large figures in the distant future look extremely small today, the author remarked as follows:

> Suppose a long-term discount rate of 7 percent (after inflation) is used . . . Suppose also that the project's benefits arrive 200 years from now. . . If global GDP grows by 3 percent a year during those two centuries, the value of the world's output in 2200 will be 8 quadrillion US dollars (a 16-figure number). But in present-value terms, that stupendous sum would be worth just 10 billion US dollars. In other words, it would not make sense for the world to spend any more than 10 billion US dollars (under 2 US dollars a person) today on a measure that would prevent the loss of the planet's entire output 200 years from now (1999, p. 128).

One of the problems with this reasoning is its presumption that social rates of discount are independent of the income forecast whose perturbation is being discounted. The underlying assumption in the passage is a massive perturbation (zero world output in 2200). This would involve a secular decline in output. However, social discount rates associated with declining consumption streams would be expected to be negative (Dasgupta and Mäler 1995). Discounting future incomes produces paradoxes only when it is not recognized that, because discount rates are themselves accounting prices, they should be endogenous to the analyses. The rates cannot be merely plucked from the air.

Institutional Responses to Perturbations
Defining policy change—for example, an investment project—as a perturbation in an economic forecast is easy enough. Identifying what the perturbation actually consists of is altogether more difficult. Any system,

human or otherwise, should be expected to respond when subjected to a perturbation. In an economy that is not pursuing an optimum policy, an act of investment can create all sorts of effects that ripple through it without being noticed by the public offices for the reason that there may be no public signals accompanying them. Tracing the ripples requires an understanding of the way markets and nonmarket institutions interact.

Many transactions take place in nonmarket institutions. I have already mentioned transactions involving environmental services as prime examples. In poor countries, further examples abound. In recent years, economists and political scientists have studied long-term relationships with the same care and rigor that they used to invest in the study of markets and the state. A large and illuminating theoretical and empirical literature is now available on the wide variety of ways in which people cope with resource scarcity when there are no formal markets for exchanging goods and services across time, space, and circumstances (Dasgupta 1999). The literature offers us a lever with which to predict, in broad terms, the way people, both individually and communally, would respond to perturbations. Unfortunately, the literature has not filtered through sufficiently to decisionmakers. I want to illustrate what I mean by providing two examples, one a local miniature and the other altogether grander and nearly global.

> Tracing the ripples requires an understanding of the way markets and nonmarket institutions interact.

For many years now, the political scientist Elinor Ostrom has been studying the management of common property resources in various parts of the world. In her work on collectively managed irrigation systems in Nepal, she has accounted for differences in rights and responsibilities among users (who gets how much water and when, who is responsible for which maintenance task of the canal system, and so forth) in terms of facts such as that some farmers are head-enders while others are tail-enders (Ostrom 1990, 1996). Head-enders have a built-in advantage in that they can prevent tail-enders from receiving water. Head-enders, however, need the tail-enders' labor for repair and maintenance of the canal system. This means that both parties can, in principle, gain from cooperation. In the absence of cooperation, their fortunes would differ greatly, so cooperative arrangements would be expected to display asymmetries, and they do display them.[5]

Ostrom also reported that a number of communities in her sample had been given well-meaning aid by donors and that canal systems had been improved by the construction of permanent headworks (Ostrom 1996). However, she observed that the canal systems that had been improved were frequently in worse repair and were delivering less water to tail-enders than previously. Ostrom also reported that water allocation was more equitable in traditional farm management systems than in modern systems managed by external agencies, such as the government and foreign donors. She estimated from her sample that agricultural productivity is higher in traditional systems.

Ostrom has an explanation for this. She argues that the construction of permanent headworks alters the relative bargaining positions of the head- and tail-enders unless it is accompanied by countermeasures. Head-enders now do not need the labor of tail-enders to maintain the canal system, so the new sharing scheme involves even less water for tail-enders. Head-enders gain from the permanent structures, but tail-enders lose disproportionately. This is an example of how well-meaning aid can go wrong if the giver of aid does not understand the institution receiving the aid.

Not infrequently, resource allocation rules practiced at the local level are overturned by central fiat. A number of states in the Sahel imposed rules that, in effect, destroyed communitarian management practices in the forests. Villages ceased to have the authority to enforce sanctions on those who violated locally instituted rules of use. State authority turned the local commons into free-access resources.

My second example—altogether more grand and fiercely debated—concerns the experience of people in poor countries with structural adjustment programs that involved reducing ing the plethora of economic distortions that governments had introduced over decades. Many have criticized the way structural adjustment programs have been carried out. They have pointed to the additional hardship many of the poor have experienced in their wake. However, one could argue that structural adjustments, facilitating as they did the growth of markets, were necessary, and proponents of the programs have argued this. What I want to suggest is that both proponents and opponents of the programs may be right. The growth of markets benefits many, but it can simultaneously make vulnerable people face additional economic hardships and thereby increase the incidence and intensity of poverty and destitution in an economy.

How and why might this happen? One way is that long-term relationships in rural communities in poor countries are typically sustained by social norms—for example, norms of reciprocity that can be practiced only among people who expect to encounter one another repeatedly in similar situations (Dasgupta 1993, 1999). Consider a group of far-sighted people who know one another, who prepare to interact indefinitely with one another. By far-sighted person I mean someone who applies a low rate to discount future costs and the benefits of alternative courses of action. Assume as well that the parties in question are not separately mobile (although they could be collectively mobile, as in the case of nomadic societies); otherwise, the chances of future encounters with one another would be low, and people (being far-sighted) would discount heavily the future benefits of current cooperation.

The basic idea is this. If people are far-sighted and are not separately mobile, a credible threat by all that they would impose sufficiently stiff sanctions on anyone who broke the agreement would deter everyone from breaking it. But the threat of sanctions would cease to have potency if opportunistic behavior were to become personally more enticing. This can happen when formal markets grow, accompanied by uncorrelated migration. As opportunities outside the village improve, people with lesser ties—for example, young men—are more likely to take advantage of them and make a break with the customary obligations that are enshrined in prevailing social norms. People with greater attachments would perceive this and infer that the expected benefits from complying with agreements are now lower. Either way, norms of reciprocity could be expected to break down, making certain groups of people (women, the old, and the very young) worse off. This is a case in which improved institutional performance elsewhere—for example, the growth of markets in the economy at large—has an adverse effect on the functioning of a local, nonmarket institution.

To the extent that local natural resources held as common property are made vulnerable by the breakdown of communitarian control mechanisms, structural adjustment programs could have been expected to be unfriendly also to the environment and, therefore, to those who are directly dependent on common property natural resources for their livelihood. This is because when the market value of a resource base increases, there is special additional pressure on the base if people have relatively free access to it (see Dasgupta 1990 for a theoretical analysis and Reed 1992 for an empirical investigation in three poor countries of some of the effects of structural adjustment programs on resource bases). Structural adjustment programs devoid of safety nets for those who are vulnerable to the erosion of communitarian practices are defective. They are also damaging to the environment unless the structure of property rights, whether private or communitarian, is simultaneously made more secure. We should not expect matters to be otherwise.[6]

> Evaluation of policy changes can be done effectively only with a fair understanding of the way socioeconomic and ecological systems would respond to the changes.

Conclusions

Policy evaluation techniques that were developed in the 1970s, while formally correct, neglected to consider resource allocation in the wide variety of nonmarket institutions that prevail throughout the world and the role the environmental resource base plays in our lives. In this essay I have argued that the evaluation of policy changes can be done effectively only with a fair understanding of the way socioeconomic and ecological systems would respond to the changes. The observation is banal, but all too often decisionmakers have neglected to model the combined socioeconomic and ecological system before embarking on new policies or keeping faith with the prevailing ones. I have provided examples to show that such neglect has probably meant even greater hardship for precisely those groups of people who are commonly regarded as being particularly deserving of our consideration. The examples were also designed to demonstrate how recent advances in our understanding of general resource allocation mechanisms and of environmental and resource economics can be incorporated in a systematic way into what are currently the best-practice policy evaluation techniques.

Notes

This essay is based on the keynote lecture delivered at the World Bank Third Conference on Evaluation and Poverty Reduction, Washington, D.C., June 14, 1999. I am most grateful to Detlev Puetz for his advice on the choice of the subject matter for the lecture. In writing the essay I have benefited from the comments of Gretchen Daily, Carol Dasgupta, Paul Ehrlich, Simon Levin, Jane Lubchenco, Karl-Göran Mäler, Peter Raven, Robert Rowthorn, and Paul Seabright.

1. To be sure, goods such as education and skills perform both functions: they are at once constituents and determinants of well-being. They do not pose problems if we are able to track the two functions and their contributions to well-being.

2. Pearce, Hamilton, and Atkinson (1996) have also suggested the use of wealth as the basis for such comparisons. Serageldin (1995) has reported empirical work done at the Bank on the use of the rule. See also World Bank (1996).

3. The social rate of discount in any period is the percentage rate of decrease over that period and the next in the accounting price of the *numeraire*.

4. Dasgupta (1982) was an attempt to put that right. The material in this section is based on Dasgupta, Levin, and Lubchenco (forthcoming).

5. In fact, a general finding from studies of the management of common property systems is that entitlements to products of the commons are, and have been, almost always based on private holdings.

6. As I am wholly inexpert on the matter, I am not offering even a sketch of the kinds of argument that can be advanced to show that the reforms that were urged upon Russia in the early 1990s suffered from a lack of acknowledgment of the role that governance plays in the operation of markets. In an illuminating work, Rose (1999) has been investigating the way social networks there have entered spheres of activity they would not have entered if citizens had enjoyed reliable governance.

References

Chichilnisky, G., and G. M. Heal. 1998. "Economic Returns from the Biosphere." *Nature* 391: 629-30.

Costanza, R. R., and others. 1997. "The Value of the World's Ecosystem Services and Natural Capital." *Nature* 387: 253-60.

Daily, G., and others. 1999. "The Value of Nature and the Nature of Value." Stockholm: Beijer International Institute of Ecological Economics.

Dasgupta, P. 1982. *The Control of Resources.* Cambridge, MA: Harvard University Press.

———. 1990. "The Environment as a Commodity." *Oxford Review of Economic Policy* 6: 51-67.

———. 1993. *An Inquiry into Well-being and Destitution.* Oxford, U.K.: Clarendon Press.

———. 1999. "Economic Progress and the Idea of Social Capital." In P. Dasgupta and I. Serageldin, eds., 1999. *Social Capital: A Multifaceted Perspective.* Washington, D.C.: World Bank.

Dasgupta, P., and G. M. Heal. 1979. *Economic Theory and Exhaustible Resources.* Cambridge, U.K.: Cambridge University Press.

Dasgupta, P., S. Levin, and J. Lubchenco. Forthcoming. "Economic Pathways to Ecological Sustainability: Challenges for the New Millennium." *BioScience*.

Dasgupta, P., and K.-G. Mäler. 1995. "Poverty, Institutions, and the Environmental Resource-Base." In J. Behrman and T. N. Srinivasan, eds., 1995. *Handbook of Development Economics,* vol. 3A. Amsterdam: Elsevier/North-Holland.

Dasgupta, P., and K.-G. Mäler. Forthcoming. "Net National Product and Social Well-Being." *Environment and Development Economics*.

Dasgupta, P., S. Marglin, and A. Sen. 1972. *Guidelines for Project Evaluation.* New York: United Nations.

Graff, J. de V. 1962. *Theoretical Welfare Economics.* Cambridge, U.K.: Cambridge University Press.

Little, I. M. D., and J. A. Mirrlees. 1974. *Project Appraisal and Planning for Developing Countries.* London: Heinemann.

Mäler, K.-G. 1974. *Environmental Economics: A Theoretical Enquiry.* Baltimore, MD: The Johns Hopkins University Press.

Mitchell, R. C., and R. T. Carson. 1989. *Using Surveys to Value Public Goods: The Contingent Valuation Method.* Washington, D.C.: Resources for the Future.

Ostrom, E. 1990. *Governing the Commons: The Evolution of Institutions for Collective Action.* Cambridge, U.K.: Cambridge University Press.

———. 1996. "Incentives, Rules of the Game, and Development." In *Proceedings of the Annual World Bank Conference on Development Economics, 1995.* Supplement to *World Bank Economic Review* and *World Bank Research Observer* 207-34.

Pearce, D., K. Hamilton, and G. Atkinson. 1996. "Measuring Sustainable Development: Progress on Indicators." *Environment and Development Economics* 1: 85-101.

Putnam, H. 1989. "Objectivity and the Science/Ethics Distinction." Working Paper 70. Helsinki: World Institute for Development Economics Research.

Reed, D., ed. 1992. *Structural Adjustment and the Environment.* Boulder, CO: Westview Press.

Robinson, J. 1964. *Economic Philosophy.* Harmondsworth, U.K.: Penguin Books.

Rose, R. 1999. "Getting Things Done in an Antimodern Society: Social Capital Networks in Russia." In P. Dasgupta and I. Serageldin, eds., 1999. *Social Capital: A Multifaceted Perspective.* Washington, D.C.: World Bank.

Samuelson, P. A. 1947. *Foundations of Economic Analysis.* Cambridge, MA: Harvard University Press.

Serageldin, I. 1995. "Are We Saving Enough for the Future?" In World Bank. 1995. *Monitoring Environmental Progress: A Report on Work in Progress.* Environmentally Sustainable Development. Washington, D.C.

Solorzano, R., and others. 1991. *Accounts Overdue: Natural Resource Depreciation in Costa Rica.* Washington, D.C.: World Resources Institute.

Squire, L., and H. Van der Taak. 1975. *Economic Analysis of Projects.* Baltimore, MD: The Johns Hopkins University Press.

UNDP (United Nations Development Programme). 1998. *Human Development Report.* New York: Oxford University Press.

Weitzman, M. L. 1976. "On the Welfare Significance of National Product in a Dynamic Economy." *Quarterly Journal of Economics* 90: 156-62.

Wolfensohn, J. D. 1999. "A Proposal for a Comprehensive Development Framework." Washington, D.C.: World Bank.

World Bank. 1996. *Expanding the Measure of Wealth: Indicators of Environmentally Sustainable Development.* Washington, D.C.

Floor Discussion: Valuation and Evaluation

Anwar Shah commented that many countries (New Zealand being the foremost example) were already applying the concept of net worth. New Zealand's government calculated its net worth on an annual basis in the form of asset valuation over time, contingent liabilities, and cash flow. A number of other countries were moving toward implementing net worth systems, because macroeconomists especially have realized that countries' deficits and debts alone do not tell them much about their fiscal situation.

Jan Piercy stated that from the perspective of someone sitting in a policymaking position, the address was sobering. She was looking at it through the lens of the current international campaign to broaden and deepen the so-called Heavily Indebted Poor Countries Initiative (HIPC). She thought that the analytical base against which indebtedness is being measured is too limited. She feared that in using that base, analysts were not capturing some of what needs to be known to understand whether debt reduction is likely to be sustainable.

Robert Picciotto indicated that much of the discussion taking place in the World Bank and elsewhere was about projects not being policy. He wondered if Dasgupta could expand his definition of policy in a way that went beyond its project components.

In response, Dasgupta asked the audience to imagine a forecast of activities that they thought were going to happen and to think of current policies as "business as usual." With some understanding of how people behave and how different sectors are likely to respond, one could derive a forecast of the economy on the basis of business as usual that referred essentially to the goods and services flowing in and out, and to which groups. Such forecasts about the economy could be as micro as one liked, depending on the availability of data.

He then asked the audience to consider an elementary policy reform, say a change in tax rates or a fuel tax. They should think of this as injecting change into the tax that was in place. A permanent tax change would be a sequence of elementary policies, in a sense. A permanent switch would be built up of temporary switches into which one could also build irreversibility by saying that once you switch, you never "unswitch."

Consider, then, a one-year change in the tax rate, which then reverts to its previous rate. This brief perturbation would alter the initial forecast. It would mean that people would have a slightly different mix of goods and services today—and, indeed, the day after tomorrow—than they started with. Tomorrow, when the policy reverted, the economy's capital stocks would be different from what had been forecast prior to the perturbation.

Elizabeth McAllister, Director of the World Bank's OED moderated the discussion.

What would have happened is a ripple effect over time. A new forecast of goods and services would be in effect.

That, explained Dasgupta, would be a project, because the forecast of goods and services had been slightly perturbed. The reason for a perturbation makes no difference. One could say that a perturbation took place because the project evaluation officers had said, "Go ahead and build that dam," or because an NGO had been set up, or because the Bank had decided to lend some money, or because the government had changed a tax regime or the property rights system, or because the village had decided to revert to a common property system or to alter the common property structure and property rights. Conceptually, Dasgupta saw no difference between these perturbations. Both a project and a policy change were really a perturbation of an economic forecast.

Another participant wanted to add some transparency to the concept of the NNP. He assumed that, according to Dasgupta, the NNP included changes not only in the stock of financial capital, but also in the stock of natural resources, health, and human capital. He noted, for example, that when economists discussed the stock of health, they had in mind potential changes in that stock that might affect, for example, malnutrition among very young children and their capacity to grow, from which they could not recover after a certain age. As one result of a crisis, say, some health indicators might deteriorate, which is tantamount to a reduction in the stock of health. Similarly, for education, when children drop out of primary school, what is the likelihood they will go back? A drop in enrollment results in a loss of potential human capital. When Dasgupta used this concept of the NNP, he suggested that it incorporate these types of stock.

Dasgupta agreed. When he discussed wealth, he meant all the assets that mattered for social well-being. A change in the flow of goods and services was really a change in assets. So an economy or a group of people who had inherited stocks from past policies carried those stocks with them, and also had certain policies that led to the flow of goods and services into the future. The kinds of capital he was referring to were physical capital and human capital. And human capital included health, education, and other components, including the knowledge base.

Finally, Dasgupta addressed the question of how we could forecast which aspects of social capital would be generated by the prevailing capital structure. When many social networks were eroding locally because of the rise of markets, in reality some sectors were gaining while others were losing. In principle, determining who the losers were was not difficult. They would be the people who were essentially outside the market system—for instance, women in villages who had children and were not very mobile. One could pick out the people who were likely to be threatened in an erosion of social capital in certain parts of the world or certain part of a particular country as a result of growth in other types of capital, local or otherwise.

Evaluation in a World of Complexity and Information Failures

Joseph Stiglitz

I have argued elsewhere that perhaps our greatest moral and fiduciary responsibility is to the billion poor people in the developing world. Our moral duty is to ensure, to the extent of our ability, that the projects and policy reforms we support will not only improve their lives but will improve them by enough to more than offset the burden of additional debt payments in the future.

This may seem like a very low threshold, but it is a threshold that, in my view, we fail to achieve all too often. Rigorous evaluation must be an integral part of our work if we are to accomplish even this modest goal, for only through evaluation can we establish whether or not we are meeting this fiduciary responsibility.

Let me comment on my use of the word "rigorous." Too often, we tend to talk about "best practices" based on unsystematic, anecdotal evidence. Of course, knowing what worked in a particular situation is useful, but what worked in one situation will not necessarily work in others. What is critical is the kind of rigorous evaluation that is the focus of the discussion in this conference.

I will focus on two observations, using the example of health care as an illustration. First, real-world problems are broad and complex, and evaluation must take such complexity into account. Second, evaluation, as well as policy and project design, must also incorporate an understanding of the information failures and limitations that are rampant in developing country markets and organizations. Such information failures and their implications were one of the main themes in this year's *World Development Report* (World Bank 1999).

Taking Account of Real-World Complexity in Evaluation

The basic methodology of modern science is to take complex problems and divide them into smaller problems. In economics we often leave it at that, content to look at the individual answers to smaller problems. We leave it to policymakers to weave these various threads together, if they can. One example from my days at the White House involved an extremely complex subject—toxic waste. Addressing the problem of toxic waste in a legal sense involved three major reforms, one of which entailed a change in legal structure. The U.S. legal system imposed what is called "joint and several" liability, and we had to find an alternative legal structure that had the enforcement properties of joint and several liability without imposing the inequities and exorbitant legal costs associated with the existing legal system. One example of these costs was that, at the time, more than 25 percent of the dollars spent on toxic waste cleanup was devoted to lawyers' fees. While this arrangement may have greatly benefited the lawyers, it was not the best investment of public money.

The first task in reforming the toxic waste cleanup system was thus to address the issue of joint and several liability, which the law and economics professions had given little thought to on any practical level. Some theorems stated that the joint and several liability system was actually theoretically equivalent to a number of other legal structures, a finding that ignored all the practical problems raised by the system. Even though legal experts had looked at several problems and had addressed them in a strictly legal context, they had not focused on how to reform the legal structure with respect to the particular problems posed by joint and several liability. The second issue was that of cost-benefit analysis, in which we had to judge just how clean a toxic waste setup needed to be. The third problem involved the insurance market, where the process of determining who had to pay for cleaning up the mess was extremely complex.

All three of these problems were intimately interrelated, and while the economics literature dealt with each of the three problems, no one had yet attempted to bring them all together. The formidable problem that faced us in a policy context was how to do just that—that is, how to integrate all three of these issues together into a single coherent framework.

What this anecdote illustrates is that even addressing a single problem like toxic waste required reaching beyond the domains of environmental economics into disciplines typically considered quite unrelated. In this case, the solution finally required an understanding of insurance markets and legal structures. Researchers, as well as large organizations, often feel the urge to confront problems with a divide and conquer strategy. Institutions such as the Bank and national governments are large organizations that, to function effectively, have to break up problems and divide the world into separate and distinct categories. At the Bank for example, we have divided the world into five networks and thirteen sector groups.

A danger arising from the subdivision of larger problems, however, is that the subdivisions create vested interests and myopic foci. Individuals in a particular region or trained in a particular discipline will tend to analyze problems only through their distinct paradigms. Yet, as I have argued, the whole is more than the sum of its parts, and as the expression goes, too often we fail to see the forest when we spend our lives examining individual trees. The CDF is an attempt by the Bank to overcome the dangers of this compartmentalized approach to development strategy and to urge developing countries to do the same in their own strategies. The CDF explicitly highlights the links between sectors and actors in the development arena. It recognizes that problems in one sector can block or undo well-designed reforms in another and that the converse is also true: progress in bottleneck sectors can release pent-up advances in another. Development strategy needs to take account of these links and, consequently, so does evaluation.

> The CDF explicitly highlights the links between sectors and actors in the development arena. Development strategy needs to take account of these links and, consequently, so does evaluation.

Let us consider the implications of this approach by focusing on one aspect of development: health. Development practitioners now generally accept that development success entails far more than a simple increase in GDP. The Bank and the rest of the development community are interested in equitable and sustainable development, particularly with regard to the very poor. Health is one of the most important dimensions of better living standards. Yet in many countries, the poor are not just in poorer health than the rich but, as figure 2.1 shows, they are in significantly poorer health. The countries in the poorest decile have much higher adult and child mortality rates than those in the richer deciles. Figure 2.1 also illustrates several other points. For example, in Bangladesh, the poorest tenth are much better off relative to the richest tenth in the country, and the inequality in health across economic classes is generally much less pronounced, than in, say, Tanzania or Uganda. Clearly some countries have been much more effective than others at achieving egalitarian health care services. This is important, because it demonstrates that improving health care for the very poor is possible.

When thinking about health care, the CDF approach urges us not to turn exclusively or reflexively to health ministries, which all too often are beholden to special interests such as health care providers, hospitals, and drug companies. This was another issue I constantly addressed during my tenure in the Clinton administration, as we reviewed proposals to reform the American health care system. Instead of looking only at providers, we attempted to ask more comprehensive questions, such as what are the

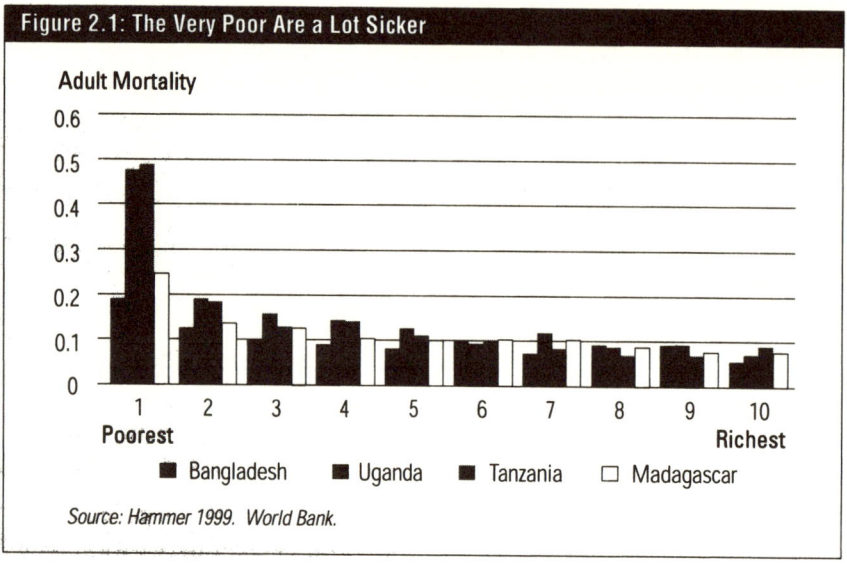

factors that most contribute to poor health, especially among the poor? What are the delivery mechanisms that will be most cost effective in addressing these factors and in improving the overall health status of the very poor? These overarching questions led us to forge a way out of the constraining boxes of subdisciplinary thinking. They allowed us to see that promoting health, rather than simply health care services, should be the policy objective.

Good health care policy will make good use of instruments that health care services do not usually deliver, such as better knowledge, improved childhood nutrition, or increased access to clean water. Take this last point as an example. Access to clean water and basic sanitation facilities is highly correlated with health status, especially the health status of infants and young children. Not surprisingly, the poorest people are also those with the most limited access to these services.

Figure 2.2 shows the strikingly inequitable distribution of access to such basic services. The top part of the figure shows relative lack of access to sanitation by level of wealth, illustrating how the richest 40 percent of people have nearly universal access to sanitation services, whereas the poorest 60 percent of people do not have nearly the same access. The same is true access to clean water by wealth: whereas almost 100 percent of the richest segments of society have access to clean water, only a small percentage of the poorest do. Hammer (1999) argues that a strategy that focuses directly on infrastructure problems such as these may be a far more cost-effective means of improving health status than actual health programs.

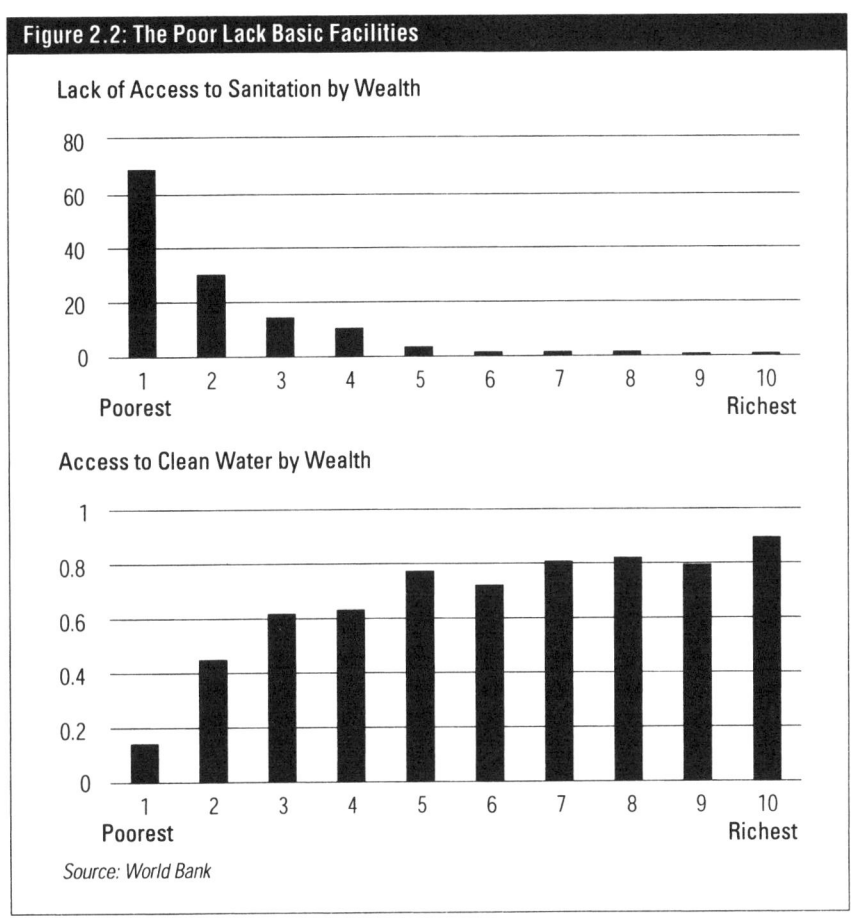

Figure 2.3 shows how the provision of both good water and sanitation could bring down the infant mortality rate markedly. Households that have both sanitation facilities and clean water experience an almost 50 percent lower incidence of child mortality than households that have access to neither—a tremendous difference.

Like infrastructure investments, investments in education can also have substantial payoffs in the health sector. For example, education programs that inform the poor about the proper location of latrines, the importance of chimneys that allow smoke to escape from their huts, the value of mosquito nets in protecting them against malaria, the value of certain precautions that will help prevent the spread of aquired immuniodeficiency syndrome (AIDS), the dangers of alcohol and drug abuse, and the possibilities offered by various birth control methods can all improve people's health status. It is not just investment in knowledge dissemination that matters but also investment in giving people the capacity to acquire

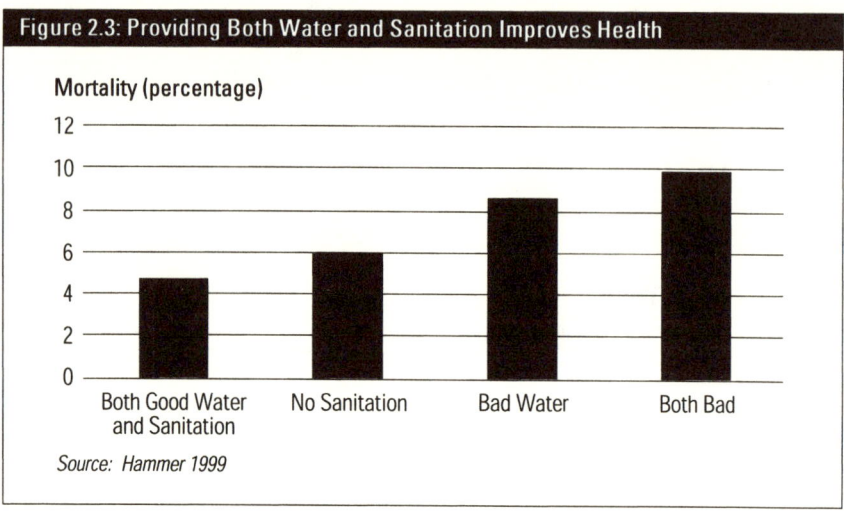

Figure 2.3: Providing Both Water and Sanitation Improves Health

Source: Hammer 1999

knowledge. The impact of education on health status is now well documented. Figure 2.4 shows the enormous impact of womens' higher education on reducing childhood mortality. Thus, at least one important set of links is intersectoral—that is, the links that bridge the health and infrastructure sectors and the health and education sectors.

A second set of links connects the different actors in the health field. For each country we need to assess what is and what is not likely to work, given the context of that country. Health care services are part of a nexus of social services, the provision of which fits into a complex set of relationships between villages, lower-level jurisdictions, the central government, and informal and formal institutions within each society. In some places, such as the Philippines, the provision of health care services in conjunction with the delivery of prenatal and obstetrical services has proven to be an effective entry point—one that, at the same time, can be an important vehicle for the social mobilization of women. A comprehensive approach to development helps countries recognize and take advantage of these economies of scope.

> Evaluators must first ask whether the project or program has kept its eye on the ultimate objective—that is, better health outcomes for the poorest rather than better delivery of health service outputs.

Evaluation of the impact of poverty-targeted health interventions must be similarly comprehensive in its scope, even as the evaluation adheres to scientific standards that were developed within a narrow disciplinary framework. Evaluators must first ask whether the project or program has kept its eye on the ultimate objective—that is, better health outcomes for the poorest rather than better delivery of health service outputs. They must ask also whether a given intervention is

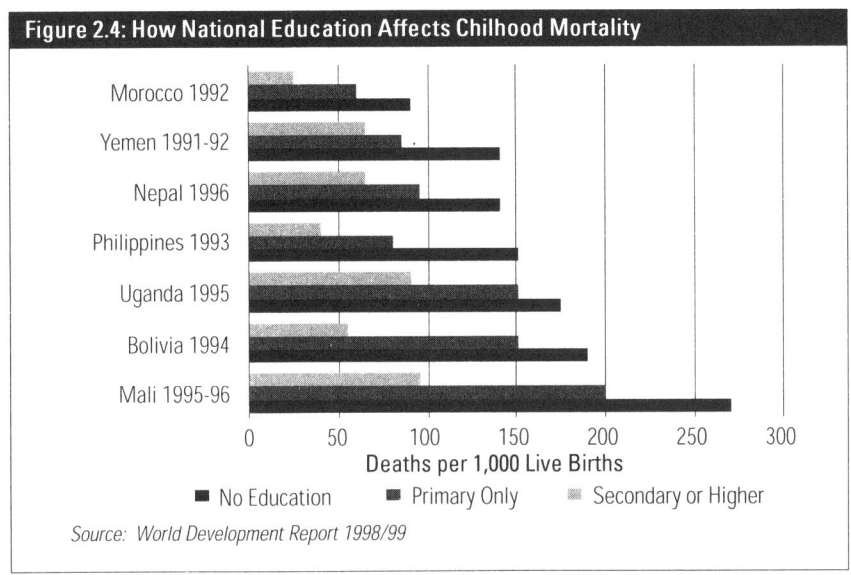

Figure 2.4: How National Education Affects Chilhood Mortality

Deaths per 1,000 Live Births

■ No Education ■ Primary Only ▨ Secondary or Higher

Source: World Development Report 1998/99

the most cost-effective vehicle for achieving that ultimate objective, considering the alternative of making health-related investments outside the health care system. Finally, they must examine whether a given actor, especially the health ministry, is the one best suited to deliver a needed service. Perhaps, given a world of information problems and poor incentives, channeling services through nongovernmental organizations (NGOs) or village administrations might be more cost-effective.

The Role of Information Failure in Poverty-focused Policy and Evaluation

The health sector is rife with market failures stemming from information problems and poor incentives, which in turn are related to moral hazard, adverse selection, and third-party payment. All these problems would seem to call for government action. In recent years, however, health economists have become more skeptical of this type of response. They have learned that information problems in the public sector can lead to massive government failure.

The problems of incentives and information asymmetries can bedevil government provision of health care services in developing countries. Government programs to provide services to the poor have often failed because governments have failed to monitor whether the services are actually provided. In poor villages, the central government may have to bear the bulk of costs for payments to the local doctor. With no incentive pay and no monitoring, the doctor has no incentive to actually provide the services.

This kind of problem arises not just in health care services but also in such arenas as education, where countries build schools but teachers do not actually come to teach. In these contexts, informal incentive schemes often arise in which the doctor or teacher receives "side payments," as they are euphemistically called. Because better-off villagers are invariably those who can afford the side payments, this means that public services are not provided to the poorest among the poor. While monitoring may be easier in urban areas, the urban users of such services typically have incomes far above the national average, and such services do not reach down to the poorest among urban dwellers. Even if they do reach the poorest urban poor, as a group they are relatively wealthy compared with the rural poor.

What does all this have to do with evaluation? Rigorous evaluation is precisely what attracts attention to these information and incentive problems. A lazy but all too natural approach to evaluating health programs would focus on intermediate outputs, such as how many clinics have been built in rural areas and how many doctors have been assigned to them. A better evaluation methodology would direct us toward the ultimate outputs and, beyond that, to outcome indicators. For example, what we want to know and measure are the quantity and quality of health services that villagers are actually receiving and whether these services have had any effect on their health status. By answering these questions and by spotlighting incentive problems, evaluation can point the way toward alternatives to the traditional means of delivering and monitoring health services.

Some alternatives to the traditional centralized approach to health care include community-based delivery and monitoring. Having services provided by members of the community who may be especially trained for that purpose can lead to more effective provision, in part because the community can use such methods as social sanctions to enforce good behavior. This is possible partly because such individuals identify with the community and its concerns. Thus, training some members of the community to provide at least basic services may be far more efficient and effective than trying to force elite doctors or paramedics to serve in local communities.

Especially when information is hard to come by, community-based monitoring of health service provision may be more effective than monitoring from a central headquarters, because the community has stronger incentives to monitor and the costs of monitoring are lower. Indeed, the marginal cost of monitoring at the community level may effectively be zero, because such monitoring may be a by-product of other activities. As the members of the community are the recipients of the service, community-based monitoring leads to demands for quality just as high as (if not higher than) demands for conventional marketed goods. Having said this, let me add that the implementing agency should complement community-based monitoring with close local monitoring, and overall supervision from the head office may also be appropriate.

Community-based monitoring has proven effective in a number of areas, especially when provided through NGOs. On a recent visit to Bangladesh I was impressed by the education and health programs carried out by the Bangladesh Rural Advancement Committee (BRAC), a leading NGO, which has shown how the pure monitoring principle underlying successful microcredit programs can be extended to other areas. The BRAC experience is also interesting in four other dimensions, as follows:

> Community-based monitoring has proven effective in a number of areas, especially when provided through NGOs.

- BRAC is now a small NGO reaching a substantial proportion of Bangladesh's huge rural population. The country's considerable success in bringing down infant mortality rates and improving the health status of the very poor has been achieved mainly through NGO programs such as those run by BRAC.
- BRAC has an active research program that focuses on the evaluation of its programs, so that it constantly studies what is working and readjusts its programs on the basis of that learning. This approach allows BRAC to fine-tune its institutional structure to make it more effective in delivering health care to the poor.
- BRAC's experience exemplifies the importance of economies of scope and demonstrates that those economies of scope exist across different programs, because BRAC began as a microcredit program but then extended itself into health and education, including legal education. This is particularly important where the transformation of social mobilization is an essential step toward longer-term development.
- BRAC's experience demonstrates that the most effective way to improve health may be to work through channels other than directly through health services and ministries.

In sectors such as health care, where information problems are extremely important, how does one go about doing good evaluation? The same information problems that plague and erode the effectiveness of the conventional market model make good evaluation extremely difficult, if not impossible. How do we conceive of the relationship between the information problems at the root of health care delivery and the market structure and information problems that we have to confront as evaluators?

To put it another way, evaluation relies on good data, and reliable data on the quantity and quality of health care services are precisely what governments often lack. If governments had that kind of data, providing the needed services in the most efficient manner would naturally be far easier. While this is an issue that needs further study, evaluation provides discipline by requiring the evaluator to look at end results such as health status and decide whether targeted programs are having an effect. This focus allows them to identify whether problems exist in an area where measuring data directly is extremely difficult, such as the quantity and quality of health services provided.

To be sure, a host of other factors affect the ultimate outcomes, so a focus on outcomes may not be appropriate for defining incentive schemes for individual service deliverers. The information needed to design an incentive scheme or an institutional structure is different from the information needed to evaluate the success of an overall program.

Furthermore, even when full-time monitoring of ultimate outputs is too costly to be feasible, mounting a one-time evaluation that does provide the necessary data may be possible. The ability to use statistical sampling methods increases the feasibility of such an evaluation. While such an evaluation may be costly and may not be used to create a better incentive structure, it will allow evaluators to assess, for instance, how well a particular institutional structure addresses information problems. Even though sampling does not permit comprehensive monitoring of individuals, it does allow evaluators to learn something about the aggregate delivery of health services.

Conclusion

The foregoing has emphasized two points. First, good evaluation of alternative policies and projects must take a comprehensive view that recognizes cross-sectoral links, such as those connecting infrastructure investment and health. Second, good evaluation must also recognize and take account of the information and incentive failures that derail government programs. Clearly these two lessons need to be applied simultaneously. While action such as increasing access to clean water can dramatically improve the health status of the poor, because information failures can easily undermine infrastructure projects, we need to carefully design programs that will deal with such failures by, for example, heavily enlisting community participation. The Bank has carried out a number of studies that support this conclusion—namely, that projects with significant community participation are not only likely to work better but are also more likely to be sustained.

Evaluating our work in development is essential not just to tell us whether a program yields benefits that exceed its costs but also to point the way toward institutions and incentive structures that promise more effective strategies for democratic, equitable, and sustainable development.

Floor Discussion: Evaluation in a World of Complexity and Information Failures

One participant noted that Stiglitz' focus on incentive structures in an authorizing environment was the right one and that the tendency to micromanage was unnecessary.

Stiglitz responded by saying that the health care sector was more problematic in those respects than the education sector, but the general point that one could get information from the choices individuals made was clear, and trying to generate institutions that reflected this idea was important.

He gave an example in the health care sector. Very different costs are associated with providing health care to individuals with very different health needs. Insurance firms, as providers, have a strong incentive to recruit the lowest-cost beneficiaries—that is, those with the fewest health care needs. Insurance firms can increase their profits more by identifying low-risk individuals with a low probability of using health care services than by improving the quality of the health care delivery mechanism. This adverse selection problem is so significant in the health care sector that the kind of choice mechanism the participant referred to would be greatly undermined.

The problem was pervasive in the health care sector, said Stiglitz, and could not be avoided, but similar issues also arose in one way or another in other social sectors, even education. It was easier and less expensive to educate a child with a strong home background than a child without one, for example. And in many places transportation costs were very high and, in local communities with only one school and one health clinic, effective competition was impossible. Even in more developed countries, the number of health or education providers in rural areas was very limited.

So while the participant's suggestion might work in certain areas, in many areas competition would not be an adequate solution.

Constance Portland, who had worked for many years in the field of paraveterinary health care, noted the tremendous synergism and potential cost savings in combining the provision of paraveterinary health care, human health care, and education. The spillover from educating people about basic health care, whether human or animal health care, was significant because many of the same principles applied.

Ravi Kanbur asked how one might evaluate assistance from different donors—for instance, comparing the Bank's money to USAID's money to some other group's money. Stiglitz had suggested that it was not right to evaluate these streams of dollars separately. "Let's go for outcomes," he had said. But institutional pressure from taxpayers is to show the productivity of individual investments. This is a real institutional problem, and, as every agency has its own evaluation group, a major problem for evaluation as a whole.

Robert Picciotto, Director-General of Operations Evaluation in the Bank and IFC, moderated the discussion.

Stiglitz responded by pointing out that the fungibility of funds (donors' dollars being ostensibly provided for one project but actually financing something else), was, in a sense, different from the issue under discussion: evaluating a particular delivery system. Who financed a health care project was not as important as the particular delivery system, about which one could talk more easily in terms of the relationship between benefits and costs. In that sense, evaluation was an important part of the program design. Evaluation did not really help ascertain the effectiveness of an institution's dollars, except by association—saying that the institution had helped push certain kinds of programs that had been very productive. One got credit by association with good projects.

Susan Stout said she had looked at the entire portfolio of World Bank health, nutrition, and population projects since 1970, and at 224 loans in depth, and had not found a single example of the Bank investing in capacity for measuring outcomes at the village or community level.

Stiglitz replied that projects were valuable to the extent that they could be replicated on a larger scale. Whether they should or should not be replicated depended on whether they were working, which was why evaluation needed to be part of what the World Bank calls the knowledge bank.

In response to a question about the institutional implications of his presentation, Stiglitz stressed that a focus on outcomes was more important than a focus on organizational issues. The Human Development Network needed to see itself, for instance, as committed to promoting health care services, whether through the health ministry or through an infrastructure project. The real point was that attention needed to focus on the outcomes. The Development Assistance Committee's (DAC) goals were to keep the focus on outcomes and to convert the notion of promoting development and reducing poverty into concrete terms. The DAC goals were inevitably somewhat arbitrary, but the very process of going through them helped focus attention on the real issues.

References

Hammer. 1999. *World Bank Research Observer.*

World Bank. 1999. *World Development Report 1999: Knowledge for Development.* New York: Oxford University Press.

Panel Discussion: Evaluation Perspectives on Poverty Reduction

Vinod Thomas, Alison Evans, Moise Mensah, Niels Dabelstein

Vinod Thomas

It is not the greatest news that a group of people is focusing on poverty as such, nor that a group of people is focusing on institutions as such. It is not the greatest news that a few people are focusing on evaluation as such. It is news that no discussion of development today can be serious without seeing the links between these areas and putting development at the center of our discussions. That is why this conference and this panel discussion are so important and why we are so fortunate to have a policymaker, an evaluator from a bilateral agency, and an evaluator from a multilateral agency to address us.

Alison Evans

I am the task manager of an evaluation that is looking at the effectiveness of the Bank's poverty reduction strategy as originally set out in the 1990 *World Development Report on Poverty.* However, the Bank's strategy has undergone some changes in focus and direction during the past eight years, as we have learned more about implementing poverty reduction projects. I will highlight some of the lessons emerging from this evaluation, which are related to lessons emerging from evaluations that other organizations are currently carrying out, and then comment on what I think this means for the evaluation frontier from the standpoint of a multilateral institution.

What has the evaluation shown us about the effectiveness of a multilateral organization, or of any development organization, that is trying to help reduce poverty? One of the first lessons is that some interventions help reduce poverty even in policy and institutional environments that do not match our criteria for good performers and, in some cases, could even be considered dysfunctional. For example, some individual social fund projects seem to have worked despite the odds against either being able to deliver basic infrastructure services or to involve poor people in defining specific needs along with projects to meet those needs. Why did these projects succeed? What can we learn from them?

Even when projects fail to meet their objectives by all our standard criteria, sometimes elements in those interventions—for example, involving poor people in making decisions and choices more effectively—provide us with important lessons for poverty reduction. Perhaps a particular water project, road project, or health intervention has clearly not met the standard objectives or criteria for project success, but it can nevertheless provide us with important lessons on how to do better in the future whatever the project was attempting to do. We must not ignore projects that seem to fail but must learn from them.

At the same time, some projects that do not have explicit poverty reduction objectives can help alleviate poverty. In the water sector, for example, improving the water supply can result in better outcomes in terms of the health status of poor people than health projects do. We need to think creatively about how we should evaluate such projects.

A third lesson is that the success of a specific intervention targeted toward the poor may depend on factors outside the project. Microfinance is a good example. Some recent evaluation work both inside and outside the Bank indicates that to get the expected increases in income from microfinance interventions, simultaneous investments in infrastructure, communication, and information dissemination are needed to achieve multiplier effects. So an intervention in one area may be critically dependent on an intervention in another.

A fourth lesson: Interventions in particular sectors or localities often have spillover effects, both positive and negative, that can either add to or cancel out project-specific effects. Consider microfinance again. Some research suggests that receiving credit through microfinance schemes can result in huge benefits, especially for women, but in some cases negative distributional outcomes in the prevailing power balance within households may cancel out the total effect in terms of well-being. In a more positive example, a specific intervention to provide rural feeder roads might produce clear direct benefits in terms of increased traffic flow and improved rural mobility, but the spillover effects in terms of employment and consumption multipliers that extend beyond the project area are all equally important and can add considerably to the overall effect of the individual intervention.

All this mean that we are still struggling to move beyond Newtonian evaluation. We have got to think beyond atoms, beyond fragmenting effects, to think more in a quantum mechanics fashion—that is, we have to think through the methodological and conceptual implications of adding up effects, effects that may be contradictory.

Of course, the challenge is how to communicate this to our policymakers and to our partners. We need to be careful that in moving to the system level we do not lose sight of the individual. Thus, the key to the quantum approach is that every small change, even at the level of the individual or the household, matters for the entire system, at the sector, country, or global level.

> We must examine the totality of an effect associated with specific interventions at the project level, the sector level, or the policy level.

We have to be prepared to take that challenge on. It means thinking systemically, but it also means living with more uncertainty in evaluation than we have been used to. This approach does not mean that we should lose sight of the individual project or the individual intervention that can make a difference to the system as a whole.

Moise Mensah

The major concern at this conference is how to go about a proper and effective impact assessment of projects, programs, and policies. Of course, the major difficulty here resides in the definition of poverty, because of its multifaceted character. One lesson we have learned is that in addition to the constituent elements that contribute to the assessment of living conditions, such as purchasing power, changes in the availability of and access to public services, changes in the level of productivity of different factors, and changes in the prices of goods and services, we must also resort to a qualitative approach, if only because the perception of poverty by the poor is of paramount importance. Indeed, the motivations of the poor to get out of poverty or to improve their condition depend on their appreciation of opportunities, risks, and their own abilities and limitations.

Furthermore, poverty reduction strategies and programs cannot be effective and sustainable unless they systematically take the perceptions and opinions of the poor into account. For example, what do the poor consider to be important within the various dimensions of poverty? Is it low income? Is it food insecurity? Is it exposure to diseases?

We must also agree with the poor on the priority they attach to poverty reduction programs and projects. For example, a survey in the rural areas of Benin showed that, to the local population, the main causes of poverty are (a) the weakness of the market because they lack access to it, and (b) the lack of solidarity within families and communities and the accompanying disintegration of society. This was news. Here we were, thinking that changes in society are conducive to progress, while the people affected considered this a component of poverty that had to be addressed.

The same survey showed that poverty is a self-propelling and self-perpetuating process. For example, a group of women was asked to give a deposit of CFAF 5,000, or some US$10, to a local credit union to gain access to credit with which to undertake income-raising activities. Their response was that if they had US$10, they would not need credit. This implies that they did not believe they could improve their condition by borrowing. We need to understand these kinds of perceptions and take them into account so that we can formulate programs that address poverty reduction effectively.

Another lesson we learned is that with the rapid urbanization of what used to be essentially rural economies, the contrast between the poverty profile in rural areas and in urban areas is growing. For example, another survey in Benin on the consumption expenditures of households in various socioeconomic categories showed that the rural poor spent 64 percent of their income on food and beverages, 6 percent on clothing, 4 percent on equipment and durable goods, and 0.7 percent on education and leisure, compared with the urban poor, who spent 30 percent of their income on food and beverages, 16 percent on clothing, 0.6 percent on equipment and durable goods, and 4 percent on education and leisure. The implications: we should try to approach poverty reduction in a targeted manner that addresses specific programs to specific groups.

As for the impact assessment of program and projects, the expected impact is normally defined during appraisal, when the indicators against which to assess impacts are also defined. However, the real issue is whether the evaluation process succeeds in identifying the real causes of any major gap between expected results and actual results and whether the lessons learned can be used to improve project performance over time.

In this connection, we should bear two things in mind. First, evaluation should be not only an end-of-project exercise but also an ongoing process of monitoring and evaluation. While this is understood in principle, it is not happening. I believe one key constraint is the training of those responsible for carrying out evaluation. This is important, because we must be able to adjust program and project components depending on evaluation findings. For example, if a women's group has been given the means to carry out staple food production as the best way to reduce poverty, but the evaluation later learned that they are better off than expected because they shifted into such income-raising activities as food processing, it should be possible to change gears and adjust. This can happen only if the evaluation findings come early enough in the life of the project.

Second, evaluation must be a participatory exercise in the same way project implementation should be. This is the only way we can identify relevant impact indicators and analyze the impact of various activities in a reliable manner, with confidence, and with a sense of ownership. This requires using appropriate communication approaches, and I suggest looking at traditional communication techniques. Evaluation is basically an exercise in good communication. You need to have the right information, and for this you need to establish rapport, confidence, and trust.

In relation to policy impact, for example, we need to analyze the impact and consistency of public expenditures as against stated policies. This is especially important with ongoing financial adjustment programs, where a variety of indicators is possible, such as per capita expenditure in the social sector or the relationship between the transportation sector and GDP. Other indicators can provide information on various improvements in the social sector in the form of numbers—for example, number of health centers established or school enrollment—but are such indicators adequate? In addition, in some cases the results you expect happen, but so do unexpected outcomes so a clear correlation between policies, actions, and results cannot be established. Therefore, the tools for assessing impact must be sharpened and attuned to various circumstances so that we can establish whether there really are correlations and, if there are, can use those correlations to formulate programs and policies more effectively.

> Evaluation is basically an exercise in good communication.

Poverty reduction is, of course, a complex process, and in Benin we have found that beyond the traditional approach to establishing safety nets—for instance, creating jobs in urban areas through public works—having a more permanent safety net is important. That has led us to the concept of minimum common social requirements or basic needs. By minimum common social requirements we mean the set of goods and services that ensures the existence of a community and enables it to participate fully in human development. To implement that concept, to learn from ongoing experience, we need to look carefully at how to carry out the type of assessment or evaluation that will enable us to draw lessons.

The complicated process of poverty reduction can succeed only if the poor are confident in their own ability to move out of poverty. Joint evaluation by all partners, including the poor, should allow us to learn from past and ongoing efforts, mistakes, and achievements to assess specific requirements for specific targeted groups. The scope of evaluation should go beyond development programs and projects. It should also address the impact of declared policy.

Niels Dabelstein

I will focus on joint evaluation. This panel was asked to look at evaluation from three different perspectives—the multilateral agency's, the bilateral donor's, and the recipient country's—which is somewhat surprising, because if we take the CDF seriously, we should all be looking at poverty from the same perspective. However, judging from the two previous presentations, we seem to share perspectives on poverty and poverty evaluation, so that is not a concern.

Basically the question we need to ask is this: Are we doing the right things and are we doing them right? However, before we can discuss this question, we have to agree on what poverty is. Do we have an agreed-upon definition or concept of poverty? I would venture a broad definition or concept of poverty—namely, the deprivation of basic human needs and rights, underscoring rights. That definition not only encompasses economic and social needs and rights in terms of consumption and access to resources and public services but also includes dignity, autonomy, personal security, rule of law, freedom of expression, and equality of opportunities.

Poverty can be viewed from four dimensions—livelihoods, resources, knowledge, and rights. Each dimension can be measured at different levels—the individual level, the household level, the community level, the country level, and even the global level. At the global level, we can compare the distribution of wealth between countries or regions, of people's access to resources, of the rule of international law—issues that are often the root causes of conflicts. If for no other reason, that is a good rationale for global redistribution and transfer of resources and, therefore, for increased development aid.

From a collective donor perspective, the focus should be on the country and, of course, our country strategies and policy dialogue should address all four dimensions of poverty. Aggregate indicators will tell us how our resources could best be distributed to address all four dimensions. However, we should also stress that as individual donors we should not necessarily address all dimensions, and all donors should not individually or collectively address only the one dimension that happens to be most popular in current development discourse. The key is coordination and cooperation, and here we come back to the CDF as a framework within which we can develop strategies so that our collective efforts with partner countries cover the ground adequately.

The individual donor and partner country would evaluate how effectively sector policies, strategies, and interventions in different sectors address the four dimensions of poverty, which is no easy task. In reality it is probably impossible as we move toward sectorwide support and budget support, where attribution to an individual donor's intervention is not feasible.

The key issue for evaluators is to carry out joint evaluations, host and donors together, to build up evaluation capacity and to create a demand for high-quality evaluations. It does not make sense to try to measure the impact of one donor's assistance at the community, household, or individual level, even though these levels are the most important, because indicators of change at these levels are the building blocks for measuring the effects of collective efforts to combat poverty.

The only truly joint evaluation of a collective intervention I have come across was the joint evaluation of the international community's response to the genocide in Rwanda, in 1996. However, that evaluation was so unique that it probably could not be repeated elsewhere, even though the need for something similar in Kosovo is obvious, not only to assess the effects of humanitarian assistance and interventions in Kosovo but also to assess the consequences for other, poorer, regions of the world of the massive diversion of funds to the Balkan region.

> The key issue for evaluators is to carry out joint evaluations.

On a much more modest scale, over the past few years, the Development Assistance Committee evaluation has tried to initiate sector evaluations as joint efforts, trying to get the five or six key donors and the host country to jointly evaluate just one sector in one country. Only now are we seeing the light at the end of the tunnel in an evaluation of the transport sector in Ghana.

Floor Discussion: Evaluation Perspectives on Poverty Reduction

Vinod Thomas opened the discussion with a reference to the panel's presentation in general and to Niels Dabelstein's remarks in particular.[1] Dabelstein had put the issue of partnership and joint work squarely on the table. The panel had highlighted the complexity of the agenda and the importance of quality, but if the participants recognized that interactions and complementarities exist, it might help donors and developing country partners deal with the complexities and feel less overwhelmed.

Ian Hopwood of the United Nations Children's Fund made three points. First, was poverty reduction as defined by Dabelstein an operational concept, given its complexity and its intersectoral reality? Second, multilateral agencies were increasingly being asked for results-based monitoring and reporting, but this created certain problems. Donors were also working on capacity building, for example, and how could that be quantified? And when donors cooperate with others, how do they apportion the credit? Third, Moise Mensah had mentioned the role of targeting. The United Nations Children's Fund was learning that nondiscretionary targeting methods might be far superior to discretionary methods.

Evans suggested that the questions asked determined the answers received. If evaluators asked simply whether a road delivered benefits to the poor, for example, they would learn whether or not a road delivered benefits to the poor. Perhaps they should ask whether donors should be doing roads at all.

As for results-based management, Evans did not think it worked against the systemic approach; however, project designers had to carefully avoid purely linear thinking. They also needed to think around corners. Perhaps by the second or third year of a project, they might find that the results chain they had anticipated at appraisal was clearly not relevant and that they would need to quickly rethink project designs. Everyone involved in project and program design needed to be flexible and adaptable and able to live with uncertainty.

Mona Bishay of the International Fund for Agricultural Development had two questions about the initial results of the evaluation of the World Bank's strategy on poverty alleviation. One finding of the evaluation was that some projects managed to reach the poor even though they took place in dysfunctional or nonenabling macroeconomic environments. The speaker wondered why and suggested three reasons why a project might reach the poor even in such an environment. First, the project might have addressed a technical constraint that was binding for the rural poor in that region. Second, the project might have targeted its interventions to the rural poor well and those

---

Vinod Thomas of WBI chaired the discussion.

interventions might have been relevant. Third, the project might have succeeded in strengthening grassroots institutions in a way that increased their ability to gain access to resources, goods, and services.

On the question of projects working even in a seemingly dysfunctional environment, Evans pointed out that OED's evidence strongly suggested that one got better outcomes for funds spent in environments characterized by good policy performance and sound institutional capability. She agreed that things could go well despite an adverse environment when technical help, effective targeting, and social organization improved conditions for the poor. In addition, the personalities of the actors could be a contributing factor, one donors could do little to influence. If a charismatic project task manager got together with an equally charismatic local NGO representative, for example, things tended to work.

Mensah strongly agreed that if donors wanted to know what worked and what did not, they had to look at processes, not just outcomes. That was the only way they could improve the design of programs, projects, and policies related to poverty reduction.

As for targeting, for most basic needs, such as education, health, and water supply, broad targeting was appropriate. For other aspects of poverty reduction, such as income generation, targeting should be rather narrowly focused.

Mona Bishay had asked a second question from the perspective of a multilateral donor. If assessing the totality of effects was more important than assessing microlevel effects, at what level of generality or complexity did one define a system? How did one deal with the issues of attribution and donor accountability?

Ridley Nelson of OED added that it was important to take resource limitations and opportunity costs into account. The challenge, in terms of both poverty interventions and the evaluation of those interventions, was that donors and developing country partners could not do everything at the same time and in the same place.

Andrew Shepherd responded that donors who were talking increasingly about looking at the totality of interventions had now begun to talk about joint evaluation and its inherent difficulties. In the 1960s and 1970s the concern was to strengthen development studies around the world. In the past 20 years or so, that basic capacity had weakened, particularly in countries that had encountered difficult economic or political circumstances. Research institutions had moved toward a narrow, market-driven approach to development studies, which serviced the needs of particular agencies rather than looking at development policies as a whole. Shepherd asked how advocacy could be facilitated and how it was constrained in development partnerships, suggesting that the tools for evaluating advocacy needed to be strengthened.

Mensah responded to the point Nelson made about resource limitations, saying that if donors were prepared to work with the poor to help them "do their own thing," the requirements for domestic resources and government financial intervention might not be as important. That is why it was so important to understand people's motivations and to design activities that reflected their needs and abilities.

Tim Frankenberger of CARE shared some of his experience with measurement and analysis. In struggling to come up with a holistic programming perspective, one might find that communities' priorities might not be the same as those of governments and donors. So one needed to take into account both normative criteria and community-relevant criteria in measuring an activity's impact on a community. The normative criteria would help determine whether an activity was having an impact on the outcomes about which one made resource decisions, but if the impact was irrelevant to the community's criteria, the community would not be fully engaged and the activity would be unsustainable.

> People sometimes confused holistic programming with holistic analysis.

CARE's livelihood security model encompassed all the components of poverty mentioned by Dabelstein. People sometimes confused holistic programming with holistic analysis. In identifying the leverage point likely to have the biggest impact on livelihoods, one could take a holistic perspective in the analysis but narrow the focus to one set of interventions to be pursued, rather than trying to tackle everything at once in something like an integrated approach to rural development. In other words, holistic analysis can be used to determine where targeted interventions would have the biggest impact.

Patrick Donkor of the Ghana National Planning Commission observed that poor people might be poor because of developments outside their own control, such as declining international cocoa prices. Evaluators should consider external factors.

Mensah said that evaluating advocacy was important because advocacy helps to change policies. Donors should help research and planning institutions look at the policy dimensions of development and strengthen their capacity to evaluate development policies.

Reflecting on a theme raised more than once, Dabelstein returned to the global enabling environment in relation to the root causes of poverty in some countries. While the Danish International Development Agency was preparing a program to improve coastal fishery capacity in Mozambique, the European Union was negotiating fishing rights for a European Union fishing fleet in Mozambican waters. There was absolutely no connection between the EU's concern about access to international resources and Denmark's local attempt to improve the livelihoods of local coastal fishermen. Donors looking for holistic approaches must look not only at what development aid agencies and money can do, but also at how economic and trade interests shape the relationship between poorer countries and richer countries.

Evans concluded the panelists' responses by emphasizing the need to link evaluation more closely to resource allocation, whether in the context of a medium-term budget framework debated at the country level or in that of a multilateral institution such as the World Bank. Evaluation had to be made an integral part of the process of deciding the level of resources and the strategic priorities to which they were allocated. Until evaluation was linked to resource allocation, it would always be difficult to incorporate lessons learned into the design of donors' work.

Thomas wrapped up the discussion by stating that in his view, the most striking and powerful points were the importance of 1) linking microlevel analysis, data, and findings to the big picture and 2) building capacity for evaluation partnerships.

Methodological Issues in Evaluation

Impact Evaluation: Concepts and Methods

Kene Ezemenari, Anders Rudqvist, Kalanidhi Subbarao

Evaluation identifies the impacts of an intervention program by analyzing cause and effect. The basic organizing principle for any good evaluation is to ask what would have happened in the absence of the intervention. What would the welfare levels of particular communities, groups, households, and individuals have been without the intervention?

Evaluation differs from monitoring. Monitoring is "the continuous assessment of project implementation in relation to agreed schedules, and of the use of inputs, infrastructure, and services by project beneficiaries" (OED 1994). The key difference is that evaluation traces causes to outcomes, whereas monitoring tracks the progress of implementation and processes, especially of inputs and outputs, to ensure that agreed targets are met.

An impact evaluation assesses the extent to which a program has caused desired changes in the intended audience: it is concerned with the net impact of an intervention on households and institutions, attributable only and exclusively to that intervention. Therefore, impact evaluation consists of assessing outcomes and thus the short- or medium-term developmental change resulting from an intervention. This chapter reviews the key concepts and tools available for conducting sound impact evaluation.

The Basic Evaluation Problem: Disentangling Project Effects from Intervening Factors

Inputs into a project lead to direct outcomes or impacts through produced output or through the impact on other variables that then affect outcomes. Intervening factors on which the project has either an observed or unobserved effect may also contribute to outcomes. In addition, other factors or events that are not caused by the project may be correlated with the outcomes. Figure 4.1 is a diagrammatic representation of the evaluation problem. Accurate and successful evaluations are those that are able to control for these effects. This task of netting out the effect of interventions from other factors is facilitated if control groups are introduced. Control groups consist of a comparator group of individuals who do not receive the intervention but have characteristics similar to those receiving the intervention. Defining these groups correctly is a key to identifying what would have occurred in the absence of the intervention.

Three steps are critical for a good evaluation:
- Defining the expected outcomes of an intervention.
- Setting performance standards and indicators at the outset.
- Defining a counterfactual.

The first step in evaluation is a prior understanding of the nature of the welfare benefits that a program is expected to generate. This step is contingent upon the nature of the intervention. Outcome indicators for judging the performance of a project need to be related to the objectives of the project. Projects may vary in their objectives. In general, projects that set too many objectives complicate the outcome indicators and cloud the evaluation. Whenever projects have multiple objectives, it is best to narrow the selection to a few key objectives and to set a few clearly defined outcome indicators. Clarifying the time period within which outcomes are to be expected is also important. Thus, for some projects, such as public employment projects, the benefits (outcomes) are consumption gains and the time is almost immediate. For others, such as a nutrition intervention, the outcomes (improvement in the nutritional status of

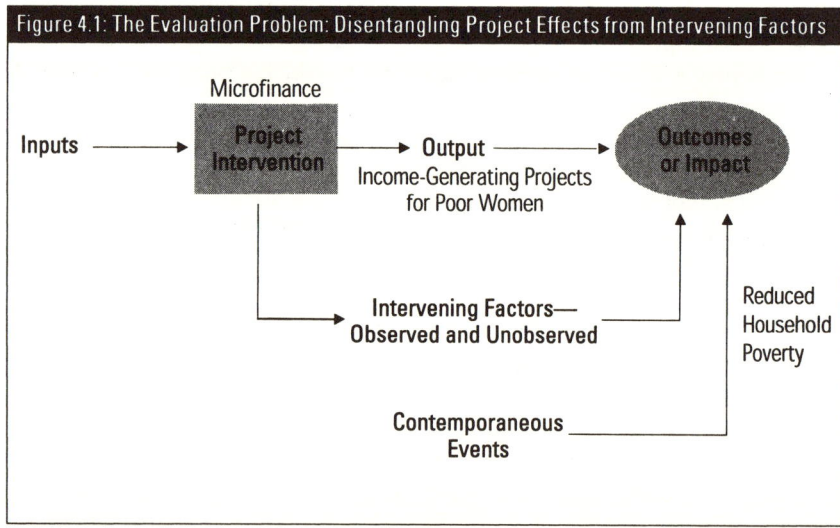

children) are medium term, four to six years. Some projects may have only longer-term goals. In such instances, a few short-term indicators should still be identified to facilitate evaluation.

Methods for Addressing Endogeneity

Endogeneity arises if other factors affect the intervention and outcome simultaneously, making it difficult to disentangle the pure effect of the intervention. The key to disentangling project effects from any intervening effects is determining what would have occurred in the absence of the program (at the same point in time). When a functional relationship is established between treatment (inputs) and outcomes in a regression equation, endogeneity manifests itself when the correlation between the treatment and the error term in the outcome regression is not equal to zero. The challenge is to identify and address the main source of endogeneity relevant to each intervention.

> Qualitative methods not only provide qualitative measures of impact but also deepen the interpretation of results obtained from a quantitative approach by shedding light on processes and causal relationships.

If the same individual could be observed at the same point in time with and without the intervention program, the problem of endogeneity would not arise. As this is not possible in practice, something similar is done by identifying nonparticipating comparison groups, identical in every way to the group that receives the intervention except that the comparison groups do not receive the intervention. Two methods can be used to identify comparison groups: experimental or quasi-experimental methods and nonexperimental methods.

Although both experimental and nonexperimental methods are grounded in the quantitative approach to evaluation, incorporating qualitative methods enriches the quality of the evaluation results. Qualitative methods not only provide qualitative measures of impact but also deepen the interpretation of results obtained from a quantitative approach by shedding light on processes and causal relationships. Related to qualitative methods are participatory methods, which can also be employed in conjunction with quantitative methods. Participatory methods require the active involvement of stakeholders, particularly at the local level, in determining the objective, indicators, and methods of an evaluation.

Experimental or Control Groups

Establishing control groups is the most straightforward way to assess the counterfactual. Identifying a counterfactual is not a straightforward task. Typically, the task manager or the analyst or both has some prior information about the counterfactual. However, the counterfactual from the participant's point of view may differ from that posited by the analyst. The best counterfactual appears to be determined by the interaction of the analyst's prior information and the participant's perceptions, which are obtained by participatory assessments prior to the formulation of the project.

The issues that arise when defining the control group include ascertaining the program's coverage, maintaining the integrity of the control, and accounting for contemporaneous events:

- A project or a policy change that is adopted throughout the country leaves little room for establishing appropriate control groups. The Bank's adjustment loans and the liberalization of a country's trade and price policy fall into this category, as do projects that target specific groups throughout a country, such as tuberculosis or AIDS patients. If the project includes all the cases in any such category, there is no scope for a control group.
- Control groups are often contaminated or may disappear altogether. One typical example is a government's extending a program into a control area. Another is the movement of people into and out of control areas. For example, a regionally targeted employment or food stamp program might induce migration from a neighboring control region, thereby compromising the integrity of controls.
- Evaluators need to account for contemporaneous events in establishing actual program impact. For example, the initial situation in a control area—no access highway—may change with the construction of an access highway, thereby compromising the comparison of outcomes between project and control areas.

Methods for Establishing Controls

Methods available to resolve some of the foregoing problems include randomized or experimental controls; quasi-experimental controls consisting of constructed (or matched) and reflexive controls; and nonexperimental controls, which include statistical, generic, and shadow controls. When successfully applied, experimental and quasi-experimental controls deal with problems of selection bias, which arise when participation in the program is related to unmeasured characteristics that are themselves related to the program outcome under study. Randomly placing individuals in treatment and nontreatment groups based on similar pre-intervention characteristics ensures that, on average, any differences in outcomes of the two groups after the intervention can be attributed to the intervention. In the case of nonexperimental methods such as statistical control, selection bias is treated as an omitted variable bias.

The choice of a method for establishing controls depends on the design of the program and the particular problem or constraint. For example, Jalan and Ravallion (1998) used constructed controls or matching to evaluate a public works program in Argentina. Conditions under the program lacked both a baseline and a randomized control group that would have facilitated an estimation of what the situation without the program would have been—for example, forgone income. Jalan and Ravallion therefore used a matching methodology to construct a control group. They began by estimating the probability of participation conditioned on a set of variables determining participation for a pooled sample of participants and comparison groups. They then calculated the predicted probability for each observation in the participant and comparison groups. Finally, they matched households by the probability of participation across the two samples.

This project was particularly amenable to matching for two reasons. First, the investigators were able to ensure that the same questionnaire was administered to both participants and nonparticipants and that both groups were from the same environment (this was greatly facilitated by piggybacking onto a national survey that was already in progress). Second, microlevel data were available to ensure that participants were matched with nonparticipants over a common region of the matching variables. Any bias could therefore be attributed to the distribution of unobserved characteristics.

Nonexperimental Methods for Controlling Selection Bias

Two forms of nonexperimental methods can be used for evaluation: multivariate analysis and instrumental variable techniques.

Multivariate Analysis. Selection bias is similar to an omitted variable bias in regression analysis. Thus, if it is possible to control for all possible reasons that outcomes might differ, this method is valid. For example, consider the following equation, where the effect of treatment (T) on outcome (Y) is measured by parameter b:

$$Y = a + bT + cX + e$$

The vector X contains variables that also determine program outcome. The parameter estimate b will be biased (or misestimated) if there are any variables that determine outcome but that have not been accounted for in X. Selectivity bias can differ across specific groups or regions.

Where influences determining program outcomes are known to the participant but not easily observed, and therefore not measurable by the researcher, the evaluation generally fails.

Instrumental Variables. This approach can also be used to control for selection bias. If variables directly affect program participation without directly affecting outcomes, then simple regression analysis will not correctly account for program impact. To account correctly for program impact, the evaluator would need to compare the outcomes of individuals who are more likely to participate with the outcomes of those who are less likely to participate, based on the value of the instrumental variables. Geographic variation in program availability can often be used as an instrument. For example, one source of bias refers to endogenous program placement. This problem arises if the criteria for placing programs in certain areas are related to program outcomes. For instance, if a program to improve health status is well targeted by placing it in a poor area, in the absence of perfect measurement of the health environment the program will appear to be less effective than it actually is.

Biases also arise when programs are targeted according to individual or geographic variables that influence subsequent growth rates of the outcome indicator (Jalan and Ravallion 1998, Ravallion and Wodon 1997). The key to handling this problem lies in finding appropriate instruments that determine program placement without also influencing program outcomes that are conditional on placement. Often a good understanding of the administrative procedure for program placement informs the choice of instruments. For example, Besley and Case (1994) used state-level political variables as instruments to identify the impact of workers' compensation on earnings in the United States. The indication was that political affiliation with the governor would influence the level of benefits of the program but not the level of wages controlled for compensation benefits.

Data Sources and Collection Methods

Information constraints can be formidable in impact evaluation. Data sources can be longitudinal, cross-sectional, baseline with follow-up, and time series. In principle, any of these types of data can be collected with quantitative or qualitative methods.

Longitudinal (panel) designs employ at least two observations in time, one made before the intervention (the baseline) and another afterward. Panel data sets are best suited for program evaluation. However, generating a panel data set is difficult and can be expensive. Serious capacity constraints for many poor countries.

Cross-Sectional Surveys. The most commonly used data sources are cross-sectional surveys: one-time sample surveys of target populations, some of whom have not received treatment. In this case, evaluators compare project outcomes for subjects who receive the treatment with outcomes for those who do not. Various statistical techniques control for differences between the two groups. Cross-sectional data are the least expensive to examine for impact; however, rigorous evaluation with a cross-sectional survey is rarely a possibility. As mentioned earlier, Jalan and Ravallion (1998) were able to use a single cross-section with a matching method to compensate for the lack of a baseline and randomization in the evaluation of the Trabajar public works program in Argentina because the evaluation could take advantage of certain project-specific conditions. For example, data collection for the project coincided with a nationwide census, which allowed for statistical matching based on observed characteristics.

Before-and-after (or baseline with follow-up) surveys are amenable to program evaluation with either full or partial coverage. The main problem with before-and-after studies is the existence of confounding factors that may obscure program impact, a problem that is tractable with panel data sets.

Time Series Data. Time-series data are probably the only data for carrying out impact assessment for programs with full (national) coverage, such as national AIDS or tuberculosis prevention programs or malaria control programs. Time-series data allow the comparative examination of trends occurring before the program with those occurring after the program. The greatest limitation is that many pre-intervention time-series data points are required for rigorous analysis of the pre-intervention trend.

Where no pre-intervention measures or information exist, everyone is covered by the program, and the coverage is uniform over place and time—virtually ruling out both randomized and constructed controls—the only way to generate information is by adopting generic controls or shadow controls. Generic controls involve comparing program outcomes with estimates based on related studies. The validity of the estimated outcomes depends heavily on the quality of controls. Shadow controls consist of the judgment of experts, program administrators, or participants. Because generic and shadow controls are often the only controls available for full coverage programs, evaluators should apply great caution when using them. Estimates of what would have occured in the absence of the program in such situations are largely speculative.

Measures to ensure the validity and reliability of data depend on the approach used to collect the data. With a quantitative approach, validity and reliability depend on the precision with which investigators collect data about the key variables of interest. The skill and training of the individuals responsible for administering a quantitative survey are important to the reliability of the data. In addition, investigators must take a large enough sample of the population of interest to ensure that the estimates are precise to a specific degree for a certain percentage of the time. Thus the key to precision with quantitative methods is appropriate sample selection and the establishment of controls.

> The skill and training of the individuals responsible for administering a quantitative survey are important to the reliability of the data.

The validity and reliability of qualitative data also depend on the evaluators' methodological skill, sensitivity, and training. In practice, observation and interviewing are fully integrated activities. Skilled interviewers are also skilled observers, because every face-to-face interview involves observation. Interviewers must be sensitive to nonverbal messages, the interview setting, and the interviewees' characteristics. Qualitative methods rely less on statistical precision to ensure validity, because the sample size is often such that statistical tests are not possible.

Therefore, investigators often use triangulation to ensure data validity and reliability. Triangulation involves the systematic use and comparison of data collected with independent methods (see box 4.1).

> **Box 4.1: Methods of Triangulation**
>
> The literature on qualitative methods of data collection identifies four basic types of triangulation.
> - **Data triangulation:** the use of a variety of data sources in a study, such as interviewing people in different occupations, status positions, or political parties.
> - **Investigator triangulation:** the use of different evaluators or social scientists.
> - **Method triangulation:** the use of multiple methods to study a single problem or program, such as interviews, observations, questionnaires, or written secondary sources.
> - **Theory triangulation:** the use of multiple perspectives to interpret a single set of data.

The objective in triangulation is to assess potential biases in particular methods of data collection and other independent methods that are likely to offset these biases. For example, in the case of data triangulation, estimates of household income obtained from direct questions may tend to underestimate income, either because respondents do not wish to admit illegal sources of income or because the respondents may forget to report certain sources. Direct observation in the home or of family diaries or more intense contact with families through participant observation could reveal the source of the bias and yield a more precise estimate of household income. The precision of the sample could be further improved by carefully selecting a small but random sample of households.

Combining Quantitative and Qualitative Approaches in Impact Evaluation

The typical quantitative approach to evaluation ideally consists of the following elements or phases: (a) experimental or quasi-experimental design, (b) quantitative data collection, and (c) statistical analysis of data. By contrast, the typical qualitative approach includes (a) inductive or "naturalistic" open-ended inquiry, (b) qualitative data collection, and (c) content analysis. Content analysis consists of describing, interpreting, and analyzing patterns observed in qualitative data, as well as the accompanying processes and causal relationships these data generate.

These two approaches can be combined in various ways to enrich the analysis of program impacts. Different combinations that can be employed include the following:
- Experimental design, qualitative data collection, and content analysis.
- Experimental design, qualitative data collection, and statistical analysis.
- Inductive or naturalistic inquiry, qualitative data collection, and statistical analysis.

- Inductive or naturalistic inquiry, quantitative measurement, and statistical analysis.

This list is far from exhaustive. In practice, a particular evaluation can include many different types of design, data, and analysis.

Participatory approaches tend to overlap more with qualitative than with quantitative methods. However, not all qualitative methods are participatory, and many participatory techniques can be quantitative. Participatory monitoring generates the basis for participatory evaluation—that is, evaluation that reflects the perceptions, perspectives, and priorities of all stakeholders. Participatory monitoring constitutes an important input and an additional perspective for impact evaluation. To fulfill the requirements of participatory monitoring and evaluation, stakeholders, particularly at the local level, should be actively involved in various or all stages of monitoring and evaluation. This includes determining the objectives of monitoring or evaluation, identifying the indicators to be employed, and participating in data collection and analysis. Participatory monitoring is a continuous process of learning and involvement on the part of the stakeholders.

A good evaluation combines both qualitative and quantitative approaches to data collection and analysis. Combining both approaches provides quantified results of program impacts as well as explanations of the processes and intervening factors that yielded these outcomes. Combined approaches enrich the interpretation or explanation of outcomes measured by the evaluation.

Quantitative. (Measurable) indicators of inputs, outputs, and outcomes are an essential part of the information base throughout project implementation and after project completion. For this purpose, the typical information gathering strategy is a sample survey of participants and nonparticipants. Ideally, a panel data set would be the best way to establish causality on the determinants of outcomes (impact). Prior to framing a questionnaire, informal discussions with stakeholders using qualitative or participatory techniques and unstructured interviews are extremely helpful, not only for asking the right questions but also for developing appropriate hypotheses.

Once baseline and follow-up survey data become available, evaluators can adopt quantitative techniques to derive an empirical estimate of the impact of an intervention on the targeted group. The quantitative approach to evaluation relies on predetermined hypotheses and assumes that the relevant variables can be identified in advance and measured. In many instances, however, knowing in advance the various factors impinging on outcomes is difficult, and without that knowledge evaluators cannot empirically isolate the role of the intervention relative to other (extraneous) factors. In this context, information on processes, institutions, and perspectives of participants and nonparticipants can be helpful. Qualitative methods are best suited for gathering this information.

Participatory. These methods are flexible and open-ended and not always restricted to a predetermined set of variables, outcomes, or questions. The participatory approach is holistic, attempting to take into account as broad as possible a range of factors and relationships. This facilitates the discovery of unanticipated consequences of an intervention, such as second-round, unforeseen, positive, or negative effects. A more direct and personal relationship between interviewers and informants promotes trust and facilitates in-depth inquiry into sensitive topics that may be difficult to approach through survey research. Furthermore, participatory approaches more directly reflect the perceptions, values, and perspectives of individuals and groups under investigation. These approaches are also well-suited to explaining in depth the reasons for, and character of, critical incidents and events and the dynamics or causality of such events when they are part of sequences or processes. Good participatory research provides rapid feedback on conclusions and recommendations, allowing investigators to modify or validate the results obtained from a quantitative analysis.

Participatory methods have been used to learn about local conditions and local people's perspectives and priorities, largely to determine the components of project interventions. However, one could go further and use participatory methods not only during project formulation but also throughout the project, especially for evaluating how the poor perceive the benefits derived from the project.

Integrated. Survey-based approaches, structured methods, and participatory and qualitative methods of information-gathering complement one another. Researchers formulate evaluation objectives, hypotheses, and research methodology from observation and knowledge of local circumstances, using qualitative or participatory methods, and develop a survey questionnaire after due pretesting. They then adopt quantitative techniques with random assignment experiments to test the hypotheses. Even after such a procedure, anomalous results from baseline surveys may require an intensive follow-up qualitative investigation, especially when translating from the general to the specific. For example, scheduled castes in India are generally worse off than other castes (a general, valid observation). Why are scheduled castes in Uttar Pradesh so much worse off in their access to public services than scheduled castes in Kerala (a very specific question)?

The integration of quantitative methods with participatory and qualitative methods can be achieved in the following ways:

- Qualitative methods can be used to determine the design of the quantitative survey questionnaire by, for example, piloting key concepts and problematic issues or questions. This allows the incorporation of the perceptions of poor people themselves.
- Qualitative methods can also be used to determine the stratification of the quantitative sample.

- A quantitative survey can be used to design the interview guide for the qualitative data collection.
- A quantitative survey can be used to determine the generality or extent (in a given area or society) of findings or phenomena identified through qualitative methods in more limited areas or samples.

Conclusions

- Identification of the counterfactual is the organizing principle of a good impact evaluation. To determine the effects of the intervention, evaluators must ascertain what would have happened without the intervention.
- In addition to identifying the counterfactual, evaluators need to clearly define control groups and identify all variables that will affect program outcomes. Ideally, the latter will be readily observable and therefore measurable; however, this is not always the case. At times, some variables that affect program outcomes are not directly measurable. Evaluators need to be aware of these variables and identify methods—whether qualitative and participatory or quantitative and statistical—that will facilitate the estimation of a proxy variable to capture their effects.

> Good participatory research provides rapid feedback on conclusions and recommendations, allowing investigators to modify or validate the results obtained from a quantitative analysis.

- Both quantitative and qualitative methods are necessary for a good evaluation. The two approaches complement each other. This note outlines how such an integration of methods can be accomplished in the context of evaluation.

References

Besley, Timothy, and Anne Case. 1994. "Unnatural Experiments? Estimating the Incidence of Endogenous Policies." Working Paper 4956. Cambridge, MA: National Bureau of Economic Research.

Jalan, J., and M. Ravallion. 1998. "Transfer Benefits from Welfare: A Matching Estimate for Argentina." Washington, D.C.: World Bank.

OED (Operations Evaluation Department). 1994. *Designing Project Monitoring and Evaluation*. Lessons and Practices 4. Washington, D.C.: World Bank.

Ravallion, M., and Q. Wodon. 1997. "Evaluating Endogenous Social Programs When Placement Is Decentralized." Washington, D.C.: World Bank.

Comments: Impact Evaluation: Concepts and Methods

Thomas Cook

The Bank wants to determine whether certain activities cause an alleviation of poverty. The key word here is "cause," to verify which requires constructing an unbiased counterfactual. To this end, one can measure a group before and after an intervention, which is rarely useful because it assumes that there is no statistical regression, that no seasonal or maturational changes would otherwise have occurred, that no historical events taking place during the same period could have caused the same outcome. However, the basic approach is sometimes useful if it is extended to create an interrupted time series—that is, many measures made over time on the same population both before and after the intervention, at all times using the same measure as the effect of interest. Then it is possible to estimate the pre-intervention trend and test whether there are any subsequent, reliable deviations from it. However, this design also requires that regression and cyclical maturational patterns do not masquerade as treatment effects, that the intervention has a sudden onset, and that the delay period within which an effect can be expected is known. These are difficult conditions to meet. Moreover, interrupted time series clearly benefit enormously from studying a control population during the same period that does not get the intervention but that does experience the same measures, with the control group being selected to maximize its multivariate similarity to the intervention group.

In the philosophy of science, only one exception to the need to use similar cases to develop counterfactuals is routinely noted: the theory of signed causes. This makes causal inference dependent on predicting a multivariate pattern of outcomes, specifying some variables that change in one way because of an intervention; others that change in other ways; and yet others that do not change at all, although they would be expected to if the most relevant alternative interpretations operated. This is the theory of cause that pathologists use to determine cause of death on the basis of examining dead bodies, observing the patterning of disease, and relating this patterning to known theories about the biological processes leading to death. It is also the theory detectives use when visiting the scene of a crime. They note the pattern among multiple clues and relate this to the modus operandi of known criminals that is either in their heads or in files, much as medical texts contain valid knowledge about signs that point to different causes of death.

A similar theory—called theory-based evaluation—has recently been reinvented in evaluation. It too has evolved to do away with the need for a credible and valid causal counterfactual. However, the theory of signed causes makes considerable demands on the specificity and accuracy of substantive theory and also requires measures that are totally valid. Thus, it is not likely to be relevant in many cases relevant to social scientists. After all, how often are our theories so specific that we can specify, for instance, which microlevel effect comes about before any other, what time lines are required for the second effect to come about, and so on down the chain of causal connections?

So some kind of control group is almost always needed. I am aware of only two conditions in the social sciences in which unbiased control groups can be created. The least known is the so-called regression discontinuity design, in which units are assigned to a treatment or not assigned, based on their score on some scale, usually measuring risk, need, or merit. In this procedure, the selection process is fully known; it depends only on the fallible classification score. More widely discussed is random assignment and its role in experimentation. In this method, units of individuals, villages, or some other grouping are randomly assigned to different intervention conditions (or to a no-treatment control group). Within the limits of sampling error, random assignment guarantees that the groups start out identically, so any subsequent differences must stem from the differences in treatment. In a two-group design with an intervention and control group, these differences must be the result of the intervention.

In the United States, it is standard procedure in method textbooks to maintain that random assignment is the best technique for creating a valid causal counterfactual. This is true in statistics, the philosophy of science, medicine, psychology, public health, microeconomics, and the work in sociology and political science on the improvement of survey research. Indeed, random assignment is now also becoming commonplace in studies to evaluate the efficacy of adult literacy programs, policing and other approaches to crime reduction, and welfare and housing policies. Congress has regularly mandated that evaluations of job training programs be conducted with random assignment. The same is true of evaluations of early childhood education, where programs are tested to see whether the delivery of educational services to poor children actually improves their scholastic performance. The Bank is active in most of these sectors, but does not use random assignment. Why?

In some sectors random assignment is not at all common—for instance, in community development projects, in much of macroeconomics, and in private sector consulting. It is also not common in U.S. studies of school reform initiatives by evaluators trained in education, although random assignment in experiments on schools are common when investigators are trained in public health, psychology, or the policy sciences. Does intellectual culture have a lot to do with reluctance to randomize? Are arguments against random assignment sometimes nothing more than expressions of an ungrounded group consensus rather than reflections of what is possible and desirable? The fact is that today evaluators in the United States who do not do random assignment must have a convincing rationale that excuses them from being different from most of the rest of the sciences, even the social sciences. The

Bank rarely carries out experiments, even though it claims to be committed to learning about the efficacy of the projects it undertakes. It therefore has a tremendous moral responsibility to ensure that it has rejected random assignment out of valid concerns, not out of habit backed by an underexamined disciplinary consensus.

One could invoke at least three arguments against the use of random assignment. The first is that it is simply not feasible. For example, in the United States twenty years ago it was the prevailing belief that random assignment simply could not be done in relation to job training. Yet organizations like the Manpower Demonstration Research Corporation (MDRC) showed routinely that it could be done. Random assignment was also considered inappropriate for evaluating options for housing policy, but now it is done. It is true, however, that it is much easier not to assign at random than to rely on self-selection or administrator selection. Random assignment is very difficult to implement well and always has to be fought for until a culture is established in which it becomes standard practice, as in medicine or agriculture today. Obviously, random assignment is not going to be fought for when an organization is dominated by employees from a discipline where such assignment is valued or has an evaluation staff chosen for its commitment to methods other than random assignment. Such people will not fight for the method, and even if they were forced to implement it, they would not have the experience to implement it well. So fighting for randomization is not just a technical matter; it also involves the intellectual and organizational culture.

Let us consider a study of a U.S. program developed to help individuals reintegrate into daily life upon their release from prison. The prison population is growing rapidly, the United States is facing the need to deal with the large number of prisoners released. The Robert Wood Johnson Foundation is working on this, but the program's designers repeatedly claimed that evaluating the program using random assignment was impractical and would lead to a long list of ethical, political, and logistical problems. The foundation, whose primary responsibilities are in health and public health, replied that in that case program funding would not be forthcoming. No random assignment, no program. So Rob Hollister was hired to help develop an evaluation model that could successfully use random assignment. Within two months a study design was implemented with random assignment. All the obstacles fell away or were surmounted.

Given organizational commitment, random assignment can be done more often than not. It cannot always be done. It should not be done sometimes. Many interesting questions in evaluation are not about causation. However, random assignment can be done more often than we think, provided that there is organizational commitment to the practice and that studies are designed by individuals and groups experienced with random assignment.

The second reason often invoked for not using random assignment is that it does not work by its own standards. Random assignment is not a panacea guaranteeing unsullied causal inference. The case for it is that it is better than alternatives when it comes to the quality of causal inferences. Indeed, there are case studies of random assignment incorrectly implemented, of treatment-correlated attrition from the study and hence selection bias, and of treatment crossovers where people intended to receive one treatment actually received some part of another through the diffusion of the treatment within a community. However, there is also a wealth of published information on how to minimize these problems, thanks to experience accumulated over the past 20 years. Moreover, it seems reasonable to assume that any residual bias left because of treatment correlation, attrition, or crossovers is going to be smaller than the bias resulting from self-selection into treatments or from administrator selection into particular treatments.

Some criticisms of random assignment are more cogent than others. It makes little sense to criticize them for substitution bias, asserting that, for instance, individuals in the control group had access to services like those to which the treatment group had access. After all, experiments answer the question of whether a treatment is better than some alternative. In this case, the alternative is whatever other services are available. If control group members have used alternative services, then the policy answer is that the intervention failed to do any better than what individuals could get for themselves without the intervention. An unbiased answer can be provided to this question but not to the meaningless question of whether the intervention is unconditionally effective.

Another objection is more cogent: that experiments reduce external validity—reduce the fit between the conditions desired for policy application and the conditions incorporated into the study. In particular, some experiments are restricted to units that are willing to be in whatever treatment group the coin toss decides for them and are also willing to tolerate the measurement burden the evaluation imposes. This is likely to be a biased subset of the relevant population. All experimenters have to believe that causal inference is so important that they are willing to tolerate on its behalf some loss of the ability to generalize. This is a genuine tradeoff. The ethos is: better a clear causal relationship of unclear applicability than an unclear causal relationship of known generalizability.

The third reason given for not doing randomized experiments is that they are unnecessary, and that the alternatives are equally adequate, if not better. This argument actually has merit in one restricted context. Imagine that my study is only about implementation, that I show only that I can deliver clean water to communities or a road into a rural community or a cheap AIDS vaccine to Sub-Saharan Africa. Many might then be willing to assume, without further testing, that positive benefits from this intervention will accrue to poor people. After all, many studies have been published on the effects of clean water and access to markets, and lower AIDS rates would clearly prevent deaths. In such cases, it may be appropriate not to evaluate the effectiveness of the services in question.

However, others argue against the need for randomized experiments even in contexts where the effectiveness of a program cannot be assumed when services are delivered well. Some maintain that substantive models can substitute for random assignment. Assuming that a particular substantive model is correct, they then specify a level of initial inputs and run this through the model and adduce a particular outcome. Philosophers of science reject this approach out of hand, because it depends on creating a hypothetical counterfactual: It relies on the rarely true assumption that the model is independently known to be true. So causal conclusions have to depend on the accuracy of the substantive theory, whatever one might do to assess its sensitivity to alternative specifications. As a means to causal knowledge, this approach is dangerous. Assuming substantive knowledge about the relevant variables and the relevant connections among them often seems more like a leap of faith or a fantasy than like an empirical product.

Still others may claim that statistical adjustment techniques work as well as random assignment. However, the most esteemed, formally trained statisticians who write about statistical adjustments for initial group nonequivalence, such as Rosenbaum, Rubin, or Holland, all prefer random assignment to the alternatives they work on, acknowledging them to be second-best, fallback options. For fallbacks, they currently favor propensity score analysis, a brute empirical way to develop and observe a selection model. More and more microeconomists prefer random assignment and, if this is not feasible, natural experiments. Natural experiments are studies where external circumstances create fortuitous group differences hardly likely to lead to selection artifacts, as when there are contrasts between students born a few days apart, the older ones being in one school year and the younger ones in another, or when the sudden and unexpected influx of large numbers of Cuban refugees into Miami alters the market for low-wage labor. Here we hope, like Francis Bacon, "to twist Nature by the tail"—that is, to use design features rather than statistical ones to approximate a better counterfactual.

Some economists persist in believing that, despite the pessimism of formally trained statisticians, statistical means can be developed to unambiguously create the missing causal counterfactual. Jim Heckman has been associated with several selection models based on instrumental variable approaches that, in the early days, could not be shown to be competent when judged against the results of true experiments on the same substantive topic. In those days, the works of Lalonde, Frake, and Maynard were important in showing that experiments and nonexperiments with selection controls did not produce the same results. A closer look at the more recent Heckman-type selection models reveals that they provide better approximations to the results of randomized experiments when certain conditions hold. These include close matching between the treatment group and a comparison group in terms of almost everything, pre-test observations on the very same measures as the outcome, and measurement of this pre-test at more than one measurement wave. Here, one is moving toward a design conception of adjustment rather than a statistical one and toward reinventing the quasi-experimental designs that Don Campbell and I have written about. There is no longer the presumption that pertained just fifteen years ago, when attempts were made to create controls for an intervention group in a particular city using data from national surveys and hence from individuals all over the nation.

The common move is toward the tradition I come from, where causal counterfactuals come through design features in the Fisher tradition in statistics rather than from the multivariate data-analytic tradition associated with Pearson. The best approximations to a valid causal counterfactual are from measuring units matched to be just like those experiencing an intervention and measuring them on multiple occasions using the same measure as the outcome. This is a minimum for responsible, fallback causal inference, and it is nothing more than mimicking what random assignment does but without the perfect controls for measured variables that such assignment provides and without any of the assurances it provides about unmeasured variables.

Lipsey and Wilson recently attempted to compare the results of experiments and quasi-experiments. They examined 74 meta-analyses on different topics, each of which consisted of multiple experiments and better designed quasi-experiments. The two types of study came to similar conclusions across the 74 studies, but the standard error for the quasi-experiments was about nine times larger than that for the experiments. In other words, the experiments were more efficient than the nonexperiments. They reached the correct answer faster and with more assurance. The implication here is that getting the same degree of uncertainty reduction about cause takes much longer in nonexperiments than in experiments. In fields where causal knowledge is already sparse, as with the Bank's work, not to do experiments reduces the credibility, validity, and efficiency of the knowledge gained. Indeed, in the field of meta-analysis, it is traditional to trust the results of quasi-experiments only if they are cross-validated by similar results from randomized experiments done on the same topic.

Any research community that still persists in not doing experiments needs not only to examine its intellectual rationale for this position but also to examine the social foundations of its intellectual culture. Has it created a social and intellectual environment that insulates itself from most of the intellectual world, whose feedback on its evaluation products would reveal the nearly universal lack of respect accorded to causal conclusions based on nonexperimental evidence? Surely there is a sociology of science component worth addressing in any culture of evaluation that, at the end of the 20th century, did not do experiments. What is the disciplinary bias prevalent in the organization? Or in the Bank's case, is it represented by just about the only two remaining evaluation subcultures that do not do experiments—macroeconomics and qualitative work emanating from anthropology and education? Only by eliciting commentary on its plans and products from these two approaches can an organization continue with a nonexperimental research agenda. Casting the net wider would be most uncomfortable, I surmise.

Thus, my conclusions are as follows:

First, if as an intellectual community the Bank does not want to do randomized experiments, then it needs a better, more up to date, and more informed rationale for not doing them than I have seen to date from the Bank.

Second, if it does not do randomized experiments, then the Bank needs to examine whether its culture of evaluation within the organization has not become insular and inbred. In particular, it might ask whether it lacks people who during the past 15 or 20 years have shown the most skill in doing randomized experiments in areas where it was assumed that they were not possible.

Third, without some randomized experiments in the portfolio, I predict that the credibility of Bank-funded projects to reduce poverty will suffer in the eyes of the larger social science community, the growing (but still small) community of policymakers who espouse random assignment, and even among younger microeconomists trained in better economics departments.

Fourth, not having rigorous evaluation is convenient if an organization is defensive about its accomplishments. Bad design guarantees some false positives that can be disseminated to the media and to policymakers, and also guarantees that any negative-seeming results can be written off as bad design.

Fifth, I am not pushing randomized experiments as a gold standard in the sense that they guarantee perfect causal inference. They do this only in the rare circumstance where a correct randomization procedure is selected and perfectly implemented, there is no treatment-correlated attrition, there are no treatment crossovers, and the conditions required to implement randomization have not lowered the external validity of a study to an unacceptable level.

Sixth, I am arguing that randomized experiments are better and more accurate than any of their alternatives.

Finally, I contend that the better alternatives are those that most accurately mimic the structural and functional design elements of an experiment that was created to give the best possible causal counterfactual. At a minimum, this is through the use of stable matching and pre-test measures gathered on the same scale as the outcome, preferably at multiple time points before and after the intervention. These design features minimize the role for statistical adjustments, without eliminating it, and so lessen the dependence on often untestable assumptions.

James Heckman

Most, if not all, of the literature on impact assessment has been marred by favoritism toward one methodology over another. I am certainly not opposed to randomization, but it is important to understand that some methodologies can play only a limited role in evaluating many of the Bank's projects and other large-scale interventions. Some seemingly ideal experiments may yield some information about certain parameters, but many of the problems the Bank is addressing are of a large-scale, general equilibrium nature. They require experiments on entire economies, where any changes in taxation or other programs can change the whole scale of the activity, and the kind of research activity promoted previously will yield only partial results.

In a forthcoming paper in the *Quarterly Journal of Economics*, I show that the job training experiment Cook mentioned actually killed the large-scale Job Training and Partnership Act (JTPA) program because of what we call substitution bias. Subjects who were randomized out of the study had excellent substitutes for the program, resulting in a gross underestimation of the program's effectiveness. Essentially, the evaluation failed to provide an adequate assessment of the program's efficacy, leading to its demise in Congress.

If we consider the larger issue of the effects of social experiments, we find that the studies conducted by Lalonde, Frake, and Maynard play a key role. In relationship to the JTPA study, these studies are often cited as examples of how bad nonexperimental estimates can be compared with the experimental estimate.

If we examine those studies more closely, we see that the data on the comparison groups and the treatment groups were actually collected with different survey instruments from different labor markets. I would favor a good matching study instead of the methodology actually employed.

A report published in *Econometrica* in 1998 established that, when comparing comparable people, using just a few basic principles—namely, collecting data in the same labor market and asking the same questions—would help eliminate the huge differences. In fact, Lalonde and I are working on a manuscript that essentially acknowledges that the previous work was dramatically overstated.

We need to recognize that we have a range of activities. Someone earlier made a statement about a strong faith in experimental models and the ability to forecast from them as long as they are correct. The identification and development of these models is a whole study in econometrics, and we are aware of the fragility of the issues at hand. If we could bypass those issues by doing randomization, no question would remain. But we cannot, and therefore we should continue to build other models. I believe that the coalition of data and evidence within the experimental tradition does not favor the summary of evidence. Too often we have seen black-box interventions that subject individuals to some randomization, and what comes out is a series of questions. Did this program work in this instance? Does this program work in that instance? But the information does not collate over different programs.

We do not reach the fundamentals, which would be to identify the structural parameters of a model with which we can establish that our experience in, for example, Argentina, Bangladesh, or Turkey would also apply more generally.

I believe alternative models play a very important role in organizing, collating, and interpreting evidence.

Floor Discussion: Impact Evaluation: Concepts and Methods

The floor discussion focused on criteria for and techniques of impact evaluation. To start the discussion, Kalanidhi Subbarao responded to a question about the appropriate timing of building models and developing counterfactuals, given the time constraints on impact assessments and the possibility of government resistance in the target country. At times, he said, randomization techniques are best in evaluation.

But government resistance can seriously undermine project evaluation and implementation. Subbarao described a case from the 1970s, of investigators accidentally discovering that vitamin A in large doses reduced mortality among children. USAID asked the government of Bangladesh to test this finding by administering doses of vitamin A in six provinces, while keeping appropriate controls in neighboring provinces. Government authorities protested the use of control groups, reasoning that if vitamin A were advantageous, not to administer it all over the country would be unethical. When the donor agreed to administer vitamin A all over the country, however, the government thwarted the effort again, maintaining that the advantages of vitamin A were unproven, so there was no scientific basis for the project. The point is that randomization may be the gold standard, but other options should be considered when there is high risk of government resistance.

Brian Wall asked how to collect valid data that could be used for comparison after a few years to decide whether a program was effective in the target areas. In his response, Subbarao used the example of an area development project in China, where data were collected in both program and nonprogram areas by engaging local residents. As a result, excellent baseline and postprogram intervention data were available. In such a case, using a control group in nonprogram areas is especially important and not especially difficult.

By contrast, Thomas Cook pointed out that of having only a single area of intervention and identifying a control area was more difficult than having the resources to intervene at random in multiple areas. Assuming that a study was focused on just one area, however, multiple control areas could be established to allow the stable, bracketed matching of the community being studied. Some areas should closely match the area under study, one should be slightly more socioeconomically advantaged than the target area, and one should be slightly less advantaged. Using multiple controls in this manner would facilitate the study of implementation, process, and outcomes and would ensure that measures were in place both before the intervention and as it progressed.

Subbarao had supported combining qualitative appraisal methods with quantitative techniques to enrich the analysis of a program's impact. Zalodo Beninni asked how one would transform the qualitative appraisal data to make it usable econometrically.

James Heckman of the University of Chicago chaired the discussion.

Subbarao explained that a qualitative approach to understanding a program area was vital to any evaluation, as it provided insight into how to frame questions. Understanding the dynamics of the socioeconomic environment a program area (its caste structures, its information flow, and so on) yielded answers that could then be used to test hypotheses and to formulate econometric models. It was important to remember that this was a two-way process: the qualitative and the quantitative enriched each other.

Cook, also strongly supporting the combination of qualitative and quantitative approaches, clarified that qualitative data helped enormously in thinking through a program's contextual location and implementation and in identifying possible side effects undetectable from the theoretical armchair. He warned, however, that integrating qualitative data after coding it into quantitative analysis was not a flourishing area of methodology in the social sciences. When Subbarao disagreed, Cook said that the integration of qualitative data into quantitative analysis had never been done well. He recommended perfecting the science of performing this kind of evaluation so the approach could be used more widely.

The participants then discussed the evaluator's role in designing and monitoring a project in such a way that an appropriate randomization or random sample could be implemented at project's end. Typically, evaluators become involved at the end of the project, not in designing the project, choosing indicators, or collecting data during implementation. This could limit the implementation of a scientifically correct randomized sample at the end of the project. Randomization is characteristically a planning tool rather than an end-of-study tool, prospective rather than retrospective. Time factors play a crucial role in evaluation. To collect a baseline indicator, for example, especially in the absence of comparison groups, the more time spent gathering pre-intervention data the better, because that information would reveal the patterns of change in a particular group more accurately.

Concurring with this argument, Subbarao elaborated that the best data collection was on a panel basis, so that information on a household, if not collected year after year, was collected every three or four years. Having high-quality panel data eliminated the need for fancy econometrics to understand program impacts. If evaluators were committed to using randomization, the work should begin at the time of project initiation to establish a baseline and appropriate controls.

Asked about the levels at which an evaluation should be pursued, Subbarao suggested that deciding whether to collect information on the individual, household, regional, or countrywide level would depend on the type of intervention under study. Some projects might require information on interhousehold effects; others might not. Because of the high cost of performing an evaluation, it is essential to identify where to stop the process. And that decision is directly related to the nature of the project.

James Heckman concluded the session by saying that what could be deduced about evaluation was that any of the questions and answers brought forth were fundamentally model contingent. That is, an evaluator had to know something about what was being evaluated before doing the evaluation. Being familiar with the study's target group and with the intervention project itself enabled the evaluator to determine the appropriate level of evaluation and to decide whether to have a long or short panel.

Heckman concluded that it was wrong to assume that there was some kind of "scientific crank" out there or that an objective body of evaluation knowledge could be externally applied to all models. Good evaluators have enough experience to be aware of the options available to them, but may tend to do more to avoid problems than to understand them. Subbarao and Cook agreed that an evaluation's effectiveness depended on how intimately the evaluators knew both the project intervention and the group toward which it was targeted.

Panel Discussion: Quantitative and Qualitative Methods in Evaluation

Timothy Marchant, Sarah Gavian, John Eriksson

Timothy Marchant

I will focus on quantitative methods of evaluation, on the limitations of quantitative surveys, and on the need to complement them with qualitative methods. I will offer four simple messages about designing and proposing methods and systems within the capacity of the countries in which these methods are established. For example, in the Africa Region, the resources available for monitoring and evaluation (M&E) are still very limited, so the systems we design should match those resources. The previous discussion on impact evaluation is riveting, but a number of the issues raised are barely relevant to the circumstances that many African countries face today.

A Variety of Surveys vs. the "Swiss Army Knife" Approach

My first message is a word of caution to the users or requesters of statistical information through household surveys. As the ambitions and challenges of impact M&E grow, it becomes an increasingly data-intensive exercise, with a need for a wider range of in-depth information.

The current focus on subnational planning, decentralization, and regionalization imposes great demands on any surveys, because the results must be presented at the disaggregated level, implying much larger sample sizes than those used in the past. This is a great challenge for national statistics offices.

In addition, time series are needed with panel studies providing the most appropriate means to develop them. Again, this is extremely challenging from the point of view of both data collection and analysis .

Finally, the multiple dimensions of poverty require increasingly weighty and complex questionnaires to catch all the dimensions influencing living standards. Questionnaires are therefore growing both in size and in complexity. Such growth places an enormous demand on national statistical systems. My first message, therefore, is to beware of trying to lump everything into a single exercise and into a single instrument. Variety is a characteristic of life, and a variety of different tools is needed. Even within the quantitative approach, evaluators should use a range of surveys.

> In the "Swiss Army knife" approach, a single survey instrument is expected to meet every information need. A better alternative for serious monitoring and evaluation is a toolbox with a range of different tools.

Furthermore, a single survey seeking all the different kinds of information required would present a compromise. Instead of this "Swiss Army knife" approach, in which a single survey instrument is expected to meet every information need, a better alternative for serious M&E purposes is a toolbox with a range of different tools.

Select the Most Useful and Pertinent Tools

If we examine the range and functions of qualitative and quantitative tools and how they complement one another, we must beware of oversimplification. The aspects and nuances of the instruments we use are multidimensional and should be slotted against a scale ranging from the subjective to the objective, as well as a scale of representation. We can create a grid using these two scales to help us select the most useful and pertinent tools (figure 5.1). On the subjective-objective scale, we would place subjective assessments at the bottom, above which come conversations, open meetings, structured interviews, qualitative questionnaires, quantitative questionnaires, and direct measurement. On the scale of representation, from left to right, we would place case studies, interviews, quota samplings, small probability samples, large probability samples, and censuses.

Of course, we can create other grids with different dimensions, but this one enables us to superimpose the different tools available for work in poverty monitoring and analysis: censuses; extremely objective measurement; complete coverage of the entire country; welfare indicators questionnaires; household budget surveys; living standards measurement surveys; sentinel site surveillance, and beneficiary assessment. Each tool can be placed at the point on the grid that shows how representative, subjective, or objective it is. My second message, therefore, is to use a variety of instruments, combining tools drawn from each quadrant of the grid.

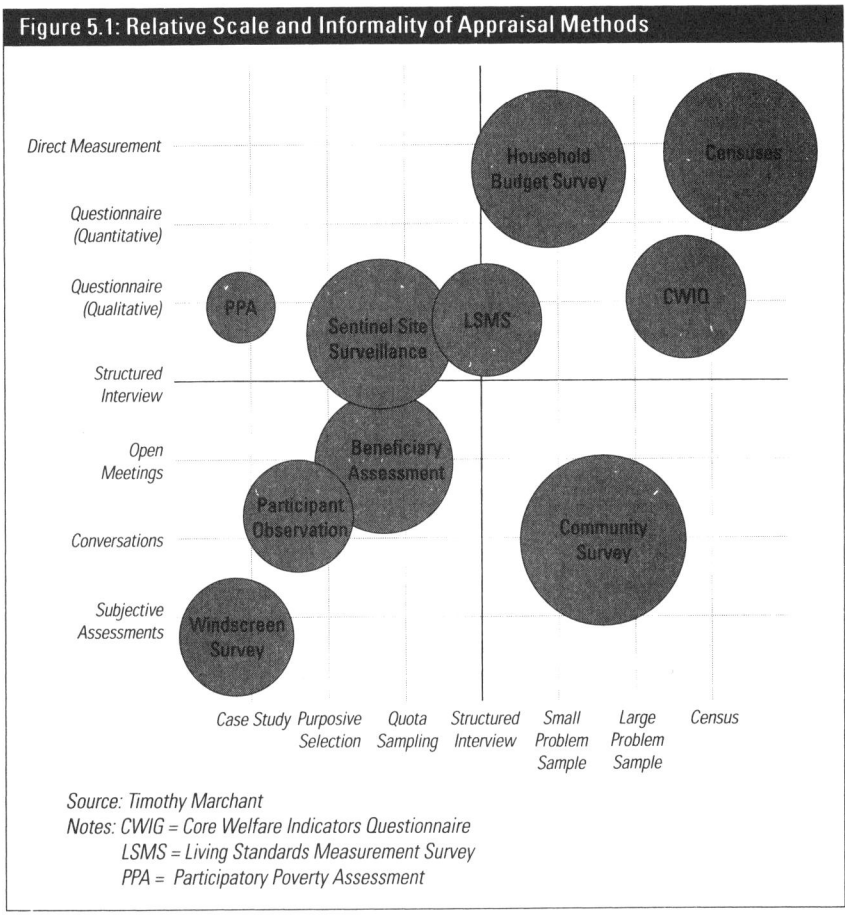

Figure 5.1: Relative Scale and Informality of Appraisal Methods

Source: Timothy Marchant
Notes: CWIG = Core Welfare Indicators Questionnaire
LSMS = Living Standards Measurement Survey
PPA = Participatory Poverty Assessment

Distinguish Between Outcome Monitoring and Impact Evaluation

In outcome monitoring, the logframe approach now in favor at the Bank has been popular with other institutions around the world for a number of years. The Bank uses this approach for all its project designs, allowing us to address a project or program in terms of inputs producing outputs, outcomes, and impacts (figure 5.2). The logframe approach is an effective tool for designing a project, but a particularly good tool for designing an M&E system for that project, in that it highlights information needs at each level.[1] It helps to answer whether the inputs are available at the right time in the right quantity; it provides a framework for monitoring the goods and services generated by the project to outcome monitoring; and it carries us to impact evaluation. There is enormous scope for more work on the monitoring of outcomes, which is where I see quantitative and qualitative tools coming together.

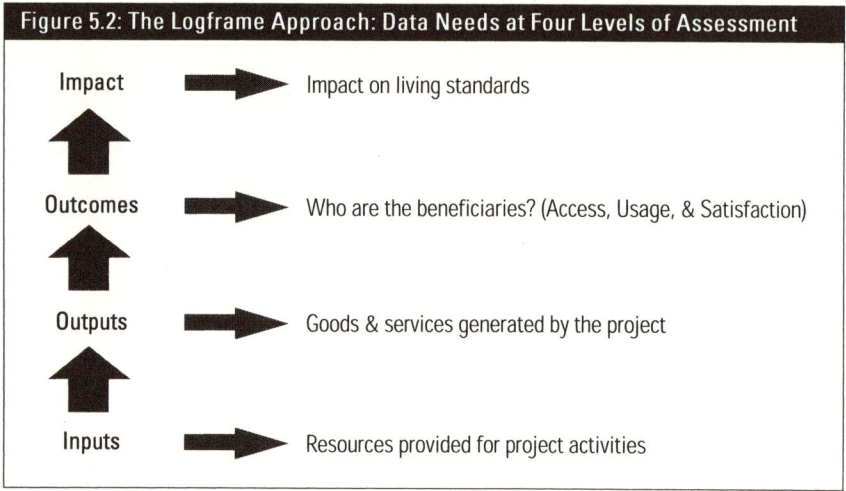

Figure 5.2: The Logframe Approach: Data Needs at Four Levels of Assessment

Monitoring Is a Question of Market Research

Monitoring outcomes is basically a question of market research. Who are the beneficiaries of the programs, the projects, the policies? Where are they located? The sorts of indicators investigators would use are leading indicators, such as access, usage, and satisfaction. Those are much easier to collect than most of the impact indicators, and they can be collected, monitored, and studied with a combination of qualitative and quantitative tools.

I will illustrate how these indicators can be and have been used by taking an example from the core welfare indicators questionnaire survey developed in Africa and recently undertaken in Ghana (figure 5.3). This survey instrument is used to monitor development objectives through the use of the leading indicators listed above.

A sample of 15,000 households received and completed the survey to monitor the leading indicators for primary education services. Survey results on access to schools—more than 90 percent across the country, with little variation between urban and rural areas or between the poor and the nonpoor—showed that lack of access is not a problem. The next indicator, usage, was measured by primary school enrollment rates. Enrollment drops to about 70 percent for the country as a whole but, again, that is not bad, and usage is pretty even across rural and urban areas and across poor and nonpoor households. For the final indicator, quality of service, households were asked to indicate whether they were satisfied with the quality of primary education services. Here, the results showed a dramatic fall: 40 percent for the whole country, dropping to less than 20 percent for poor, rural households. Immediately, this very simple tool signals an alert.

The survey includes a follow-up question about the reason for the dissatisfaction. In most cases, the response was poor facilities and lack of books; this varied both by group and by region.

The importance of this survey instrument is that it provides an early warning system or a mechanism for highlighting an issue, which can then be followed up by some more qualitative study through other channels. In other words, it provides rapid early feedback for managers and even policymakers within the country. Repeated annually, the survey can build a time series of these key indicators, so that their evolution can be observed.

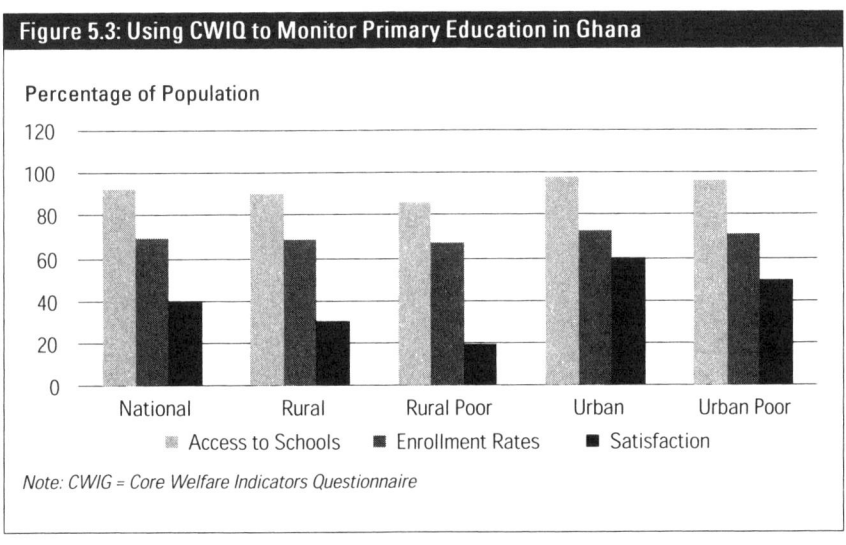

Figure 5.3: Using CWIQ to Monitor Primary Education in Ghana

Note: CWIG = Core Welfare Indicators Questionnaire

Conclusions

In conclusion, I would like to reiterate my four main messages. First, we should be cautious using household surveys to gather statistical information because of the increased complexity of the information sought by these surveys. Using one lump survey for all levels of information from the households interviewed may present a serious challenge and compromise to those in pursuit of information. Second, to avoid a Swiss Army knife approach, we should employ a variety of tools, with varying degrees of subjectivity, objectivity, and representation. Third, we should distinguish between outcome monitoring and impact evaluation. In outcome monitoring, the logframe approach highlights information needs at multiple levels. Finally, monitoring outcomes is a question of market research. We can learn from a survey by using leading indicators to identify an area of concern for policymakers, thereby opening the door to follow-up studies using both quantitative and qualitative tools.

Sarah Gavian

From the world of designing models and collecting data to study the impact of programs and policies on poverty alleviation, I would like to shift gears to the operational challenges of using available data and qualitative information to monitor changes in the poverty-related phenomenon of food security.[1]

The Famine Early Warning System Project

I work for the Famine Early Warning System (FEWS), a U.S. Agency for International Development (USAID) early warning and food security project covering 17 countries in Africa. Our mission is to monitor the effects of various actual—and uncontrolled—events on the food security of people in those countries. Some of the realities we have struggled with in culling qualitative and quantitative information to answer our questions may prove relevant to the topic of impact assessment.

The FEWS project evaluates the food security of national and subnational populations. Food security is a condition in which a population has physical, social, and economic access to sufficient, safe, and nutritious food over a given period to meet its dietary needs and preferences for an active life. The concepts and techniques for assessing food security are similar, but not identical, to those for evaluating poverty. An individual's food security depends not only on the physical availability of food but also on that person's ability to obtain access to adequate food and to use it in a manner that meets dietary needs. The access component of food security involves an evaluation of incomes and, in that sense, resembles measures of poverty. However, the definition of food security itself, because it also includes the physical availability and biological use of food, extends beyond the definition of poverty.

Monitoring Food Security

To monitor a population's often changing food security status, FEWS pulls together its quantitative and qualitative indicators of availability, access, and use. As we do not have the mandate, staff, or funds to collect primary data, we rely on various sources of secondary data and qualitative information. We use remotely sensed (satellite) data pertaining to meteorological and vegetative conditions, as well as information (as quantified as possible) on crops, livestock, off-farm incomes, health, nutrition, and demographic conditions.

Our method for measuring food security has evolved greatly over the nearly 15 years of the FEWS project. During the project's early phases, we used a convergence of indicators approach, checking the trends in each of the available data series to see, more or less, if a population was likely to be food secure or insecure. While this back-of-the-envelope method is conceptually muddy and opaque, some find it the most intellectually honest, given the paucity of reliable data needed to support more complicated modeling attempts. Over the years, FEWS has made conceptual advances in assessing food security, drawing in great measure from research conducted at the International Food Policy Research Institute (IFPRI) and by field practitioners such as Save the Children in the United Kingdom and the World Food Program. Our need to generate an ongoing and up-to-date view of food security conditions for all major populations in a country has led us to avoid mathematical and econometric models. We have focused instead on developing a rigorous, transparent, and replicable method for pulling together disparate sources of quantitative and qualitative data to determine who is vulnerable to food insecurity and why.

Although food insecurity is ultimately an individual issue, it is nearly impossible to monitor at an individual level. So we back up, drawing inferences about household food insecurity from district-level information on food availability, access, and use.

As users of secondary information, we often use the results of sample survey data, such as household expenditure surveys and census data. Generally, however, most of our information comes from the official statistics generated by government ministries. Such data are often fairly poor, with a confidence interval of plus or minus 20 percent. Increasingly often, during this period of deficit cutting and structural adjustment, official data collection efforts have withered. Even basic agricultural production statistics and trade and price data are no longer available in certain African countries. Attempts to substitute locally generated information with satellite data to predict agricultural production have been problematic. The quantitative components of our analyses are often fairly limited.

Once we have the best possible picture from available quantitative information for the districts, we use qualitative information to refine our understanding. From expenditure surveys, rapid rural appraisals, or pre-existing studies, we determine how each of the identified populations derives its livelihood, and we evaluate each of those livelihood sources relative to a norm. The qualitative assessment is done mostly through interviews with NGOs or representatives from the communities, usually in the capital city or during brief field trips to affected areas.

The results of a FEWS food security analysis indicate where there may be food-insecure populations and the causes of problems. FEWS itself does not assess exact food needs in any particular area and does not implement food aid programs. The analysis provides the information needed to plan follow-up emergency needs assessments.

Lessons from the FEWS Experience

FEWS does not conduct surveys, nor does it assess the impacts of planned development interventions. We monitor the effect of natural and man-made shocks to the national and local food economies. In so doing, we try to marry quantitative and qualitative information—often seen as apples and oranges—in a rigorous analytical argument.

Two issues arise in this context. The first concerns the absolute paucity of reliable information in many of the countries FEWS works with, worsened by the degradation of the institutional capacity for collecting that information. Governments with limited means are often unable to fund data collection activities. Donors, however, are often the major users of such information. Until demand for reliable statistics can be generated internally, national data collection activities will require donor support.

The second issue concerns the need for organic partnerships between donors and a country's food security community. This is important for generating consensus, to both identify the problem and effect a solution. Many people, decisionmakers and technicians alike, are skeptical about data and models. Our analysts and our partner organizations resist the standard economic practice of making simplifying assumptions or quantifying qualitative indicators. Yet decisions must be made about food aid interventions, both emergency and developmental, regardless of weaknesses in the information. Our challenge is to identify needy populations with sketchy information and to build a consensus for action.

For FEWS, developing institutional capacity and consensus within a country on matters of food security is even more important than perfecting our analytical methods. The one or two FEWS analysts who work within the countries work in local partnerships to collect information, analyze food security, and link the assessments to the response planning process. This effort involves getting the community of food security teams to agree on the analysis done by the various NGOs, government agencies, and donors; establishing a common view of the problem; and planning appropriate responses. The lesson FEWS has learned is that the assessment and intervention process must have local credibility and ownership.

John Eriksson

My remarks are drawn from a paper, "Aid Coordination—Moving Toward Partnership—the Challenge of Measurement," that was prepared as part of an OED evaluation called *Aid Coordination and the Role of the World Bank*. The approach is one that can be applied to the systematic measurement of qualitative processes in many areas, including poverty reduction.

The paper illustrates some of the basic principles of process measurement methodology as applied to aid coordination. It is important, first, to define objectives as clearly as possible and, second, to distinguish between objectives and measurable indicators. A process as multidimensional as aid coordination typically requires more than one measurable indicator to measure the changes in each objective adequately.

A further challenge is to identify a feasible number of indicators that are representative, clear and straightforward, cost-effective, and participatory.

The first of the eight objectives of aid coordination is "government in the center of the process," which relates to the ownership of aid coordination processes. Table 5.1 shows the eight objectives and illustrates a full set of related concepts for the first objective and a selected set for the other objectives.

Several kinds of baseline indicators, or indicator questions, measure the different dimensions of government's central involvement in the aid coordination process. These indicators culminate in a broad question: How do government and donors assess the centrality of the government's role and why?

For a number of questions, the respondent has the option to indicate briefly why a particular response was given or not given. These indications can yield some important insights.

Aid coordination fora should be concerned with key development issues. Showing the relationship between aid coordination processes and development impact is difficult methodologically, but at least one can ask if aid coordination fora are concerned with key development issues. This is the second objective.

The third objective relates to the availability of quality information on development plans and activities. A frequent complaint we have heard, both from governments and from donors, is that only limited and poor-quality information is available from their counterparts.

The fourth objective is coherent donor support for the national budget and the national development strategy. Some indicator questions include the following: To what extent is donor financing channeled through the national budget? What is the response from the government if a donor proposes a low-priority project as opposed to one within budget?

The fifth objective calls for donors to provide assistance efficiently—that is, to minimize transaction costs in the delivery of aid. Indicator questions include the following: To what extent are sectors crowded with a large number of donors? What proportion of total sector aid do the three largest donors provide? To what extent are donor appraisal, supervision, and evaluation missions harmonized, as opposed to being ad hoc and separate? One measure of this indicator question could be the number of joint missions as a percentage of total missions during the previous twelve months. (Note the importance of the time period here.)

The flip side is embodied in the next objective, regarding donor views of the quality and transparency of such key recipient government processes as budgeting, accounting, and auditing. Who audits government accounts?

Table 5.1: Sample Objectives, Indicators, Measures, and Methods

Objectives	Indicators (selected baseline questions)
1. Government is in the center of the process.	Is there a coherent national development strategy, with clear priorities and countrywide ownership?
	Is strategy linked to development impact objectives, e.g., international goals, as articulated in DAC *21st Century* document?
	Is there a locus of aid coordination responsibility within the government?
	Who convenes and chairs aid coordination meetings (within or outside country)?
	Who does preparatory/analytical work for aid coordination meetings?
	How do government and donors assess the centrality of government's role and why?
2. Aid coordination fora are concerned with key development issues.	How do participants assess adequacy with which a.c. for address development issues?
3. Good quality information about development plans and activities of participants is easily available.	How do participants assess the quality and availability of information and why?
4. Donors provide coherent support to the national development strategy.	How do government and donors assess the coherence of donor support and why?
5. Donors provide assistance efficiently, minimizing transactions costs	How do government and donors assess overall efficiency of donor aid delivery and why?
6. Donors have confidence in quality and transparency of government budgeting, accounting, and reporting.	How do donors and government assess government transparency and why?
7. Donors contribute to improved government institutional capacity for aid management and coordination.	How do government and donors assess the quality of aid for capacity building and why?
8. Concerns of civil society and private sector are addressed in aid coordination processes and outcomes.	How do participants and stakeholders assess the extent to which concerns of civil society and the private sector are addressed and why?
9. Overall Assessment of "Aid Coordination Quality."	How do participants and stakeholders assess "aid coordination quality" overall?

Measures	Methods
Scale 1-to-5: Priorities: "lacks-to-clear" Ownership: "very low—widespread"	Documents, observation, and interviews
Scale of 1-to-5, "weak-to-strong"	Documents, interviews
"Yes"=1; "No"=0 Name(s) of unit(s)	Observation, documents, and/or interviews
No. and % of total, for each chair, previous 12 months.	" "
No. and % of total, each party, previous 12 months	" "
Scale of 1–5, "not at all–great extent" plus brief narrative	Survey (questionnaires and/or interviews)
Scale of 1 – 5, "poor – excellent" plus brief narrative	Survey of participants
Scale of 1 – 5 for each; "poor – excellent" + brief narrative	Survey of participants in aid coordination processes
Scale of 1- 5, "poor –excellent" + optional narrative	Survey of government and donors
Scale of 1 – 5, "poor- excellent" + optional narrative	Survey of government and donors
Scale of 1 – 5, "poor – excellent" + optional narrative	Survey donors and government
Scale of 1 – 5, "poor-excellent" + optional narrative	Survey of government and donors
Scale of 1 – 5, "not at all – very well" + optional narrative	Survey of *all* participants and stakeholders (civil society and private sector)
Average of the last measures of each of the eight objectives	Indicator 1.6 could be given more weight

How timely are they and what is their quality? Does the government consistently use internationally accepted procurement procedures?

The seventh objective is donors' contribution to improving government institutional capacity for aid management and coordination. Attempts to do this have been mostly supply driven and largely ineffective, often because they have ignored institutional rules and incentive structures.

The eighth objective concerns the extent to which the concerns of civil society and the private sector are addressed in aid coordination processes and outcomes.

The last objective is really an average of the first eight: an overall index of aid coordination quality.

The indicator questions were framed as baseline questions. After an interval of a year or two, one might ask the respondents' views about changes in some of the critical indicators.

Note

1. A project logframe is a conventional tool for project planning to better link the project's ultimate goals to its outputs and inputs and to identify key indicators for monitoring and evaluation.

Floor Discussion: Quantitative and Qualitative Methods in Evaluation

The floor discussion focused on the flow of information from the community to the national level and on the subjectivity of information gathered at the community level.

John Eriksson had outlined eight important objectives in aid coordination. Regarding two of these—keeping government central to the process and ensuring coherent donor support for the national development strategy—one audience member wondered how NGOs should be expected to channel their aid. Eriksson observed that many of the indigenous NGOs worked directly with target populations, whereas many of the international NGOs channeled their aid through the governments of target countries. In addition, NGOs themselves were often capable of conducting evaluations, although they tended to use more qualitative tools.

Another discussant asked whether baseline indicators should be changed or adjusted, depending on the type of government in a target country. Eriksson advised that the government, as a key participant and stakeholder in aid coordination should be asked to identify critical objectives and indicators on which adjustments could then be made, based on government priorities.

Marchant had emphasized the need to use a variety of instruments in collecting information as part of the task of monitoring outcomes. A participant asked if any methods were available to identify the unintended benefits of intervention programs. Marchant replied that monitoring outcomes was generally concerned with measuring where a change occurred rather than with determining its cause, and that expected or unexpected changes warranted more detailed follow-up studies.

When the discussion turned to an examination of how community-based information was channeled upward toward the national level, someone made a pivotal comment about donors' interest in resource distribution. In many cases, when donors are involved in investigations at the national level, the input of local beneficiaries becomes less direct or less likely to affect centrally made decisions.

One participant suggested that especially where decentralization was taking place, a bottom-up strategy might be more appropriate, or an investigation at the community or individual level.

Marchant observed that some countries had shown an increasing tendency toward regional rather than national decisionmaking, but that this trend might present a significant challenge to evaluation of needs or program impact. In particular, a community-based information system, though essential for generating the information that would facilitate decisionmaking, was extremely difficult to put into practice.

Gavian added that if decisions about donations and intervention programs for communities and individuals were made at the national or international

---

James Heckman of the University of Chicago chaired the discussion.

level, it could also be difficult to identify the beneficiaries and their needs. Similarly, the danger in gathering resources at the national level and tailoring them to meet local needs was that direct input from the beneficiaries was more likely to be excluded.

Taking Gavian's point further, Heckman noted that in a fully decentralized environment the community should have enough reasonably objective knowledge and debate to make informed decisions without formal statistical apparatus. In other words, some kind of community-based information system should already be in place in a decentralized environment. There were two problems with information collecting at the community level. First, if a community had a system for collecting information, it should also be able to analyze the information and apply it in decisionmaking, which was not always the case. Second, the information generated at the community level might be more qualitative and therefore more subjective. This subjectivity affected the reception of information by the central government, to which donor funds might still be transferred. Often there was a propensity at higher levels to mistrust reports that were seen as subjective, because allocating funds on the basis of a subjective evaluation would encourage people to misreport their subjective opinions. However, complete objectivity was nearly impossible to establish, even with more quantitative methods.

Heckman added that there were elements of subjectivity at several other stages: deciding the values at the center of a study, establishing who composed tools such as survey instruments, and deciding which questions should be asked of the group under study, among others. In addition, there might be gaps between survey respondents and the people who interpret the results of survey instruments. Even identifying a control group could present a problem: assuming that the control group was identical to the area under study involved some degree of opinion. What made the difference between qualitative and quantitative approaches more evident was that subjectivity was simply more open and easier to see in the more qualitative approaches.

Several discussants suggested solutions to the problem of channeling subjective information to the central government. One said that collaboration with NGOs on a long-term basis could lend more credibility to information gathered at the community level. Another suggested that benchmarking across fairly similar regions could permit comparisons of the various mechanisms used, thereby providing an opportunity to build a consensus. A third said that several different stakeholders could jointly evaluate the quality of the information gathered, providing another opportunity for consensus building about the nature of the intervention needed. Finally, one participant recommended that while qualitative participatory approaches on the community level helped "add flesh to the skeleton," aggregating from the particular to the general should be avoided. Qualitative information should at most serve to enrich a study. The study should ultimately draw on different sources of information.

6

Theory-Based Evaluation: Theories of Change for Poverty Reduction Programs

Carol H. Weiss

Theory-based evaluation is a mode of evaluation that brings to the surface the underlying assumptions about why a program will work. It then tracks those assumptions through the collection and analysis of data at a series of stages along the way to final outcomes. The evaluation then follows each step to see whether the events assumed to take place in the program actually do take place. Figure 6.1 is a simple model of a program theory as applied to a specific project.

I want to apply the ideas of theory-based evaluation to programs that seek to reduce poverty. My first example is a set of programs in the United States with which I have been working. These are comprehensive community initiatives designed to help low-income communities improve their economic, social, and political conditions. After I discuss theories of change in these programs, I will present a theory of change in the Bank's social funds program. I am currently working with Soniya Carvalho of OED on a design for evaluating the social funds. The work I will present is preliminary, and subject to some revisions down the road.

Underlying Assumptions for Comprehensive Community Initiatives

Figure 6.1 depicts comprehensive community initiatives that large foundations and the federal government are funding in a series of communities and neighborhoods around the country. The assumptions underlying these initiatives are twofold. One major theory is that services should be coordinated so that residents get all the care they need without having to

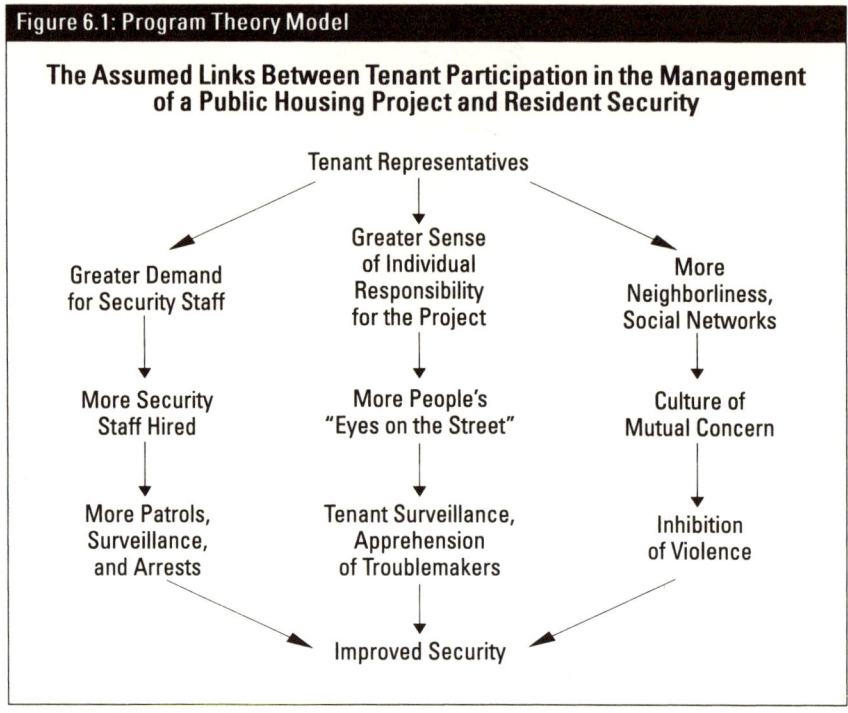

Figure 6.1: Program Theory Model

The Assumed Links Between Tenant Participation in the Management of a Public Housing Project and Resident Security

apply and prove eligibility in many different places. Social service agencies have to work together with common eligibility criteria, common data collection, easy referrals to other services without long waiting periods, mutually convenient locations, and so on. The assumption here is that if agencies coordinate their services to the whole family, each member of the family will be better off. Children will do better in school, adults will be able to get and keep jobs, and so on.

One particular comprehensive community initiative was designed to improve the condition of adolescents in the community. The program theory is shown in figure 6.2. Coordination of services is expected to save time for the family which can go to one or two locations rather than chasing all over town. The agencies see each family member's problems in the context of the whole family, and so understand the problems better. The services offered are more complementary: health services, mental health services, and drug abuse prevention services are provided in ways that make them mutually supportive. With a coordinated set of services, professionals can identify any missing services and take steps to fill the gaps. With this kind of coordination, services become more appropriate for residents and missing services are supplied. The improved quality of the services gives the professionals involved greater satisfaction and boosts their morale. Most important, now that services are more convenient and more appropriate for the residents' needs, they attend regularly and do what they are supposed to do (take medication, attend homework help programs, and so on). The end result is improved functioning of the families and healthy, productive adolescents.

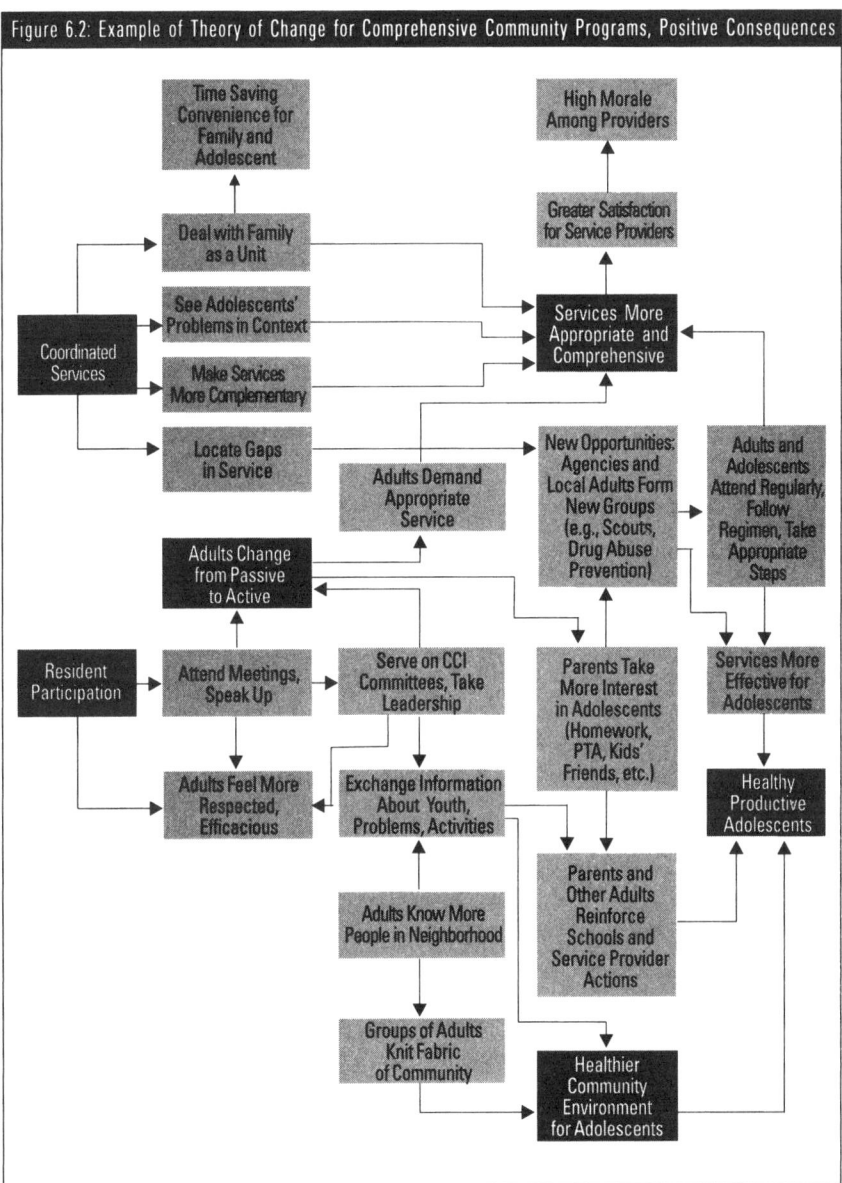

Figure 6.2: Example of Theory of Change for Comprehensive Community Programs, Positive Consequences

The other branch of theory in relation to comprehensive community initiatives is that residents should have a greater say in managing their community and its services. They are invited to community meetings to express their desires for the community. They speak and take part in community planning. They demand more appropriate services. They take more interest in their own children and adolescents. They come to know other parents and share information with them so their children cannot say such things as "everybody else's family lets them do it." Adults keep track of who their children are associating with, work together for the good of the community, and support and reinforce the services of schools and service agencies. The end result again is expected to be improved development and behavior of adolescents, the goal of the program.

Implications for Evaluation

These are the theories underlying the current community initiative movement. For the evaluators, the big advantage of bringing these theories to the surface is that it shows where to check program progress. It identifies the points at which data should be collected and the kinds of data needed. For example, do residents attend community meetings? Do they take on leadership responsibilities in the community? Do they give more time and attention to their own children? Do they share information with other parents? Thus, long before the four or six or eight years that it will take to produce desired effects in the form of healthier adolescents, the evaluators can tell whether the expected sequence of steps is happening. For example, if coordination of services does not yield more appropriate services and greater client satisfaction, then the program is unlikely to produce its desired long-term consequences, at least by that route.

Three big advantages for pursuing a theory of change evaluation are as follows:

- A theory of change evaluation allows evaluators to give early word of events without having to wait until the end of the whole program sequence.
- The evaluators can identify which assumptions are working out and which are not. They can pinpoint where in the theory the assumptions break down. This should enable the program to take corrective action before too much time goes by.
- The results of a theory of change evaluation can be more readily generalized across programs. Seeing the successes and the failures between closely linked assumptions, such as between greater parental attention to children and better child behavior, is easier than between, say, parenting education programs and better child behavior.

Many kinds of programs aim to increase the time that parents spend with their children, and if evaluators of these different programs collect data on parental time actually spent with the child and desired outcomes, the data are more likely to be comparable. By paying attention to the intervening steps in the process of change, the evaluators not only have more to tell the program but can also aggregate results across programs more readily.

Another methodological advance that theory-based evaluation can provide is the identification of unanticipated and undesired program consequences. We all know that programs not only do what they intend to do, at least some of the time, but also set in motion forces that lead to things they did not want to do.

Figure 6.3 presents theories about possible negative consequences of the same comprehensive community initiatives. We start with the same two major strands of programming, coordination of services and enhanced resident participation, but these theories develop untoward effects. Coordination may lead to bureaucratic wrangling over resources and control when each agency wants a bigger slice of the pie and more say about how the coordinated services will be run. If gaps in service are identified, municipal and project resources are too small to fill the gaps. Available resources are spread thin, and services become diffuse and unfocused and perhaps decline in quality. If redundant services are discovered, the funding agents may seek to cut back funding. Moreover, coordination is a time-consuming process. Service providers have to spend much time meeting with collateral agencies about such matters as eligibility rules, reporting rules, data systems, procedures for initiating and terminating service, and so on. They have to spend time in joint planning of the services a family should receive, understanding the complexities of the whole family and its members, keeping records up-to-date so that other providers will know what has gone on, and so on. Such time demands can reduce the actual amount of service provided. As a consequence, the services provided under the coordinated system may be less appropriate and less effective for the families they serve.

Take a look at the other strand: resident participation. Things can go awry here as well. If residents do become engaged and active, they may get embroiled in arguments and conflicts with one another. The community climate may become more contentious rather than more positive and consensual. If they do get down to planning, residents may make plans that are unrealistic and unfundable. When the authorities turn down the plans, residents may become frustrated and angry or they may withdraw from participation entirely. Resident planning may lead to demands for more services than agency budgets can sustain, and the demands may create conflicts with the agencies and the city. The whole community environment may be fragmented and hostile. The effect on youngsters may be to engulf them in community feuds and factions, perhaps drawing them into the conflict and, in general, having negative effects on their development.

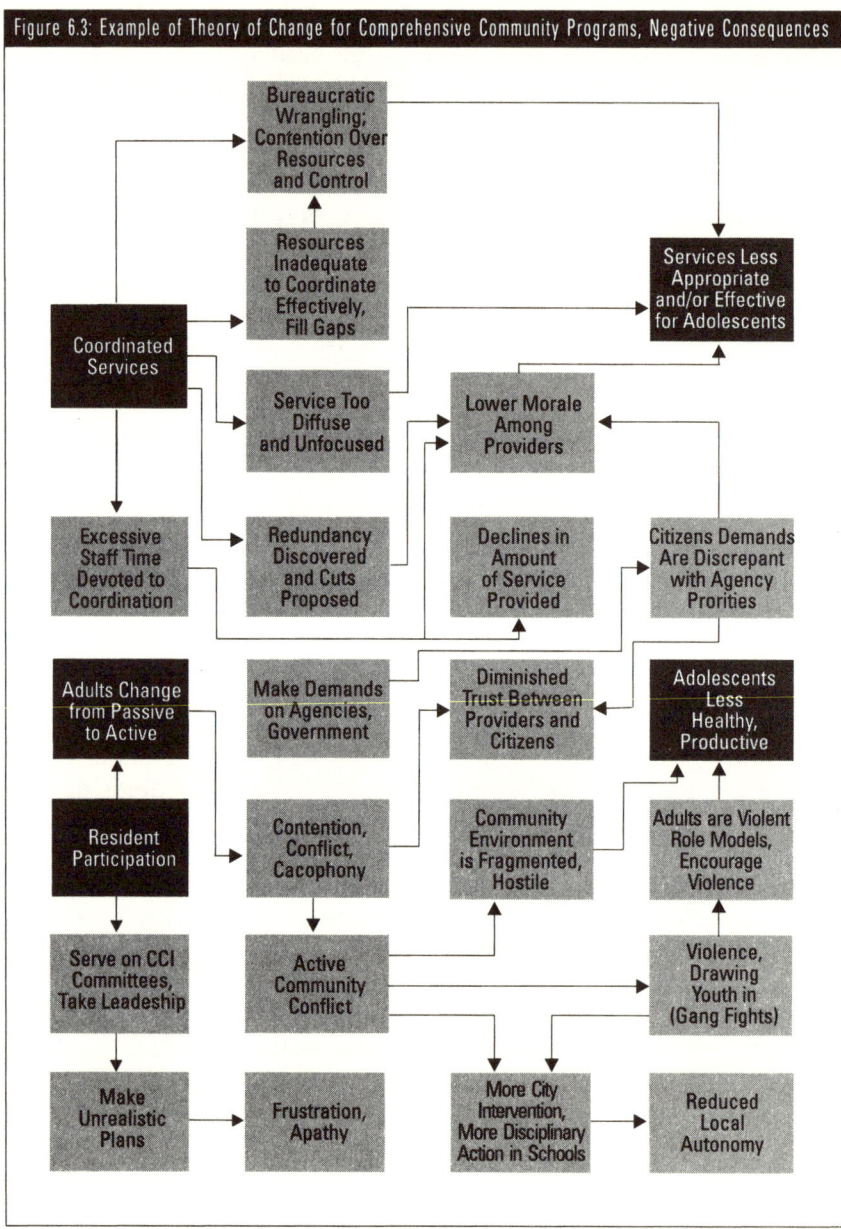

Figure 6.3: Example of Theory of Change for Comprehensive Community Programs, Negative Consequences

The reason for laying out this kind of program theory is to alert the evaluators to the unplanned effects the program may have. A program is not successful if it creates as many problems as it solves. Therefore, sensible evaluators track the onset of negative consequences in the same way they track the emergence of positive consequences. Then if the program does not have good effects, evaluators do not have to speculate about the reasons. They have data that help explain why the program went astray and, again, they can share this information with other evaluators and other programs to gain a better sense of the obstacles to goal achievement.

Applying Program Theory to Social Fund Evaluation

Let us now turn to the preliminary program theory that I have been developing with Carvalho for social fund evaluation (figure 6.4). Drawing on the extensive research and evaluation that have been done on social funds, I have laid out the sequence of assumptions, as I understand them, that underlie their operation as a poverty reduction program.

Theory posits that social funds are a mechanism decentralized to the community level and demand driven to meet the needs of residents,

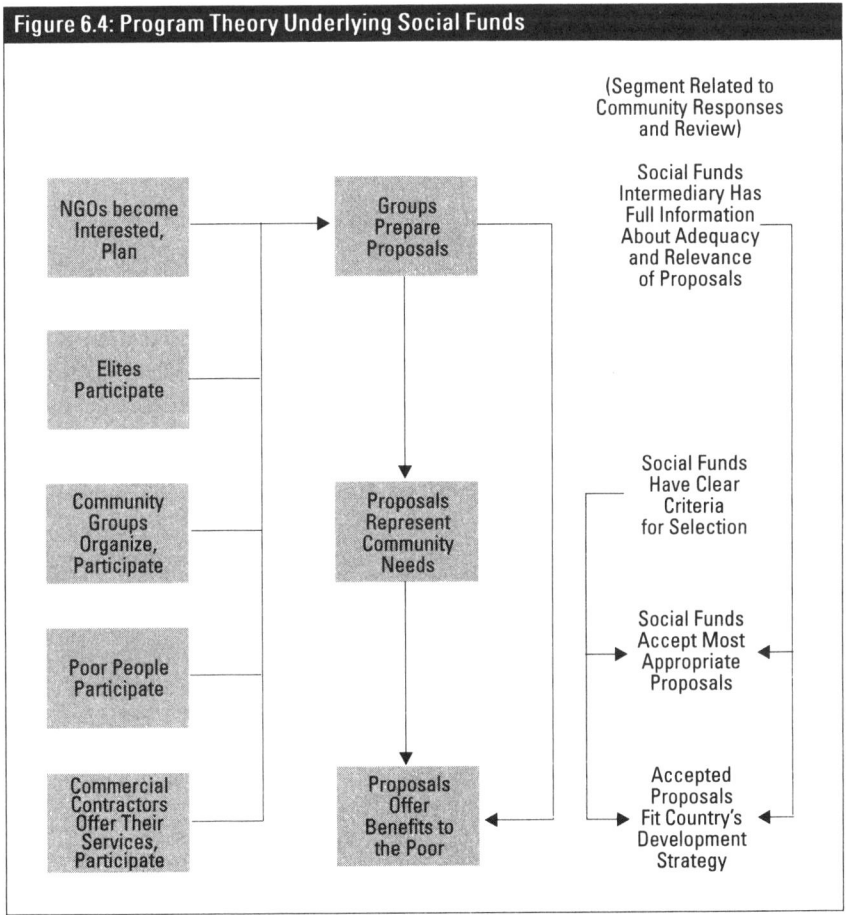

especially the poor. Social funds are expected to respond to community demand and avoid the drag of bureaucracy. Therefore, projects funded by social funds are expected to operate more quickly and more efficiently than centralized projects; be more sustainable; and bring benefits to communities, especially poor communities. The table sketches out what I see as some of the assumptions on which these expectations rest. I am sure we will improve this statement as we proceed. The implication for evaluation is that each column represents a point at which data can be collected to test the assumptions, and the statement in each cell indicates which kinds of data are needed.

Figure 6.4 takes a segment of the full theory of change and shows some key points at which an evaluation might concentrate its data collection. In the evaluation study that Carvalho is now undertaking, analysts are going to compare how social funds operate with the operation of other funding mechanisms. The evaluators will have to find a way to collect comparable data on the key assumptions of demand-driven investment fund projects, municipal development fund projects, sectoral projects, and community development fund projects. An important aspect of their work will be to see which elements in the theories underlying each of these mechanisms are similar and which are distinctive and to construct a design that homes in on both the similarities and the differences. Then when the theoretical assumptions are clarified, collecting data and analyzing outcomes in light of the underlying assumptions become possible.

Finally, I would like to suggest a rather different version of program theory. So far we have been talking about program theory that deals with the how question: How is the program assumed to work to reach its goals? There is also a why question: Why does the program expect that things will work out as assumed? The why question I am asking in figure 9.5 is why community members would propose projects that benefit the poorest of the poor. A number of theories might explain why people in the community plan for the needs of the poor. As the figure suggests, one might be that helping the poor is a religious tenet—that is, people plan poverty reduction projects because of their religious convictions. Another theory is that they are altruistic, not necessarily because of their religious beliefs but because they have a social conscience. A third theory might be that community groups and NGOs want to get funding for their organizations and their staffs. They have no particular commitment to the poor, but if benefits to the poor are a condition of funding, then they will plan projects for the poor. Another theory might be that organizations want to maintain good relations with the Bank. They may have other goals for their dealings with the Bank, so if the Bank is determined to work on poverty reduction, they will go along, and so on.

Evaluations can be designed to answer "why questions" like these. Getting answers will be especially illuminating when expected processes do not happen, when communities do not propose projects that serve the needs of the poor.

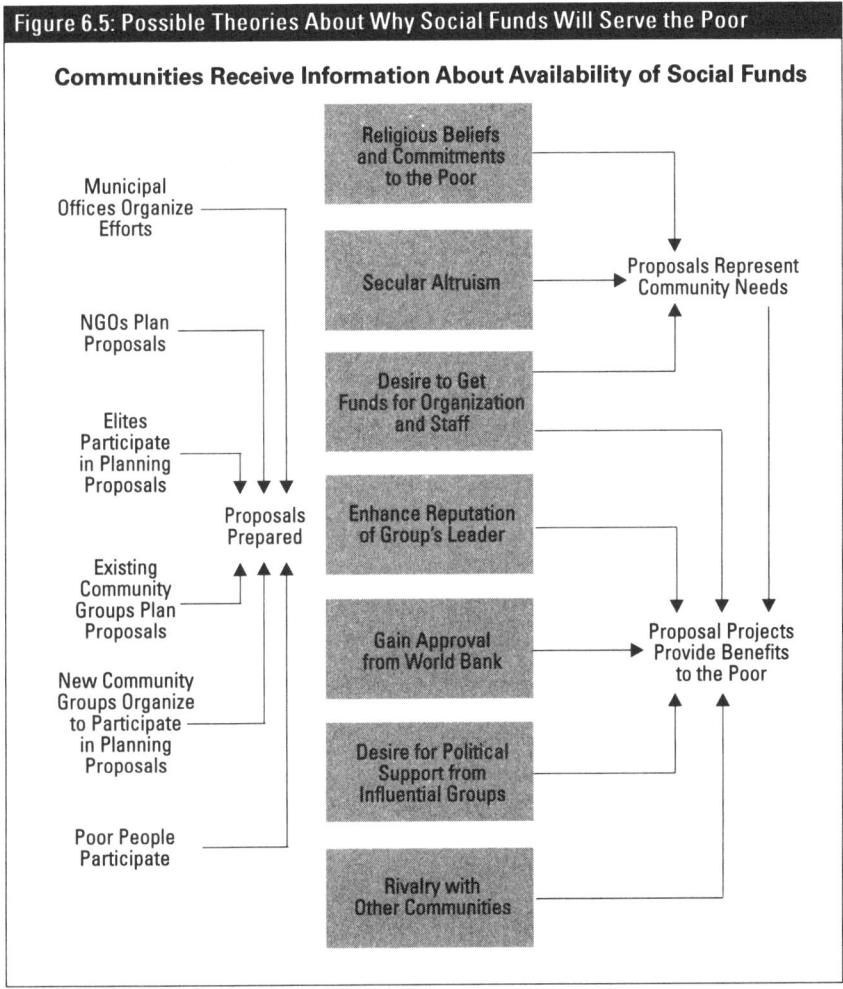

Figure 6.5: Possible Theories About Why Social Funds Will Serve the Poor

Part IV

Participatory Evaluation: Costs and Benefits

The Front-End Costs and Downstream Benefits of Participatory Evaluation

Edward T. Jackson

To a greater or lesser extent, explicitly or implicitly, donors, government, and NGOs all subject their decisions on investing in poverty reduction projects to an assessment of its costs and benefits. Considerable front-end costs are associated with participatory development strategies, but the downstream benefits are significant and usually outweigh the costs considerably. Development agencies must also assess the costs and benefits of participatory evaluation (PE), a form of participatory development. Less well understood is that beneficiary stakeholders do their own cost-effectiveness analysis of their involvement in antipoverty projects, and withdraw their support of a project if concrete results are not forthcoming. Evaluators must understand better the relative perspectives of different stakeholder groups on cost-effectiveness.

Participation and results are both crucial to poverty reduction. Poverty and exclusion persist in a world of volatile change. The unpredictability and complexity of the present era demand that citizens and institutions in all societal spheres—civil, state, and private sector—combine their knowledge and action to solve evolving problems rapidly and efficiently.

The past five years have seen two parallel trends in the corporate and programming strategies of development agencies, governments, and NGOs. First, there is now broad consensus that stakeholders' participation in poverty reduction interventions helps increase their commitment and ownership and helps reduce the risks of failure. A diverse range of methodologies is now available to practitioners for engaging and facilitating stakeholder participation. The second trend, which has been under way in development for some time, is a shift from activity-based to results-based management (RBM). The emphasis on results has prompted more precision in thinking about (a) types of results (short-term outputs in less than a year, medium-term outcomes of one to five years, long-term impacts of five years or longer), (b) levels of results (microlevel for individuals, households, and communities; mesolevel for institutions; and macrolevel for policy), and (c) patterns of results generated by different intervention approaches over time (Jackson 1998). Integral to RBM regimes is a related emphasis on flexibility, learning, and decentralized authority (World Bank 1999). What is generated is more important than how it is generated. An adaptive, learning orientation is essential for an effective RBM system (Rondinelli 1993).

The World Bank has made a strong corporate commitment to participation and results, and is clarifying what this means in practice. The Bank's Committee on Development Effectiveness (CODE) recently observed that "the Bank is at an early stage of practicing result-based management, which is both a management system and a reporting system. RBM provides a coherent framework for learning and accountability in a decentralized environment." Furthermore, participation and results will have to become integral elements in operationalizing the country-focused CDF advocated by World Bank President James Wolfensohn as a new direction for the Bank's engagement with borrowing countries. (World Bank 1999, p. 48).

Opportunities for Participatory Evaluation Under Results-based Management

Participatory evaluation has attracted interest among development practitioners worldwide. PE can be defined as self-assessment, production of collective knowledge, and cooperative action in which the stakeholders in development interventions participate substantively in identifying evaluation issues, designing evaluations, collecting and analyzing data, and acting on the results of evaluation findings. The stakeholders thus build their capacity for participatory development research and evaluation in other areas. PE seeks to give preferential treatment to the voices and decisions of the least powerful and most affected stakeholders: the local beneficiaries of intervention. This approach to evaluation employs a wide range of data collection and analysis techniques, both qualitative and quantitative, involving fieldwork, workshops, and movement building (see Jackson and Kassam 1998).

This definition is generally supported by two separate streams of PE practice. The transformative tradition of PE seeks to promote the democratization of knowledge and social change in favor of the poor and marginalized in society, while the pragmatic tradition seeks to increase the stakeholders' commitment to using evaluation and improving interventions

(Cousins and Whitmore 1998). Currently, both sides appear to be willing to exchange views and experiences and, where possible, blend their approaches and techniques.

The 1990s saw a virtual explosion of guides, manuals, toolkits, and other aids for carrying out PE (see, for example, Gariba 1998, IDS 1997, Lusthaus and others 1999, UNDP 1997, World Bank 1996). Organizations that have become centers of excellence in PE include the International Development Research Centre (IDRC) in Ottawa, the Institute of Development Studies (IDS) at the University of Sussex, and the Society for Participatory Research in Asia, based in New Delhi. Books, networks, conferences, and web sites have all begun to map and advance this growing field.

Like development professionals in all fields today, PE practitioners are following the discourse on and policy shifts toward RBM with great interest. Some are skeptical, concerned that RBM could render PE more technocratic and top down. Others view RBM as an opportunity to place stakeholders, especially local citizens, at the center of the evaluation process: "In fact, the ultimate beneficiaries of a development intervention—the poor, the disadvantaged, the disempowered—can, and should, lead the effort among stakeholders to define the results to be achieved by a given intervention. And they should be the leaders in reviewing performance on these results, as well" (Jackson 1998, p. 52).

How can poor citizens drive the definition and assessment of results? Generally, professional facilitators must ensure the space, voice, and choice for the poor to articulate their views and produce new knowledge in the PE process. Specifically, results can become (and often are) the focus of the widest range of PE activities carried out by citizens: interviews; workshops; committee meetings; community meetings; theater and other popular media and cultural events; mapping; transect walks; willingness-to-pay exercises; site visits to specific services; study tours to other communities; computerized analysis of quantitative survey data; and the preparation of verbal, written, and visual reports of findings. Other stakeholders can participate in some of these activities as well.

> RBM provides an opportunity to place stakeholders, especially local citizens, at the center of the evaluation process.

The network of stakeholders for a typical poverty reduction project funded by the Bank in a rural area might include the country's taxpayers and government; the line ministry; and alternatives such as social funds, local governments, NGOs, village development organizations and leaders, wealthy and landless farmers, the unemployed and workers in the informal economy, and the Bank's senior managers, task managers, specialists, and consultants. Each stakeholder group is itself made up of diverse interests, and each has a particular agenda. Understanding the different costs and benefits to each group is important.

The Benefits of Participatory Evaluation for Development Projects

Practitioners of PE report that it "democratizes and enriches the assessment of development. At the same time, participatory evaluation enhances the capacity of interventions to achieve impacts that benefit the stakeholders engaged in the process" (Jackson and Kassam 1998, p. 2). PE's proponents argue that it produces better, more accurate knowledge about development performance than nonparticipatory methods. Practitioners at the IDS point to the limitations of nonparticipatory evaluation approaches and find that PE's inclusive approach "can reveal valuable lessons and improve accountability. . . . By broadening involvement in identifying and analyzing change, a clear picture can be gained of what is really happening on the ground" (Guijit and Gaventa 1998, p. 1).

> IDRC, a longtime supporter of PE in many forms, has found that it "improves the quality, performance, and effectiveness of projects" and is thus an important management tool. By involving those who are most affected, project outcomes become much better understood by external agencies, national officials, and the beneficiaries themselves. The process of participatory evaluation can also develop or enhance the communities' capacity to recognize the various strengths, weaknesses, and alternatives in project activities. This enables them to plan for the future and to assert their interests in future activities affecting their well-being. In this way, participation, and the capacity building it encourages, can make an essential contribution to the much sought-after sustainability of projects and programs (Cummings and others 1997, p. 4).

IDRC's evaluation unit has been a leader in taking a learning-based approach to evaluation and encouraging its partner research institutions to undertake rigorous, systematic self-assessments of their own performance. Rather than emphasize the evaluation of projects, IDRC emphasizes systematic self-evaluation by institutions on four dimensions: capacity, motivation, environment, and performance. It has found that institutional self-assessment—a mesolevel application of PE—is a powerful process that often generates fundamental changes in the mission or structure of organizations as well as improvements in systems, programs, and projects (Carden 1997; Gupta, Sohani, and Dhamankar 1997; Lee-Smith 1997).

There is some evidence that scaling up PE to the national level is also possible and can generate important policy change. Instances of national processes and benefits are emerging in both the South and the North (Gaventa, Creed, and Morrissey 1998). One of the more promising areas of macrolevel application is participatory poverty assessment (PPA), which the Bank now uses in half of its poverty assessments in borrowing countries. Although technically not PE processes, PPAs are macrolevel investigative initiatives. Using flexible, participatory research methods, PPAs engage the poor on the ground in an analysis of poverty and seek their insights on such issues as vulnerability, lack of security, and powerlessness. PPA findings are then often used to influence national policy. They can be especially effective in countries where civil society is actively engaged in policy dialogue with the government (Robb 1999). Participatory methods have also been used at the national level to build common policy frameworks and research projects among disparate groups in war-torn societies (Stiefel 1998).

> Some evidence indicates that scaling up PE to the national level is also possible and can generate important policy change.

> Scaling up participatory evaluation requires effective champions in the institutions themselves, leaders who have the capacity to take the risks of creating a space for creative questioning, learning, and conflict. It also requires certain levels of social capital or at least a commitment by groups to work together despite differences. It requires creating and supporting within communities and organizations new cultures and environments where learning both for program accountability and for broad community and institutional change can occur (Gaventa, Creed, and Morrissey 1998, pp. 93-94).

Moderating the Costs of Participatory Evaluation

From the perspective of development agencies, one of PE's major costs is time. Writes Whitmore,

> It cannot be rushed. We can condense human learning and the change process just so much. The problem is that we operate in a system that tends to demand measurable results in the short term. Even administrators committed to participatory approaches find themselves having to convince superiors to hold off and allow the process to work (1998, p. 98).

Institutional self-assessments, or mesolevel PE processes, take a particularly long time and require the extended involvement of the staff, members, and other constituents of the institution (Carden 1997). Extended time, of course, creates uncertainty and delays project-related decisions and perhaps disbursements. The consequent pressures on the managing development agencies and government officials to respond are persistent and very real.

Another factor is the cost of the evaluation studies themselves. External consultants or facilitators are likely to be engaged, foreign or domestic, and the fee rates of the former are almost always double or triple those of the latter, not to mention the greater travel costs. Local field workers and research assistants may also be needed, generating additional costs in fees, transportation, and accommodations.

While these costs are significant, they may not exceed those of a conventional evaluation. The difference is time. As Anderson and Gilsig observe: "The dollar value of an investment in participatory evaluation may not appear any greater than that in expert evaluation, but the overall costs to society when people's time is included are undoubtedly much more" (1998, p. 165).

The most effective long-term strategy to enable development professionals to manage PEs' costs is to realign thoroughly development agency rewards and incentives—salaries, benefits, promotions—with results and participation. Project success, driven by stakeholder engagement and a focus on outcomes, should be rewarded; rapid disbursement and top-down management should not. The institutional change, in culture as well as in systems, required for such realignment is, to be sure, challenging and complex; however, not achieving such change is even more problematic in the long run.

Establishing a network of centers of excellence in participatory evaluation throughout the developing world could organize and aggregate local specialists, set common professional standards, promote best practices, and exchange experience and technologies. Their work should focus on results-oriented M&E and balance quantitative and qualitative methods. The centers would require endowed funds to work independently on long-term impact analysis. Overall, such a network should significantly moderate the costs to donors, national governments, NGOs, and citizens. It could also support efforts to design and implement the Bank's CDF at the country level.

A helpful short-term strategy might be to engage a senior champion of PE to provide support within the agency system. A network of professional allies inside and outside the agency sponsoring the PE initiative could help moderate costs. So could a communications strategy that disseminates information about the general merits of PE and about the progress of specific PEs, both vertically and horizontally inside the organization. Web sites, videos, technical papers, colloquia, and workshops can all be useful in this regard. Finally, if staff time permits, sponsoring several PEs at the same time in a given manager's portfolio of ongoing projects may make sense. These will take variable amounts of time and can probably be managed in the sequence in which they are completed.

As for budget expenses, one principle for limiting costs is to keep the engagement of foreign experts to a minimum or not to use them at all. Today virtually every developing country has sufficient local professional expertise to facilitate PE processes competently, although this expertise is not always institutionalized. In addition, in most capital cities of developing countries, and in an increasing number of outlying regions, internet communications are now possible. Project teams should make the fullest use of this facility, along with sophisticated computer software for managing and analyzing evaluative data and project resources.

Benefits and Costs from a Citizen Perspective

The development community's terminology is inadequate to reflect the reality and intent of participatory development. The term "beneficiary" is somewhat patronizing, as today's participatory approaches seek to empower poor citizens with a voice and choices. Citizen engagement in development interventions better describes these approaches (Graham and Phillips 1998). "Primary stakeholder" is another term with some currency.

Development results mean a great deal to citizens who live in poverty. A new school, clinic, or road or access to credit can change the lives of the members of a household or community. Citizens are probably the most results-oriented stakeholders in any project network. Generally speaking, they are little concerned with bureaucratic systems and development strategies. Instead, they want to see concrete, useful results as rapidly as possible. They predicate their engagement on an understanding that PE will lead to development results. Otherwise, contributing their time and ideas makes little sense to them. The opportunity costs are too high.

> Citizens are probably the most results-oriented stakeholders in any project network.

Levin reminds us that all costs are opportunity costs: "The value of what is given up represents the cost of an alternative" (1983, p. 48). All costs represent the sacrifice of an opportunity that has been forgone. "Technically, then, the cost of a specific development intervention [is] the value of all the resources it uses that might have otherwise been assigned to their most valuable alternative use." This notion of opportunity cost lies at the base of cost analysis in evaluation. "By using resources in one way, we are giving up the ability to use them in another way," and so we incur a cost.

What is important here is that different stakeholders in an intervention assess opportunity costs through different lenses. For a farmer, attending a PE meeting during the harvest season carries a greater opportunity cost than attending a PE meeting during some other time of the year. For government officials or consultants who do not farm, seasonality is probably not a factor in calculating their opportunity cost of attending the same meeting. Table 7.1 lists some of the activities citizens engage in during PE and some of the costs they incur in doing so.

The concept of opportunity cost underlies the methodology of cost-benefit analysis (Sugden and Williams 1978). In this technique, benefits "refer to those results or outcomes of an intervention that can be assessed in monetary terms" (Levin 1983, p. 108). Infrastructure projects lend

Table 7.1: Citizens' Opportunity Costs for Engaging in Participatory Evaluation	
How They Spend Their Time	**What They Forgo**
• Listening and talking in interviews, focus groups, committee meetings, workshops and seminars, community meetings • Analyzing data and problems: mapping, transect walks, willingness-to-pay exercises, computerized data analysis • Engaging in cultural activities such as theater, dance, storytelling, radio productions • Traveling to and from meetings, making study tours to other communities • Waiting for leaders, outside experts, decisions, funds	• Time for productive activities, depending on seasonal factors • Time for reproductive activities • Lost time for other development initiatives • Time for political processes • Cash outlays for budgeted expenses spent on food, transportation, and accommodations • Freedom from the resentment of rival groups or elites • Freedom from intimidation or violence during travel

themselves to this type of analysis. However, for many types of interventions, placing a monetary value on results is complex, time-consuming, and costly in itself.

A different concept underlies cost-effectiveness analysis, which "refers to the evaluation of alternatives according to both their costs and their effects with regard to producing some outcome or set of outcomes . . . When costs are combined with measures of effectiveness and all alternatives can be evaluated according to their costs and their contribution to meeting the same effectiveness criterion, we have the ingredients for a [cost-effectiveness] analysis" (Levin 1983, pp. 17-18).

In poverty reduction interventions, which seek to achieve a wide range of development results, cost-effectiveness analysis appears to have more potential for useful assessments. An even better term might be cost-results analysis. Cost-results analysis can and must be applied from the perspective of each separate stakeholder group. In practice, each stakeholder group in a poverty reduction initiative, including the citizens, conducts its own cost-results analysis on its own terms informally and continuously. Projects that do not deliver real outcomes that matter to the stakeholders are viewed as unaffordable ventures. Stakeholders withdraw from their engagement, and the projects rapidly lose the support and momentum derived from the alliances and coalitions that usually hold interventions together.

Valuing the Intellectual Capital of Citizens

Experience with PE, and indeed with other forms of participatory development, demonstrates how citizens' knowledge can make or break a project. Citizens' analysis of local conditions and problems and their resourcefulness in implementing solutions are decisive factors in enabling the evaluation process to generate appropriate adjustments to an intervention. The lessons learned from numerous PEs worldwide demonstrate that citizens' knowledge is often much more valuable in helping the evaluation process produce results than the knowledge of other project stakeholders. However, poor citizens' knowledge and time are undervalued by market dynamics. Evaluators are thus faced with the problem of valuing the intellectual capital of citizens.

Research on knowledge-driven enterprises in the private sector is helping define intellectual capital. One definition is as follows:

> Intellectual material—knowledge, information, intellectual property, experience—can be put to use to create wealth. Intelligence becomes an asset when some useful order is created out of free-floating brainpower—that is, when it is given coherent form (a mailing list, a database, an agenda for a meeting, a description of a process); when it is captured in a way that allows it to be described, shared and exploited; and when it can be deployed to do something that could not be done if it remained scattered around like so many coins in a gutter. Intellectual capital is packaged useful knowledge (Stewart 1997, p.67).

The purpose of poverty reduction interventions is to create a range of development results, not only wealth. When we attribute to citizens, say, 50 percent of the total influence over the success of a US$20 million project, can we then say that the value of their time, labor, and knowledge is equivalent to US$10 million worth of project results? Perhaps not, but the measurement issue is important. The Bank should bring together economists, sociologists, anthropologists, and others to study how to assess and track the intellectual capital of the primary stakeholders of poverty interventions: ordinary citizens.

Areas for Future Research

In connection with future research, at least six issues are at the forefront of investigation into the effects of PE on participation and results:

- *Citizen-oriented cost-results analysis.* Detailed research is needed on how various groups of primary stakeholders assess the costs of and payoffs to their participation at different points in the intervention cycle in both qualitative and quantitative terms. How do different categories of primary stakeholders judge the results that matter to them against their costs?

- *Returns on citizen investment.* To what extent do the citizens who are supposed to be the beneficiaries of development projects receive a return on their direct investment of time, money, ideas, and other resources? How do they judge an acceptable rate of return? How can external agencies understand and track citizens' decision processes? What rates of return is it possible to achieve, in what sectors, and under what conditions?
- *Ways to value the intellectual capital of citizens.* If citizens often exert the greatest influence over a project's success, how should their time and knowledge—their intellectual capital—be valued in comparison with those of other stakeholders?
- *Citizen-defined indicators of development results.* Within and across sectors, what sorts of results indicators are most important to primary stakeholders? To what extent are these indicators aligned with, or divergent from, those of local and external development agencies? How can such indicators be integrated into the M&E processes of development interventions?
- *Reward systems for development professionals.* What reward systems and incentives are most effective in encouraging officials in development agencies to facilitate and support participatory processes at various points in the intervention cycle? Specifically, how can their salaries, bonuses, and other incentives be linked to behavior that encourages participatory antipoverty actions?
- *Agency reporting on development results.* How can development agency reporting systems, indicators, and protocols regarding development results and effectiveness achieve a reasonable and insightful balance among the interests of the primary stakeholders and the interests of the other stakeholders in the intervention network?

Conclusion

In the final analysis, stakeholders make strategic choices about whether to become involved in PE processes, how much time to devote to these efforts, and what ideas they will contribute. Specific groups of stakeholders make these strategic choices on the basis of their own assessment of the costs they will incur, balanced against the results they expect to benefit from, either as a group or as individuals. Stakeholders make similar strategic choices in their decisions to engage in other forms of participatory development. Development practitioners must come to a better understanding of the analysis underlying these strategic choices for all stakeholders, and especially for citizens, who are the primary stakeholders in poverty reduction interventions.

Note

1. The author is grateful for inspiration, advice, and assistance in the preparation of this paper from a number of colleagues, including Frances Abele, Françoise Coupal, Sulley Gariba, John Gaventa, Katherine Graham, Budd Hall, Yusuf Kassam, Fran Klodawsky, Huguette Labrosse, Barbara Levine, Shona Leybourne, Robert Mitchell, Florence Ombaso, John Saxby, Magda Seydegart, Norean Shepherd, Cathie Slatford, Ian Smillie, Terry Smutylo, and Elizabeth Whitmore.

References

Anderson, and Gilsig. 1998. "Participatory Evaluation in Human Resource Development: A Case Study from Southeast Asia." In Edward T. Jackson and Yusuf Kassam, eds., *Knowledge Shared: Participatory Evaluation in Development Cooperation.* West Hartford, CT: Kumarian Press.

Carden, Fred. 1997. "Giving Evaluation Away: Challenges in a Learning Based Approach to Institutional Assessment." Paper presented to the Participatory Monitoring and Evaluation Workshop, International Institute for Rural Reconstruction, Manila.

Cousins, J. Bradley, and Elizabeth Whitmore. 1998. "Framing Participatory Evaluation." In Elizabeth Whitmore, ed., *Understanding and Practicing Participatory Evaluation.* New Directions for Evaluation 80. San Francisco: Jossey-Bass.

Cummings, F. Harry, and others, eds. 1997. "Participatory Evaluation of Development Programs and Projects." *Knowledge and Policy* 10(2).

Gariba, Sulley. 1998. "Participatory Impact Assessment as a Tool for Change: Lessons from Poverty Alleviation Projects in Africa." In Edward T. Jackson and Yusuf Kassam, eds., *Knowledge Shared: Participatory Evaluation in Development Cooperation.* West Hartford, CT: Kumarian Press and IDRC.

Gaventa, John, Victoria Creed, and Janice Morrissey. 1998. "Scaling Up: Participatory Monitoring and Evaluation of a Federal Empowerment Program." In Elizabeth Whitmore, ed., *Understanding and Practicing Participatory Evaluation.* New Directions for Evaluation 80. San Francisco: Jossey-Bass.

Graham, Katherine A., and Susan D. Phillips, eds. 1998. *Citizen Engagement: Lessons in Participation from Local Government.* Toronto: Institute of Public Administration of Canada.

Guijit, Irene, and John Gaventa. 1998. "Participatory Monitoring and Evaluation: Learning from Change." *IDS Policy Briefing* 12:1-4.

Gupta, Ranjit, Girish G. Sohani, and Mona Dhamankar, eds. 1997. *Monitoring and Evaluation for Strategic Management and Organizational Development: Proceedings of an International Workshop.* Pune and Ottawa: BAIF Development Research Foundation and IDRC.

IDS (Institute of Development Studies). 1997. *Participatory Monitoring and Evaluation: An Introductory Pack.* Brighton, U.K.: University of Sussex.

Jackson, Edward T. 1998. "Indicators of Change: Results-based Management and Participatory Evaluation." In Edward Jackson and Yusuf Kassam, eds., 1998. *Knowledge Shared: Participatory Evaluation in Development Cooperation.* West Hartford, CT: Kumarian Press.

Jackson, Edward T., and Yusuf Kassam. 1998. "Introduction." In Edward T. Jackson and Yusuf Kassam, eds., 1998. *Knowledge Shared: Participatory Evaluation in Development Cooperation.* West Hartford, CT: Kumarian Press.

Lee-Smith, Diana. 1997. *Evaluation as a Tool for Institutional Strengthening: Proceedings of the Regional Workshop.* Nairobi and Ottawa: Mazingira Institute and IDRC.

Levin, Henry M. 1983. *Cost-effectiveness: A Primer.* New Perspectives on Evaluation. Thousand Oaks, CA: Sage Publications.

Lusthaus, Charles, and others. 1999. *Enhancing Organizational Performance.* Ottawa: IDRC.

Robb, Caroline M. 1999. *Can the Poor Influence Policy? Participatory Poverty Assessments in the Developing World.* Directions in Development. Washington, D.C.: World Bank.

Rondinelli, Dennis A. 1993. *Development Projects as Policy Experiments*, Second ed. London: Routledge.

Stewart, Thomas A. 1997. *Intellectual Capital: The New Wealth of Organizations.* New York: Currency.

Stiefel, Matthias. 1998. *Rebuilding After War: A Summary Report of the Wartorn Societies Project.* Geneva: United Nations Research Institute for Social Development.

Sugden, Robert, and Alan Williams. 1978. *The Principles of Practical Cost-benefit Analysis.* Oxford, U.K.: Oxford University Press.

UNDP (United Nations Development Programme). 1997. *Who Are the Questionmakers? A Participatory Evaluation Handbook.* Office of Evaluation and Strategic Planning. New York.

Van Wicklin, Warren A. 1999. "OED Participation Process Review Design Paper." Washington, D.C.: Operations Evaluation Department, World Bank.

Whitmore, Elizabeth. 1998. "Final Commentary." In Elizabeth Whitmore, ed., *Understanding and Practicing Participatory Evaluation.* New Directions for Evaluation 80. San Francisco, CA: Jossey-Bass.

World Bank. 1996. *World Bank Participation Sourcebook.* Environmentally Sustainable Development. Washington, D.C.

_____. 1999. *1998 Annual Review of Development Effectiveness.* Operations Evaluation Department. Washington, D.C.

Comments: The Strategic Choices of Stakeholders: The Front-End Costs and Downstream Benefits of Participatory Evaluation

Nicoletta Stame

Measuring Results and Costs

Pluralism spreads through Jackson's paper in many guises: he recommends the use of mixed methods (qualitative and quantitative, local observation, and computer-based analysis), of mixed approaches (the transformative and pragmatic traditions in participation), and of mixed aims (results and participation). These dichotomies have so far limited our understanding, and it is refreshing to see how Jackson has bridged many of them.

Two main themes cut across his paper: mainstreaming participation and reversing conventional wisdom. Mainstreaming participation means participation is not opposed to, and different from, good social research but part of it. It means participation is needed not only for certain types of programs—mainly social, short-term, or local—but for all types. Jackson shows this when he says that participatory evaluation (PE) can be used for output that can be detected soon; outcome that asks for a real engagement of time and energy; and impact, which may take even a generation to become evident. PE is used not only at the microlevel of anthropological work but also at the mesolevel of institutional self-assessment, and even at the macrolevel, as in the Bank system of participatory poverty assessment, or PPA (Robb 1999).

> Participatory evaluation (PE) can be used for output that can be detected soon; outcome that asks for a real engagement of time and energy; and impact, which may take even a generation to become evident.

Reversing conventional wisdom means turning upside down Whitmore's (1998) witty expression: "The donor wants measurable results in a short time." This makes it sound like only external experts can produce results, and that participatory evaluation takes time and still produces unreliable, unmanageable data. Jackson isolates the elements in Whitmore's sentence and for each one shows how important participation is.

First, donors are not all alike, and there are more actors (whom Jackson calls primary stakeholders or citizens) involved in a development partnership than just donors and institutional stakeholders. If the voices of partners at all levels are heard, it is possible to understand better what poverty means in different areas (and to understand links and causality across areas), so one can readjust goals. Hearing all voices will also help in the selection of indicators and the discussion of effects.

Second, to be meaningful, results must measure not only what appears to be easily counted but also aspects and viewpoints. Conventional wisdom holds that donors are interested in results, which can be measured, and the poor are interested in participation, which is hardly measured. This is nonsense. The poor are even more interested in results than donors are; otherwise, they would not bother to participate. As Jackson says, each group of stakeholders "conducts its own cost-results analysis on its own terms informally and continuously." Moreover, results refer not only to goods produced but also to overcoming conditions of powerlessness (illegality, corruption, inefficient institutions). Results should also be measured in terms of sustainability and institutional development, a task to which PE as Jackson conceives of it contributes well.

Third, time is complicated, short and long are relative concepts, and evaluators must assess the value of time for the donor and for the citizen. Conventional wisdom holds that experts are outside evaluators whose high salaries and traveling expenses make it unwise to use them in PE. Jackson concedes that PE need not necessarily take long and that local experts could be trained for the job.

Paying the Costs

Jackson then proceeds on a more daring offensive. If we agree that PE produces better information, a greater sense of ownership, and greater accountability, we should accept the costs and be prepared to pay for them. Jackson is full of suggestions.

First, we should reward officials in development agencies who introduce participation into evaluation with bonuses and other incentives. Finding a way to do this should not be difficult.

Second, we should assess the value of the collective knowledge of the primary stakeholders and the local facilitators who contribute to the production of a good evaluation. The value of participation is not just information to be stored in a statistical series but new knowledge provided through interaction.

Participatory evaluation is not an easy issue to tackle. It is one thing to pay the personal costs of specific evaluation by specific individuals; it is another to reward the collective intellectual capital of the primary beneficiaries who participate in evaluation. And how does one distinguish between local facilitators (who articulate the voices of the poor) and citizens (who hold values and beliefs about the facts being interpreted)? The work of local trained personnel has a market value that can be easily calculated, but how do you calculate the value of time citizens spend in meetings and informal gatherings offering their insights and ideas? Jackson offers a blunt alternative. If we considered the market value of the citizens' opportunity costs, it would probably be low. If we considered the contribution we are willing to acknowledge (if, say, we feel that people's knowledge contributed 50 percent to the success of a program), we might not be prepared to give the primary stakeholders a proportional reward. Where do we draw the line?

Valuing Participatory Evaluation

As for collective resources, I suggest we draw on tacit local knowledge based on social relationships among family, friends, and the working community. I would draw less attention to assessing individual costs (how to reward inputs by single bearers of knowledge) and more to considering everyone involved (favoring the use of social ties and building local PE capacity).

Let me clarify my point with a comparison from a different literature. Industrial districts in the center-north of Italy and local socioeconomic systems in southern Italy (Cossentino, Pyke, and Sengerberger, 1996; Meldolesi 1998) specialize in high-quality "made in Italy" goods (those produced in such traditional sectors as textiles, garments, furniture, mechanical products, and musical instruments). Production is divided among many small- and medium-size firms, usually family based, and the producers simultaneously compete and cooperate. The literature recognizes the importance of the mix between, on the one hand, scientific knowledge about technology and organization and, on the other hand, local and tacit knowledge about traditional crafts that depends on social relationships of trust for organizational flexibility and for adjusting to external market changes (including global competition).

> If the benefits of participatory evaluation are better information, a greater sense of ownership, and higher accountability, then we should face its costs and be prepared to pay for them.

Various policies have been suggested to help introduce advanced technology while strengthening the social factors of cooperation in such functions as buying and selling, training, providing financial services, and providing aid to small family firms. The rationale for these policies is that social capital is not required for development and is not something the lack of which dooms you to underdevelopment. Rather, it is an easily available resource (as are kinship relationships or traditional crafts) whose potential has to be put to use for development.

Here I see a useful comparison with participatory evaluation. In PE the citizens contribute local, tacit knowledge about poverty, how they have been used to coping with it, and how they could use the programs to work with the evaluators, who contribute a general view of how to funnel those ideas into a system of goals and indicators. The social capital that the citizens bring to PE is something that has to be elicited and put to use. To accomplish that, it is necessary to analyze the situations in which PE has worked well and with what results and then design programs that build on the lessons learned.

References

Cossentino, F., F. Pyke, and W. Sengerberger. 1996. *Local and Regional Response to Global Pressure: The Case of Italy and Its Industrial Districts.* Geneva: International Labour Office.

Meldolesi, L. 1998. *Dalla Parte del Sud.* Bari: Laterza.

Robb, C. M. 1999. *Can the Poor Influence Policy? Participatory Poverty Assessments in the Developing World.* Directions in Development. Washington, D.C.: World Bank.

Whitmore, Elizabeth, ed. 1998. *Understanding and Practicing Participatory Evaluation.* New Directions in Evaluation 80. San Francisco: Jossey-Bass.

Floor Discussion: Front-End Costs and Downstream Benefits of Participatory Evaluations

Richard Gerster said he had become aware of the importance of participatory evaluations ten years earlier, when he evaluated a project to launch a buffalo milk cheese factory in the hills of Nepal. When he asked the Swiss donor about the project, they said it was a complete failure. Their measure of success was the alternative energy for the factory, biogas and solar energy, which did not work. The factory was run on wood. When Gerster asked the Nepalese partner, the area development corporation, about the project, they said it was wonderful. Their criterion was processing buffalo milk into cheese, and since that is what happened, the project was a success for them. They did not care about the energy supply. The perspectives of various stakeholders can differ tremendously, and should be integrated.

Gerster was also intrigued by the contradiction between Jackson's presentation of the costs incurred by citizens and Stame's statement that participatory evaluation should be mainstreamed. In traditional types of evaluation, where just knowing the results is a completely donor-driven exercise, bothering citizens with donors' concerns seems somehow illegitimate.

Donors have used contingent evaluation methods to assess nonmarket goods and services and environmental concerns, but they have structured evaluation within an existing price system. One participant wondered whether this was really very useful at the local level.

Rosalind David, commenting on the need for time, said that in her experience, it was important for people who participated in a project to see that the project was flexible and that their opinions were taken into account. In northern Uganda she had seen that a project's impact could be felt in a much shorter time than 5 to 25 years, particularly when people facing emergency situations in extremely dire circumstances had moved to areas where their cultural environment, social attitudes, and social behavior were changing.

Suley Gariba agreed with David about a project's impact being felt fairly readily, especially if participatory evaluation were mainstreamed. Mainstreaming participatory evaluation would probably also reduce costs. The issue of doing several participatory evaluations simultaneously is related to how a series of participatory evaluation exercises is linked to convergence in a comprehensive development framework.

Anwar Shah said that most investments in participatory monitoring helped strengthen community capacity in ways that might not benefit the immediate projects, because it takes time to build capacity, but might have a multiplier effect, strengthening the community's voice, access to information, and leverage with the state and the market. Sustainability also improved, as local

---

Richard Gerster of the Swiss Development Cooperation chaired the discussion.

capacity lasted beyond the project period. Shaw did not think donors had a good handle on developing independent, ongoing country capacity for participatory monitoring.

Pointing out some of the constraints associated with good participatory evaluation, Warren Van Wicklin said that on mission he has about one week per project. He can get to perhaps four to six villages and can spend four to six hours at each village. But this is lightning evaluation. It costs more if he tries to set up local capacity to carry out some kind of primary stakeholder self-evaluation after he leaves, but his budget is limited. At the same time demands are increasing, to add more studies, to respond to more questions, and to do all this not only cheaply and faster, but better. Bringing other development institutions—bilateral and multilateral donors, NGOs, and so on—into World Bank evaluations costs even more time and money. In reality there are some very human and financial constraints on participatory evaluation.

Jackson proposed some solutions. He would advocate better funding, if the management of donor agencies were really serious about participation and the evaluation of participation. One step forward would be to have a network of centers of excellence on participatory evaluation around the world. These centers could achieve substantial economies of scale, which might help moderate some of the costs of participatory evaluation.

Building Local Capacity for Participatory Monitoring and Evaluation

Rolf Sartorius

"Most of the time, the outside experts fly in and out without taking the time to listen to the people. In this evaluation, they really listened to us and respected our opinions. We all worked together to make the project stronger" (local participant, Honduras forestry project evaluation).

Participatory monitoring and evaluation (PME) offers development organizations a host of opportunities to improve the performance of poverty alleviation programs and to build the management capacity of local partners. Few outside "experts" who evaluate poverty reduction programs have the skills to employ PME approaches, and fewer still are able to design and implement effective PME systems. PME encompasses a wide and expanding range of philosophies, tools, and methodologies that can often be married to more traditional approaches.

The Rationale for PME and Its Distinction from Conventional Approaches

PME is widely recognized for its potential to:
- Improve the performance of development and poverty alleviation programs
- Enhance local learning, management capacity, and skills
- Build partnerships and local ownership of projects
- Build consensus among project staff and partners about project goals and objectives
- Provide timely, reliable, and valid information for management decisionmaking

- Increase the cost-effectiveness of M&E information
- Empower local people to make their own decisions about the future.

PME is a broad constellation of approaches and methods that means different things to different people at different points in time and is highly specific to context.

Cousins and Whitmore (1998) posit two principle streams of PE: practical and transformative. They compare them on dimensions of control, level, and range of participation. Feuerstein (1986) and Pretty and others (1996) distinguish among various kinds of evaluation by the extent to which local evaluation stakeholders influence decisions about evaluation processes and the degree to which evaluation activities build local capacity for learning and collective action. Feuerstein outlines four major approaches to evaluation in relation to her work in community development:

- **Studying the specimens.** The community has a limited, passive role.
- **Refusing to share results.** The community receives selected information and feedback.
- **Locking up the expertise.** PE is guided.
- **Partnership in development.** The project builds local capacity to carry out PME.

These frameworks help us see how and where we can deepen and expand participation in our ME work.

Designing PME Systems

Integrating PME systems into the design of poverty alleviation projects from the start increases the likelihood that PME will be fully integrated in a project's operations and that important benefits, such as participatory learning and action aimed at project improvement, will be realized throughout the project's life. It is best to be flexible and to include the four key elements below (Larson and Svendsen 1997). A PME facilitator can work with stakeholders as a team during a project's inception to develop a project logical framework (logframe) and a written PME plan. (A project logframe is a conventional project planning tool to link goals to outputs and inputs and to identify key indicators for ME).

A Collaborative Team

Responsibility for PME is shared within a group of project and partner organization staff. The team comprises key PME stakeholders—people who are committed to PME and who are willing to take responsibility for it. Roles and responsibilities for each team member are spelled out in the written PME plan.

The PME Worksheet

Central to designing a PME system is a planning worksheet, or project logframe, to help the team identify and organize the key information needed in the ME plan (table 8.1). The worksheet helps stakeholders generate consensus on the project's objectives, define practical indicators, and, most important, anticipate who will use the higher-level results. The PME facilitator works with the stakeholders to fill the worksheet with elements important to them. In workshops and planning meetings, the facilitator helps the team think carefully about who will participate in each stage of PME, how information will be used to improve the project, what training and PME training and capacity building activities are needed, and how lessons will be shared.

In work with illiterate or semiliterate groups, the worksheet is used loosely as a conceptual framework. Symbols and pictures may be substituted for the written word and decisions may be recorded on newsprint. This design approach draws heavily on participatory rural appraisal (PRA) or participatory learning and action methods to support the PME system.

Figure 8.1: PME Planning Worksheet

Project Objective (Goal, Purpose, Outputs)	Indicator	Data Collection						Data Analysis and Use			
		Source of Info	Baseline Data Needed	Who Is Involved	Tools and Methods	How Often	Added Info Needed	How Often	Who Is Involved	How Info Is to Be Used	Who Gets Info

A Written PME Plan

In well-designed PME systems, project teams develop a brief, written PME plan through a series of planning meetings whose agenda all participants are aware of and agree on. Ideally, these meetings take place during the project's start-up phase, when the major stakeholders, including the project staff, are available. The plan describes how the activities listed in the PME worksheet will be carried out and should include the following items:
- A description of the key users of PME information and their specific information needs
- A list of the PME team members and their responsibilities

- The project's logframe and PME worksheet
- A description of the project's approach to PME and the process used to develop the PME plan
- The PME training plan
- An annual implementation schedule
- A schedule of project reports, assessments, and evaluations
- The budget for PME activities.

As the plan takes shape, the team may work with a local artist to produce illustrations that show how to use the simple PME tools. The various pieces are put together in a basic set of operational guidelines for the PME team.

Annual Project Self-Assessments

Self-assessments should be made annually in participatory workshops that use data gathered through the participatory monitoring system. These workshops allow participants to reflect on project activities and gain insights into aspects of the project that have or have not worked well, and why. Self-assessments are conducted by project staff and partners and may involve outside resource people. The workshops can last one to three days, depending on the size and complexity of the project. The results are action plans for improving project performance. Performance improvement planning (PIP) is one methodology for this kind of assessment.

The following checklist could be applied during and at the end of the design process to ensure that a PME system is complete and sustainable.

Box 8.1: Checklist for Designing a PME System

- Is the PME system based on a clear understanding of the project's objectives?
- Is it based on a clear understanding of the information needs of key stakeholders?
- Is it based on indicators defined by the participants?
- Can it be incorporated into the structure of the collaborating agencies?
- Does it involve the participation of all key stakeholders in every stage of the PME cycle: planning, data collection, analysis, and use?
- Do the people responsible for PME have all the necessary skills?
- Do the data collection tools fit the skills of the collectors?
- Is the amount of required data collection manageable and conducive to timely analysis and use of the results?
- Is there a plan for testing and adjusting the system?
- Have annual self-assessments been planned?
- Have impact evaluations been scheduled?
- Will the system be sustainable once the project has ended?
- Is it cost effective?
- Is it documented so that everyone knows what it contains?
- Other?

Source: Adapted from Larson and Svendsen (1997).

Conducting Participatory Evaluations

Although PME systems are not practical for all projects, PE is. If PME systems are in place, then PEs will naturally follow. PEs can offer many of the benefits of PME systems, but if they are one-time-only events, they will do little to build sustained capacity for local learning and collaborative action. Therefore, decisions about where PME should be introduced should be made carefully. PME should be used where it has the greatest potential to succeed with adequate resourcing and political commitment. The following five tips will help make PME more effective in supporting poverty alleviation programs.

Determine Whether PME Is Appropriate for Your Program

Knowing the rationale for and the differences between conventional and participatory ME allows an assessment of the conditions necessary for PME systems, their appropriateness for a program, and the extent of financial and human resources and political commitment. PME is much easier to establish in a project that is already using a participatory approach. Good PME work requires a commitment to empowering local people, relinquishing some control, using simple data collection methods, and sharing results with all key stakeholders immediately. In addition, to be most effective, PME systems require active support from project and organizational management. Without these factors, expectations for PME might be reduced or scarce resources devoted to other projects. Larson and Svendsen (1997) summarize the conditions that are usually necessary to develop an effective PME system:

> Good PME work requires being committed to empowering local people, relinquishing some control, using simple data collection methods, and sharing results with all key stakeholders immediately.

- A shared understanding among the project's partners of the project's objectives and approach
- An attitude of partnership characterized by mutual respect between the project staff and the community
- The commitment to use a participatory approach in all phases of ME, along with patience, flexibility, and willingness to allocate resources to the process
- Participatory project management and decisionmaking to help ensure that the input from all participants into the ME process will be taken seriously.

Become or Recruit an Evaluation Facilitator

Evaluators facilitate stakeholder participation during each stage of the evaluation process, from designing the evaluation system through implementing and testing it to training and building the capacity to ensure that the stakeholders can own and manage the system. Facilitators operate in a way that contrasts with that of the traditional outside expert. International agency staff may be members of the PME team and contribute valuable perspectives about the agency's ME requirements, but they need to work collaboratively with the facilitator and the local stakeholders while the PME system is designed. Staff from international agencies must listen closely and become sensitive to working with local people and their realities.

Use Appropriate Variations of the Logical Framework

The results-oriented logframe gives agencies and local groups an evaluation tool for use in many different settings and with various less formal methods. Its use with illiterate stakeholders is inappropriate, because it puts them at a disadvantage. With literate stakeholders, the logframe can be applied in large, mixed groups in a wall-sized visual format to clarify project objectives, review project performance, and generate ideas for actions to improve the project. PIP is one such approach that can be used for midterm reviews.

Use Less Extractive, Less Formal Approaches to Data Collection

In all PME work, less extractive approaches to data collection are best because they focus on the generation of information for immediate decisionmaking and on action by the groups who will take the action. In other words, the experts do not take information away from the communities. Rather, the communities generate and own information, and because of this they have a greater commitment to learning and action. Less extractive approaches include community meetings and group discussions, drama, storytelling, before-and-after photos and drawings, community mapping, and wealth rankings. The attitudes and methods of PRA and participatory learning and action are especially useful.

Start, Stumble, Self-correct, and Share

Evaluation facilitators need to respect local knowledge and learning. They need a personal repertoire of skills in using simple PE tools and methods and a willingness to take risks and make mistakes. PME is one of a family of approaches for reversing centralization, standardization, and top-down development. It empowers the poor to do more of their own analysis, to take control of their lives and resources, and to improve their well-being as they define it.

> PME is one of a family of approaches for reversing centralization, standardization, and top-down development.

Therefore, a good facilitator:
- Is self-aware and self-critical
- Embraces error

- Hands over the stick
- Sits, listens, and learns
- Improvises, invents, and adapts
- Uses his or her own best judgment at all times.

Who lectures? Whose finger wags? Whose knowledge, analysis, and priorities count? Ours? Theirs, as we assume them to be? Theirs, as they freely express them? Good PME learns from mistakes and so spreads and improves on its own (see Chambers 1994).

Four Examples of PME

The following four examples fit within Feuerstein's (1986) typology of evaluation approaches, from guided PE to partnership in development.

PME System in Tanzania

The United Nations Capital Development Fund (UNCDF) launched several initiatives to improve project quality and stakeholder participation in its project cycle. One of these initiatives focused on improving project evaluation and introducing PE systems for selected UNCDF field projects. An external facilitator conducted two days of training for headquarters staff to provide an overview of PME and to map out a strategy for introducing PME systems to UNCDF's projects. During the training, the UNCDF staff outlined steps for pilot testing PME systems and introducing operational guidelines for integrating PME into its project cycle.

In another initiative in Tanzania, a PME system was designed and implemented for a local development project in Mwanza District. The facilitator met with a range of evaluation stakeholders from the village level up through district authorities to determine their information needs and to assess local ME activities already under way. With a good deal of redundancy, the district was generating roughly 35 reports for central authorities. In a two-day workshop, the facilitator helped local stakeholders identify and prioritize practical indicators for the project. A local artist helped to illustrate PRA methods, many of which were already in use at the district level, to support the PME system. A simple operational guide was developed, the PME team was trained, and a medium-term plan for the rollout of the system was finalized. UNCDF, the project management team, and the local and district authorities all supported the effort.

PIP in Sri Lanka

The United Kingdom's DFID conducted a midterm PIP review of its relief project for people displaced by Sri Lanka's civil war. Thirty participants at a four-day workshop for local and international NGOs and DFID assessed the project and developed action plans to improve its performance. Using a wall-sized visual depiction of the logframe, the participants first analyzed the project's goal, purpose, outputs, and assumptions. Second, they clarified the project's objectives and measurable indicators and removed the objectives and indicators that they decided were no longer relevant. Third, in group discussions they identified performance gaps that were preventing the project from reaching planned performance levels. Finally, they developed strategies for improving performance and action plans with clear roles and responsibilities for each strategy. The PIP process refocused the project's objectives, built partnerships among the implementing agencies, and led the partners to actions that got the project back on track. The NGOs adopted the PIP techniques, and within a few months PIP was adapted in local languages and applied in the local communities, which used it to improve grassroots project and nonproject activities.

PE in Rose Place, St. Vincent and the Grenadines

A community sanitation project in Rose Place, in St. Vincent and the Grenadines, uses photography and simple written commentary from community members to monitor and evaluate the project's progress (DFID 1997). Photos have been taken at different stages throughout the project. A cheap scrapbook has been made into a photo album to tell the story of the project in chronological order. Photos have been put in by community members, and children and adults have written comments to explain what is happening in Rose Place. Many photos are before-and-after shots. Some show the problem; others show the solution. The visual difference has a strong impact. Newspaper articles, radio announcements that community members helped write, and notes about their goals have also gone into the book, giving a good overview of the project. The book has generated a great deal of interest because it is attractive, tangible, immediate, and accessible—and it belongs to the community.

Participatory Planning and M&E Systems in Nepal and India

In the past six years, the World Bank has worked with the governments of Nepal and Uttar Pradesh, India, to develop a new generation of community-based water supply and sanitation programs that rely heavily on participatory methods for planning and ME. A pilot project in Nepal and the National Rural Water Supply and Sanitation Program project begun there in 1993 enabled IDA to test methods and approaches for large-scale participatory programs. Communities participated in designing and implementing water and sanitation schemes and also acted as project managers to carry out their own situational analysis, planning, execution, and ME. They used SARAR and PRA methods systematically to develop community planning and monitoring systems and combined these with conventional ME. (SARAR, a participatory approach to training, builds on local knowledge and strengthens local ability to manage development activities. The acronym stands for self-esteem, associative strength, resourcefulness, action planning, and responsibility for follow-through.)

During community planning and monitoring, a set of 24 participatory tools were developed and adapted to the needs of the users in Nepal. These were tested in the pilot project with about 24 NGOs in 113 communities spread across 12 districts. Healthy Homes, a PRA tool, proved highly effective in villages, where women gained status as they took charge of choosing indicators and monitoring personal, domestic, and environmental hygiene and sanitation practices in their communities' households and public areas. This work enabled them to participate more actively in water and sanitation committees. The approach has now been expanded to more than 220 additional communities through several cycles and should reach 900 communities by the end of the National Rural Water Supply and Sanitation Program project.

In Uttar Pradesh, India, the approach was replicated and adapted to the specific needs of the Uttar Pradesh Rural Water Supply and Environmental Sanitation Project. This project has been notably successful in having NGOs systematically apply SARAR and PRA methods in project field areas. The project has used participatory planning and ME tools as it has expanded in the Uttar Pradesh hills and Bundelkhand areas to reach 1,000 communities with rural water supply and environmental sanitation services. Of particular note is the use of public spaces to document the results of the participatory tools. Maps and project information are graphically displayed in schools and clinics. The methods used have been powerful stimulators of local will to design, build, and monitor these community facilities. The initial success of the project has led national authorities in India to call for replication of the approach in other states.

These two projects in Nepal and India and attempts to adapt their approach in Bangladesh have demonstrated that participatory ME can function effectively in large-scale programs if they are supported and nurtured. There is a learning curve to develop the capacities of support organizations such as the NGOs and to adapt the specific tools and methods needed for each project, but the effort has proven promising (Pfohl 1986).

Conclusion

PME is a broad constellation of approaches, methods, and techniques that development agencies can use to strengthen their poverty alleviation programs, ensure accountability, build local management capacity, and foster an environment of partnership and collaborative learning. The best place to start with PME is to design PME systems into new projects. PME works best in an environment of participatory management and shared decisionmaking. Leadership attitudes of respect for local knowledge and partnership with local agencies are vital to the success of PME.

Not all projects are ready or appropriate for PME. Rather, PME activities should be chosen carefully, and then sponsoring agencies should fully commit the time, resources, and leadership needed to ensure that PME activities succeed.

References

Aaker, J. 1994. *Looking Back and Looking Forward: A Participatory Approach to Evaluation.* New York: Participating Agencies Cooperating Together.

Aubel, J. 1993. *Participatory Program Evaluation: A Manual for Involving Stakeholders in the Evaluation Process.* New York: Participating Agencies Cooperating Together.

Cameron, E., and K. Page. 1998. *Facilitation Made Easy: Practical Tips to Improve Facilitation in Workshops.* New York: Participating Agencies Cooperating Together.

Casely, D., and K. Kumar. 1987. *Project Monitoring and Evaluation in Agriculture.* Baltimore: The Johns Hopkins University Press.

Chambers, R. 1994. *Note for the Staff of Bilateral and Multilateral Aid Agencies and of Northern NGOs on Participatory Rural Appraisal.* Brighton, U.K.: University of Sussex, Institute of Development Studies.

──── . 1994. "Participatory Rural Appraisal: Analysis of Experience." *World Development* 22(9).

Cousins, J. B., and E. Whitmore. 1998. "Framing Participatory Evaluation." In E. Whitmore, ed., *Understanding and Practicing Participatory Evlauation.* San Francisco: Jossey-Bass.

DFID (Department for International Development). 1997. *Participatory Monitoring and Evaluation Guidelines.* Dissemination Note 1. London.

Feuerstein, M. 1986. *Partners in Evaluation: Evaluating Development and Community Programmes with Participants.* London: Macmillan.

Forster, R., ed. 1996. *ZOPP Marries PRA?* Eschborn, Germany: Gesellschaft fur Technische Zusammenarbeit.

Gosling, L., ed. 1995. *Toolkits: A Practical Guide to Assessment, Monitoring, Review and Evaluation.* London: Save the Children.

Goyder, H., and R. Davies. 1998. *Participatory Impact Assessment.* Somerset, U.K.: ActionAid.

Harding, P. 1991. "Qualitative Indicators and the Project Framework." *Community Development Journal* 26(4): 294-305.

IDS (Institute of Development Studies). Internet participation subject page <http://nt1.ids.ac.uk/eldis/pra/pra.htm> Brighton, U.K.: University of Sussex.

Isham, J., and D. Narayan. 1994. *Does Participation Improve Project Performance?* Washington, D.C.: World Bank.

Kaner, S. 1996. *Facilitator's Guide to Participatory Decision-making.* Gabriola Island, BC: New Society.

Kumar, K. 1987. *Rapid, Low-cost Data Collection Methods for USAID*. Washington, D.C.: USAID.

Larson, P., and D. Svendsen. 1997. *Participatory Monitoring and Evaluation: A Practical Guide to Successful Integrated Conservation and Development Projects*. Washington, D.C.: World Wildlife Fund.

Marsden, D., and P. Oakley, eds. 1990. *Evaluating Social Development Projects*. Oxford, U.K.: Oxfam.

Mayo-Smith, I. 1987. *Achieving Improved Performance in Public Institutions*. West Hartford, CT: Kumarian.

Narayan, D. 1993. "*Participatory Evaluation: Tools for Managing Change in Water and Sanitation*." World Bank Technical Paper 207. Washington, D.C.

Narayan, D., and L. Srinivasan. 1994. *Participatory Development Tool Kit*. Washington, D.C.: World Bank.

Norwegian Agency for Development Cooperation. 1989. *The Logical Framework Approach: Handbook for Objectives-oriented Project Planning*. Oslo.

Participating Agencies Cooperating Together. 1998. *Participatory Monitoring, Evaluation and Reporting*. New York.

Patton, M. Q. 1997. "Toward Distinguishing Empowerment Evaluation and Placing It in a Larger Context." *Evaluation Practice* 18(2).

_____. 1997. *Utilization-focused Evaluation: The New Century Text*. Beverly Hills, CA: Sage.

Pfohl, J. 1986. *Participatory Evaluation: A User's Guide*. New York: Participating Agencies Cooperating Together.

Pretty, J., and others. 1996. *Participatory Learning and Action: A Trainer's Guide*. London: International Institute for Environment and Development.

Rugh, J. 1986. *Self-evaluation: Ideas for Participatory Evaluation of Community Development Projects*. Oklahoma City, OK: World Neighbors.

Sartorius, R. 1991. "The Logical Framework Approach to Project Design and Management." *Evaluation Practice* 12(2): 139-47.

_____. 1996. "The Third Generation Logical Framework." *European Journal of Agricultural Extension* (March): 49-61.

Comments: Building Local Capacity for Participatory Monitoring and Evaluation

David Marsden

A clear and evolving relationship is apparent between PME and RBM. The challenge is to try to marry them coherently in the pursuit of inclusive and accountable institutions. This is clearly articulated in the paper by Sartorius. Other issues highlighted in his paper are the context specificity of much of this work, the importance of ensuring that it is built in from the beginning, and the need to be less extractive in the ways we collect and manage information. I think we are really talking about a shift in paradigm that relates to the nature and place of measurement.

Emerging Themes

The work of the German sociologist Ulrich Beck on the perception of risk and the British sociologist Tony Giddens on reflexive modernity provides a basis for reflecting about the future. The changing focus of our work in development revolves around four related themes:

- The shift from long-term, full-life employment to more contractual types of employment and the management of diverse portfolios
- Gender, which has received inadequate attention in our work on poverty reduction
- The challenge of environmental assessments related to both global concerns and the local use and management of natural resources, coupled with the assessment of environmental risk
- Governance in an era of increasing decentralization, with calls for both local integrity and more effective forms of global governance.

The challenge of decentralization is not just better delivery of goods and services but also the establishment of more transparent rules of the game (about who benefits and who does not) and of organizations that involve more stakeholders in decisions about how those goods and services are appropriated.

We need to reflect on how we perceive "truth"—not necessarily as something extracted from statistically robust measurements but from the contextual negotiations Guba and Lincoln discuss in their work on "fourth generation evaluation." They argue that truth is a matter of negotiated consensus, that facts have no meaning except in some framework of values, and that the counterfactual may be counterproductive in that it distracts us from other types of activities and engagements. Interventions are not stable, change is nonlinear, and evaluators are partners with stakeholders in creating data and facilitating negotiation.

Where We Stand Now

How do we measure the process of development? How do we move from the measurement of outputs to the measurement of outcomes? How do we effectively combine qualitative and quantitative techniques? How do we evaluate institutional and organizational development? We have had some success building first-generation participation, by engaging community-based and other organizations, but how do we scale this up to address the institutions and institutional arrangements that govern how organizations deliver services? How do we build second-generation participation in which the implementing agents serve more as facilitators of processes over which the poor have more control than as police officers or deliverers? We need to understand how to measure achievements, impacts, and institutional and organizational capacity. Who should be involved in that measurement? When, why, and how?

Traditional approaches have focused on producing rationally designed operational tools perceived as value neutral and objective. Their aim has been to increase managerial control and standardize procedures, replicate models and norms, and reduce subjectivity. Thus evaluations are often perceived as negative and external instead of as interpretive negotiations of value. We have reached a consensus that we cannot advance along that traditional path.

Recognizing that there may be no absolute or objective criteria, we see also that circumstances and contexts are never neutral and are always informed by a history and a culture of evaluation. Evaluation should be interpretive rather than judgmental. We are coming to see evaluators as facilitators rather than as judges, which means that we need to provide for dialogue, encourage multidisciplinary cooperation, and recognize the relative perspectives people have on their lives. In recognizing all stakeholders, we must see evaluation as a process of negotiation.

Some Challenges of Evaluation and Participation

Are evaluation and participation separate categories of activity? Do we negotiate value? If so, what issues are implied in that negotiation for the relative positions of the parties to the negotiation? Consider this example: the Bangladeshi government, not understanding the value of vitamin A, postponed the development of a health project for some ten years, so people were not informed that it was acceptable. What are the implications—for knowledge production, management, and dissemination—of saying knowledge is emergent rather than facts to be extracted?

In the production of robust indicators that measure validity, legitimacy, and institutional maturity, the challenges to participatory evaluation are understanding the changing nature of the relationships between outsiders and insiders and building trust and mutual partnerships between unequal allies.

We must develop mechanisms for interventions at all levels. At the macro level, the country assistance strategy and comprehensive development framework are instruments for systematic consultation and joint learning about policy. To encourage second-generation participation, we might take concrete steps to develop institutions for independent specialist evaluations, perhaps with a rights-based approach, and a social audit capacity within countries or states. At the meso level, we need to develop approaches that give the poor, the marginalized, and the vulnerable a voice and leverage in issues before the reoriented public sector bureaucracy. At the micro level, we are familiar with the bottom-up approaches that have traditionally informed the debates about participatory methods. At all three levels, we should encourage the development of systems for exchanging jointly learned knowledge and for involving all stakeholders in the design and implementation of projects and programs.

Floor Discussion: Building Local Capacities for Participatory Monitoring and Evaluation

The floor discussion centered on the capacity of both donor agencies and client countries to carry out participatory evaluation.[1]

One participant noted that although much had been done at the Bank to make project preparation and implementation more participatory, little had been done to make monitoring and feedback to decisionmakers more participatory during implementation.

Another participant wanted to know what process could be used to build participatory monitoring and evaluation systems.

Rolf Sartorius responded that there were two reasons why project monitoring and evaluation systems were not really being implemented by institutions that otherwise generally pay attention to participation. First, project officers get few rewards for devoting extra time and attention to designing participatory monitoring and evaluation systems with stakeholders during project appraisal. Second, many development institutions lack the skills to do more participatory design, although they may be gaining experience in it. Design work receives attention because development institutions want to get projects approved and funded, but building evaluation—especially participatory monitoring and evaluation—into implementation is less well understood. It is also fairly complicated to blend results-based and participatory systems, especially if no earlier participatory appraisal work provides a context for it.

Marrying results-based and participatory approaches boils down to real field work, said Sartorius. The most practical approach is to have facilitators negotiate among the different stakeholders in evaluation about the indicators important to them. The donor institution might prefer using indicators standard for that institution. It is the wedding of those realities—the negotiation of indicators in workshop settings and discussions—that helps people reach agreement. The negotiation of indicators is, by and large, the most technical and challenging part of discussions among stakeholders. Reaching agreement on objectives is generally more straightforward than finding specific ways to measure objectives and show that they are being met. That negotiation involves blending competing perspectives on whose reality counts and what is important to whom.

Another participant asked if Sartorius had any experience involving illiterate and semi-literate communities in participatory evaluation, and if so what the consequences were for capacity building?

Sartorius said that a wealth of experience and resources, views, methodologies, and tools were available. They were used in various pockets of the Bank, but were not widely known outside those pockets.

Richard Gerster of Swiss Development Cooperation chaired the discussion.

Finally, a fourth participant wondered how Sartorius envisaged dealing with the two complementary functions of evaluation, namely, accountability (reporting to the donor on results, outcomes, and impacts) and evaluation as a management tool used almost on an ongoing basis to establish how far the project had come and what should happen next year. The question was, how could traditional approaches to evaluation best be crossed with participatory approaches?

The distinction between traditional monitoring and evaluation has broken down, said Sartorius. There is now a continuous process—a cycle—of learning, with data collection, analysis, and action cycles all continuing until people agree that they have reached an activity's intended impact. At the front end, there should be a common vision of what that impact should be, then a learning cycle to support that vision. That is essentially what a monitoring and evaluation system is about now. It could be a very simple and informal system. It does not have to be bureaucratic or overly technical.

The same participant said that the phrase "ombudsman-type function" sounded to her like a control. She wondered if there was a place for that in Sartorius's participatory evaluation framework.

Sartorius explained that what he had in mind when he mentioned an ombudsman function was how evaluation could support the empowerment of the vulnerable and the excluded. Those who are vulnerable and excluded simply need a way to appeal. The question is, what is the nature of the appeals process? How can people get redress for wrongs or get a hearing when they feel they have a limited voice? In this connection he was thinking, in particular, of many of the infrastructure projects with which the Bank is involved, in which decisions about where a road or a dam goes have huge implications for many people whose voices remain unheard. For this kind of problem, it is important to institutionalize some sort of appeals process within the evaluation framework

Part V

Poverty-Reducing Growth

9

Africa and Asia: Evaluation of the Poverty Alleviation Impact of Alternative Development Strategies and Adjustment Responses

Erik Thorbecke

The incidence of relative poverty has increased in Sub-Saharan Africa (SSA) and fallen significantly in both East and South Asia, according to large-scale, international data sets compiled to examine changes in poverty until 1993 (Chen, Datt, and Ravallion 1994; Ravallion and Chen 1997). Subsequently, country-level information on the incidence of poverty suggests that the trend toward a reduction in poverty continued unabated throughout Asia until the 1997 financial crisis, while the picture in SSA was much more mixed, with some countries showing a slight improvement and others showing a further increase in various poverty measures (headcount ratio, poverty gap, and poverty gap squared).

The Asian financial crisis brought to an end the successful poverty reduction trend in most East and Southeast Asian countries. For example, the headcount ratio in Indonesia rose from 11 percent in 1997 to an estimated 14 to 23 percent in the last quarter of 1998, while in the Republic of Korea, the proportion of urban households below the poverty line rose from 7.5 percent in 1997 to 22.9 percent during the same period (Subbarao 1999). Nevertheless, the Asian model of poverty alleviation offers useful lessons for the developing world, particularly SSA.

The first objective of this chapter is to explore why East and South Asia have been so much more successful in alleviating poverty than SSA and to what extent this performance can be ascribed to different initial conditions and radically different rural development strategies. The second objective is to critically review the various evaluation procedures and methodologies available to estimate the net impact on poverty incidence of alternative development strategies and of policy measures and institutions while controlling for different initial conditions.

Successful Development Strategies for Alleviating Poverty

Half a century of development experience has led to a broad consensus on the major strategic elements that have contributed to poverty's retreating faster in some regions than in others:

- Rapid poverty reduction has been much more likely in countries and during periods characterized by rapid economic growth.
- An outward orientation and a strategy of export-led growth based on labor-intensive manufactures is particularly conducive to poverty alleviation.
- Emphasizing agricultural and rural development at an early stage and encouraging the adoption of green revolution technologies helps to create productive employment and lower food prices, thereby benefiting the poor.
- Investment in physical infrastructure and human capital adds to the resource endowment of poor, unskilled households.
- Institutions need to give farmers and entrepreneurs the right incentives, including property rights and a reliable and transparent judicial system.
- Social policies should promote health, education (especially female primary education), and social capital, as well as minimum safety nets to help protect the chronically poor and households caught in transient poverty (Asian Development Bank 1997, World Bank 1999).

Comparing the overall development performance of Asia and SSA shows the strikingly divergent rural development paths these two regions followed. At a relatively early stage of development, when agriculture is the center of gravity of the economy, an appropriate rural development strategy is fundamental to progress and poverty alleviation. Much of the rather dismal performance of SSA in reducing poverty can be ascribed to the particular rural development path it adopted. Why did the rural sector in SSA evolve so differently from that in other regions, particularly Asia? A combination of initial conditions, policies, institutions, and cultural and community norms appears to be at the heart of Africa's rural development path. Platteau and Hayami provide a comprehensive and systematic explanation of why "Sub-Saharan Africa appears as a perfect counter-model to the East Asian experience."

Their thesis is that:

Differences in population density are responsible, through short- or medium-term physical and economic effects or through (varied) long-term social and cultural effects (effects on cultural values and norms mediated by social and family patterns), for most of the divergence observed between rural development performance in SSA and Asia (1996, p. 3).

Physical and Technological Environment

The physical and technological environment in SSA was significantly less favorable to development than that in Asia. The initial resource endowment, particularly access to land, is likely to be a crucial determinant of the pattern of agricultural development a country or region will follow. In Asia, land resources relative to population and labor force are much scarcer than in Africa. As Platteau and Hayami argue, this had the effect of forcing Asia to focus more on productive agriculture:

> The high population density and the unfavorable land-labor ratio induced more intensive land use, resulting in high percentages of land used for agricultural production...by building better land infrastructure...above all, irrigation. The better land infrastructure created suitable conditions for the introduction of modern land-saving technologies such as high yielding varieties and chemical fertilizer (1996, p. 4).

If the amount of arable land per agricultural worker is taken as a measure of access to land, the latter ranged from 0.3 hectare of arable land per agricultural worker in East Asia to 0.8 in South Asia (and 0.5 for the whole of Asia) to 1.2 in Africa in the early 1990s.[1]

Africa is also characterized by a great scarcity of physical infrastructure, particularly road networks in rural areas (including farm-to-market roads) and between rural and urban areas. There is also tremendous underinvestment in irrigation projects: only 4.6 percent of agricultural land in SSA is irrigated, compared with 38.4 percent in Asia (Khan 1997, table 5). The quantity and quality of the road network play a crucial role in facilitating trade at all levels: intraregional, interregional, and international. This network is tremendously underdeveloped in SSA and is a major cause of (a) extremely high transportation costs, (b) high spreads between producer and consumer prices, (c) segmented agricultural product markets, and (d) lack of market orientation on the part of small African farmers, who produce largely for subsistence, with little marketable surplus.

These interrelated factors—together with technological constraints and discriminatory policies against agriculture—go a long way toward explaining the essentially stagnant agricultural production in SSA over the past three decades. In addition, the extent of market integration for agricultural products is much more limited in Africa than in Asia.[1] Average producer prices, as a percentage of final consumer prices, range from 30 to 60 percent in the African countries, but from 75 to 90 percent in Asia. In addition, the regional price differences within countries are substantially larger in Africa than in Asia (Ahmed and Rustagi 1984).

As a logical consequence of high transportation costs and segmented markets, the relative size of the marketable surplus is significantly higher in Asia than in SSA. In other words, African small farmers tend to be much more subsistence oriented than their Asian counterparts. Clearly, a number of specific elements, such as the large price spread from farm to consumer (reflecting high transportation and transaction costs) and the scarcity of road infrastructure operate as binding constraints on the supply response of small farmers.

Still another crucial constraint for Africa is the extreme diversity of agroclimatic and soil characteristics, as well as the diversity of farming systems and socioeconomic conditions. This diversity exists not only across SSA countries but also within countries. Moreover, agricultural production in SSA occurs almost completely on rainfed land. Given these characteristics, Africa is at a great technological disadvantage compared with Asia. The green revolution technologies have been extremely successful in creating new high-yield varieties of rice, wheat, and maize grown on irrigated land but have had only limited success in developing new rice varieties and other crops that can grow on rainfed land. Thus, given the diversity of crops grown in SSA on rainfed land that is itself agronomically heterogeneous, a standard technical package using a single rice variety, which works so well in Asia, will not succeed in the African context.

A final environmental feature worth noting is that land is much more unequally distributed in SSA than in Asia. In many African countries, there is little connection between the small subsistence farmers and the large estates (a legacy of the colonial era) that produce cash and export crops. Unequal land distribution impedes growth and is a significant explanatory variable contributing to poverty (Deininger and Squire 1996). Conversely, the Asian economies that were able to implement large-scale land reforms early in the development process, such as Taiwan, China and Korea, achieved high growth rates and equitable income distribution.

Policies, Institutions, and Cultural and Community Norms Affecting the Rural Sector

The major mechanism to obtain the resources needed for industrialization at an early stage of development is an intersectoral transfer out of agriculture. Developing countries typically tax their agriculture sectors heavily through both direct and indirect taxation. Direct taxation usually involves turning the internal terms of trade against agriculture through such interventions as artificially low consumer prices for food and high input prices, while indirect taxation is mainly through the impact of an overvalued exchange rate on agricultural tradables. In a careful empirical study of intersectoral resource flows, Teranishi (1998) showed that the degree of direct and indirect taxation on agriculture did not differ significantly among four regions—East Asia, South Asia, Latin America, and SSA—but that the differences in infrastructure investment in agriculture were enormous. In East Asia, and to a lesser extent in South Asia, the adverse effects of direct and indirect taxation of agriculture were counterbalanced by government efforts in agricultural development, particularly in the area of infrastructure investment, resulting in a relatively low overall policy-based resource shift from agriculture. The explanation given by Teranishi for the radically different treatment of agriculture in Asia and in SSA, and the consequent disparate agricultural growth performance, is that in SSA, incumbent political regimes selectively rewarded the agricultural actors who supported them, regardless of their contribution to production.

A large-scale research project by OECD Development Centre that evaluated the effects of policies and institutions on agricultural performance over time in six poor developing countries—four in Africa and two in Asia—reached similar conclusions (Thorbecke and Morrisson 1989). That analysis also found that in countries where foodstuff prices were the most depressed because of government actions, aggregate output either fell or stagnated. In Tanzania, for example, the sheer magnitude of the burden imposed on both the domestic food crop and cash crop export sectors short-circuited the development process and, more specifically, jeopardized the desired industrialization. Extremely low regulated food prices on the official market led to a booming parallel market where, at one time, prices were eleven times higher. In sum, while East and Southeast Asian countries followed an agricultural development-based industrialization strategy, SSA relied on a forced import-substitution industrialization strategy that discriminated heavily against agriculture.

Institutions as well as policies can have a major effect on agricultural performance. There are a number of examples in SSA of the agriculture sector being damaged by inappropriate institutions, often because of social and institutional experimentation based on ideological beliefs. Perhaps most extreme was the forced villagization and collectivization program imposed in Ethiopia, which wreaked havoc with agricultural production incentives (Khan 1997). The villagization program led to massive resettlement and dislocation, which was compounded by government intervention in both production and distribution, thereby helping to trigger a vicious cycle of cumulatively worsening agricultural performance.

In a study of the evolution of states, markets, and civil institutions in rural Africa based largely on four countries (Guinea, Malawi, Mozambique, and Tanzania), Sahn and Sarris (1994) concluded that state-mandated and state-sponsored systems of production failed dismally. Production and yields plummeted in some cases and stagnated in others.

Finally, one can argue that the different physical and socioeconomic conditions in SSA and Asia have led to the evolution of different norms, growth-retarding SSA and growth-enhancing Asia. Specifically, the abundance of land and corporate land tenure conditions in Africa have constrained capital accumulation and helped foster egalitarian redistributive norms, while the scarcity of land and individual property rights conditions in Asia have encouraged cooperative actions and reciprocity norms (Platteau and Hayami 1996).

Evaluation of Poverty Impact

In a recent methodological note on impact evaluation, Ezemenari, Rudqvist, and Subbarao (1999) concluded that the organizing principle of a good impact evaluation is identification of the counterfactual. To determine the effects of an intervention, evaluators must identify what would have happened without the intervention. Clearly, if the intervention consists of a specific investment, technical assistance project, or safety net, operational methods are available for comparing the impact on poverty with and without the intervention. The more specific the intervention, the easier the task. But how do we evaluate the effects on poverty alleviation of a long-term development strategy that consists of a whole set of interrelated interventions, policies, and institutions; or a medium- or short-term structural adjustment and stabilization strategy; or a strategy in response to a financial crisis that combines a variety of fiscal, monetary, trade, and safety net measures? How do we determine a valid counterfactual and what methodologies and techniques are available to judge how these strategies affect poverty?

Retrospective Historical Comparisons

In the case of a long-term strategy, there appears to be no substitute for sound retrospective historical comparisons of the socioeconomic performance of groups of countries that followed alternative strategies. The relevant counterfactual scenario, in this case, would be the growth or poverty outcomes achieved under a strategy different from the one actually implemented. Here we enter the domain of economic history and political economy, where practitioners paint with a broad brush and use a combination of quantitative and qualitative approaches to arrive at an overall assessment. The discussion in the previous section comparing the rural development strategies of Africa and Asia is an example of this method.

Perhaps the quintessential example of this approach is *The East Asian Miracle* (World Bank 1993). At the outset, this report raised the key question of whether some selective interventions were good for growth and, by extension, for poverty alleviation. As the book made clear, in addressing this question the authors had to face a central methodological problem:

Since we chose the high-performing Asian economies for their unusually rapid growth, we know already that their interventions did not significantly inhibit growth. But it is very difficult to establish statistical links between growth and a specific intervention and even more difficult to establish causality. Because we cannot know what would have happened in the absence of a specific policy, it is difficult to test whether interventions increased growth rates.... Thus, in attempting to distinguish interventions that contributed to growth from those that were either growth neutral or harmful to growth, we cannot offer a rigorous counterfactual scenario. Instead, we have to be content with what Keynes called an "essay in persuasion," based on analytical and empirical judgments (World Bank 1993, p. 6).

Such "essays in persuasion" are more convincing the higher the quality of the underlying information and statistical data and the greater the competence of the analysts. A good example of an analytical evaluation of the impact of alternative agrarian policies on development over an extended period of time is that of Binswanger and Deininger (1997). Using a semiformalized approach, these authors provided a strong rationale for the rural development policies East and Southeast Asian countries followed.

Comparing the performance of countries at relatively similar stages of development and with similar resource endowments that pursued different development strategies can also be enlightening. Thus, comparing the performance of Tanzania and Kenya in the 1970s and early 1980s can shed some light on the impact of a socialist strategy based on agricultural collectivization and state-sponsored industrialization in contrast with a more free market-oriented strategy. Similarly, a comparison of the policies and institutions that enabled Taiwan (China) to withstand the Asian financial crisis in the 1990s much more successfully than Korea also provides lessons that might be transferable to other countries (Thorbecke and Wan 1999).

Cross-Sectional and Time-Series Statistical Inferences

In a much more limited sense, statistical inferences about impact on poverty alleviation can be derived from large-scale, cross-sectional, and time-series (sometimes pooled) observations. This approach should ideally build an underlying structural and behavioral model to yield a reduced form equation that is subsequently statistically tested. In many instances, the underlying model is not explicitly presented, so the multiple regression equation specification that is empirically tested appears to be—or is—ad hoc. In any case, the number of explanatory variables that can be used to estimate the effects on poverty alleviation, either directly or indirectly, is limited. Therefore, this approach can be used only to explore the impact of a few specific policies (such as an outward orientation) and specific initial conditions (such as the extent of inequality in initial resource endowment, for example, land) on poverty alleviation. This approach is clearly ill suited for comparing the impact of broad-based development strategies.

Only a few examples of this approach will be mentioned here. Ravallion and Chen, using household surveys for 67 developing and transition economies over 1981-94, conclude that

> There is a strong association between the greater growth in average living standards and the rate at which absolute poverty fell. In terms of elasticities, the response of the poverty measures to changes in average consumption is even stronger for lower poverty lines. The benefits of higher total consumption appear to be spread quite widely, on average (1997, p. 380).

Likewise, on the basis of a new large-scale data set of 682 observations covering 108 countries, Deininger and Squire conclude that

> Aggregate growth was associated with an increase in the incomes of the poorest quintile in more than 85 percent of the 91 (growth) cases.... Our data suggest no systematic relationship between growth of aggregate income and changes in inequality as measured by the Gini-coefficient... [E]specially because changes in inequality tend to be relatively modest, we find a strong link between overall growth and a reduction in poverty. This link supports the hypothesis that economic growth benefits the poor in the large majority of cases, whereas economic decline generally hurts the poor (1996, p. 588).

Finally, in another paper Deininger and Squire regress growth on initial gross domestic product, a measure of initial income inequality, investment, a black market premium, and education. They reach the following conclusions:

> First, we find that initial land inequality is important for the poor...but not for the rich, whose income growth is not significantly affected by this variable....Second, we find that [while] investment is significant for all individual quintile groups...the poor are likely to benefit disproportionally from aggregate investment....Growth-enhancing policies are... at least in the medium term, not inconsistent with the goal of poverty alleviation.... The policy conclusion that emerges directly from this discussion is that the accumulation of new assets is likely to be a more effective way of reducing poverty than efforts to redistribute existing assets (1998, p. 284).

Notwithstanding the robust results yielded by these studies, one should be aware of the limited and largely ad hoc specification of the regression equations on which they were based. In particular, correcting for fixed country effects includes so many unobserved and omitted variables that one should be careful in interpreting the findings.

Computable General Equilibrium Models and Macroeconometric Models

When the set of policy measures actually implemented (or to be implemented) is not too extensive and occurs during a specific and relatively short period of time, computable general equilibrium (CGE) models provide an analytical methodology for simulating the impact of a counterfactual scenario and comparing it with the scenario resulting from the actual set of policies.

This tool has been widely used to explore the impact of adjustment and stabilization policies on equity and poverty (Bourguignon and Morrisson 1992). Perhaps the most well-known examples are the OECD research program on adjustment and equity and the work of the Cornell team (Sahn, Dorosh, and Younger 1996) on the effects of adjustment on poverty in SSA. By using country-specific general equilibrium models that reflect the underlying socioeconomic structure of the country and the behavior of the major actors, including the government, the impact of counterfactual scenarios, including the consequences of the country's not adjusting or adjusting only marginally, can be simulated. Under the OECD project, researchers built five country models, including a large-scale Indonesian model integrating a real and financial sector built by Thorbecke (1992a). In general, the researchers found that adjustment was not inconsistent with more equitable income distribution and poverty alleviation (Bourguignon and Morrisson 1992). Similarly, the Cornell project, based on five CGE models (Cameroon, Gambia, Madagascar, Niger, and Tanzania), concluded that adjustment had not hurt the poor (Sahn, Dorosh, and Younger 1996). The CGE methodology potentially corrects for the major drawback of the so-called before-and-after approach. Thus, these studies show that a worsening of socioeconomic conditions after adjustment, compared with the situation prevailing before adjustment, cannot necessarily be ascribed to or causally linked to adjustment. Conditions might have deteriorated even further in the absence of managed adjustment.

Because CGE models are fully calibrated on the basis of an initial-year social accounting matrix that provides a set of consistent initial conditions (and does not contain information on income distribution among groups of households at different socioeconomic levels), conventional CGE models can only simulate the impact of a shock or a package of policy measures on the representative household in each group. This amounts to the implicit assumption that the variance of income within a group is zero. To the extent that poverty is pervasive and is likely to affect many household groups at different socioeconomic levels (albeit to different degrees), any analysis of the impact of an exogenous or policy shock on poverty must start with information about intragroup income distribution. As more income and expenditure surveys become available, researchers will increasingly be able to generate the within-group income distributions prevailing in the same base year used in the social accounting matrix to calibrate the general equilibrium model.

Thus, a major weakness of existing CGE models used to derive the distributional impact of various macroeconomic interventions is that they can derive poverty only in an indirect way—that is, (a) by using an arbitrary socioeconomic classification that distinguishes between such categories as rural poor households and rural nonpoor households or between urban poor households and urban nonpoor households or (b) by solving for the mean incomes of the representative households. Another weakness of conventional CGE models used to derive distributional effects is that the specification does not permit an endogenous determination of the poverty line.

A recent paper by Decaluwe and others (1999) goes some way toward remedying these drawbacks. This is done by specifying intragroup distributions that conform to the different socioeconomic characteristics of the groups, and by postulating a poverty line based on a basket of basic needs commodities. Because commodity prices are endogenously determined within the model, the monetary value of the poverty line is also endogenously determined. These innovations help shed more light on the black box pertaining to the dynamics of poverty following a shock.

However, investigators need to recognize that in general, CGE models are relatively blunt, inflexible instruments that are not very customer friendly and require experienced, mature analysts to translate their results so that they are operationally useful to policymakers. Although they may still be the best method for obtaining counterfactual results under certain conditions, one can agree with the conclusion a recent critical evaluation of CGE models by De Maio, Stewart, and van der Hoeven reached:

> We believe there is a place for CGE models in the analysis of the effects of adjustment. They need to be accompanied, however, by extensive use of sensitivity analysis to test how far the conclusions depend on particular assumptions; by consistent, careful, empirical checking of parameters and functional forms; by appropriate categorization of groups for poverty analysis; and by continuous monitoring of the actual changes, checking these against the predictions of the models (1999, p. 465).

References

Ahmed, R., and N. Rustagi. 1984. *Agricultural Marketing and Price Incentives: A Comparative Study of African and Asian Countries.* Washington, D.C.: IFPRI.

Ali, A. A. G., and E. Thorbecke. 1997. "The State of Rural Poverty, Income Distribution, and Rural Development in Sub-Saharan Africa." Paper prepared for the Conference on Comparative Development Experiences in Asia and Africa, African Economic Research Consortium, November, Johannesburg, South Africa.

Asian Development Bank. 1997. *Emerging Asia: Changes and Challenges.* Manila.

Binswanger, H. P., and K. Deininger. 1997. "Explaining Agricultural and Agrarian Policies in Developing Countries." *Journal of Economic Literature* 35 (December).

Bourguignon, F., and C. Morrisson. 1992. *Adjustment and Equity in Developing Countries.* Paris: OECD Development Centre.

Chen, S., G. Datt, and M. Ravaillon. 1994. "Is Poverty Increasing in the Developing World?" *Review of Income and Wealth* 40(4).

Decaluwe, B., and others. 1999. "Poverty Analysis within a General Equilibrium Framework." Paper prepared for the African Economic Research Consortium, Nairobi, Kenya.

Deininger, K., and L. Squire. 1996. "New Data Set Measuring Income Inequality." *World Bank Economic Review* 10(3).

_____. 1998. "New Ways of Looking at Old Issues: Inequality and Growth." *Journal of Development Economics* 57.

De Maio, L., F. Stewart, and R. van der Hoeven. 1999. "Computable General Equilibrium Models, Adjustment and the Poor in Africa." *World Development* 27(3).

Ezemenari, K., A. Rudqvist, and K. Subbarao. 1999. "Impact Evaluation: A Note on Concepts and Methods." Washington, D.C.: World Bank, Poverty Reduction and Economic Management Network.

Khan, A. R. 1997. *Reversing the Decline of Output and Productive Employment in Rural Sub-Saharan Africa.* Issues in Development Discussion Paper 17. Geneva: International Labour Office.

Platteau, J-P., and Y. Hayami. 1996. "Resource Endowments and Cultural Endowments in Agricultural Development: Africa vs. Asia." Paper presented at a roundtable conference on the Institutional Foundation of Economic Development in East Asia, International Economic Association, December, Tokyo.

Ravallion, M., and S. Chen. 1997. "What Can New Survey Data Tell Us about Recent Changes in Distribution and Poverty?" *World Bank Economic Review* 11(2).

Sahn, D. E., and A. Sarris. 1994. "The Evolution of States, Markets, and Civil Institutions in Rural Africa." *Journal of Modern African Studies.*

Sahn, D. E., P. Dorosh, and S. Younger. 1996. "Exchange Rate, Fiscal, and Agricultural Policies in Africa: Does Adjustment Hurt the Poor?" *World Development* 24(4).

Subbarao, K. 1999. *Financial Crisis and Poverty: Adequacy and Design of Safety Nets for the Old and New Poor in Korea.* Washington, D.C.: World Bank.

Teranishi, J. 1998. "Sectoral Resource Transfer, Conflict, and Macrostability in Economic Development: A Comparative Analysis." In M. Aoki, H.-K. Kim, and M. Okuno-Fujiwara, eds., *The Role of Government in East Asian Economic Development: Comparative Institutional Analysis.* Oxford, U.K.: Clarendon Press.

Thorbecke, E. 1992a. *Adjustment and Equity in Indonesia.* Paris: OECD Development Centre.

———. 1992b. "The Anatomy of Agricultural Product Markets and Transactions in Developing Countries." Working Paper 43. Washington, D.C.: Institute for Policy Reform.

Thorbecke, E., and C. Morrisson. 1989. "Institutions, Policies, and Agricultural Performance: A Comparative Analysis." *World Development* 7(9).

Thorbecke, E., and H. Wan. 1999. *Taiwan's Development Experience: Lessons on Roles of Government and Market.* Dordrecht, Netherlands: Kluwer Academic Publishers.

World Bank. 1993. *The East Asian Miracle.* New York: Oxford University Press.

———. 1999. *Poverty Reduction in the World Bank: Progress in Fiscal 1998.* Poverty Reduction Board. Washington, D.C.

Note

I acknowledge with thanks the research assistance of Yun H. Chung.

1. The discussion in the remainder of this section is based largely on Ali and Thorbecke (1997) and Thorbecke (1992b.)

Comments: Africa and Asia: Evaluation of the Poverty Alleviation Impact of Alternative Development Strategies and Adjustment Responses

Richard Gerster

Thorbecke says that "much of SSA's rather dismal performance in reducing poverty can be ascribed to the particular rural development path that it adopted." Talking about policy failures presumes the existence of political will to reduce poverty. What Thorbecke did not mention was that in some countries there still is no such will. In Cameroon, the Democratic Republic of Congo, Nigeria, and Togo—to name but a few important cases—the dismal performance is a question not of policy but of corruption, the misuse of public funds, and bad governance. In that respect, the African experience is very different from the Asian experience, where exploitative governance was less widespread.

Policy failures assume that a government could have adopted different policies and was not limited by policy constraints. For the misguided industrialization policy or the forced villagization program, this assumption seems justified. For the enormous resource transfers from rural to urban regions through taxation and underinvestment, this may also be the case, although the political consequences may be doubtful. But innovative policies cannot overcome the serious and persistent constraints of soil and climatic conditions or their implications for communities and cultures.

> Talking about policy failures presumes the political will to reduce poverty. In some countries there still is no such will.

Consider also how the international economic environment constrains Africa's development. Let us start with one of Africa's success stories. One factor in the development of Mauritius has been the export of sugar, its traditional crop. The Sugar Protocol of the European Union secured for Mauritius not only market access but also a preferential price for 80 percent of its annual harvest. Since 1974—for the past 25 years—Mauritian sugar exporters got a price that was, and still is, in line with what the European Union pays its own sugar farmers in Europe. For a long time, this has been about double the world market price. Because of this special situation, the terms of trade for Mauritius are slightly positive, at 103, using an index of 1987 = 100 (UNDP 1998). In addition, good governance and good policies have ensured that these massive transfers were invested soundly on the island.

By contrast, most of the rest of SSA suffers from a structural underfunding of policies and programs. The terms of trade for SSA fell by more than one-third between 1977 and 1993 (UNCTAD 1998), so SSA had to increase exports by more than 50 percent above 1977 levels just to be able to import the same amount of goods. This would have been a difficult challenge for even an economically advanced country. Closely linked to this dramatic erosion of trade benefits is the long-looming debt crisis. Each year SSA countries use a significant proportion of their GNP to service their foreign debt. The Heavily Indebted Poor Countries initiative will save Mozambique precisely $10 million a year out of a burden of $120 million. The remaining debt servicing cost is still twice what it spends on running its health service (*Financial Times* 1999). Under such conditions, winning the confidence of foreign and local investors is impossible, and overall official development assistance is falling. The result is a constant drain on resources, which undermines even well-designed adjustment and development strategies.

As I am not an expert on evaluation methodology, my remarks have so far concentrated on development strategies and adjustment responses. However, I will make three remarks about the evaluation of poverty impacts:

- A positive statistical relationship between economic growth and income poverty reduction performance is a fact. The question is whether there is a causal relationship and, if there is, in which direction. During World War II British citizens who prayed were not hit as often by German bombs. Is praying therefore effective? Or did more of the religiously active population live in rural areas? Obviously, clarifying causes and effects is of primary importance for policy conclusions. Lipton (1998) estimates that variations in gross national product explain 35 to 50 percent of the variation in poverty incidence across countries. If this is correct, growth as an instrument for poverty reduction is at best only moderately effective. Poverty reduction can be made more effective by strategies specifically designed for that purpose and, in cases of conflicting objectives, we should remember that what we want is pro-poor growth, not simply economic growth.
- In recent years, a new consensus has begun to emerge that poverty is a multidimensional phenomenon. The poor themselves have related poverty to powerlessness, to insecurity, and to vulnerability, to name but a few key words beyond income and consumption. The process matters as much as the results. Still, evaluation methods have not yet adequately integrated these more qualitative concerns. If investigators measure poverty reduction using CGE models, macroeconometric models, and cross-sectional and time-series data, they may miss major changes, good or bad, in the life of the poor. Retrospective historical comparisons may offer opportunities to catch changes of a more qualitative nature.
- As Thorbecke correctly notes, retrospective historical comparisons of countries can be enlightening. What I advocate goes beyond comparisons of Kenya and Tanzania to include comparative historical studies with the industrial countries. Let us consider Switzerland when it was a developing country. For decades, Swiss industry—in particular, the pharmaceutical sector—opposed the patenting of inventions. In the sector's view, not patenting gave it free access to technology and imitation as a basis for new research, obviously quite a successful recipe for development.

Historical comparisons can widen the horizon beyond existing national and international socioeconomic settings and, for example, reveal the effects of rules and regulations such as trade-related intellectual property rights, which are part of an international framework that sometimes enables, but sometimes impedes, development.

To conclude, the success of development and poverty reduction strategies does not depend only on technical design. It depends as much on political decisions taken at the national level and by the international community.

References

Financial Times. 1999 (June 12–13).

Lipton, Michael. 1998. *Successes in Anti-poverty.* Geneva: International Labour Office.

UNCTAD (United Nations Conference on Trade and Development). 1998. *Trade and Development Report.* New York and Geneva.

UNDP (United Nations Development Programme). 1998. *Human Development Report.* New York.

Floor discussion: Africa and Asia: Evaluation of the Poverty Alleviation Impact of Alternative Development Strategies and Adjustment Responses

Michael Walton opened the discussion by reminding conferees that two issues were being discussed: what kinds of development strategy were effective in reducing poverty and what kinds of evaluation techniques could be used to evaluate impacts in a country as opposed to the impact of a specific intervention.

Robert Picciotto said he liked the first part of the presentation, in part because it reflected his own bias toward looking for an explanation in the rural sector. He wondered if Thorbecke had looked at other explanations in contrasting Asia and Africa—for example, at knowledge, education, and technology, in which Asia had clearly invested so much more than Africa, and at sound macroeconomic management, which might be as powerful an explanation as the rural one. He was curious why Thorbecke had decided on a partial explanation.

Thorbecke accepted all Robert Picciotto's points about the importance of education, sound macroeconomic management, technology, and so on. As for whether he was being politically correct in not mentioning the extremely poor governance in most of Africa, Thorbecke said he was very much aware of it. He recalled Platteau's statement that in Africa there is no loyalty to the national government, only to the tribe. Platteau, who spent years studying Africa as an economic anthropologist, had provided many examples of the conflict between national and tribal interests.

Commenting on structural inequality, Walton described an experience from the field. He had been surprised to learn, when working on East Asia until just before the crisis, that some Japanese scholars were shifting their interpretation of East Asia's success to give greater emphasis to rural development's central role in the political economy. It seemed that the governments that had come into power after World War II had had to strike an alliance with the peasantry to ensure their own political survival. Walton linked Indonesia's extraordinary expansion of social services to its political economy and, in an admittedly gross oversimplification, to the sources of the crisis. We are now seeing the beginning of the breakdown of a political economy based on support from the peasantry. Mature societies were arising with totally new demands. New interactions—between new urban elites and an urban middle class, and between industry and global forces—were the proximate source of the crisis.

Thorbecke said he was sure that some African countries had somewhat less artificial boundaries and the beginnings of a nation state and national sentiment. But in his experience, and certainly in the literature, there seemed

---

Michael Walton of the World Bank chaired the discussion.

to be more loyalty to a region or clan than to the nation. He had researched the large number of ethnic groups in Indonesia, for a paper for the International Economic Association's 1996 meeting in Tokyo on the institutional foundations of macroeconomic stability, and learned that the Javanese made up about 60 percent of the population, along with people from Sulawesi. The Javanese were not only culturally dominant but also peaceful, which made building a nation state easier. He was not sure whether one could generalize from this, however.

A discussion followed on political economy as a way of "taking on board other disciplines," the multidimensional nature of poverty, and counterfactuals. A Bank staff member said that certain types of general equilibrium models built in recent years could probably start addressing issues of political economy. He wasn't sure about the benefit-cost ratio of building such models, but with a sound socioeconomic base—which most countries in the world, including many African countries, increasingly had—would make a good deal of disaggregation unnecessary. With perhaps six socioeconomic rules, six production sectors, and four or five actors, one could start addressing important issues about the relationship between growth and poverty.

A few audience members expressed concern about the direction the discussion was taking. One participant pointed out potential contradictions in some of the points made in the afternoon session, stating that the counterfactual could take conferees away from a more disciplined approach. To compare Indonesia and the Philippines contradicted what Sheperd had said in his session. The point was not to talk about absolute truths but to feel out what might be the right approach.

Perhaps the task was misspecified, suggested Sheperd. Evaluators did not need a single approach to the evaluation of poverty reduction; they needed to tailor their approach and methodology to circumstances. In discussing a single specific case he had tried to suggest some issues of possibly wider relevance in evaluating poverty education, but he did not claim any sort of model.

> If the development community really wanted poverty reduction, how it engaged the group was perhaps more useful than what happened to the group.

One of the challenges conferees faced, said Alam, was to move beyond projects and programs to development outcomes. Projects might be extremely successful in building institutional capacity yet make little difference in terms of development change.

Returning to an earlier point by Salehuddin Ahmed, another participant asked what conferees were evaluating. Ahmed had said that evaluators were not looking enough at process. Looking only at accountability would not reveal why something did or did not work. He thought Ahmed's point was valid. Much poverty work had been oriented to target groups and impacts. If the development community really wanted poverty reduction, how it engaged the group was perhaps more useful than what happened to the group.

Thorbecke followed up on a point made earlier by Dasgupta. To examine the impact of a project's civic intervention, one should really examine a vector of outcomes. An irrigation project, for example, might increase outputs, create more employment, and affect the incomes of different groups. But what kind of weight should be assigned to those different objectives? Poverty alleviation could not be the exclusive objective. How did one deal with intertemporal issues? What if a project did relatively little for poverty alleviation, but raised output for the next period, which then led to significant poverty alleviation? Some kind of assigned weight of preference should be used to look at the impact of a project in subsequent years.

In this connection, another participant thought the development community had become increasingly intolerant of losers. In the 1960s, when he had started working in development, one always accepted that there would be losers, but one considered the good of the country or community as a whole. Today safeguard policies were used.

After a statement about the need to balance tradeoffs, participants discussed the merits of evaluating efficiency and suggested various ways to carry it out, such as donor partnerships, client-focused evaluation, theory-based evaluation, the development of country evaluation capacity, and thinking about scale. In reference of scale, Thorbecke said one major development in the last decade had been the availability of information about the various dimensions of poverty and about what he called "poverty profiles." He was co-coordinator of a large-scale project on poverty analysis in Sub-Saharan Africa, in which 12 country teams were currently spending two years building a poverty profile of the countries based on large-scale surveys of income and expenditures—and partially on participatory poverty assessments. In addition, demographic and health surveys had provided a huge amount of information on nutritional and health status for about 29 other countries. Information was now available at the regional and socioeconomic levels. Sample sizes for the surveys ranged from 10,000 to 200,000 households (in Indonesia). In Africa, for some five countries at least two surveys permitted comparisons over time. Evaluators should be sure to use this type of information. One problem the project faced was that although the central statistical bureau often said it would not release the information, evaluators later learned that the World Bank had it. Maybe the World Bank should become a depository for this type of information and provide it to bona fide researchers and evaluators.

One participant remarked on the market for evaluators who were underpaid and under pressure to produce results—and on the relationship between the policy research agenda and the efficient use of information. Ethiopia was cited as an example of failure to learn and retain knowledge gained from evaluation. Was knowledge management a solution? At the crux of the efficiency dilemma, another participant suggested, was the relationship between the demand for, and the supply of, evaluation. What was needed was more synergy between self-evaluation and independent evaluation, between accountability and learning. If an organization was a learning organization, the transaction costs of evaluation fell drastically.

A participant from the Bank stated that renewal in the Operations Evaluation Department focused on producing the supply when the demand existed instead of producing the supply regardless of the demand.

> If an organization was a learning organization, the transaction costs of evaluation fell drastically.

Another participant compared evaluation with business, in which entrepreneurs must know their market and follow it. Evaluators who are evaluating without knowing their markets are not good evaluation managers. Good evaluators look at reality first, try to understand what really happened, then question the policy paradigm that policy researchers have come up with. Evaluation should challenge the policy researchers and the policy researchers should challenge evaluation, which is very much what is happening at the Bank. This competition between policy research and operations evaluation is healthy.

10

Lessons Learned from Evaluation of DFID's Aid Program

Andrew Shepherd

In September 1997, several months after coming to power in the United Kingdom (U.K.), the new government commissioned an evaluation of the U.K.'s bilateral aid program. In November 1997 the Department for International Development (DFID) published a white paper, *Eliminating World Poverty,* that focused the U.K.'s aid program on the goal of eliminating world poverty.[1] The terms of reference for this evaluation reflected officials' concerns as they moved toward a new approach to foreign aid. The evaluation was to be forward looking, contributing to a policy debate that was to take place during the next two years. This created an especially difficult context for evaluation, because the audience was changing rapidly. Note that the findings and lessons of the DFID evaluation are still tentative. This was the first formal DFID evaluation to ask whether the aid program had made a difference to poor people, the aid program's explicit goal since 1994.[2]

The terms of reference specified three steps: a policy review, three country studies (India, Uganda, and Zambia), and a synthesis. Mozambique was added later as an example of a country recovering from complex emergencies. Key thematic concerns were participation, gender, and sustainability.

Evaluation Approach

DFID considered three evaluation approaches:
- Develop a model of a poverty-reducing bilateral aid program and measure a country program against it (see Cox and Healey forthcoming).

- Measure performance and impact against the donors' stated goals (the traditional project evaluation approach).
- Develop an interpretative approach with preconceptions specific to context (country, province, and so on) and time (1990-97).

The evaluation team chose the third approach, as it found considerable variation in approaches to poverty reduction, poor people's own perception of poverty, and DFID's definitions of poverty. Thus, the purpose of the study was not to develop a representative database of country programs or to compare one with another but rather to study the aid program in a range of poverty situations and policy contexts. The choice of countries reflected this approach. India had the largest, and ostensibly most poverty-focused, program; Uganda was a good performer on economic reform and growth; Zambia was a poor performer with low growth; and Mozambique was a good performer in a context of recovery from a complex emergency. The evaluation team hoped to:

- Ascertain the influence exerted by the aid program
- Understand the range of concepts of poverty and poverty reduction and where the aid program stood in relation to those concepts
- Explain the relationships between macroeconomic management, economic growth, and poverty reduction
- Derive a portfolio of interventions to facilitate impact assessment, learn lessons, and identify good practices.

The evaluators felt that during the 1990s DFID had approached poverty reduction in the way outlined by the Bank in its 1990 *World Development Report* (World Bank 1990). They therefore felt it was appropriate to ask about the contribution of macroeconomic and sector-level work to poverty reduction, as well as to focus on direct or targeted interventions.

Methods

The evaluation employed both quantitative and qualitative methods, although it was somewhat biased toward qualitative approaches. No uniform set of methods was prescribed for each study, but findings were triangulated as far as possible. The evaluators recognized that attribution would be highly problematic, especially where donors operated together, as in program aid or sectorwide approaches. In such cases, judgment could only be qualitative, focusing on a program's contribution, and the United Kingdom's contribution, to poverty reduction. Approaches and methods varied somewhat at the country level, the program or sector level, and the project level.

The synthesis team reviewed all material by sectors and themes and generated statements, along with the evidence to support them. It then prioritized statements depending on

- The significance of the issue
- The general or restricted relevance of the statement

- The level of confidence with which the statement could be supported
- The possibility of weaving the statement into a consistent "story line."

Some degree of quantification was obtained by expert scoring of the performance of 14 projects intended to reduce poverty "directly" against a variety of indicators (see box 10.1).

Methodological Changes Along the Way

The findings of the policy review were taken into account in developing the approaches and methods for the country studies and synthesis. The review suggested that centrally developed policies were weak instruments to guide or determine the content of country programs and perhaps not adequately based on country program experience. The country studies confirmed these findings.

> **Box 10.1: Preliminary Findings from the Evaluation of Selected DFID Antipoverty Projects**
>
> The country teams selected nonrandomly for in-depth evaluation a small sample of 14 DFID projects that aid officials had designated as both "direct assistance to poverty reduction" and "women in development." Nine of the projects involved NGOs, perhaps consistent with the reliance on NGOs to deliver direct poverty interventions. Five had been through some kind of impact assessment, thereby allowing a degree of confidence in the findings. Included were rural and urban development, safety nets, health, education, water and sanitation, and microfinance projects.
>
> The analysis suggests that the projects performed consistently well in terms of targeting, access, participation, and impact but consistently worse in coverage, poverty analysis, learning, and influence. The evaluators judged that the most important indicators of effectiveness for poor people were impact, coverage, and influence. There was a degree of tradeoff between impact and coverage. Projects that succeeded in terms of impact but had low coverage needed to achieve some influence, both within the aid program as a whole and within the country or region, to justify the normally high and unreplicable levels of resourcing. However, influence was most often the weakest link in the chain.
>
> The absence of good-quality poverty analysis at entry level in several projects may have resulted in activities that had a limited range of poverty reducing components. This may be especially significant for reaching the poorest people. Only one of the projects had a comprehensive range of activities, and the evaluators judged it to be particularly successful for poverty reduction. This limited evidence may challenge the prevailing wisdom that integrated development projects are not successful, a view expressed, for instance, in a recent study of Dutch-funded comprehensive, integrated area development projects (NEDA 1999). The Dutch study broadly confirms the generally disappointing results of integrated development projects in earlier reviews. However, the U.K. aid program's relatively positive experience with integrated urban and rural development suggests that this subject deserves further consideration.

Organizational factors were critical in developing capacity to address poverty reduction. The key organizational features were the development of professional groups (that is, technical advisory groups in specific areas) and consequent intersectoral and interprofessional group relations and decentralization. This meant that the evaluation partly studied DFID's capacity to work on poverty reduction. There is scope for a research project comparing the organizational cultures of aid agencies and the relationship of organizational cultures to the capacity to address poverty reduction.

The policy review also discussed the importance of influence as an aspect of effectiveness. DFID staff were keen to examine the extent of international influence over the Bank through the Special Programme for Africa. (The U.K.'s partnership with the Bank had been strong but conditionalities were being written off as a mode of influence.) The country studies were also to include an explicit study of influence.

Finally, the synthesis team discussed the importance of comparing the poverty reduction record of the Overseas Development Administration (ODA) with that of another bilateral aid agency. This led to a small benchmark study with the Swedish International Development Authority (SIDA), an agency with a reputation for a poverty focus.

Adopting a Forward-Looking, Best-Practice Approach

Evaluators can easily pick out the negative, focus on the constraints, and identify underachievement. Explaining the negative and imagining the positive are more challenging. Because evaluation has historically been a critical activity, focusing on the positive does not come naturally to evaluators. In this case, dwelling on the positive was essential for several reasons. First, poverty reduction involves a complex, and sometimes conceptually contested, set of issues that cannot be resolved by an evaluation. Second, aid agencies generally pursue several objectives at the same time, and non-poverty-reduction activities might have important positive consequences for poor people. Third, establishing the goal of poverty reduction for the aid program as a whole meant that staff were concerned about the validity of cherished ideas and approaches to work.

Given that poverty reduction was not main program goal at DFID until 1994, the evaluators could have written a short and extremely critical report that would have served little purpose. Instead, the evaluators looked for cases of good practice at both the country and program levels, from which current programs could learn, to build confidence in the organization's potential contribution to poverty reduction (box 10.2).

Emerging Lessons on Poverty Reduction

A number of provisional lessons can be drawn from the country studies and a synthesis of the evaluation results.

Lessons from the Country Studies

The lessons that emerged from the country studies varied considerably from program to program. This is not surprising, given that the countries were chosen because they represented different approaches, histories, and performance levels on such critical development indicators as economic growth, perceived success in economic reform, and spending on antipoverty programs. The country case studies helped identify strengths and weaknesses that might or might not be replicated elsewhere because of differences in countries' policy environment and aid history.

A general conclusion from the country studies was that none of the DFID country programs was optimally designed for poverty reduction. This is not to say that individual projects had no impact but that, taken as a whole, they did not add up to a substantial impact. Given that programs were not

---

Box 10.2: A Chronicle of Good and Improving DFID Practices 1990–97

Program Development
- A remarkable shift in poverty focus within the constraints of the neoliberal consensus
- The understanding of poverty evolving per international trend toward multidimensionality and multisectorality
- Importance of joint work with other donors recognized in the context of the Special Programme for Africa
- A substantial shift to basic services with potential for including the poor
- Examples of sector reform focusing on pro-poor service outcomes
- Useful combinations of sector- and project-level interventions to ensure that sectorwide work focuses on the poor
- Examples of good impact, targeting, and participation in direct interventions
- The utility of enterprise development and microfinance portfolio development
- Achieving influence through a combination of knowledge products, appropriate institutional context, and operational practice
- Increased awareness of the importance of analytical capacity for understanding socioeconomic, cultural, and institutional barriers to utilization, demand, and access
- Increased awareness of social sectors as safety nets

Improving organizational practice
- Decentralizing the office
- Making a serious attempt to incorporate gender analysis, despite the intrinsic difficulties
- Following up on the rare operalization of gender
- Creating some space for slow poverty- and gender-focused project work
- Engaging progressively with governments, moving outward from macroeconomic support to public sector reform and sector aid
- Building the India program impact assessments into a picture of program impact and using them to move projects along.

explicitly designed to have a maximum impact on poverty but had poverty reduction as one of several objectives, the finding is not surprising. It does indicate, however, that if poverty reduction is really their goal, programs and projects need to recognize that as the starting point for operations.

Despite this general conclusion, the quality of programs in India and Zambia improved dramatically during the 1990s. This included improvements in focus and coherence, in the intellectual inputs devoted to project management, in the innovativeness of projects, and in the increasing seriousness with which poverty issues were discussed (see table 10.1). Improvements in Mozambique and Uganda came much later.

Evaluation Synthesis

Once the policy review and country studies had been carried out, the most difficult part of the job was to synthesize the results and to produce useful lessons for DFID. A long list of findings and lessons that cut across country programs or were peculiar to particular countries was easily produced; but it was not easy to work out which were the most important, which might involve changes in approach or operations, and which were necessary to contribute more significantly to poverty reduction. The procedure was to cluster lessons into groups, so that each cluster would link a set of strategic or policy lessons with organizational ones (systems, procedures, culture) to provide operationally useful results.

Balancing the social and productive sectors. A number of lessons clustered around the need to achieve some balance, and possibly coordination or integration, between the social and productive sectors. Working through the productive sectors enabled greater participation by poor people, so this was the key entry point for enhancing social or political capital. The following observations seemed important in this regard:

- Spending on the social sectors, especially health, had grown dramatically, while expenditure on potentially pro-poor productive activities had remained even.
- Economic growth did not automatically translate into improved economic opportunities for poor people without complementary public and private investment.
- Participatory work repeatedly identified poor people's priorities as improvements in employment opportunities, incomes, and access to domestic water. Because participatory work is a way to build social and political capital, which is important for progress toward poverty reduction, constructing participatory arrangements and building social capital around poor people's priorities rather than around social sector activities is likely to be easier.
- No systematic work on safety nets had been undertaken.

Table 10.1: Key lessons from Two Country Studies

Country	Key Lessons
India	1. Analytical, critical engagement with the "Indian consensus" on income poverty reduction is a necessary part of a quality aid programme.[1] 2. Given the government's emphasis on income poverty reduction, donors' emphasis on human development was logical, but a sectoral mode of agency (and government) organization should not be allowed to obscure the drivers of human development. 3. Decentralised aid management allows engagement with context, intellectual discourse, and imaginative programme development with creative partnership. Further decentralization would allow multi-sectoral, multi-level, multi-partner (including donor) interventions. 4. Inclusive participatory arrangements were easier to develop around productive activities than around social sector activities. 5. Developing evidence-based analytical approaches to project and programme management (impact assessment, gender strategies) could improve aid quality in the short term. 6. Influence was best generated by the combination of knowledge products and mainstream project work; "insider" status conferred by longevity of commitment, networking capacity, and staffing patterns (especially employment of Indians).
Zambia	7. The degree to which an intervention addressed not only economic but also social and political dimensions of the problem was crucial to its effectiveness (impact and influence) and sustainability. 8. Efforts which had the support of powerful stakeholders were likely to be more successful; however, where vested interests were challenged, progress could be made either if interventions attempted to influence state structures and behavior, or to build the political capital of the poor. Political-institutional analysis was critical. 9. Policy leverage through disbursement conditionality and associated pressure is an over rated art, at least for a bi-lateral donor. 10. Thought had to be given to how the synergies between improving livelihoods and strengthening social and political capital within the successful CARE projects might be emulated in other fields (such as health and rural infrastructure). 11. The stop-and-go nature of reform in Zambia constrained the effectiveness of cutting edge donor approaches - the use of program aid to fund the government budget and SWA to provide financial support. 12. Thought also had to be given to extending the successful process approach to project management beyond the small number of projects actually operating within this framework.

Source: Evaluation of DFID Support to Poverty Reduction: India Country Studies

[1] DFID India debated this point strenuously, arguing that there was less consensus than the study proclaimed. The evaluators maintain the existence of a consensus on income poverty reduction in the late 1990s although there had been competing schools of thought in previous decades. There is little consensus on human development and social and political capital issues.

The separation (and even competition) between sectors had inhibited intersectoral collaboration in the past. For example, work on renewable natural resources needed to be firmly linked to enterprise development and rural infrastructure. Some organizational restructuring might facilitate these links. In addition, aid management considerations—in particular, limiting country programs to a few sectors because of a scarcity of sectoral advisers—had inhibited logical choices between sectors based on poverty analysis. A reversed flow of decisionmaking and better intersectoral collaboration might be furthered by more understanding of the context.

The studies clearly supported the view that even development interventions focused on improving livelihoods rarely support the poorest. Social services by themselves are unlikely to be enough. Safety nets are essential. Donors should become involved with public sector safety nets, small improvements in which were likely to have substantial benefits. Community-based safety nets and recovery programs run by NGOs need exploration.

The need for multilayered and multisectoral approaches to poverty reduction requires a much more painstaking analysis of a donor's place in a complex policy and program jigsaw and comparative advantage within this institutional matrix. Clearly a single donor, however large, need not do everything. But establishing comparative advantage with any methodological rigor is difficult and time consuming.

Lessons for the Social Sector. During the 1990s development experts saw improving social service outcomes as the key intervention (along with economic growth) to reduce poverty. In this context, the evaluation synthesis derived a second cluster of lessons:

- Sectorwide approaches focusing on improving the quality of service, access, service outcomes, and accountability had the potential to include the poor.
- Small but critical improvements in service outcomes had a greater impact on poor people than more difficult system improvements that might take longer to achieve.
- Participatory and analytical work reflected the importance of curative and emergency health services as well as preventive health services and of secondary schooling as well as primary schooling. This suggests the power of balanced sectorwide approaches to permit local priority setting.
- There were inherent dangers of donors swinging with fashion trends in favor of particular approaches.
- Donor willingness to fund recurrent costs, which is necessary to rehabilitate social services in poor regions and countries, is likely to depend on the improvements in public expenditure management sought by the Special Programme for Africa.
- Civil service reform agendas have not been adequately linked to social sector policymaking.
- Civil society organizations are likely to play a key role in helping poor people overcome barriers to using social services. In this context, donors could help NGOs play a more strategic role rather than that of alternative service providers.
- Reducing the barriers to the use of social services by the poor is best done in the context of priority or productive sector programs around which poor people organize themselves more easily.

Enabling Poverty Reduction Through Macroeconomic Interventions.
Much U.K. aid to poor countries took the form of program aid or macroeconomic support for structural adjustment programs. Another strong focus was good governance, generally through support for civil service reform and reforms of the judiciary, revenue collection, and police functions of the central government.

One major finding of the country studies was that although macroeconomic interventions and governmental stabilization were likely to be necessary for sustained poverty reduction, they needed to be accompanied by complementary measures. On occasion, however, such measures could work against poor people's interests—for example, cutting back on the number of teachers and health workers or requiring cost recovery for basic services without improving revenue collection in general or finding ways to exempt the poor.

Even where analysis addressed such issues, it was not always used, perhaps because of the leadership of reform programs by the international financial institutions. Even collectively, bilaterals find influencing these juggernauts difficult. The Special Programme for Africa created a valuable forum in which such dialogue was possible, and some influence was achieved. However, influencing the Bank through the program required a strategy that included funding pilot activities in Bank country programs, funding and managing studies and secondments, and providing trust funds to enable Bank staff to carry out activities for which loan funds were not appropriate. U.K. program aid brought little influence over policy beyond adding the United Kingdom's voice to that of the international financial institutions, whose impact varied from country to country and was always constrained by the interests of the political elite. Influence beyond the confines of macroeconomic management was extremely limited.

Good governance rarely extended to support for decentralization. In any case, decentralization is no panacea for poverty reduction because local governments may be captured by local elites. Still, decentralization could provide a forum that local elites and interlocutors for the poor can use constructively to build alliances with poor people.

In the case of post-conflict reconstruction as an enabling form of aid, economic growth was clearly the key to recovery. However, macroeconomic stabilization alone could not deliver the kind of economic growth that could reduce poverty widely. For this, a more complex model of recovery was needed than was available in the international literature or through consensuson aid, which subsumed recovery under a model of conflict prevention. An attempt to graft new forms of social organization onto the chaos of resettlement was one of the few admissions that recovery was a complex, poorly understood process that required more than the donor community was apparently able or willing to offer.

Lessons for Evaluation Design
The lessons learned from DFID's experience should be taken into careful consideration in designing evaluations of poverty reduction strategies.

Poverty Reduction: A Complex, Multidimensional, Interorganizational "Project"

Evaluating programs intended to reduce poverty is an intrinsically difficult exercise, more difficult by far than classic project or policy evaluation. One reason for this is that poverty reduction is complex and involves many actors and economic and societal processes that are not easy to control, or even to influence.

- **Lesson 1.** Synthesizing information and conclusions from varied activities is a subjective activity. The commissioner of the evaluation must have a great deal of confidence in the evaluators, and a close collaborative relationship is required throughout the evaluation. Some degree of independence is necessary, though unlikely, under these circumstances.
- **Lesson 2.** Unless the lessons learned help agency staff recognize themselves, they are little more than an informative but dull list. The complexity needs not only to be brought out but explained.
- **Lesson 3.** The problem of attribution suggests that joint evaluations need to be given far greater operational weight. These could be joint donor or joint donor-government evaluations. Joint evaluation would help reduce the conflict of loyalties involved in simultaneously commissioning and being the object of evaluation.
- **Lesson 4.** In the necessarily complex field of poverty reduction, influence is a key component of effectiveness for a medium-size donor. However, the study of influence is not well developed.
- **Lesson 5.** Program management needs to incorporate far more evaluation and impact assessment. Too few strategic decisions about the direction of country programs are informed by any such evaluative studies. For agencies to commission large-scale, semi-independent, ex post studies is no longer sufficient. Country program evaluation should be a routine part of any agency's strategic thinking and planning cycle. This is also a way to engage in local discourse about poverty reduction.

The Poor Are Unrepresented: The Search for Interlocutors

Another difficulty in evaluating poverty reduction programs is that the agencies involved do not generally include representatives of poor people or interlocutors for the poor.

- **Lesson 6.** Interlocutors for the poor are neither readily available nor free of their own interests. Evaluators should interact with a variety of potential interlocutors and use existing participatory assessment processes.

- **Lesson 7.** Interlocutors who have not been involved with a program over a period of time will not be able to represent the views of poor people in an evaluation study easily. Evaluations should rely on existing, authentic participatory processes and civil society organizations for such information.
- **Lesson 8.** Evaluation is not normally perceived to be about organization or organizational change, but organizational factors seemed to have been extremely influential in permitting or inhibiting effective poverty reduction. Many of the most important messages to emerge from the evaluation concerned systems, procedures, and organizational culture.
- **Lesson 9.** Any organization is likely to be sensitive about singling out particular groups within it; however, some groups may see themselves as interlocutors and as more poverty-focused than others. Even without clearly demarcated groups, the contested nature of poverty reduction means that evaluation occurs in a context of conflict, which obviously makes it difficult. An inclusive evaluation strategy demonstrates that good practice exists in a variety of forms, not attached to any single group, sector, or program.

The Specificity of Poverty: Is It Relevant?

Poverty reduction has rarely been the only goal of an aid program. In a multigoal context, program design has to be balanced with pressures to achieve other objectives. Any evaluation probably needs to distinguish between effectiveness in general and capacity to contribute to poverty reduction in particular. The evaluation approach made much of the specificity of poverty and of approaches to poverty reduction. This was largely confirmed by the following examples:

- **Lesson 10.** The difficulty of understanding the situation of displaced people returning home led to a number of questionable assumptions about recovery programs. Some generalizations may be possible, buth the politics of intergroup relations and the degree of institutional and market destruction will influence the speed of rehabilitation.
- **Lesson 11.** Debate about the nature of poverty and how to reduce it is substantial. Indian development practitioners, for example, agreed on the need for income poverty reduction, while those in Mozambique focused on structural poverty.
- **Lesson 12.** The findings of poverty assessments, especially participatory poverty assessments, were often specific. The Zambia case study, for example, showed that widows' lack of access to land and other assets was a critical cause of poverty.

The growing view that the distribution of social capital affects economic growth is another example of the importance of context. But exploration of the relationship between social capital and poverty reduction is still in the early stages. The evaluation argues that politics is also neglected as an explanatory factor in analyses of constraints on, and possibilities for, poverty reduction. Programs need to address assumptions that the poor will participate if they are given the opportunity, that democratic structures ensure their representation, that removing subsidies will improve their access, that markets will open up opportunities for them, that they will be able to compete for resources in education and health, and that they will gain access to and use basic physical or socioeconomic infrastructure. All these assumptions may be easily undermined by vested interests that may be linked politically to elite interests. It is important to think through strategies to ensure that not only the nonpoor benefit.

Stakeholder Involvement: Evaluation's Contribution to Strategic and Organizational Change

Evaluation has a dismal record in contributing to change. In the U.K. aid program, old-style project evaluations had little impact at a country program, policy, or strategic level and usually came too late to affect the course of a project (Flint 1997, Flint and Austin 1993). Newer, topical, synthesis evaluations that have addressed particular professional groups or sectors and exposed their work in a holistic (nonproject) way to senior management have probably been more influential. For example, a synthesis evaluation of water and sanitation projects (White 1997) concluded that projects' health benefits were not being realized because of weak intersectoral linkages. This led to a stronger relationship between project engineers and health advisers.

It is too early to assess the impact of the current evaluation. However, it has played a role in resourcing the country programs studied, raising key issues, forcing the debate, and contributing expertise.

Lessons on the findings and impact of the study are listed below:

- **Lesson 13.** The more general or abstract the finding, the more acceptable it has proved. Specific findings and lessons were challenged, although the evaluators' arguments have gradually been accepted more. In making these arguments, the evaluation contributed to the organizational change currently under way.
- **Lesson 14.** The audience for this evaluation has been in transition from one policy environment to another. Program managers fully engaged with current programs have sometimes been impatient with a retrospective study. The demands on the study to be up to date have therefore been heavy. The findings and lessons of the study have frequently confirmed changes already in process rather than contributing new ideas and information.

Notes

1. DFID was established in May 1997 to handle international development issues; its predecessor, the Overseas Development Administration (ODA), had been largely concerned with aid delivery. This evaluation covers the period 1990 to 1997.

2. The opinions expressed in this paper are the author's and do not necessarily represent the views of DFID. The analysis draws from work in synthesizing the evaluation findings by the synthesis team, which included Kate Bird, David Booth, Alicia Herbert, David Hulme, and Tina Wallace, with help from Howard White, to all of whom thanks.

References

Cox, A., and J. Healey. Forthcoming. *European Development Cooperation and the Poor.* New York: St. Martin's Press.

Flint, M. 1997. "Report on a Survey of Evaluation Users. Development Assistance Committee Expert Group on Aid Evaluation: Review of Processes for Evaluation of Development Assistance."

Flint, M., and C. Austin. 1993. "Learning Lessons: A Review of ODA Evaluation Impact." London: Overseas Development Administration, Evaluation Department.

NEDA (National Economic Development Authority). 1999. "Integrated Area Development: Experiences with Netherlands Aid in Africa." *Focus on Development* 10.

White, J. 1997. *Rural Water and Sanitation: A Synthesis Evaluation.* London: DFID.

Comments: Lessons Learned from Evaluation of DFID's Aid Program

Octavio Damiani

I will start by highlighting three features of the methodology applied in the evaluation:

- *The use of best-practice cases.* Did the evaluation look only at successful cases or did it also compare the successful cases with projects that did not work well in each of the countries analyzed. If it did not consider relative project failures, how was the evaluation able to identify the key factors that led to good project performance?
- *The context-specific way in which the evaluation considered the problem of poverty.* In other words, the evaluation analyzed the aid program in a variety of poverty and policy contexts on the assumption that poverty may have different roots in various regions and countries and that different policy contexts may influence the evolution of interventions to alleviate poverty in a variety of ways. In that regard, I would have liked the evaluation to address the issue of context more specifically, explaining, for example, why and how a project might do well even in adverse macroeconomic circumstances and even when project performance is affected by politics.
- *The consideration of influence as a key component of program effectiveness.* I have a slightly different perspective on influence. Shepherd defines it as the capacity to shape other programs without imposing conditionalities, a definition which implies that the program has a design that is already effective. I like to see a project as a learning experience, which if it succeeds can show governments possible interventions they could implement in the struggle against poverty. Thus, influence would be measured as the adoption in national programs or policies of the principles of a program or project.

In turning to the paper's findings I will refer to my own experience—specifically, in rural poverty in Latin America.

I believe any program evaluation should consider, especially for projects addressing the problem of rural poverty, first, how can projects that promote economic transformation simultaneously address rural poverty? The evaluation mentioned the lesson about the need for a closer relationship between social and productive projects. During the past decade, most international donors decreased their support to programs that targeted rural poverty, partly because the integrated rural development projects popular during the 1970s and 1980s had performed somewhat poorly. They turned their attention mainly to macroeconomic reform, government reform, decentralization, and privatization. In the late 1980s and early 1990s, development economists became interested in late industrialization, focusing on the East Asian countries and arguing about what policies would promote the development of manufacturing. The problem of rural poverty became more closely associated with the social sectors, so projects began to support services and social funds.

Since rural poverty remains important after a decade of these efforts, donors concluded that rural poverty should be targeted specifically. So we seem to be returning to the question development economists posed in the 1950s and 1960s: Should the problem of rural poverty be targeted exclusively through community development and social fund programs? The paper mentioned that at least one integrated rural development project had succeeded. What was the difference between this project and other integrated rural development projects? What difference does it make when the provision of extension services is private rather than public, or when credit is provided through farmer associations rather than banks? What types of programs can promote dynamic agricultural growth and reduce poverty at the same time? What would be the key interventions? Reforming land tenure systems? Promoting the creation of nonagricultural firms? Promoting the adoption of new crops and technologies among small farmers? Or implementing contemporary rural development projects with the private provision of extension and other services and with self-administered credit?

Developing countries have substantially integrated with the global economy, opening their markets and increasing their exports. In Latin America, common markets have developed in the southern cone, in the Andean region, and with North America, and countries are interested in developing a broader common market. At the same time, many Latin American developing countries, such as Argentina, Brazil, Chile, Costa Rica, and Guatemala, have been able to create dynamic agricultural export sectors, often based on nontraditional crops. What types of projects could help the rural poor avoid the possible negative effects of globalization and take advantage of it?

The evaluations of cases of growth in nontraditional export crops have often stressed the exclusionary characteristics of a growing export-oriented agriculture. According to these evaluations, small farmers have a problem growing high-value crops such as fruits and vegetables because of the considerable demand for credit, complex technologies, economies of scale, and limited access to market channels. In addition, the literature analyzing the recent growth of nontraditional export crops in developing countries often stresses its negative effects on wage workers, because such crops are often mechanized and may demand substantial amounts of labor only during certain times of the year. Arguably, workers receive low wages and work under poor conditions.

In contrast, other authors have found cases in which small farmers have been able to grow nontraditional export crops that have created employment, increased wages, and improved working conditions. What types of interventions might lead small farmers to grow nontraditional export crops? Should programs to support such interventions focus on providing extension services or credit? Should they focus on improving the conditions of production—through extension and credit—or emphasize the demand side—through helping small farmers find market channels?

In the case of wage workers, some nontraditional export crops have led to increased employment and wages and better working conditions. In such cases, how is the outcome affected by different factors such as the type of crop, how the product is marketed, and the nature of local institutions such as rural unions?

Shepherd presented the results of an evaluation that posed important questions and applied an interesting methodology. However, it lacked detail about specific cases and left unanswered questions which, although they were not the objective of the evaluation, would be of interest to international donors and to others designing future aid programs.

Floor Discussion: Lessons Learned from Evaluation DFID's Aid Program

Walton opened the discussion by observing that Shepherd's paper and Damiani's discussion dealt with three kinds of issues: What kinds of public actions make sense in reducing poverty? What influence can an external donor agency have? And, in discovering what has the greatest impact on poverty reduction, what do we learn about evaluation techniques and methodologies?

Adding to what Shepherd had said about learning from evaluation, Colin Kirk of DFID explained that this had been an innovative evaluation for DFID, partly because of the scope of the subject matter, but also because of the way it was tackled internally. In the past, the Evaluation Department had tended to deliver and disseminate the product, identify the lessons, and then try to promulgate the lessons. In this case, it tried to take the DFID along with it because of the nature of the subject matter. Poverty reduction is an enormous topic, and Evaluation Department staff believed that everyone from top management down to the country program staff should understand what the evaluation was trying to achieve. The evaluators managed that to some extent, but inevitably some misunderstandings arose, and there were still defensive reactions to some of their findings. Their number one priority was to establish a basis for communication from the very beginning and throughout evaluation, not just at the end. They have not reached the end yet and are still communicating. Throughout evaluation, the evaluators sought a broad understanding of how issues were connected, not just lessons learned at the end of the process.

Kirk said it had been a particularly difficult time for the evaluators to deliver lessons within DFID. Two years earlier, the U.K. government had changed and DFID had replaced the old Overseas Development Administration. The aim of DFID was to explicitly focus on poverty reduction. The advantage of this focus was that it elicited a great deal of interest in what the evaluation would have to say. The disadvantage was that people were extremely impatient and wanted the results before the evaluation had even begun. Shepherd was now coping with the difficult task of supplying goods that had been asked for two years earlier. However, the department had moved on and had found its own answers to some of the questions the evaluation had set out to address.

Anneke Slob from the Dutch Ministry of Foreign Affairs asked about the global environment in which the evaluation had taken place. First, in the four case study countries, had the evaluators investigated the relationships between their poverty reduction objectives, their policy objectives, and DFID's objectives? Had there been coherence among these objectives? How had they influenced DFID's policy? Her questions were also related to the issue of good governance.

Michael Walton of the World Bank chaired the discussion.

Second, Slob was working on an evaluation of a Dutch program in Mali, where the whole aid system has tremendous influence, especially on poverty reduction, which is really a country issue. If every donor comes in with its own strategy, how does this influence a country's approach to poverty reduction? An OECD and Development Assistance Committee review of the Mali program noted that the aid system was inefficient, ineffective, and definitely not sustainable. What does the donor do under such circumstances? Basically the donor stuck to its own procedures, since it was accountable to its own departments. Slob had to report to the Dutch parliament, which reported to the Dutch taxpayer.

She described an interesting experience in Burkina Faso and in Mali, where her organization carried out studies of villagers' perceptions. The villagers said they knew about this whole aid business, which involved the government, civil society, and aid agencies, and from which sometimes some things trickled down to the village level. That was fine, the villagers said, but it did not really influence their lives much. What were donors doing about such perceptions? She doubted whether more evaluation was needed. Rather, as Shepherd had said, more information was needed. Maybe donors needed to learn better from each other.

About DFID's methodology, Shepherd said, given the resources available for the study, the evaluators would not be able to go for the rigorous sample-based studies that would give them the kind of generalizable conclusions for which some of the conferees were looking. The study had to be more qualitative than that. For example, the 14 projects were not chosen on the basis of a random sample. They were chosen because they seemed to be important in the context of the countries the evaluators were studying and they could bring up themes and lessons from which they might be able to generalize if they were later able to do a wider study. However, the tradeoff was that where the evaluators were producing lessons, they were able to produce them with a reasonable degree of certainty by using a number of different methods. As much as possible, for example, they used participatory methods or linked up with participatory processes and backed those up with whatever quantitative material was available through impact assessments and so on. So they worked at getting the best results they could, not generalizing, but bouncing any significant learning points off the organization and getting a sense of whether people thought they would apply elsewhere.

Walton felt that not nearly enough evaluation of the right kind was being done. An enormous amount of effort went into assessing projects, but few evaluations assessed the consequences of a program relative to the counterfactual consequences of a program's not having taken place. So donors were not really learning from the process of development.

One participant expressed interest in the notion of context-specific evaluation and a context-specific template. Did this mean that only context-specific lessons were available, so that India, say, could learn nothing from Bangladesh or Indonesia, or vice versa?

Shepherd responded that the evaluators had started off feeling that development practitioners were coming up with many indicators, especially from the participatory studies the World Bank and other donors had sponsored, in which NGOs had been involved for some time. Poor people themselves thought about their situation differently in different places, and somehow DFID needed to take these perceptions into account in evaluating poverty reduction programs. In the 1994 Zambia poverty assessment, for example, the vulnerability of widows was shown to be a strong dimension of poverty, so the evaluators would have expected to see that factor reflected in the development programs in Zambia. In another example, an urban safety net project that was working with women's groups had highlighted some quite new issues of access to land, of property grabbing, and so on. That became an example of good practice, addressing context-specific analysis with some positive results.

But the evaluators were looking at the process over a period of time and, in moving from the program's first phase to its second phase, were losing some of those gains out of concern about focusing on aspects of the project's infrastructure that were clearly appreciated and could be replicated. Replicating the slower, more qualitative group processes was much more difficult. One of the things the evaluators observed was how the dynamic of upscaling and replication led to a downscaling of some factors learned in the participatory assessment. This meant that if one were moving into a second, upscaled phase, one needed to think about how to retain those qualitative factors that had been identified on a relatively small scale.

This made generalizing difficult, but one would not expect the same poverty situation and programs to appear everywhere. Nevertheless, DFID thought that significant learning points for the organization could come out of a context-specific investigation.

One participant felt the presentation was interesting because it showed the interaction between the evaluators and the agency. There seemed to have been a kind of horse-drawn effect—that is, the observations by themselves were to improve performance. Time would tell whether this hypothesis was true.

Another conferee asked whether DFID planned to link learning from evaluations to salary incentives. He thought organizational culture was the most crucial point of learning. Another said that, to matter, evaluations should be linked to resource allocation. This participant was not sure if this was the right approach, because evaluations were often donor driven, and such an incentive would make them all the more so.

Walton closed the discussion with three comments. First, evaluators were pushing hard to combine structured quantitative methods with qualitative methods. Second, to foster evaluation, donors should subsidize evaluation, treating donor programs as experiments in learning, because they are a genuine public good. Finally, evaluators have to ensure that donor agencies feed the learning back into project design.

References

World Bank. 1990. *World Development Report 1990: Poverty.* New York: Oxford University Press.

Sectoral and Microlevel Interventions

Evaluating Microfinance's Impact: Going Down Market

Monique Cohen

In the burgeoning field of microfinance, policymakers and practitioners are focused on how best to deliver financial services to the poor on a sustainable basis. With the push toward financial sustainability and outreach, client-level impact assessment has been marginalized in favor of the assessment of institutional performance. However, donors, policymakers, and practitioners have begun to demand middle-range approaches to impact assessment that are at once credible, cost effective, and useful.

Evaluations of the performance of microfinance institutions (MFIs), with their emphasis on sustainability and outreach, place a premium on financial criteria. Conventional wisdom suggests that clients will automatically follow if the services are made available, and that high rates of repayment and repeat borrowing indicate client satisfaction and a positively valued service. However, such measures fail to answer the persistent and central questions: Whom do these programs reach and do they make a positive difference in clients' lives?

Meanwhile, a growing number of rigorous impact assessments offer valuable insights into the benefits associated with participation in particular programs:

- Employment is generated primarily among the larger microenterprises.
- Households invest in housing and education across income levels.
- Benefits are often greater for better-off clients than for poorer clients.

Linking levels of client participation in programs to how the programs affect them reveals the following trends:

- The cumulative value of loans may be an important determinant of positive change.

- While clients may use first loans for working capital for lower-risk, existing, or known economic activities, once they have a steady flow of income, they may use subsequent loans for housing and riskier investments.
- To mitigate risk, the poor split the use of their loans between production and consumption.

These generalizations are at best tentative. Many mediating variables make programs differ noticeably in whom they reach, the range and types of services they provide, and the environments in which both the clients and the programs operate.

Given the challenges facing microfinance evaluation, this paper looks at some innovative approaches to lower-cost impact assessments. The paper also considers the preliminary findings on the impact of microfinance on poverty alleviation from the research commissioned for the *World Development Report* on Poverty (see Sebstad and Cohen forthcoming). This work represents one of the evolving attempts to understand client perspectives on impact and to develop low-cost impact assessment methods.

Client-Level Impact Evaluation: The Emerging Agenda

Existing microfinance impact assessments cluster around two poles. First, a limited number of large-scale, methodologically rigorous, quantitative impact assessments have used sophisticated econometric analyses. Many of these have been donor driven, with the goal of proving that resources have been well spent and that the results conform to the donor's priorities. A disproportionate number have been undertaken in Bangladesh. Second, a large number of small-scale impact assessments have used less sound methods. The designs have often lacked control or comparison groups and a time perspective. They have employed either quantitative or qualitative instruments or have mixed them. Even though the funding for such studies usually comes from outside, their agendas may reflect an unarticulated mix of donor and practitioner objectives.

> Donors, policymakers, practitioners, and researchers have different priorities, standards, approaches, and uses for impact assessment.

Meanwhile, a middle-range approach is starting to emerge. Donors and practitioners are finding that large-scale assessments are too expensive, and they are pushing to lower costs. Advocating low-cost approaches puts the onus on evaluators to develop reliable instruments that can measure impact more cost-effectively and credibly.

Hulme's (1997) continuum of objectives for impact assessment—which extend from proving impacts for the purpose of measuring the results of an investment to improving the operations of an MFI—suggests that donors, policymakers, practitioners, and researchers have different priorities, standards, approaches, and uses for impact assessment.

Donors and Policymakers

Policymakers guide the climate for investment in microfinance, while donors are a principal source of investment funds. Both want proof of the effectiveness of financial services in relation to their development objectives. In addition to looking for measures of program sustainability, outreach, and deepening financial markets, they want to know whether their services are reaching the poor, helping alleviate poverty, and putting clients on the road to self-sufficiency. Positive results provide evidence of the value of investment in microfinance services and indicate whether they are helping the poor get out of poverty. Failure to demonstrate positive results raises the prospect that donors and policymakers will reprogram their funds for other uses.

Practitioners

As recipients of grant funds, practitioners are often required to show that their programs are contributing to the donors' strategic objectives. At the same time, practitioners have an interest in impact assessment to establish whether financial products are responding to clients' needs and improving their lives. Most practitioners recognize a strong link between program performance and client impact: a loan to a client with a stable and growing income base can make for a repeat borrower who will add to the long-term health of an MFI. For clients, knowing that the institution will be around for a while and that they have access to credit may, by itself, place them in a better position to make riskier investments than they might otherwise make (Diagne 1997). Practitioners have noted that as a management tool, impact assessments can

- Identify which clients are receiving more benefits and which are receiving fewer and reveal the reasons why
- Provide information about the growth, decline, and saturation of different sectors in which clients are working
- Inform institutional understanding of what products and services clients prefer, what barriers they face, and what they value in a program (Cohen and Gaile 1997).

Impact assessments document any changes in clients over time. Combined with client feedback on program services, an impact assessment can amplify practitioners' understanding of the underlying meaning of performance criteria. Understanding clients' behavior and their changing needs interests many institutions, especially when repeat borrowing rates are lower than hoped for or ratios of new to old clients are higher than desired. The findings can inform product development. A comparison of clients and nonclients can offer insights into whom programs and products reach and do not reach and can suggest strategies for attracting new clients.

Researchers

Researchers with support from donors looking for accountability in the use of their funds conduct the most rigorous impact assessments. In a field that requires complex methodologies and is plagued by conceptual problems such as client self-selection bias, fungibility, and attribution, researchers have made key methodological contributions (see Gaile and Foster 1996). However, their studies often have limited applicability for many practitioners. Because they often ignore details about services accessed, length of program participation, levels of arrears, and the volume or size of loans, the impact assessments can appear to be unrelated to MFI operations. Furthermore, from a practitioner's perspective, such studies cost too much, demand analytical methods that are difficult to replicate, and rarely generate timely results.

A growing body of literature reveals what microfinance can and cannot do, but we still have far to go, particularly in terms of understanding the relationship between microfinance and poverty alleviation. Outside Bangladesh, little research has been done on this issue. Rhyne (1998) recently noted that very little is known about the poverty levels of clients in various microfinance programs. But perhaps this is not surprising, because few microfinance programs have received the rigorous statistical evaluations necessary to prove that microfinance can alleviate poverty (Morduch 1998).

Moving Toward Lower-Cost Impact Assessment

At the center of the search for robust lower-cost approaches is the relation between methodological rigor and the reliability of results. Consensus is growing that the overall effectiveness of lower-cost impact assessments depends on credibility, usefulness, and cost-effectiveness (Sebstad 1998). A series of virtual meetings conducted by the Impact Assessment Methodologies Working Group of the Consultative Group to Assist the Poorest (CGAP) proposed that lower-cost or middle-range impact assessments should include the following:

- A small set of key hypotheses grounded in a solid conceptual framework
- A series of well-defined, contextually meaningful variables
- A set of reliable measures that reflect the degree of precision needed
- A comprehensive assessment of the program and of local contextual factors

- Clients at all stages of the impact assessment
- A longitudinal design
- Control groups
- A mixture of quantitative and qualitative research methods
- A systematic analysis of the data (Sebstad 1998).

The highly participatory process that had built this consensus by the working group was as important as the conclusions. The working group began in 1996 with six donor members and two members of the CGAP Policy Advisory Group. The working group's initial agenda was to debate in a series of virtual meetings methodological options for undertaking impact assessment. The group commissioned a discussion paper that reviewed the issues and drew on voluntary submissions of case studies by group members. Following distribution of the discussion paper, working group members held a two-week virtual meeting in April 1997 with 22 participants from nine countries and a moderator. Out of this meeting came a consensus that while many methodological options were available, guidelines were needed for credible, useful, and lower-cost impact assessments.

A second virtual meeting in April 1998 was held to build consensus on the guidelines listed above. By this stage, the number of the working group's donors had grown from 6 to 11, many of whom contracted with 20 researchers and practitioners either to undertake impact assessments or to participate in the meeting. Seventeen countries were represented.

USAID is now ready to test the guidelines in the field. Several of the donors and practitioners are completing impact assessments in accordance with the guidelines. The next virtual meeting took place in October 1999 to produce a manual based on the field tests and the debates. Meanwhile, donor membership has grown, the virtual meetings have become well known outside the working group, and a number of practitioner organizations have asked to participate. They have been asked to submit papers that use the guidelines as a framework. A product should be ready for general circulation early in 2000.

Building consensus on impact evaluation in microfinance in this way has proven advantageous as an end in itself, but the process has had other benefits, as follows:

- The virtual meetings have engaged a global mix of policymakers, donors, practitioners, and researchers, as well as staff, managers, evaluation specialists, and many younger players who might not have attended a conventional conference but were able to contribute intermittently from their home bases.
- People actively engaged in fieldwork were able to provide practical suggestions on both substance and methods.
- The group's deliberation has led to a strong debate on tradeoffs in going down market, an issue that lies at the center of this topic.
- Meeting costs were lower for everyone because they were shared.

- Limiting e-mail contributions to two paragraphs constrained verbosity, promoted a pointed debate, and strengthened the participation of non-English speakers.

Impact Studies As "Advanced Market Research"

Data from a range of MFIs indicate that they mainly reach the poor who are concentrated around the poverty line. MFIs seeking to broaden their client base—downward to the extreme poor, upward to the vulnerable nonpoor, or simply outward with their clients—will have to look more closely at their clients' behavior and deliver new products and services that respond to the differing needs of these various strata of the population. This calls for innovative loan products and other services such as savings and insurance. The key will be flexibility to ensure that each stratum of clients can gain access to needed loans in a timely fashion with terms of repayment that correspond to its capacity to pay.

Many practitioners recognize the need for a deeper understanding of client behavior. Some MFIs—the Small Enterprise Foundation in South Africa; Freedom from Hunger in the United States; Freedom from Hunger International, a French NGO; and many of the large MFIs in Bangladesh—are developing the in-house capacity to better understand their clients and how financial services can be used to improve their money management. These practitioners understand how impact assessments can inform an institution's strategic planning and improve its performance. Donors are providing the financial support for practitioners to experiment with different approaches.

An important goal of USAID's Assessing the Impact of Microenterprise Services (AIMS) Project is to develop affordable impact assessment tools that can generate credible and useful results. SEEP, a membership organization of microenterprise and microfinance institutions, took charge of developing a package of quantitative and qualitative instruments to service a combination of program improvement and impact objectives. The instruments include a household survey, an exit survey, a loan and savings use tool, focus group discussions on client satisfaction, and focus group discussions on empowerment. Numerous NGOs will review a draft manual based on pilot testing in Honduras and Mali to be published in English, French, and Spanish in 2000.

An Ongoing Study of the Impact of Microfinance on Poverty and Vulnerability

Many defenders of microfinance give the impression that it can help the poor climb out of poverty and raise their living standards. Clearly the real world is not so simple. While practitioners tend to agree that microfinance can make a positive difference to people's lives, even when the margin of change appears to be small, hard data to confirm this are limited. Overselling the benefits of microfinance can raise unrealistic expectations and create disillusionment.

Even where data are credible, the methodological complexities associated with client self-selection and fungibility issues have ensured controversy. This is exemplified by a recent study by Morduch (1998). Using a data set of clients and nonclients from three Bangladeshi institutions (Grameen Bank, the Bangladesh Rural Advancement Committee, and the Bangladesh Rural Development Board's Rural Development Program) that other researchers had previously analyzed (Khandker 1998), Morduch arrived at contradictory conclusions. He argued that microfinance had little effect on alleviating poverty but was important in reducing the vulnerability of the poor through consumption smoothing and in moving labor from casual work to self-employment.

Framing the Issues

Outside Bangladesh, the number of sound studies is limited, and generalizing from them to the rest of world would be inappropriate. The remaining microfinance literature has largely focused on income poverty indicators and outcomes, with much less research on the dynamics of how clients use services to reduce their vulnerability and improve their standards of living. This attention to the poverty impacts of microfinance was the background for the USAID-led microfinance contribution to the World Development Report (WDR) 2001. The focus of the research on microfinance and reducing vulnerability parallels the central themes of this WDR: listening to the voices of the poor and considering the nonincome dimensions of poverty, such as how assets help the poor cope with risk and reduce their vulnerability to shocks. While USAID designed and managed this contribution, a consortium of donors (USAID, CGAP, and DFID) funded it, and multidisciplinary field teams in four countries collaborated virtually throughout the design, implementation, analysis, and review process. The research encompassed seven MFIs in Bangladesh, Bolivia, the Philippines, and Uganda, countries where research on the impact of microfinance services has been done or is in progress.

USAID Study's Approach for the WDR 2001 Contribution

The USAID study started with selected nonincome dimensions of poverty—those related to risk, vulnerability, and assets. The study built on elements originally articulated in Sebstad and others (1995) and later elaborated as a household resource management model based on Chen and Dunn's (1996) household economic portfolio model. Chen and Dunn defined risk as a chance of loss, and vulnerability as the ability of an individual or household to cope with risk. They defined assets broadly to include financial, physical, social, and human. They categorized sources of risk as structural factors, such as natural disasters or economic reform; crises, such as death and sickness within the family and loss of income by household members; and life cycle factors, such as marriage and the education of family members. They distinguished between strategies people use to protect against risk ahead of time and those they use to cope afterward in the face of a shock.[1]

The central thesis of the study was that financial services reduce vulnerability by making "chunks" of money available to clients. This enables them to protect themselves against risk because they can fulfill their needs, take advantage of opportunities, and cope with economic loss from crisis, shocks, and downward pressures (Rutherford 1999). The USAID study hoped to clarify the relationship between assets and vulnerability.

The premise was that the money microfinance provides permits households to accumulate financial, physical, social, and human assets that allow them to withstand shocks. Over time, this accumulation both reflects and contributes to income stability and positive change, enabling poor households to emerge slowly from poverty.

USAID's study addressed four questions:
- Whom do microfinance programs reach?
- What kind of risks do poor clients confront?
- What strategies do clients use to reduce their vulnerability?
- What role do microfinance services play in this process?

The research design was relatively simple, and generated both a substantial body of information and findings that were consistent across the four countries. It involved a mix of qualitative and quantitative data on poor clients and nonclients. In budget terms, each of the field studies fell within the cost limits of a middle-range impact assessment.

All the field studies addressed a core set of questions relating to building, managing, and controlling assets. At the same time, the design's flexibility enabled the field experts to pursue other issues in relation to the impact of microfinance in reducing risk and vulnerability that were relevant to their program or country contexts or their research interests, as in the following examples:
- The 1998 floods in Bangladesh provided a context for looking at how clients use financial services to cope with shocks.
- The Bolivia study honed in on the role of microfinance services in coping with the risk of financial loss.
- In the Philippines, the field team explored the importance of social assets in mitigating risk among CARD Bank clients.
- In Uganda, the investigators examined savings and empowerment.

Preliminary Findings

A ranking of microfinance clients by household wealth indicates a heterogeneous population. Other impact studies have shown that microfinance programs reach a wide range of poor people, whether or not targeting is used (figure 11.1).[2] In the four countries covered by the USAID study, most clients fell within the categories of vulnerable nonpoor and moderately poor. The extreme poor were an important, but not always major, group of clients. Programs that explicitly targeted poorer segments of the population tended to have a greater percentage of the extreme poor. None of the programs reached the destitute. While these categories may suggest discrete categories of income, in reality they reflect a continuum along several dimensions of poverty, of which income is only one.

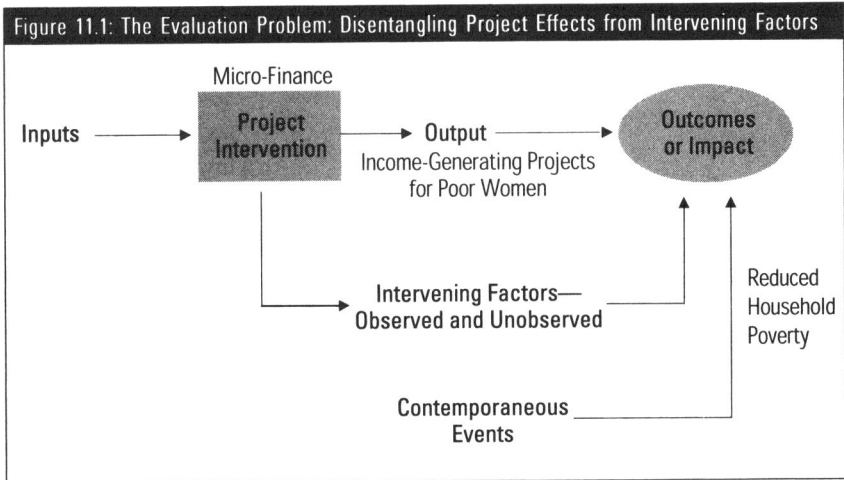

Figure 11.1: The Evaluation Problem: Disentangling Project Effects from Intervening Factors

Microfinance clients at all poverty levels are vulnerable to a wide range of risks, of which illness, death, and loss of a household earner are the most prominent. These unanticipated emergencies can rapidly plunge a household further into poverty, sometimes taking the vulnerable nonpoor from the middle class back into poverty. The vulnerability of low-income women who are heads of households may be compounded by their lack of control and ownership of assets. In Uganda, many women noted the importance of using financial services to save for land and housing and to acquire utensils to protect themselves should their husbands abandon them or take another wife.

Taking a loan is a risk in itself, yet it is one that clients willingly bear. They ascribe a high value to continued participation in a credit program. Failure to repay means default and loss of access to valued financial markets as well as loss of self-esteem, confidence, and social assets. This can be especially true for women, for whom participation in an MFI can be empowering. By increasing their contribution to household income, they reduce their households' vulnerability and strengthen their own decisionmaking role within the household, their control over assets, their involvement in social networks, and in turn their options for dealing with shocks.

Maintaining access to credit is integral to many clients' risk management strategy. By making chunks of money available, microfinance services provide clients and their households ways to protect themselves against risk and to take advantage of opportunities as they present themselves. Not surprisingly, clients go to great lengths to repay, even when confronted with a crisis or shock. Repayment can lead eventually to new loans and to starting on the road to recovery to restock a microenterprise, rebuild a house, or pay school fees.

The preliminary findings of the USAID study highlight a wide range of strategies used by the poor to protect against loss and confront shocks. The study identified three broad strategies that the poor use ahead of time: increasing their income base; building a portfolio mix of short-term, medium-term, and long-term assets; and strengthening their coping mechanisms. Financial, physical, social, and human assets figured heavily in both their before-risk and after-risk management scenarios, as did the creative management of cash and the other resources of the household economic portfolio. Once the poor experience a loss, they make immediate adjustments to their household expenditures, including reducing and modifying their consumption and improving their family budgeting.

Clients are more likely to use microfinance services to protect against risk than to smooth consumption following a shock. In coping with loss, clients give priority to conserving productive assets and thereby maintaining their income-earning potential. Across the countries studied, clients were reluctant to withdraw their children from school, cash in their savings (particularly savings linked to loan size or earmarked for future investments), or sell productive assets. They accessed MFI services only when other strategies were exhausted or had failed.[3]

While clients at all poverty levels use microfinance services to reduce their vulnerability, many of the programs do not readily allow a response to unanticipated shocks. A year-long loan is neither timely nor flexible. Meanwhile the poor, like everyone else, need chunks of money and reserves to manage emergencies. With fewer resources to draw on, the poor can find that a stressful event easily becomes a crisis. Depleting their few assets can mean forfeiting any capacity to generate income. To cope with risk, they need products and services that are flexible enough to allow them to respond to emergencies, timely enough to give them access to cash when they need it, and structured enough to allow repayment in bite-size pieces.

For the extreme poor who have no assets and irregular incomes, the downward pressures are continuous. Continuous demands on their scarce cash indicate the need for accessible savings and insurance as well as credit. The terms of the financial products and services that MFIs offer should correspond to the priority the poor place on stabilizing their income and should allow them to build up assets that will help them protect their fallback positions.

Conclusion

Impact assessment in the area of microfinance is a work in progress. As a result of pressure from both donors and practitioners, recent years have seen a movement toward developing lower-cost, credible, and useful approaches. Academics—some of whom are more resistant than others—need to be convinced because this work calls for methods that require compromise and deviation from conventional approaches.

In developing a lower-cost impact assessment method, the USAID WDR 2001 background study has shown the value of building on previous impact work and of using a simple conceptual framework, a small set of hypotheses, and well-defined, contextually meaningful variables. Qualitative and quantitative research are equally important in this process. The study also shows the benefits of cross-country studies: they can explore similar hypotheses in different places to generate findings that deepen our understanding of the dynamics and contexts of programs. While the findings are not comparable in a strict sense, they do provide a perspective on similarities and differences that can both justify and improve goals of impact assessments. The WDR 2001 study also suggests that methods that emphasize client perspectives and their proactive involvement in assessment are invaluable. Programs can succeed only if their products and services help clients achieve their own economic goals.

Comments: Microfinance Impact Evaluation: Going Down Market

Mohini Malhotra

Monique Cohen referred to CGAP, a microfinance program with 24 donor partners and a secretariat based in the Bank. CGAP invests in selected microfinance institutions (MFIs) worldwide, works on policy issues, and works with donors to come up with a common set of best practices on how to invest their money in microfinance activities. As CGAP's manager until recently, I am not an entirely neutral party. I am a "partner in crime" with Cohen because, under the auspices of the Impact Assessment Methodologies Working Group, CGAP collaborated on and cofunded this initiative. I have four comments to make about her paper.

First, Cohen said that impact assessment in microfinance has largely been biased toward institutions rather than clients. My view is that client-level impact assessments are largely irrelevant for microfinance. The real concern in impact assessments is getting a development bang for the development buck invested. The development dollar has an opportunity cost, which could be invested in other activities that might have higher returns. The only way to know whether an activity is having an impact is through an impact assessment.

But microfinance does not fall into the traditional mold for development projects because, in principle, the good institutions become self-sustaining within three to seven years, are off the public dollar, and no longer require subsidies to provide services. At that point, they pass the acid test: the clients, who are paying full price for services, vote with their feet and come back for more. Poor clients are borrowing, saving, repaying, and returning to purchase additional services at above-market interest rates. That is as honest an impact assessment as I need. The questions we ask at the level of institutional performance are these: Are the clients poor? Are they paying back their loans? Are they coming back for repeat loans—that is, are they voting with their feet? Is the institution expanding its outreach to enlarge its client base? Notice that I am saying "clients," not "beneficiaries," because these individuals are paying a higher cost for capital than any of us.

> Poor clients are borrowing, saving, repaying, and returning to purchase additional services at above-market interest rates. That is as honest an impact assessment as I need.

Another question we ask is whether the institution is moving toward becoming self-sustaining within three to five years. That is, is it earning its revenues from its clients? This is one of the most significant departures from traditional development projects.

Second, as Cohen correctly pointed out in her presentation, donors are still grappling with the issue of justifying the initial use of public sector funds. To justify any initiative in microfinance, the development agencies need to know what they are getting for these funds in the long term. Donor staff still need to make the case for development impact to get the seed capital needed to help MFIs get started. So the initiative Cohen has described (speaking to the intermediate issue) is useful. We need an argument even to make an investment in this field in the first place.

Cohen said that impact evaluations are difficult, costly, and time consuming. They are a huge drain on resources. Could we not just do a limited number of valid, useful, in-depth, methodologically sound evaluations of a few institutions that could then be generalized to the broader industry? Do we have to invest the resources and time to evaluate every little institution or every bit of money invested? I think we can reach a compromise between those who think we need only institutional assessments and those who think we need to do client-level assessments for every dollar invested in microfinance.

Third, in relation to impact evaluation, there is much debate about whether microfinance makes the poor not poor, and few claim that it does. As Cohen said, the strongest indications we have from the a number of impact assessments is that microfinance makes the poor less poor. It reduces their vulnerability by smoothing consumption, and an emerging body of evidence indicates that microfinance helps people move from casual or seasonal employment to self-employment. But nothing indicates that microfinance helps poor people stop being poor.

Fourth, we talk about impact and poverty alleviation, but in microfinance, the unanswered question is really, "Who are the clients?" There is no debate at all about whether the nonpoor benefit from these programs or participate in these institutions. The question is, how poor are the participants, not whether they are poor or not. Under the auspices of CGAP and with the International Food Policy Research Institute, we have recently undertaken a research program to identify the participants. This is a burning question for the donor agencies, whose objective is to reach the poorest.

I contend that we should not put too many resources into impact assessment. The more pressing need is to make services available to the people who have amply demonstrated that they are eager to get them and willing to pay full price for them.

Notes

The views expressed here are the author's own and do not reflect USAID's.

1. USAID used a broad definition of poverty that considered both income and non-income dimensions. Income poverty relates specifically to household income and consumption levels. Vulnerability, while related to income poverty, is more specifically a household's capacity to deal with risk. This, in turn, is a function of a household's asset levels, its mechanisms for coping with crises, and the number of its income earning sources. Income poverty can be reduced at the household level by smoothing income and consumption, by increasing income, and by increasing consumption. Vulnerability can be reduced at the household level by strengthening coping mechanisms, increasing income-earning sources, building household assets, and empowering women.

2. While some microfinance service providers specifically target the poor through a wide range of means test measurement systems, others set loose eligibility criteria and assume that the small loans will serve as targets. The study encompassed institutions that used both approaches.

3. This study encompasses only clients who have remained in a program following a shock. In the absence of information about dropouts, we can merely speculate that clients default on loans only when they have exhausted all their other options, which slows down their recovery from the shock.

References

Chen, Martha Alter, and Elizabeth Dunn. 1996. *Household Economic Portfolio Model.* AIMS Project. Washington, D.C.: Management Systems International.

Cohen, Monique, and Gary Gaile. 1997. *Highlights and Recommendations of the Virtual Meeting of the CGAP Working Group on Impact Assessment Methodologies.* AIMS Project. Washington, D.C.: Management Systems International.

Diagne, Allou. 1997. "Impact of Access to Credit on Poverty and Food Insecurity in Malawi." Paper prepared for the Symposium on Rural Financial Institutions for and with the Poor: Relating Access and Impact to Policy Design, August 10-16, Sacramento, California.

Gaile, Gary, and Jennifer Foster. 1996. *Review of Methodological Approaches to the Study of the Impact of Microenterprise Credit Programs.* AIMS Project. Washington, D.C.: Management Systems International.

Hulme, David. 1997. *Impact Assessment Methodologies for Microfinance: A Review.* Manchester, U.K.: University of Manchester, Institute for Development Policy and Management.

Khandker, Shahidur R. 1998. *Fighting Poverty with Microcredit: Experience in Bangladesh.* Oxford, U.K.: Oxford University Press.

Morduch, Jonathan. 1998. "Does Microfinance Really Help the Poor? New Evidence from Flagship Programs in Bangladesh." Cambridge, MA: Harvard University.

Rhyne, Elizabeth. 1998. "The Yin and Yang of Microfinance: Reaching the Poor and Sustainability." *MicroBanking Bulletin.*

Rutherford, Stuart. 1999. "The Poor and Their Money." Institute for Development Policy and Management, Manchester, UK: University of Manchester.

Sebstad, Jennefer. 1998. *Towards Guidelines for Lower Cost Impact Assessment Methodologies for Microenterprise Programs.* AIMS Project. Washington, D.C.: Management Systems International.

Sebstad, Jennefer, and Cohner. Forthcoming. *World Development Report 2001.*

Sebstad, Jennefer, and others. 1995. *Assessing the Impact of Microenterprise Programs: A Framework for Analysis.* Washington, D.C.: USAID and Management Systems International.

12

Evaluating Targeted Versus Nontargeted Approaches to Poverty Reduction

Joachim von Braun, Mona Bishay, Sohail J. Malik

Joachim von Braun

Most people believe that targeted interventions are good and nontargeted interventions are bad. I am going to argue about that. I am under the impression that the Bank is particularly interested in targeted interventions because they allegedly are efficient and nontargeted ones are inefficient. Targeted interventions are approaches that attempt to directly help the poor improve their economic, physical, or social conditions. Nontargeted interventions are universal provisioning approaches and are costly: everyone gets something.

I would like to make two conceptual remarks. First, increasingly, situations are arising that affect the poor in a way that forces international development cooperation to provide for them universally. I am referring to the growing numbers of refugees. You do not target in refugee camps.

Universal provisioning also involves programs that deliver public goods relevant to the poor. I argue that this is also of increased relevance. In addition, universal provisioning involves creating markets and rights that are particularly relevant for the poor but also apply to everyone, which is an untargeted or fairly untargeted approach.

Second, we all know about means testing based on incomes, indicator targeting based on regions, and self-targeting based on actions that address commodities or jobs that are relevant for the poor. Within self-targeting or within targeting at large there are two concerns—the widely quoted type one and type two errors. A type one error is failure to reach the targeted group. A type two error is reaching excessively into the nontargeted population. My perception is that development agencies are overly concerned with type two error and insufficiently concerned about reaching only a subset of the poor.

Related to all this is the cost of targeting. Targeting costs money, uses administrative funds, incurs the costs of incentive distortions and disutility of the target group, and sometimes implies political costs. The cost components of targeting are complex, but we need to minimize them, and there are tradeoffs between more targeting and less targeting. Thus, I am calling for optimal targeting, not nontargeting versus targeting. Optimal targeting involves reaching the target at the lowest cost and accepting the tradeoffs between targeting and nontargeting.

The following alternative to focusing on targeting versus nontargeting brings me to evaluation. First, evaluate broader-based actions to reduce poverty. Second, within such actions, search continuously for ways to optimally target the poorest and consider the cost of targeting in that context. I will give four examples of broadly evaluating poverty-reducing actions, and in the process, zeroing in on the poorest and thereby achieving optimal targeting. Two examples relate to pro-poor technology development and dissemination and two to pro-poor public goods provisioning.

> Evaluate broader-based actions to reduce poverty.

The first example is the classical case of improved seed varieties. These typically benefit all farmers who grow them, rich or poor, but for some time targeting has focused on seed varieties grown by the poor and the poorer. The Consultative Group for International Agricultural Research (CGIAR), cosponsored by the Bank, is looking into this.

The second, newer, example relates to information and communications technology. My institute, together with Grameen Telecom, has looked into the Grameen groups' use of cellular telephones. How do you target telephones? You can do that the way Grameen did, by not leasing them to just anyone. You lease them selectively to poor women, thereby handing over technology to poorer people. Our evaluation shows that the poor use the telephone as a tool for increasing productivity.

With the first example of public goods provisioning, I argue for broad-based evaluation of public health services. Take nutrition, for instance. If you want to identify those most affected by poor nutrition, you have to weigh all infants and children. Once you have identified those most affected, you then give them special treatment if they fall below cutoff points. Thus, targeted interventions require broad-based approaches first to reach out efficiently to the poorest. An attempt right from the outset to identify only the malnourished and give them special treatment may misinvest in services that are useless to the rest of the population.

My last example is that of labor-intensive public works—that is, self-targeting through low wages to build infrastructure. Evaluating the impact on the poorest by looking only at the workfare side and not at the intersectoral effects of public works programs would be misleading.

The bottom line is not to get carried away by too narrow a focus on targeting. If you do, you lose sight of the larger development impact.

Mona Bishay

I will call my contribution to this panel "Issues in Targeting Rural Poverty: Evaluation Findings."

Since its inception 22 years ago, the International Fund for Agricultural Development (IFAD) has had a mandate to alleviate rural poverty and to target well-defined groups in rural areas. IFAD does this through relatively small and well-defined investment projects in rural areas.

A conceptual distinction must be made up front between a target group and targeting. All IFAD projects have a clearly specified target group and are aimed at one or more specific groups of rural poor. However, targeting involves much more than specifying a target group. It involves a conscious and deliberate effort to discriminate among potential beneficiaries or clients of project interventions in favor of some clearly specified poor group. Hence, targeting must include a clear elaboration of the actions, mechanisms, and institutions required to distinguish between eligible and ineligible beneficiaries.

The preliminary findings of the first phase of an ongoing review of targeting in IFAD projects based on evaluation results in general indicate that agricultural and rural development projects that achieved a positive outcome in poverty reduction succeeded in targeting the poor. However, not all well-targeted interventions produced positive effects on poverty reduction. The review defines success in targeting as good coverage of the intended target groups and low leakage of project benefits to nontargeted groups. Success is defined along an ordinal scale—high, medium, low—in relation to the targeting level stipulated in a project's design.

IFAD uses three categories of the wide variety of mechanisms for targeting the poor, as follows. They can be distinguished according to their basic administrative requirements.

- **Individual assessment mechanisms.** These require applicants to satisfy certain criteria to be eligible. Such criteria can be based on gender, landholdings, asset ownership, per capita income, or the like.
- **Group-based targeting mechanisms.** These grant benefits to all groups that share a common, easily identifiable characteristic. For example, a geographic group criterion can be residence in a given village or particular region. Another criterion might involve all those who cultivate land under a small irrigation scheme or all those who share a

particular economic activity—for example, nomadic pastoralists or artisanal fishermen.
- **Self-targeting mechanisms.** These rely on individual decisions by potential beneficiaries. This is a screening device because participation in a program normally involves time or even monetary costs. The logic is that these costs should be lower for targeted groups so that they will find that applying for the benefits is beneficial.

The main findings of the review reveal that targeting as part of rural poverty alleviation projects occurs both during project design, through the selection of the project site and components, and following project site and component selection. There is a tradeoff in the scope of before-and-after targeting. Better-targeted projects—that is, those that design targeting into their identification and inception stages—often entail less targeting effort during implementation. However, this does not imply that targeting should always be pursued in poverty alleviation projects without considering the costs involved, even when it is deemed essential.

Another finding is that the quality of the design of targeting mechanisms at the project preparation stage is strongly related to the quality of target group specification. A good description of the rural poor includes a good characterization of the variables that are strongly correlated with poverty and a good analysis of the dynamic poverty processes and risk-related behavior, the nature of the poverty traps, and the coping mechanisms of the poor. The review also reveals that the quality of target group specification is strongly related to the quality of the available data. This implies that resource limitations early in the project cycle may limit the proper description of target groups, which is needed for adequate targeting during implementation. This also underscores the importance of building capacities for data collection and poverty analysis in borrowing countries.

One important finding is that all well-targeted projects involve local communities or grassroots institutions or both in defining poverty, identifying the poor, and directing project resources. As a rule, effective targeting is associated with the adoption of participatory approaches during design and implementation. This has been particularly prevalent in recent IFAD-supported projects.

The review's analysis of targeting issues during project implementation also highlights that whenever the project design specifies the methods of targeting well, targeting is likely to be conscious and screening tests are likely to be applied and monitored during implementation. To avoid excessive leakage, any prescribed screening tests for targeting during implementation must be reviewed during the design phase for their correlation with the poverty status of the intended beneficiaries. The review reveals that the main type of project for which screening tests can be applied rigorously is credit projects.

However, extensive and complex targeting mechanisms can be counterproductive. The review identified cases in which complex eligibility criteria to exclude nontargeted groups were difficult to apply, costly, and so time-consuming that project implementation suffered from prolonged delays and target group coverage was limited. There is always a tradeoff between results and complexity.

In short, an examination of the attributes of successfully targeted projects reveals that they are distinguished by a good specification of the target group at project design, an understanding of the dynamic poverty processes before project implementation, the adoption of clear and simple targeting criteria, the specification of an appropriate M&E system for targeting, the participation of beneficiaries and the community during project design and implementation, and the rigorous screening of beneficiaries. The review also found that some leakage of project benefits is unavoidable and that a certain degree of leakage is often necessary to ensure good coverage of the poor.

While IFAD is continuing its efforts in this field, a number of issues that emerged during the review will be investigated further during the follow-up phase. First, proper targeting involves costs during both project design and implementation. At the design stage, targeting requires careful diagnostic studies and surveys to specify the socioeconomic characteristics of the target group and the dynamic processes that determine the causes and consequences of poverty. This requires additional expenditures, and it also increases the length of the project design cycle, which implies further indirect costs. While the evidence suggests that some investment in better data collection and analysis of poverty at the design stage is profitable for IFAD because it facilitates the design of targeting instruments, debate continues about whether large investments in this area are justified in the context of the rapidly changing socioeconomic environment of the poor. Some argue for flexibility in shifting the detailed design of targeting to the implementation stage, when project staff and implementing agencies come into direct and close contact with the poor and their communities. This shift may enable targeting to better reflect and capture the rapidly changing realities of the poor. Empirical evidence and further studies are required to verify whether this is indeed the case.

Second, at the implementation stage the administrative costs of targeting incurred by the implementing agencies consist of implementing the means test and other quantitative criteria to ensure that ineligible groups are excluded from project benefits. Identifying the extent of these administrative costs is not easy, especially if several institutions are involved in the intervention. Verifying the targeting criteria for each prospective applicant to a program can be costly and is often difficult to determine accurately because of cost content and interpretation issues. For instance, if one beneficiary is selected from among three applicants, then the targeting cost per beneficiary is three times as high as the targeting cost per applicant. What is the relevant frame of reference? Ideally, the overall cost of targeting should also take into account the opportunity cost of those participating in the targeted activities. Can these costs be estimated? The required support and strengthening of the agencies responsible for targeting (government or nongovernment) are often large additional costs.

Third, the administrative costs might be lowered through universal targeting practice—namely, administering a program to all those in an easily identified group, such as those living in a particular region with a lower average per capita income than others. However, this runs the risk of omitting all the deserving poor in other regions and providing benefits to the nonpoor in the selected region. All these targeting costs must be compared with the benefits of targeting. As IFAD projects deal mostly with chronic poverty, they almost always have to handle several types of intervention simultaneously that relate to access by the rural poor to productive resources and services. Therefore, the cost efficiency of targeting is much more complicated under such programs than under simple social welfare programs, particularly because the actions often pass through complex institutional structures. Methods of assessing the costs and benefits of targeting for rural poverty alleviation are areas for further investigation.

Fourth, another issue is the depth versus the width of targeting. What are the merits of concentrating support on a smaller number of beneficiaries versus spreading resources thinly over a large number of households? There are obvious tradeoffs. The two approaches should be compared in light of the per capita resources required to overcome the poverty trap; the importance of increasing the ability of the poor to cope with poverty (as a minimalist approach); the need to reach a certain level of real income per capita for sustainable poverty alleviation; and the importance of demonstrating and learning from useful poverty alleviation approaches through well-defined, thorough, and replicable interventions. Here again we need to increase our field-based knowledge.

Finally, the evaluation findings in general indicate that success in making a difference in the life of the poor, particularly in low-potential areas, depends also on how donors' interventions are coordinated. When a number of donors operate in low-potential areas, which is increasingly the case, and when each concentrates on a particular aspect of the constraints and handles it in close coordination with the other donors, they are more likely to have a positive effect on the lives of the poor.

Sohail J. Malik

Von Braun made an important observation when he noted the lack of sufficient evaluative evidence for whether targeted interventions perform better than nontargeted ones for poverty reduction. I will try to address his observation by presenting some comparative evidence from OED's database on the Bank's Program of Targeted Interventions (PTI). Since 1992 the Bank has classified projects as falling under PTI if their designs meet one of two criteria: the project includes a specific mechanism for identifying and reaching the poor, or the participation of the poor in the project significantly exceeds the countrywide incidence of poverty. The Bank has also classified adjustment operations as poverty focused if they meet one of two criteria: the reform program corrects distortions that are detrimental to the poor—for example, labor market distortions—or the program involves a reorientation of public expenditures toward social or infrastructure services for the poor. The data indicate that the percentage of satisfactory projects in terms of outcome is consistently higher for projects that fall under PTI (PTI "Yes" projects) than for projects that do not (PTI "No" projects) in all regions except Eastern Europe and Central Asia, as shown in table 12.1 for the 228 projects for which outcome ratings are available. Table 12.2 presents OED's ratings of sustainability. The percentage of projects with a likely sustainability is almost equal for PTI "Yes" and PTI "No" projects. The major difference is in the uncertain rating, where the percentage of PTI "Yes" projects is higher. Note that the percentage of PTI "No" projects rated as having an unlikely sustainability is significantly higher than the percentage of PTI "Yes" projects.

Table 12.1: OED's Outcome Ratings for PTI Projects				
Region	PTI	Satisfactory	Unsatisfactory	No. of Projects
AFR	Yes	87.9%	12.1%	33
	No	73.5%	26.5%	34
ECA	Yes	81.0%	19.0%	21
	No	84.6%	15.4%	26
EAP	Yes	100.0%		7
	No	85.7%	14.3%	21
LCR	Yes	93.8%	6.3%	16
	No	86.1%	13.9%	36
MNA	Yes	100.0%		5
	No	81.8%	18.2%	11
SAR	Yes	100.0%		7
	No	63.6%	36.4%	11
ALL				228

Table 12.2: OED's Rating Sustainability for PTI Projects

	PTI Yes (n=90)	PTI No (n=145)
Likely	56.7%	56.6%
Unlikely	3.3%	11.0%
Uncertain	38.9%	27.6%
Not Rated	1.1%	4.9%
Total	100.0%	100.1%

Table 12.3: OED's Rating of Institutional Development Impact for PTI Projects

	PTI Yes (n=91)	PTI No (n=145)
Substantial	34.1%	40.7%
Modest	51.6%	43.4%
Negligible	12.1%	12.4%
Not Rated	2.2%	3.4%
Total	100.0%	99.9%

In terms of institutional development impact, however, PTI "Yes" projects do not fare as well in the substantial rating as PTI "No" projects (table 12.3).

Projects targeted at the poor are generally considered riskier and more complex. The OED evaluation database indicates that PTI "Yes" projects

Table 12.4: OED's Rating of Riskiness for PTI Projects

	Yes (n=40)	No (n=68)
High	47.5%	23.5%
Substantial	25.5%	44.1%
Modest	22.5%	29.4%
Negligible	5.0%	4.4%
Total	100.0%	99.9%

Table 12.5: OED's Rating of Complexity for PTI Projects

	Yes (n=40)	No (n=68)
High	27.5%	23.5%
Substantial	40.0%	44.1%
Modest	32.5%	29.4%
Negligible		2.9%
Total	100.0%	100.0%

generally have higher risk but are only marginally more complex than PTI "No" projects (tables 12.4 and 12.5).

In summary, the available data suggest that PTI "Yes" projects have better overall outcomes than PTI no projects and do just as well on sustainability but less well on institutional development impact. While the percentage of high-risk projects among PTI yes projects is significantly higher, the percentage rated as highly complex is only marginally higher. While the numbers are merely indicative, they do give rise to a number of questions. For example, does a project that gets a PTI classification encounter increased supervision and better management of resources that in turn lead to a better outcome? Do better managers generate more PTI projects? Are PTI "Yes" projects typically soft-sector projects with outputs and outcomes that are less tangible and harder to measure, so that the evaluations are biased? These questions all require further research and good data. As more evaluative evidence accumulates, we will be able to state with greater confidence whether targeted interventions do better than nontargeted ones.

Floor Discussion: Evaluating Targeted Versus Nontargeted Approaches to Poverty Reduction

Nurul Alam reminded conferees that, according to the panelists, targeting was neither a panacea nor an unmixed blessing. He called attention to von Braun's statement that one should evaluate broad outcomes and then zero in on specific target groups to see the particular impact; to Bishay's remark that targeting was necessary, but not sufficient; and to Malik's numbers, which were interesting and relevant to the conclusions of the other panelists.

One participant agreed with von Braun that perfect targeting was not a good idea on the basis of cost, but said that the benefits that accrued to the nonpoor might be a price one had to pay to get political support. Political economy was not unimportant.

Another participant said the discussion of microfinance showed clearly that if one gives money to the poor, one should not be concerned about how they spend it.

Interjecting evaluation results on targeting, Cohen said that when the Bank put the Program for Targeted Interventions in place in about 1991, it recognized that PTI was an imperfect tool. It started with the hypothesis that targeted projects would require more complex designs, would demand more from both the Bank and the borrower, to ensure that benefits flowed to poor people, and could be riskier institutionally and financially, which could affect project outcomes overall. If outcomes were slightly less than satisfactory, that would be tolerable. As it happens, the data show that none of this seemed to be true. On average, PTI projects seemed to be slightly riskier, but not necessarily more complex in terms of the number of components. In terms of outcome, PTI projects seemed to do better, but the Bank did not know why. This was a self-selecting sample, so the results could be spurious. Cohen welcomed any insights from the audience.

In response to a question about whether she was referring to two criteria or to an either-or situation, Cohen said she was referring to the latter. Either it had a mechanism or it covered more than the average number of poor people in the country.

Another participant asked for examples. Cohen produced a sectoral breakdown showing that even in agriculture, 58.1 percent of all projects were targeted; in health and nutrition, 66.9 percent were targeted. The criteria were applied on a case-by-case basis after discussions with the Bank's task manager. If a particular project or component with a poverty focus accounted for less than 25 percent of the total project, that project did not get a PTI consultation.

Bishay wanted to know if there was any positive correlation between outcome in terms of targeting and poverty alleviation. Malik said that was a

---

M. Nurul Alam of the United Nations Development Program chaired the discussion.

wider question, and so was whether this increased focus on poverty alleviation led to better indicators and monitoring. These were long-term policy research issues that needed to be looked at on an ongoing basis.

A member of the audience asked Bishay if IFAD was doing a similar consultation. Bishay replied that all IFAD projects were targeted – IFAD's mandate was to design projects targeted toward a specific part of the rural population. One particularly important fringe benefit of targeting was that if the design included good diagnostic studies or surveys of the socioeconomic characteristics of the target group, the poverty line, and the constraints on poverty, these contributed valuable baseline data for monitoring and evaluation.

She added that the projects IFAD designed had a certain amount of leakage. IFAD never assumed that leakage would be zero. In more recent projects, targeting was done with the communities, so IFAD realized some benefits would trickle down to the elite, by definition. IFAD could not operate on the basis of an exclusion mechanism. Bishay reminded the participants of Mensah's remark in the opening panel that leakage could have a direct multiplier effect if used properly—if not used for conspicuous consumption, for example.

Bishay emphasized that the cost of targeting during implementation was higher than during design, because IFAD relied more and more on NGOs and on some government departments to implementing targeting mechanisms. Unless these agencies had the capacity, they could not target properly, so IFAD had invested a good deal in building the capacity of the agencies involved in targeting. Whether this investment was justifiable was a question IFAD was now trying to answer.

One participant commented on how targeted aid sometimes benefited a nontargeted group. He used the example of a school lunch program in a community with skewed income distribution. It was leakage if the children were fed more than they needed at school. Leakage depended on the structure and distribution of poverty, its seasonality, and the instruments of poverty under consideration. He also asked how one assessed the cost of institutions. How could the benefits of microfinance credit associations for building rural health services or rural insurance schemes be calculated when they start playing an agent role? Institutions designed for narrow targeting do not produce major effects.

Another participant expanded on this theme, saying he was not convinced that targeted projects were always the most desirable. The immediate benefits of a nontargeted irrigation project might go to medium-income farmers, for example. Output would increase, leading to a demand for landless workers, who would then get wages, but a greater output of food might pull prices down. As a poverty alleviation mechanism, this might ultimately be more important to the poor than a well-targeted scheme in which the immediate benefits went to the poor. He felt evaluators should think more in terms of a general equilibrium framework and indirect effects.

Bishay replied that targeting was difficult where assets were skewed in favor of a particular minority. In an irrigation scheme, in particular, if the intervention were not targeted, either the large landowners or those at the front end of the irrigation line would benefit more.

Malik concluded by saying that part of the reason the discussion had shifted to whether targeting was good or bad was the unclear basic definition of what the conferees were aiming to reduce, the specific design, and intertemporal aspects.

Social Funds and Safety Nets

13

What Are Social Funds Really Telling Us?

Judith Tendler

This presentation is based on research I carried out in northeastern Brazil, often together with my graduate students, and on a careful reading of the vast evaluation literature on social funds produced by the donor community and others. In this presentation, I question the magnitude of resources being allocated to social funds and the enthusiasm for social funds today on the part of the donor community. These questions were raised both by the field research and the donor evaluations.

Why are social funds important? Why are they interesting? As many of you know, the World Bank, the Inter-American Development Bank (IADB), and the European donors spent close to US$5 billion on social funds between the late 1980s and the mid-1990s, and more of these funds have emerged since the recent Asian economic and financial crisis. Social funds are alive and well.

Donors have lauded social funds for making two important contributions to development. First, as part of the arsenal of safety net instruments, they reduce poverty by creating employment and by extending services and public works projects to poor communities. The funds often constitute part of the safety net of a larger structural adjustment package. Second, social funds are considered an exciting and interesting new model of service delivery that works better than traditional government because it is more demand driven and decentralized.

Moreover, social funds present an empirical window on the workings of a set of issues that are currently of great interest to the development community. These include government reform in developing countries, decentralization, participation, demand-driven approaches, and the contracting out of services at the local level (or what could be called partial privatization). In a certain sense, social funds combine all these elements in different degrees.

My skepticism about social funds is based on two somewhat different bodies of evidence. One, donors themselves and some outsiders have recently issued a handful of studies that suggest that social funds have a fairly insignificant effect on poverty and employment, particularly in comparison with other kinds of interventions. The other body of evidence concerns social funds as a service delivery model. I have focused more attention on this issue because I have been interested for many years in how to improve government and in what we can learn from experiences in building sustained institutional capacity. This body of evidence is actually quite mixed on whether social funds really represent a sustainable improvement on service delivery by government.

I conclude from my own research project and the reading of this vast evaluation literature that social funds, while accomplishing some things, have as many flaws as traditional government. Some shortcomings of social funds, also noted in donor evaluations, are surprisingly similar to those of traditional government. Finally, the recommendations of the donor evaluations to resolve these problems would make social funds more like traditional government. Unfortunately, this would compromise the very traits that are considered to be the strengths of the social fund model.

What are these strengths? The proclaimed strengths of social funds can be seen as the flip side of the problems that afflict traditional government. Traditional government is commonly portrayed as overcentralized, overcostly, overbureaucratized, rigid, unresponsive, and supply driven, and characterized by the worst features of an unregulated monopoly: failure to reach the poor, poor-quality services, and high unit costs and overhead. Social funds, in contrast, are said to deliver numerous small infrastructure projects and service projects with faster rates of disbursement and project completion. They have lower unit costs, lower overhead, and leaner organizations without the excessive staff that tends to characterize traditional governments. They also consult with project beneficiaries.

How are social funds able to do this? In many cases, they are autonomous from government and hence disentangled from bureaucracy. In this sense, social funds are like parastatals and state enterprises, many of which were created in the 1960s with donor encouragement and financing. Like the parastatals, the social funds are often free from government regulations, particularly with respect to procurement and civil service regulations, salary determination, and employee hiring and firing. Social funds often pay higher salaries and hence attract better people. Another difference is that the management and staff of many social funds often come from private firms or NGOs—that is, from outside the public sector.

Many, though not all, social funds are said to be demand driven and participatory. This means that communities get to choose whether they want a well, a school, or an irrigation project. This kind of user choice introduces a new dynamic that leads to ownership by beneficiaries and other local actors and therefore to a concern about operation and maintenance, better cost recovery, and, ultimately, sustainability. The benefits of greater user choice are key to today's thinking about the desirability of decentralization, given that the problem of ownership and sustainability seriously affects the investments and services traditional government provides.

Finally, social funds represent an important experiment in contracting out to private actors part of what government usually does itself. This reduces the problems and inefficiencies of government as a faraway monopoly provider. The provider is closer to the user and is more accessible and more vulnerable to the dissatisfactions of the user. In addition, healthy competition among providers is introduced. All this, it is presumed, will improve quality and yield a customized and more appropriate result, drawing on local knowledge and circumstances.

I will now compare the view of social funds presented in the previous paragraphs with findings from field research.[1]

First, as is reflected in donor evaluations of other social funds, many of the funds are erroneously described as participatory and demand driven. When communities are asked how they decided to choose a well, for example, rather than a school or an electrification hookup, it often turns out that the community did not make the decision and that no consensual or collective process was used. Other actors, instead, made or induced the decision. These actors include: social fund staff, as in the old model; local politicians; and interesting new private sector actors on whom we have less research—private project design firms, equipment suppliers, and building contractors. Therefore, in a sense, what was new about these situations was not that they were demand driven. They were still supply driven, but the supply-driving cast of characters was enlarged to include the private sector, in addition to the more familiar government staff and politicians. Another finding, which is rather worrisome, is that the donor evaluations of social funds tend uniformly to give social funds low grades on sustainability, ownership, and maintenance and support of other operational costs. The same serious problem afflicts traditional government programs.

In this study, we discerned how communities decided on the use for the funds, particularly with respect to the new private actors, because less is known about this. When we went into the communities and asked them how they decided, their answers often had to do with firms. Project design firms, equipment contractors, or building contractors went to them and said, for example, "I can get you a well," depending on the specialization of the particular firm. The communities did not know that they had other choices. The same process also took place with politicians, something that is more familiar to us.

These firms, in turn, standardized the project design because it allowed them to do more projects more quickly. Therefore, their designs were not particularly tailored to local conditions. This was less problematic for projects that could be standardized, like school construction, than for those requiring local knowledge and adaptation, like wells.

The firms also wanted to minimize the number of visits they made to a community to minimize costs, salaries, vehicle operating costs, and per diems. Sometimes the firms managed not to go to the community at all to save travel costs and time, and simply met with the community leader or another local powerholder when that person came to town. These circumstances obviously were not conducive to any participatory or other inclusive demand-making process. In addition, and for the same reasons, the projects tended to be spatially clustered in the vicinity of firms' offices, because this also minimized the firms' travel time. Finally, the set of firms working in the project area divided the market among themselves, acting as local spatial monopolies.

One of the interesting results of this process was that communities often said that they had "chosen" a power hookup or a well. They did not choose these, though, because they wanted or thought that they needed them the most; rather, they thought they had the highest probability of getting it, among the possible choices, because that is what that particular firm or politician was offering or specialized in. They therefore signed on for a well, even though what they really wanted was a school, because they perceived their chance of actually getting the well as greater.

Thus, the market mechanism in terms of this partial privatization was actually working properly in the sense of causing firms to reach for economies of scale, to standardize, and to reduce costs. In addition, more decentralized decisionmaking was taking place. However, both worked, contrary to expectations, to limit choice and information and to ration the demand for these projects in undesirable ways. So what we had thought was demand driven turned out to be supply driven, like traditional government services, albeit with a different cast of characters, private sector and local.

Social funds, then, often operate in ways that are different from how they are portrayed. This makes it difficult to learn lessons from the experience, not only about the problems or the failures but, more importantly, about the successes and what explains them.

Two examples are the Chilean Fund and the Bolivian Fund. The Chilean FOSIS (Fonds de Solidaridad e Inversión Social) is often cited as one of the star social funds. Yet, it is more different from than similar to most social funds. It is not autonomous, but integrated with line ministries. It observes procurement regulations and civil service regulations rather than circumventing them. The salaries are not higher than government salaries. Until recently the fund did not operate in a participatory manner. This sounds more like traditional government than the popular image of a social fund.

The Bolivian social fund, a second example of a star fund, is actually quite centralized as an agency. It was also not participatory until recently, when it was induced to become so by the larger political environment that produced the law on popular participation.

In conclusion, the current portrayals of social funds are making it difficult to understand which ones are working, which ones are not, and why. They overestimate the strength of the social fund as an institutional model, and they may be deluding us into thinking that they make reform easier. Let us look at the experiences of the successful funds or the successful pieces of social funds with a more open mind. Similarly, the attention and resources devoted to social funds are distracting attention from the opportunities for reform and for reform experiments within governments and are therefore depriving them of support.

Note

1. Some of these findings are drawn, in part, from an excellent case study (and master's thesis) by one of my graduate students, Rodrigo Serrano. See also Tendler and Serrano (forthcoming) for the detailed argument and evidence on which this short presentation is based.

References

Tendler, J., and R. Serrano. Forthcoming. *The Rise of Social Funds: What Are They a Model of?* New York: UNDP.

Comments: What Are Social Funds Really Telling Us?

Soniya Carvalho

Judith Tendler's work is provocative and timely. Current estimates of upcoming social fund projects show that the Bank will have committed almost the same amount of lending to social funds during the next five years as in the entire preceding decade. Tendler's paper suggests that we pull in the reins and question again some of the basic premises on which this approach is based. This paper's energy is invigorating and uncommonly fresh.

Tendler's single most important contribution is to document the complexities of consumer choice. The one who expresses a choice may not be the one who actually makes that choice, and what is chosen may often reflect what one thinks one is likely to get rather than what one really wants and is willing to pay for.

Tendler questions a number of assumptions about providing service through social funds—for example, that inviting project proposals locally gives beneficiaries more voice in designing them and greater community ownership. These assumptions were not realized in the Brazilian projects reviewed because of several intervening factors and actors, including private contractors and mayors with their own preferences and predicaments, perpetrators of information distortion, and creators of new kinds of information asymmetries.

Tendler's questioning of these assumptions leads me to mention an evaluation of alternative service delivery instruments that we are undertaking in OED with a new evaluative technique called theory-based evaluation. Carol Weiss of Harvard, the architect of this evaluation technique, is advising on its practical application. The idea in theory-based evaluation is that the theoretical assumptions underlying an intervention can be expressed in terms of a phased sequence of events: causes and effects, a program theory, and a chain of causal linkages—for example, that teacher training leads to better teaching by teachers, which in turn leads to students absorbing more learning, which in turn improves students' learning achievement. Investigators collect data to examine how well each predicted event in the sequence is realized. If the sequence has broken down somewhere along the way, the evaluation can tell where and when, and what the final impact is likely to be. For example, the assumption that better teaching leads to students absorbing more learning may break down if poor health interferes with the students' ability to absorb the messages being transmitted, even if improved teaching ensures the effective transmission of the messages.

In our evaluation of alternative service delivery instruments, the assumptions are as follows: first, that households hear about the offer of funds, that the terms of the offer are conveyed to the households without bias, that the households are able to organize themselves into a cohesive group, and that the group resolves any internal conflicts that arise and reaches a consensus on the common use of funds. We assume that the poor are included in the group and have a say in the group's decisionmaking, that the group has full information about the options and is aware of the operations and maintenance implications of its choice, and that the group is capable of preparing a project proposal in the required format.

We assume further that, if the group cannot prepare the proposal, intermediary agencies can help the group and can act in its best interests, that the group agrees on a proposal without alienating the group's members, that the proposal reaches the right authority on time, that the authority chooses the most viable proposal, and that it releases funds to the group efficiently. Finally, we assume that the group makes its share of counterpart funds available; that public and private groups are adequately coordinated for effective implementation, operations, and maintenance; that the group finally uses the service, feels its ownership, and operates and maintains the service; and that this ultimately leads to improved living conditions.

It is not difficult to see how many slips could occur between the two endpoints. The causal linkages are by no means automatic and could break down for a variety of reasons, depending on the socioeconomic and institutional environments and the behavioral responses of those involved.

Tendler's paper makes a valuable contribution by identifying the leap of faith we often make in assuming that our program assumptions will be borne out.

I would suggest a slightly different view from Tendler's characterization of programs as either demand driven or supply driven. Tendler's paper characterizes social funds as demand driven and traditional government projects as supply driven. This classification is perhaps misleading and an unnecessary polarization. That social funds invite beneficiaries to make project proposals does not make them demand driven. Demand is the quantity of goods and services that consumers want at a given price.

In the tradition of the water supply and sanitation sector, a project is driven by demand to the extent that it offers clients a range of options to choose from, provides information to help them make an informed choice, and requires evidence of the clients' commitment and interest through cash or in-kind contributions as a condition of project approval and release of funds. Not all social funds incorporate these features in their design, and practice is often very different from theory.

Also, the offer of resources in social funds includes the imposition of supply-side constraints. Eligibility criteria, targeting mechanisms, appraisal criteria, and project menus all constrain free choice. Moreover, government projects may also offer beneficiaries choice and may also require cost sharing.

In other words, the so-called demand-driven programs are not purely demand driven, and the same is true on the supply side. In most cases, effective service delivery must combine elements of both demand and supply in varying proportions and intensities, depending on the country and sector and on the nature and scale of the services being provided. It is the particular balance between demand and supply that is critical. The key is to identify the right combination of demand and supply for specific contexts. The next step is to develop solutions. In my opinion, these solutions will inevitably involve mixing and matching demand and supply rather than requiring either-or decisions—in other words, various shades of gray rather than stark black or bold white.

Floor Discussion: What Are Social Funds Really Telling Us?

A conferee asked Tendler if she could name one thing social funds did especially well.[2] Tendler replied that social funds are often credited with getting the money out quickly. If this were true, it would indeed be an accomplishment. But social fund programs are run under heavy pressure and getting the money out is the easy part; the hard part is getting it back. Her concern was sustainability. If social funds do one thing especially well, it may be that they challenge traditional ministries, saying in effect, "Look, this can be done, and you are not doing it, so we did it." In Tendler's opinion, government reform often happens this way, with some upstart challenging traditional agencies, although she could find little verification of this effect in the economic literature.

Patrick Donkor, a participant from Ghana, complimented Tendler for describing the range of actors, especially those on the ground, and for opening the way for participants not involved in traditional supply-driven service delivery who might be able to affect decisionmaking.

Within the various shades of gray, Donkor continued, a great deal of learning is going on. Ghana, for example, tends toward a blend of sector agencies and government institutions participating quite actively in developing projects. Social funds are often started in collaboration with those agencies, so some institutional links are already in place. Distance comes at the time of implementation.

Finally, Donkor said that in Ghana in the past four or five years much of the activity with social funds had involved trying to build demand responsiveness in the community. One could not expect this to happen instantly. For communities that had been marginalized for many years, even the capacity to receive messages was an important milestone. In Ghana, more than 5,000 user groups had formed around water projects alone, and those communities were now capable of making choices about other sectors, not just water.

In response to another question, Tendler said that based on evaluations, she could not say projects had succeeded because of more or less integration with the central government. What bothered her about social funds, however, was that they tended to start from scratch and then to try to make a clean sweep. They often disregarded the pockets of real capacity in government and the people who were extremely dedicated or had a clear idea of how to bring about reform but were unsupported by their superiors and by the system because of political interference. In other words, what disturbed Tendler about social funds was not just what they did, but what they did not do. They did not start by identifying these pockets and saying, "We want to make the system work better. What are your ideas about that?" What social

---

Soniya Carvalho of the World Bank's Operations Evaluation Department facilitated the discussion.

funds were trying to achieve would be more sustainable if they worked with people who were already working within a sustained government system.

Tendler found it interesting that the World Bank literature for dealing with some of these problems with social funds was full of recommendations for more monitoring, more evaluation, more staff presence in the countryside, and more training and participation. If all those recommendations were acted upon, social funds would become more like traditional government agencies instead of remaining lean and mean, with low unit costs. One reason people prefer to start from scratch is that working with pockets of government is messy. It is not neat and clean, or new and exciting, like setting up something new.

Other participants wondered if Tendler's work allowed her to generalize about whether the initial objectives of social funds had been fulfilled after they had changed in response to structural adjustment. They also wondered if Tendler had examined the differences between the sustainability of social funds and the sustainability of the projects initiated by the social funds. Had social funds done more harm than good? At what point did projects supported for a few years by social funds cease working, necessitating a return to government-dominated and more supply-driven approaches? Was Tendler recommending still trying to work with governments? One participant found that generalization tempting, but felt one had to be cautious about extrapolating anecdotal evidence from one fund across all funds or pushing analysis too far.

Tendler responded that her conclusions were based not only on her own field work in northeastern Brazil. She had read a number of donor evaluations to see how her findings fit into the larger picture. Evaluations of several funds showed the importance of social funds in places outside of Latin America. And a paper by Andrea Cornia provided a much more damning critique of social funds than anything Tendler had written. The data Cornia worked with showed that social expenditures in countries with social funds had not returned to precrisis levels. Many poverty problems came about because countries failed to spend on safety nets and other poverty-reducing measures, failed to extend social security to the countryside, and failed to extend unemployment insurance to the informal sector. Any government concerned about reducing poverty should start paying attention to those issues.

Carvalho wrapped up the session with three comments. First, the evidence on cost recovery indicated that poor people were willing to pay for services of good quality. In many countries poor people were already paying three or four times the market price of water to private vendors, for example. If a social fund were to provide them with clean water at the market price, poor people would be willing to pay for it.

Second, there was some evidence that social funds often missed the very poor, who might not even hear about social funds being offered. And if they did hear about the funds despite their isolation in the mountains in a remote part of their country, they might not be articulate enough to prepare a project proposal. So social funds often missed the poorest groups. If a social fund could reach a truly poor area, there would be ways to work out waivers or exemptions for certain people, but the fund would have to be carefully and strictly enforced and administered, which could raise the program's administrative costs.

Third, many countries had undertaken two-stage targeting. Peru, for example, had first identified poor areas and then, within the poor areas, had identified the poor people willing to pay, which was the strongest indication they wanted a service. Services were then targeted to the poor people willing to pay. Such two-stage targeting had worked quite well to reach groups who were genuinely interested in a service. It also addressed the problem of contractors and other intermediaries biasing demand.

14

Economic Crises and Social Protection for the Poor: The Latin American Experience

Nora Lustig and Arianna Legovini

Macroeconomic crises have recurred in Latin America and the Caribbean for the past twenty years. In the 1980s, Mexico's debt crisis spread throughout the region on the back of trade shocks and weak public finances. In 1995 Mexico's liquidity crisis spread to Argentina. In 1998 and 1999 contagion from the Asian and Russian crises and low commodity prices on the back of weak public finances and financial sectors hit Brazil, Ecuador, and Venezuela particularly hard. In the 1980s the crises were accompanied by sharp declines in living standards. The impact of the fall in real incomes (40 percent in Argentina, 11 percent in Brazil, and 15 percent in Chile) and of rising unemployment on the incidence and severity of poverty (doubling in Argentina and rising perhaps as much as 20 percent in Brazil and 30 percent in Mexico) is well recorded. Similarly, in the 1990s unemployment rose (to around 18 percent in Argentina and 9 percent in Brazil) and so did poverty (by 50 percent in Argentina). In addition to the effect that economic crises have on current living conditions, they may have long-term consequences for economic growth. Falling incomes affect households' decisions about their investment in children's schooling, health, and nutrition, which in turn affect their capacity to generate future income.

Downturns in income can undoubtedly have a more devastating effect on individuals who live below or close to subsistence level. In addition, evidence suggests that a recessionary period associated with a crisis may be more detrimental to social indicators than an equivalent period of growth. Clearly, the best way to avoid the social costs associated with macroeconomic crises is to prevent them by means of prudent macroeconomic policy and sound financial systems. Countries with low fiscal deficits and coherent monetary and exchange rate policies are less likely to face macroeconomic crises and are more likely to withstand the effects of volatile capital flows and contagion. Similarly, countries with a financially strong banking sector and adequate prudential regulation are less likely to face financial debacles such as the ones witnessed in East Asia, Latin America, and Russia in the 1990s. Even if countries do everything right, adverse shocks from volatility in capital markets or sharp turns in commodity prices are likely. Although macroeconomic management and global financial systems are key to reducing the potential social costs of economic crises, specific responses to them can provide more sensitive or less sensitive protection for the poor.

The Social Costs of Economic Crises in the 1980s

Economic indicators have been tracked in detail for Mexico in the 1980s (Lustig 1998). The debt crisis led to a sharp fall in GDP in 1983 from which Mexico did not really recover until after 1988. From 1983 to 1988, real wages cumulatively fell by between 36 percent and 46 percent, depending on the sector, and minimum wages fell by 49 percent. Social spending fell by 33.1 percent, with spending on health falling by 23.3 percent and spending on education by 29.6 percent. A targeted food stamp program replaced general food subsidies, and targeted programs suffered from important exclusions. Spending on targeted programs was cut by more than the total in noninterest spending. General subsidies on corn derivatives, beans, rice, noodles, cooking oil, and eggs were justified from an equity point of view. The number of free textbooks available per student declined, and programs targeted to the extreme poor in rural areas were cut disproportionately, with some programs eliminated.

Mexico's poor may have suffered a long-term impact on their capabilities, as social indicators show for the 1980s. The number of infants suffering from slow fetal growth and malnutrition increased both in absolute terms and in proportion to total diseases; infant and preschool mortality increased after years of decline; the percentage of children entering primary school as a ratio of the total number of children in the relevant age cohort declined; dropout rates from primary school declined for urban children but rose by 40 percent in rural zones; and the proportion of graduates at each school level who entered the subsequent level declined, particularly after junior high and high school.

Macroeconomic crises also hit households hard in other countries in and outside the region in the 1980s. In Argentina real wages fell by close to 40 percent and poverty doubled. In Chile real wages contracted by about 15 percent, and open unemployment shot up by 9 percentage points within a year. In Brazil real wages fell by 11 percent and poverty rose between 10 and 20 percent. Social spending was widely cut back. Social indicators such as infant mortality rates and average years of schooling continued to improve in Latin America but more slowly than during the previous decade. In Chile the data on low birthweight infants and undernourished children followed the trends in economic conditions after systematic improvement in the 1970s. In Venezuela the literacy rate for people aged 15 to 19 fell in the 1980s. These trends imply that investment in human capital also probably became more skewed, making the observed increase in inequality more entrenched. No wonder this period became known as the "lost decade."

Measured by headcount, moderate poverty in Mexico rose in the 1980s from 28.5 to 32.6 percent, and extreme poverty rose from 13.9 to 17.1 percent, while inequality measured by the Gini coefficient rose from 0.47 to 0.53. Poverty and inequality also increased in Brazil, Guatemala, Panama, and Venezuela and in the urban areas of Argentina, Bolivia, Chile, Honduras, and Peru. Similarly, poverty and inequality rose sharply in urban Argentina during the 1995 crisis and in Mexico nationally. In the 1995-96 episode, real wages in Mexico fell by more than 30 percent, and in Argentina unemployment increased by 6 percentage points and remained at around 18 percent for more than two years. Although the poorest quintile of the population was not always hurt disproportionately, their average income fell. The income downturns had a more devastating impact on those living close to subsistence, while in country after country hit by the crisis, the income share of the top 10 percent increased, sometimes substantially (Lustig 1995).

Because of the increase in inequality during the 1980s, the poor suffered more from the impact of the economic contraction in that decade than they had benefited from the growth of the 1970s. For example, estimates indicate that a 1 percent decline in per capita GDP in a recession eliminated the gains in urban and rural poverty reduction achieved by, respectively, 3.7 percent and 2 percent growth in per capita GDP in the 1970s (De Janvry and Sadoulet 1999). Recession has a particularly strong ratchet effect because subsequent growth is unable to compensate for the higher level of inequality recession generates.

The role of the international community left much to be desired in the 1980s and 1990s. Labor and capital were treated asymmetrically. Whereas capital could always find a safe-haven country, labor could not freely enter other countries in search of higher living standards. The international financial institutions sided with creditors in debt management strategy, at least until the Brady Plan was announced in 1989. The multilateral financial institutions did not press or persuade countries to protect or implement safety net programs.

The Relationship Between the Social Costs of Economic Crises and Policy Choices

Are increases in poverty and inequality and in the deterioration of social indicators the result of economic crisis or of the policies that governments implement afterward? The answer has at least three dimensions: (a) whether the macroeconomic policy mix is harmful to the poor, (b) whether the specific measures introduced to achieve fiscal targets are biased against the poor, and (c) whether the government introduces new programs or uses existing programs as safety nets to protect the poor from the impact of the adjustment process.

The Macroeconomic Policy Mix

In any typical macroeconomic crisis, capital inflows fall sharply, the interest rate on external and internal debt increases, and international reserves are depleted. Recent macroeconomic crises have also been accompanied by banking crises. To the extent that a country must rely on foreign savings to grow, the cutback in capital inflows translates into a fall in GDP or, at best, a fall in GDP growth. Likewise, the disruption of the financial system and high interest rates curtail economic activity. Higher interest rates on public debt also imply that the government must increase its primary surplus, whether or not its fiscal stance before the crisis was adequate. This fiscal retrenchment is recessionary. Finally, the depletion of international reserves leads to a currency devaluation that can be contractionary in the short run, depending on the amount of external financing available from the International Monetary Fund (IMF), the development banks, and bilateral and other such public sources.

In the 1980s, when Latin American and Caribbean countries faced large fiscal imbalances and sharp exchange rate misalignments, they typically reduced the government deficit and devalued domestic currency. Some argue that relying on exchange rate adjustment to restore balance in the current account and to build up international reserves erodes confidence in private capital markets. In the 1990s, when fiscal imbalances were pervasive no longer and the countries were highly integrated with international financial markets, the countries relied more widely on short-term interest rate spikes to restore balance in the macroeconomic account. Some argue that interest rate spikes impose a heavy toll on the domestic banking system and can cause bankruptcies and wipe out distressed debtors, but may be the only way to attract private capital. In times of severe crisis, governments may also consider whether to default on their obligations or, less drastically, impose a unilateral moratorium; to introduce capital and exchange controls; or to do both. While mainstream economists and international financial institutions agree that such measures are inadvisable because they may cause irreversible damage to a country's reputation, they are less critical of some forms of such capital controls as a tax on short-term capital inflows introduced during good times. The consequences of introducing capital and exchange controls in Malaysia will tell us more. Which response is the right response depends on the country's circumstances.

Clear-cut answers as to how alternative macroeconomic policy combinations affect growth and income distribution are desirable, but unavailable. Clearly, the macroeconomic policy mix will involve tradeoffs. One tradeoff is that some policy combinations might result in a sharp contraction of GDP in the short run followed by quick recovery, while other policy combinations might result in a gradual emergence from a crisis. Another tradeoff is distributive. Some poor may be hurt by currency devaluations, high interest rates, or reductions in the fiscal deficit while others may not. Devaluation may affect the urban poor differently than the rural poor, for example. Such tradeoffs make designing poverty-sensitive macroeconomic policies difficult. The difficulty is compounded by how little we know about the best analytical tool for assessing these tradeoffs and their order of magnitude for specific countries.

Fiscal Adjustment

How governments raise revenues and cut public (nondebt) spending has important implications for who bears the burden of the adjustment process and whether the poor are protected. While public spending is characteristically distributed unequally before a crisis, concern is widespread that spending on primary education and health care and, in particular, on programs targeted to the poor is not protected from fiscal retrenchment. This is because the fiscal adjustment has to be undertaken quickly and under immense political pressure from the groups who have access to the government's budget. Proportional cuts are easier to implement from both a technical and political economy point of view. Some perceive that fiscal adjustment in a crisis bails out the rich (externally or internally) rather than protecting the poor from asset losses.

Safety Nets

Latin American governments have responded to the social costs of economic crises with food assistance programs, unemployment insurance, social funds, health care coverage for the unemployed, scholarships for children, training and retraining programs, and workfare programs. However, policymakers too often devote their energy only to restoring macroeconomic stability and implementing structural reform. Even when the response is designed to cushion the social costs of economic adjustment measures, the beneficiaries are not necessarily those most affected by the crises. In Mexico and elsewhere, general subsidies were cut without introducing effectively targeted alternatives. Core education and health services were supported poorly in Latin America in the 1980s, as evidenced by the irreversible losses in human investment mentioned above. Argentina waited until 1997 to introduce an emergency employment program despite the sharp rise in unemployment during previous years and despite the fact that the existing severance payment and small-scale unemployment insurance schemes were not safety nets for the unemployed poor. Evidence suggests that implementing programs before crises hit is better for protecting the target population than instituting ad hoc emergency measures (Lustig and Walton 1998).

At present, most Latin American and Caribbean social investment funds are more effective at building small-scale social infrastructure than at creating employment opportunities for those hurt by emergencies. Most countries in the region lack effective private or public insurance markets that could protect the poor from output, employment, and price risks associated with systemic shocks. A recurring problem is that responses have to rely on improvisation or on programs designed for purposes and beneficiaries other than those affected by crises. Emergency responses to emergency situations often lack the time for technical analyses to clarify the socioeconomic profile of the most vulnerable groups and to assess the cost effectiveness of different social protection options.

The 1980s showed that programs that were not always expensive and that benefited the poor were sometimes eliminated or cut in the same proportion as other budget items. With the possible exception of Chile, Latin American countries did not have mechanisms to protect the poor from the impact of fiscal adjustment policies. The international financial institutions, including IMF, IADB, and the Bank, devoted most of their energy to stabilization and to the elimination of price distortions rather than to careful assessment of how fiscal cuts would affect the poor and to the introduction of adequate safety nets. The notion of protecting pro-poor programs, in real terms, was introduced in the fiscal adjustments in Argentina and Mexico in 1995. More recently, the Venezuelan government has agreed to undo a budget cut on programs targeted to the poor as a result of the Bank's involvement. In recent loans for Argentina, Bolivia, and Brazil, the governments have agreed on real fiscal targets for several safety net programs. Also, the implementation of consumption- or income-smoothing safety nets is now taken more seriously. The employment programs *Trabajar* ("Work") in Argentina and *Programa de Empleo Temporal* ("Temporary Employment Program") in Mexico are examples of this. Evidence suggests that the cost of safety nets should be manageable even under more severe fiscal constraints. Improvisation, however, is still common, and budgets to introduce countercyclical components do not always exist.

Developing Adequate Responses

Social Monitoring and Early Response

Governments should put into place social monitoring and early response systems to provide themselves and donors with rapid, real-time qualitative information on crisis-related conditions and on the operations of social safety net programs in urban and rural areas. This was recently done in Indonesia. The system could enable community monitoring of crisis response programs, disseminate information about the design and intended operation of safety net programs, and establish specific mechanisms for query and feedback. It would give countries the capacity to make rapid field assessments of danger signals and to mobilize research on specific social crisis issues, such as household coping mechanisms, migration and support networks, and gender differences. Finally, such a unit could use a range of qualitative techniques (rapid appraisals, participatory rural appraisals, key informant interviews, and focus groups) to produce quick turnaround reports.

Assessing the Impact of Macroeconomic Policy

To design macroeconomic policies that cause less harm to the poor, governments must determine how their different fiscal and monetary choices and exchange rate adjustments affect different groups, especially with regard to labor demand, prices, and the value of assets. They should identify the tradeoffs between external and internal financial workouts, between external and internal confidence, and between efficiency and the present and future fiscal burden. They should determine precisely how structural reforms—trade liberalization, price reforms, privatization, opening to foreign investment, and labor market reforms—affect different groups in the short and medium term and should systematically evaluate the costs and benefits of alternative sequences. Their analysis should be based on at least a qualitative assessment of the overall distributional effects of a crisis or, alternatively, the allocation of the costs of a shock and the required adjustments in relation to changes in labor demand, prices, and the value of assets. CGE macro or micro models of adjustment and transition are useful but generally highly sensitive to parameters. Until satisfactory tools are available, the effects of economywide developments, especially labor demand and relative price changes, can be linked to the profile of key socioeconomic groups, drawing on existing poverty profiles and survey information (see Kanbur 1986). There will be no substitute for tracking outcomes for different groups.

Designing Poverty-Sensitive Fiscal Adjustments

Direct public action, linked to public spending, is the most obvious area for pro-poor adjustment with the largest set of lessons from experience, but is complicated by weak information, political pressures to preserve fiscal support to the nonpoor, and institutional rigidities that often make it difficult even to conduct comprehensive public spending reviews in large countries. The design of a pro-poor fiscal adjustment should be based on the assessment of the impact of the macroeconomic policy outlined above. Separating overall services from safety net instruments is useful, although in practice these are linked. The design analysis, which should include an assessment of the distributional effects of spending on social and economic services in terms of both labor demand and service provision, can draw on a number of incidence studies and work on the role of public services. The spending lines that are of particular value to the social and economic conditions of the poor—basic education, preventive health, rural roads, irrigation, water and sanitation, and slum upgrading—should be inventoried, and their continued support ensured. Determining what spending lines can be reduced or delayed to expand, or at least preserve, during crisis the programs that have been identified as pro-poor is equally important. Because reducing middle-class services or subsidies is also a question of managing the political economy, political action will be necessary to garner and sustain support for such reductions.

Introducing Social Safety Nets

Whatever their form, efficient and cost-effective safety nets to cope with emergencies can be of great value in the quest for greater social equity in the region. Models for safety nets to deal with both the individual and systemic risks the poor face can draw on past and ongoing work for their optimal design. Because information and capabilities may be limited in a crisis, designs that have self-targeting properties are particularly important.

One option to explore is the institutional basis for a significant expansion of workfare, which is generally the instrument of choice for poor workers, as with the Argentinian Trabajar program. A second option might be to increase subsidies for poor households to keep their children in school, such as the Bolsa Escola in Brazil, the Program of Family Assistance in Honduras, or Progresa in Mexico. A third option is to expand programs affecting early childhood development, such as mother and child feeding programs. Transfers can be provided to the poor who cannot work, who include the old, the sick, and the disabled. Programs, such as severance payments, can also be designed or activated for the nonpoor suffering from layoffs, as long as the programs do not involve labor market distortions or divert transfers from the poor.

Raising Institutional Capacity

Because short-run responses often encounter issues of institutional capacity, reasonably effective core central, or especially local, government agencies that are not subject to corruption or political capture are vital for effective administration of pro-poor programs in times of crisis. Safeguards must be put in place to prevent the worsening of weak or corrupt government institutions and the loss of governmental credibility as resources and salaries decline during political transition. Multiple channels and local participation should be used to increase both effectiveness and accountability. The Social Monitoring and Early Response Unit has these objectives. The crisis can also be used as an opportunity to pursue the longer-term objectives of decentralization and increased accountability of government and other agencies. In addition, governments can look to social funds as viable short-run alternatives if the social funds support, rather than undermine, longer-term institutional objectives, and they can look to parallel institutions that can, during crisis, be swiftly integrated into core government structures. Also, including the richer sectors of society in the consensus-building part of formulating pro-poor crisis response strategies will improve the chances of successfully designing and implementing the strategies.

Maintaining Labor's Rights

While development banks have traditionally steered clear of taking a position from a rights perspective, much of the actual engagement in developing social protection relates to core rights. A broad labor market perspective could assess how policy choices can increase the degree to which the adjustment takes account of the interests of all workers and their employment opportunities and labor conditions. With respect to specific rights, a reasonable approach could be to assess whether either the crisis or the response is likely to lead to a deterioration of core rights. Existing rights to association and collective bargaining should be respected during crisis. It is also vital that unions and representatives of informal workers be included in the debate about which policy directions to take in confronting a crisis. In addition, labor market reforms, which may reduce the acquired rights of formal sector workers, can be designed both to foster better overall labor prospects and to arrive at reasonable settlements for those adversely affected by the financial crisis.

Countries should also be aware of a heightened risk of exploitative forms of child labor during crisis and should implement specific policies to deter it. A combination of subsidies (notably to keep children in school) and civil society engagement may reduce this risk. Similarly, countries should be aware of the heightened possibility that women will be subjected to discrimination or abuse in the workplace during such times and can look to unions or civil society for prevention or remedies.

Assessing Effects on the Social Fabric

Countries must assess the capability of existing community-based or risk-management mechanisms (a dimension of social capital) to cope with severe countrywide crisis. Such mechanisms may come under heightened pressure under crisis and may not provide the social protection they provide under other circumstances. Policies must be formulated to compensate for this and to supplement these traditional mechanisms. National distributional conflicts may be exacerbated by economic crisis and should be taken into account when designing policies. The effectiveness of the existing societal mechanisms for conflict resolution should also be determined, as well as the potential for violence, including within families, as a consequence of worsening economic conditions and services. If such a link is found, mechanisms for direct action should be designed and put into place.

Developing Information, Diagnosis, and Public Debate

Both in and out of a crisis, information is central to understanding changes in welfare and the effect of alternative responses to them, the societal debate on options, and the accountability and transparency of programs in civil society and communities. A minimum set of key indicators for tracking the conditions of core socioeconomic groups should be established and incorporated in the monitoring of quick disbursing operations to support countries in crisis. Statistical services must make current information on the shifting pattern of welfare and vulnerability publicly available. Good participatory surveys of individual and community conditions and developments should be designed and carried out to complement quantitative information. Similarly, a sound structure using a range of quantitative and participatory techniques is necessary to evaluate the impact of programs on an ongoing basis. Public information on the intended and actual use of programs is vital to increase their transparency and accountability. Finally, countries must develop effective systems to assess, synthesize, and debate issues and policy options. Short-run outside action can both support the generation and sharing of information and foster longer-term institutional development.

Building Permanent Structures for Crisis Management

Crises either across an economy or geographically concentrated will always be with us—whether from the weather or financial shocks—no matter how much we learn from the latest crisis. Rather than thinking about ways to respond when hit by a crisis, we have to build the countries' development strategies, including strategies for short-run adjustment responses, to deal better with the human dimension of future crises. The key is to design institutional structures for reducing or managing the risks that households face. Many of the elements of such structures are known but tend to be introduced in a rush in the midst of a crisis, when they are least effective. They are too often too little, too late (or too much, too late). Managing risk should be as much a part of a long-term strategy as investing in economic or social services. This is likely to require more understanding of how alternative macroeconomic policy mixes affect growth and income distribution. It will also require a structure of safety nets that can expand countercyclically when shocks occur, without creating longer-term distortions; a menu of piloted activities that could be expanded, and spending lines that could be cut, when aggregate fiscal cuts are required; and information systems to track changes and impact over time.

References

De Janvry, A., and E. Sadoulet. 1999. "Growth, Poverty, and Inequality in Latin America: A Casual Analysis, 1970-94." Paper presented at the Conference on Social Protection and Poverty, IADB, February 4-5, Washington, D.C.

Kanbur, R. 1986. *Structural Adjustment, Macroeconomic Adjustment, and Poverty: A Methodology for Analysis.* Discussion Paper Series 132. London: CPER.

Lustig, N., ed. 1995. *Coping with Austerity: Poverty and Inequality in Latin America.* Washington, D.C.: The Brookings Institution.

_____. 1998. *Mexico: The Remaking of an Economy,* 2nd ed. Washington, D.C.: The Brookings Institution.

Lustig, N., and M. Walton. 1998. "East Asia Can Learn from Latin America's Travails." *International Herald Tribune*, May 29.

_____. 1999. "Crises and the Poor: A Template for Action." Paper presented at the Conference on Social Protection and Poverty, IADB, February 4-5, Washington, D.C.

Comments: Economic Crises and Social Protection for the Poor: The Latin American Experience

Raghav Gaiha

The paper by Lustig and Legovini is a rich and illuminating exposition of the macro and institutional aspects of protecting the poor during economic crises in Latin America and the Caribbean. More can and must be said about the political aspects of policy reform and poverty alleviation.

Let me comment, first, on the political consequences of market-oriented policy reforms launched in response to an economic crisis in a democratic setting. Usually, reforms proceed in spurts, advancing, stumbling, retreating, and advancing again (Prezeworski 1995). Even with a stop-and-go cycle, reform can be far reaching, but in the process, as opposition mounts, the subversion of democratic institutions cannot be ruled out.[1] Building coalitions, political parties, unions, and other professional associations may be vital for sustaining not only reform but also democratic institutions.

It is easier to agree that the poor must be protected during the transition to a new policy regime than to agree why. Some promote social protection out of compassion, some from a sense of Kantian justice, thinking "I might have been them." But policies designed to protect the poor may also provoke strong resistance, depending on how much other parties expect to gain or lose. Generalizations are risky, but De Janvry, Fergeix, and Sadoulet (1992) offer important insights into the political feasibility of policies to alleviate poverty. Using a sophisticated methodology, they have constructed a political feasibility index from a wide range of antipoverty interventions, taking into account alternative financing possibilities.

Whether some coalitions matter more than others can be inferred from the coalitions' ranking. First, the rural rich on their own are not an effective coalition. Second, coalitions of rural and urban poor are ineffective in general but are more decisive when they enjoy state support. Third, coalitions of all rural groups, with or without state support, are ineffective against coalitions of all urban groups. However, all rural groups can form an effective coalition when the gains to both the rural poor and the rural rich are substantial. This political flexibility index is important because it illustrates the complexity of policy choice, even when there is agreement on protecting the poor. Clearly, we need to know much more about how coalitions are formed and whether some of them gain strength over time. Besides, a case could be made for strengthening a coalition of rural poor on normative grounds.

Some recent studies conducted at the Bank and elsewhere have emphasized that organizations designed to protect the poor also matter. Little is known, though, about the conditions under which such organizations are effective. My own analysis of *panchayats* (Gaiha 1999; Gaiha and Kulkarni 1999) suggested a few impediments. Panchayats are elected village bodies in India that could and should play a major role in alleviating poverty. Despite a constitutional amendment to overhaul and revitalize them, however, their performance has been largely unsatisfactory or disappointing, for the following reasons:

- The domination of official agencies and blatant violation of provisions of state acts often hamper panchayats. The incompatibility of their incentives leads to inordinate delays in implementing antipoverty programs, such as rural public works. If common performance indicators could be devised and adhered to, some of this incompatibility could be reduced or eliminated.
- There has been a large-scale diversion of funds because a few influential persons, including chairpersons, have captured village panchayats by tightly controlling information about program outlays and disposition.
- The emphasis in state acts on panchayats' accountability to higher authorities is not matched by concern about their accountability to village communities (Gaiha, Kaushik, and Kulkarni forthcoming). So the capture of village panchayats remains unchecked and uncontested.

We must not overlook such deficiencies in the design of rural organizations. It is not enough to design organizations to serve the poor in an environment of acute inequality of endowments. It is equally important to create the conditions that allow such organizations to function. Clearly, a strong coalition of the rural poor is imperative. How to promote such a coalition is not obvious, but some evidence suggests moderate but sustained economic betterment as a way to initiate the rapid empowerment of the poor (Gaiha and Kulkarni 1999).

In short, protecting the poor may depend not merely on whether appropriate protective measures and organizations are in place. It may be equally important that the poor can affirm their collective interests.

Note

1. Decree powers were used extensively to get reform packages adopted in Bolivia, Ecuador, and Peru. Of the 675 laws promulgated in Peru between 1980 and 1984, for example, 463 were executive decrees (Prezeworski 1995).

References

De Janvry, A., A. Fergeix, and E. Sadoulet. 1992. "The Political Feasibility of Rural Poverty Reduction." *Journal of Development Economics* 37.

Gaiha, R. 1999. "Do Anti-poverty Programmes Reach the Rural Poor in India?" Paper presented at the World Congress of the International Economic Association, August, Buenos Aires, Argentina.

Gaiha, R., P. D. Kaushik, and Vani Kulkarni. Forthcoming. "Participation or Empowerment of the Rural Poor? The Case of *Panchayats* in India." In V. Damodaran and M. Unnithan-Kumar, eds., forthcoming. *The State, Development and Representation.* Thousand Oaks, CA: Sage Publications.

Gaiha, R., and Vani Kulkarni. 1999. "Policy Reforms, Institutions and the Poor in Rural India." *Contemporary South Asia* (June).

Prezeworski, A. 1995. *Democracy and the Market.* Cambridge, U.K.: Cambridge University Press.

Floor Discussion: Economic Crises and Social Protection for the Poor: The Latin American Experience

Arianna Legovini opened the discussion by noting the significant loss in human capital brought about by not addressing the issue of poverty. One reason Latin America had been able to withstand the recent crisis better than the rest of the world was that it had been able to address governance issues. Much remained to be done, but the various rounds of market liberalization and public sector reform had improved governance. Corruption still existed and funds were still being diverted, but things were moving in the right direction.

In response to a question about the essential scope of safety net programs, Legovini replied that all types of employment programs in Latin America, from training to employment insurance to public employment, reached not even 1 percent of the population, although poverty rates were between 20 and 50 percent and unemployment rates were between 5 and 20 percent. Was that enough? Probably not, but it depended. In Brazil, for example, the federal and state governments spent a lot of money but evaluations of expenditures told a sad story. Only 3 percent of the unemployment insurance in Brazil reached the bottom two quintiles of the population. Unemployment insurance was really targeted to middle-class workers who were skilled or semiskilled. Perhaps it was time to rethink the rationale for some of these programs.

There were good theoretical and practical reasons for having unemployment insurance systems cover everybody, and there were ways to finance those systems that did not require transfers from the government to the unemployed. One was unemployment insurance savings accounts, in which some level of forced savings by employed workers went into personal savings accounts that workers could draw on during a period of unemployment, using the balance when they retired. Workfare programs were gaining attention because they used subtargeting to identify very poor unskilled workers. Workfare programs generally did pretty well at targeting the right people, but they were expensive. Also missing from the safety net were children's programs not based on schooling. With school-based children's programs, street children were being left out and parents were not being reached. Access to institutions was essential for access to such social programs.

In response to questions, Legovini said development institutions were increasingly aware of the cost of not paying attention to the poor during times of crisis. People in development institutions, who had seen poverty increase dramatically and had seen a complete decade without growth, were asking, "What have we done wrong? Should we look at the next crisis in a different way?" The countries themselves found it politically useful to implement

---

Johan Helland chaired the discussion.

programs at some point, but some very targeted programs had always suffered from a lack of middle-class support. The crisis's effect on growth had heightened awareness of the need to protect and develop human capital.

In Asia, the basic difference between countries at similar stages of development that were then left behind was a large increase in human capital. There was no parallel in Latin America.

Gaiha said that his review of India's employment guarantee scheme showed the self-targeting mechanism did not work well when conditions were difficult. It was often taken for granted that a work requirement would ensure that only the poor would participate, but that was not true of public works in India. During a slack period, the opportunities were so few that even relatively affluent people considered working on public works to be a fairly attractive option.

Part VIII

Development Effectiveness in Health, Nutrition, and Population Services

15

Delivering Social Services: Lessons on Health, Nutrition, and Population

Susan Stout

The World Bank is now the largest source of international financing for the health sector, with commitments of more than US$14 billion since 1970. Support for the sector has expanded rapidly since about 1988. Although during the 1970s the Bank lent a total of US$400 million, lending is currently averaging US$1.3 billion per year. Lending for individual projects has increased concomitantly. The average loan size has increased from approximately US$25 million per project to a current average of approximately US$80 million per project.

Throughout the years, the Bank has helped strengthen health, nutrition, and population (HNP) policies and services in some 92 countries worldwide. To assess the effectiveness of these efforts, OED recently carried out the first comprehensive study of Bank assistance to this sector. Our main concern when we embarked on this endeavor was to draw lessons from the past to improve the effectiveness of the Bank's work as it embarks on increasingly complicated and comprehensive approaches to health sector reform.

We started by reviewing what the Bank and others had already done to evaluate effectiveness in the sector. Because most funds have been lent to this sector since 1990, by 1997 only a third of projects had been completed and evaluated. Thus, the scope of our evaluation needed to include both completed and ongoing projects. We started out with the idea that we would evaluate according to the use of services but then began to think about whether this was a correct indicator of performance. This led us to a major review of the literature on health project evaluation.

Some work had been done on individual programs—for instance, evaluations of a nutrition project in India and an OED review of work on population—but a broad look at the entire portfolio was lacking. Moreover, our review of the evaluation literature in the sector showed that, despite an extensive literature on the evaluation of particular health program interventions (particularly for family planning, immunization, and nutrition interventions), there is little experience in evaluating efforts to improve the performance of multiple programs or the capacity of the health system as a whole.

We then developed the conceptual framework to provide a context for the evaluation of development effectiveness in the sector (figure 15.1). The framework suggests that the likely impact of Bank, or any other international, assistance on health outcomes is far from direct. Impacts are likely to occur through two major paths, each complex and multifaceted. First, projects and policy advice might work through influence on two important dimensions of a country's health care system: (a) the actual physical structure, or the number of clinics, the number of private providers, the number and location of hospitals, and the number and kinds of staff that these facilities have, and (b) the institutional environment, or how these resources are managed, which in turn results in a particular level of health system performance (which includes accessibility to the poor, service quality, consumer satisfaction, and economic efficiency).

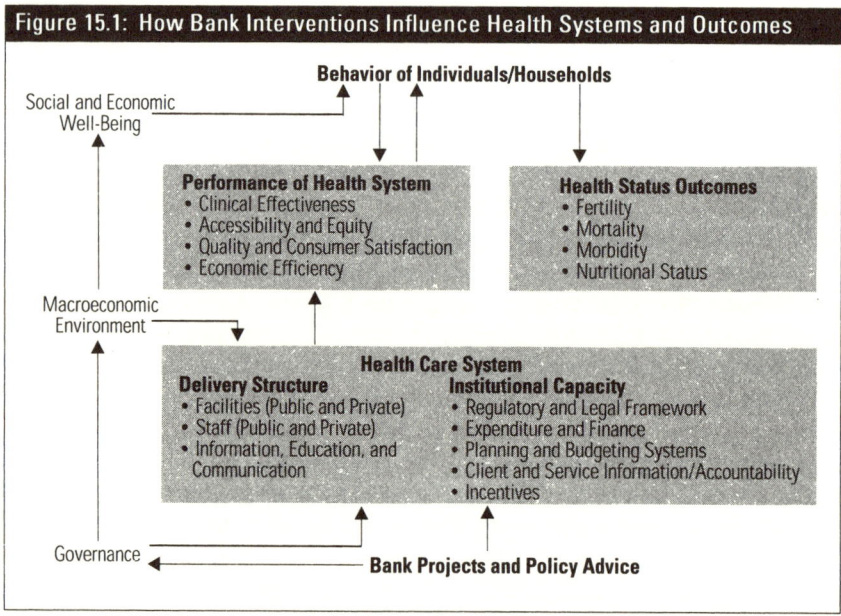

Quality as perceived by the consumer is central to effectiveness, because if consumers do not want a service, they will not make use of it. If consumers do not make use of it, the service is unlikely to achieve an outcome.

The framework illustrates a second major point, which is that external assistance can influence these determinants, but that the form and levels of impact are highly indirect, are not the focus of interventions defined within conventional definitions of sectoral boundaries, and are ultimately mediated through the behavior and responses of individual households. The major correlates of health are income; education; the quality of the environment, including access to safe housing, clean water, and sanitation; and individual and community practices related to nutrition, sanitation, reproduction, and alcohol and tobacco use. That is, they are behaviors shaped by culture and by social and economic status and not by the use of medical care. Thus, if interventions focus only on the health care system, they ignore many other determinants of health. In this connection, we found that the Bank had emphasized the establishment of a delivery structure and strategically tended not to focus on the other determinants of health. Although the Bank moved more toward work on institutional and policy issues in the 1990s, the bulk of lending has nevertheless gone toward delivery mechanisms.

> Bank interventions have emphasized the delivery of medical interventions over other determinants of health.

We applied this framework to our review in two primary evaluative exercises. First, we conducted a comparative analysis of the entire HNP portfolio, using content analysis and a coding format designed for the study to analyze all the project appraisal and completion reports for projects approved between 1979 and 1997. We assessed each project in terms of project quality at entry—that is, the kind of work that had gone into project preparation—and extracted common themes and observations about performance from the Bank's own supervision reports on project implementation, as well as from all available completion and project performance audit reports. We used this information, combined with data on Bank inputs and other characteristics, to model project performance. Second, to gain greater insights into how nonlending activities, including formal sectoral analyses and policy dialogue, add to the value of specific investment projects, we prepared four country studies of the evolution and history of Bank-supported HNP activities in Brazil, India, Mali, and Zimbabwe.

Findings

Figure 15.2 shows trends on standard OED measures of project performance. Outcome indicates whether projects were satisfactory or unsatisfactory as defined by the Bank; institutional development refers to whether

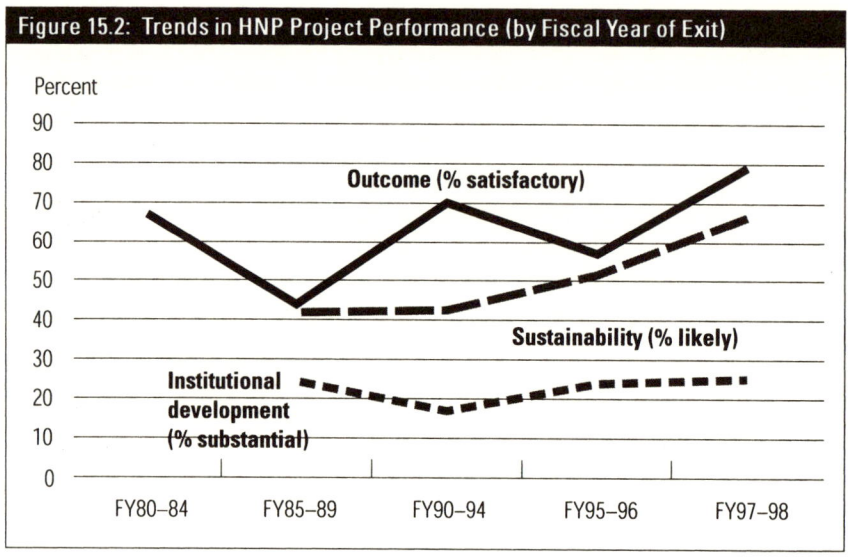

Figure 15.2: Trends in HNP Project Performance (by Fiscal Year of Exit)

or not projects achieved their institutional development goals. As the figure shows, from a lower rate of success in the 1980s, 79 percent of projects completed in fiscal years 1997-98 achieved their development objectives satisfactorily, and approximately 66 percent were likely to be sustainable. Yet one-third of ongoing HNP projects were rated as at risk by the Bank's portfolio monitoring system, and high rates of completion of physical objectives disguise difficulties encountered in achieving policy and institutional change. Only 25 percent of health projects achieved their institutional development objectives. This is lower than in any other sector in the Bank and lower than in the other social sectors.

In explaining these results, our first major (and unsurprising) finding was that the most important determinant of project outcome was borrowers' performance, yet borrowers' performance is not entirely independent. The borrowers' implementation capacity and certain environmental characteristics tend to be beyond the Bank's control, but the Bank's analysis of institutional and political issues that influence borrower performance can make a difference. The Bank can control for project quality at entry, and, if the Bank has successfully analyzed institutional capacity and the mechanics of implementation, projects are more likely to succeed.

Unfortunately, the Bank's work on institutional analysis has been weak, which brings us to the second most important determinant of HNP project outcome: countries' institutional context, including prevailing levels of corruption. Almost all HNP projects identify low capacity as a risk to project success, but we found that few project designs clearly specify how risks are to be managed. For instance, only one-third of health sector projects included an in-depth analysis of implementation capacity or took into account possible political obstacles to implementing anticipated reforms or programs. If these were considered, the issues were not specified in the formal project documentation. Of the two-thirds of projects that did discuss institutional obstacles to performance, only about 30 percent anticipated any political or other opposition to change. Many projects, for instance, aim at adjustments to the health work force, but few projects discuss the views and possible opposition of professional associations to undertaking changes, or propose strategies to overcome it.

> Many projects, for instance, aim at adjustments to the health work force, but few projects discuss the views and possible opposition of professional associations to undertaking changes.

Forty percent of the projects promoted some form of decentralization, but less than half addressed the mechanics of decentralization, which is external to the health sector. For example, we have been advocating decentralization in Indonesia for 15 or 20 years. Only in the past seven years or so, though, have we started working systematically with macroeconomists and other people working with public expenditures to understand how the budgeting environment for the government as a whole influences the likelihood that the ministry of health will be able to decentralize.

Another important observation concerns the incorporation of stakeholders' views in project design. Until the past two years, we did not really do any formal analysis of the interests and concerns of key stakeholders in the sector. In particular, we rarely discussed or analyzed the regulatory environment and the incentives that influence the behavior of the health work force. The consequences of these omissions can be dire. In Zimbabwe, for example, a series of family health projects was successful in achieving its physical investment objectives and establishing 16 new, well-equipped district hospitals. However, changes in the macroeconomic environment during the construction period exerted pressures on public wages. This resulted in a deterioration in the conditions of work for medical and nursing professionals in the public sector so that, with construction of facilities completed, the government is finding it difficult to pay the people needed to staff the new facilities, some of which are therefore seriously underutilized.

The second largest expenditure after salaries is for the purchase and distribution of pharmaceutical and medical supplies, but in another example of weak institutional analysis, we found that the Bank has generally failed to assess the difference between public and private interests in the pharmaceutical industry. What are the guidelines that govern the purchase, distribution, and logistical arrangements for drugs? For instance, a large drug project in West Africa covered only the public sector, but sales of pharmaceuticals in the private sector were 250 times greater than sales in the public sector. Therefore, even if the project had been successful, it would have affected only a small part of the market.

The core objectives of many Bank-financed health projects are to improve maternal and child health, family planning, and primary health services. Accordingly, project designs in the health sector often assume that project beneficiaries will be primarily poor women, so a large proportion of health projects are characterized as poverty oriented. However, few of the projects discussed specific strategies for targeting the poor. The projects tended to employ geographic targeting but did little microlevel analysis to ascertain whether the poor really would have access to the services. We also found little analysis of the impact of various health financing reforms on poverty, so projects tended to prescribe cost recovery without analyzing of exemption policies to help protect the poor.

The third major finding concerned the Bank's performance. The evaluation found that the most important element was project quality at entry, particularly the quality of institutional analysis, followed by the quality of supervision. As already noted, quality at entry has improved in recent years, but institutional analysis remains weak. The most common problems related to unsatisfactory projects included inadequate assessment of borrower capacity and commitment, insufficient Bank supervision, little or no monitoring and evaluation (M&E), and excessively complex project design. In relation to M&E, we found that while almost all the HNP projects defined technically appropriate indicators, few started with any estimate of a baseline value or anticipated what the project would actually be able to accomplish. Of the completed projects, 70 percent were not able to report on specific output or outcome accomplishments because well-intentioned plans to build and employ M&E components were ultimately not implemented. Moreover, the logic underlying the project design, as well as M&E plans, typically reflects an inadequate analysis of the possible causal links between the inputs to be provided by the project and likely changes in outputs or outcomes. Few project designs include efforts to specify measures of the nature and extent of expected organizational or policy change, making tracking of achievements toward institutional objectives difficult.

Projects rated as having substantially achieved their institutional objectives shared the following characteristics:

- **Institutional objectives.** Project designers promoted consensus about priorities and approaches among stakeholders and, if necessary, developed strategies to anticipate and reduce resistance.
- **Project design.** Project designers combined sector work, earlier evaluations, and dialogue with key stakeholders to reveal impediments to project success and developed realistic strategies to combat the constraints.

- **Project implementation.** Bank staff and borrowers regularly reviewed progress toward institutional objectives and addressed problems proactively, modifying projects during implementation as necessary.
- **Governance and macroeconomic context.** Projects supported institutional and organizational development.

Figure 15.3, which measures the complexity of project designs by the number of objectives in the project, provides a way to summarize our findings. It shows that the Bank tended to use extremely complex designs, which are likely to be the most difficult to implement and the most demanding of institutional capacity, in exactly those settings with low institutional capacity and the greatest need for change. Our hypothesis about why this happens is that Bank and borrower staff working in countries with low capacity feel a need to do everything—provide training, finance reform, set

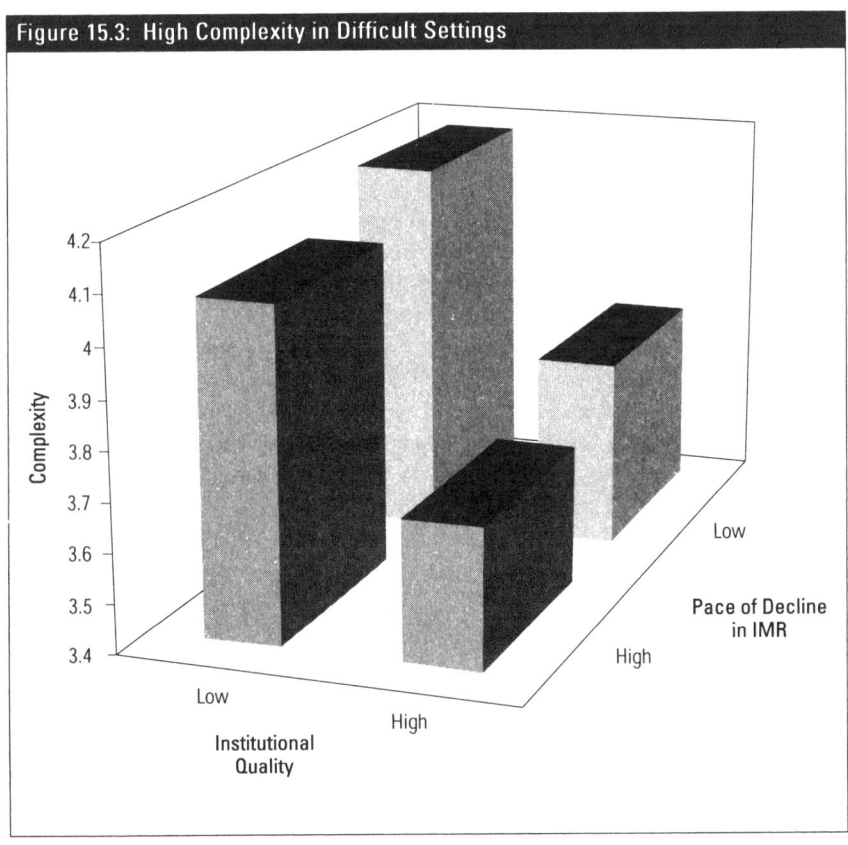

Figure 15.3: High Complexity in Difficult Settings

up information systems, build hospitals—in response to the dismal initial conditions. Knowledge of how best to sequence and phase inputs, as well as policy and institutional change, is limited. The result is the evolution of a complex design that far exceeds the borrower's capacity to implement or the Bank's capacity to supervise.

Lessons Learned

Bank support has helped expand access to basic health services, sponsored training for service providers, and provided other important inputs to basic health services. The Bank has also promoted dialogue and policy change on a range of key issues, such as family planning and nutrition strategies. Clients appreciate the Bank's broad strategic perspective, and the Bank has increased its role in donor coordination. Despite an initial focus on government health services, the Bank's focus has increasingly shifted toward insurance, regulation, and service delivery by the private sector and NGOs. It has also increased its emphasis on client ownership and beneficiaries' views on project design and supervision.

The evaluation revealed the following lessons:
- Projects' institutional impact has been disappointing.
- Monitoring and evaluation has been weak.
- Intersectoral coordination has been weak.
- Flexibility and learning have been insufficient.

In terms of changing policies and institutions, the Bank is relatively good at diagnosing problems but less successful at developing solutions. Its sectoral analyses and appraisal reports are relatively effective in determining technically sensible suggestions for improving sectoral performance. They are not as effective in identifying the underlying causes of performance problems or in anticipating the consequences of the incentive and information failures typical of the sector. When it comes to building capacity, Bank project designs tend to equate low capacity with the need for training and technical assistance. Therefore, the correlation between statements of low capacity and the percentage of loans attributed to technical assistance is high. Unfortunately, however, capacity constraints are often not skill constraints but rather problems of incentive and institutional arrangements.

The Bank also tends not to evaluate effectively the institutional and organizational environment that governs capacity weaknesses. For example, it tends to focus on the health sector while ignoring the macroeconomic environment, so it encounters problems at the work force level.

In addition, many Bank projects and much of its sector work and policy dialogue argue persuasively for better donor coordination but tend to be vague on specifying practical steps for improving coordination. The projects ignore the problems of coordination within and among the major actors within the sector itself.

We conclude that much of the work done so far in the HNP sector on M&E is unduly focused on extracting data—for example, explaining to the Bank or other donors what has happened rather than establishing systems to promote the use of data in the context of local planning and budgeting procedures. In addition, Bank projects have not paid sufficient attention to the challenge of improving the borrowers' capacity to measure and subsequently steer by outcomes. Analysis of the strengths and weaknesses of systems for ensuring accountability within the sector are typically weak or nonexistent. This gap is apparent in terms of understanding the relationships, expectations, and rules of the game for measuring and following up on performance measures on the supply side (among and between various levels of government or provider groups, for example) and on the demand side. The second dimension of this is the tendency to emphasize accountability. For example, if a province makes some expenditure, how can the central level be sure that it was the right expenditure? In addition, the Bank does not think about consumers in relation to accountability. Project designs tend to define consumers in terms of the behaviors they are expected to change or modify as a result of program interventions—for example, wider acceptance of family planning services or changes in health-related behaviors. The designs also define the consumers as targets, not as individuals who might have some expectations of what the system should be providing and, therefore, have an ability to use their voice to help change the quality of the system's performance.

The main recommendation of the evaluation is that the Bank should do better, not more, and should focus on selectivity and quality, with increased attention to institutional development in project design and to supervision and substantial improvements in M&E. The Bank should also strengthen its efforts in health promotion and intersectoral interventions; renew the emphasis on research; attempt greater understanding of stakeholders' interests; and forge strategic alliances with development partners at the local, regional, and global levels.

Having stated these lessons, I would characterize Bank HNP projects as full of good intentions but with insufficient focus on measuring results. Bank and borrower staff focus primarily on getting the appraisal right and on getting the concept of what should happen in the future correct but expend considerably less effort on establishing whether the good intentions achieved the expected results. However, before we spend too much effort on getting technical and methodological details of evaluation right, we need to understand why someone would want to use an evaluation. If we do not focus on use, technical precision will not be any help.

A major conclusion of our evaluation thus takes the form of a new question. How can the Bank or other donors rebalance the concentration between the appraisal of good intentions and accountability for specific results? This point is directed not simply at borrowers but also at donors.

Some work in this area is occurring in USAID as well as elsewhere in the U.S. government and also in the United Kingdom. We need to find ways to build evaluation infrastructure not just for the Bank but also among borrowers. If borrowers are not steering by outcomes, donors are also not going to succeed in redressing the gap between providing input planning and achieving results on the ground.

Health and other social sectors must find ways to close the large gap between our understanding of good practice and theory and the reality on the ground. Evaluations and evaluation processes can help close that gap. If we think about the consumers as being the ones who have the greatest interest in the effectiveness and quality of health service delivery or the delivery of any other social service, we should be focusing much more of our evaluative efforts on understanding what would help them to hold health policy and program decisionmakers accountable for achieving results. Evidence is available, for instance, from the successful work on the eradication of smallpox that developing measures of outcome that are meaningful to consumers and providers, as well as to technocrats, is a key step in this direction.

Recommendations

Recommendations fall into two major categories. In the first category, organizational strategy, recommendations are to:

- **Enhance the Bank's orientation toward quality assurance and results.** The Bank should continue its efforts to improve the quality of portfolio monitoring. It should also establish mechanisms to provide timely support to project design and supervision work. A critical factor in enhancing borrowers' M&E capacity is strengthening incentives to achieve results and to use information, within both the Bank and client countries.
- **Increase learning from both lending and nonlending services.** Given the weak institutional performance in the health sector, the Bank should establish appropriate tools, guidelines, and training programs for institutional and stakeholder analysis.
- **Strengthen partnerships and increase strategic selectivity.** The Bank should choose a few strategic areas in which to improve its intersectoral coordination, including macroeconomic dialogue and health work force issues. At the international level, the Bank could strengthen its partnership with the World Health Organization to address such priorities as enhancing M&E and performance-based health management systems in client countries.

In the second category, policy and practice, recommendations are to:

- **Increase the focus on health promotion and behavior.** This includes emphasizing information, education, and communication campaigns along with broader policy and regulatory changes.

- **Avoid excessively complex project designs.** The Bank needs to assess implementing organizations' capacity in this respect and make a greater effort to rank and sequence interventions.
- **Increase the emphasis on targeting the poor.** More work needs to be done to analyze the causes of ill health among the poor and to select interventions that are likely to be the most effective in reducing the disease burden of the poor.
- **Develop the consensus and the broadly based coalitions needed to achieve change.** This includes understanding the political context of reform and recognizing stakeholders' interests, along with facilitating community involvement in HNP program planning, implementation, and management.

Comments: Delivering Social Services Lessons on Health, Nutrition, and Population

Margaret Goodman

Stout's presentation was excellent and to the point. From my experience, if we had changed the name from World Bank to Inter-American Development Bank, the paper would just as accurately have reflected the status of IADB's evaluation programs.

The two banks have many similar problems in reviewing projects to determine what went as planned and where predictions were wrong. It is amazing that after so much time, projects are not developed to plan for the contingencies that repeatedly happen and can be expected.

I am talking about how and where we should look at evaluation. One thing evaluation looks at, for example, is other projects, but perhaps evaluation should also look at history, to learn how and where the disadvantaged have gained better service from the government. We all know that the poor do not get service through good evaluations; they get service when they get political power, a factor that is never reviewed in evaluations.

Bank evaluations tend to examine things from a technical viewpoint, striving for objectivity, but development does not happen that way, especially not in areas relevant to poverty alleviation. Poverty is alleviated not through social services but through money. And the way people get money, especially in Latin America, is to use the political system to demand jobs, better income distribution, and more and better skills training. The banks really do not work at the political level, except to provide money and tell people what to do.

Sometimes projects are implemented well and sometimes they are not. What we evaluate is the process. But even when we come up with fairly negative evaluations the banks never say a country will be denied a loan because the loans the country already has are not performing well. No penalty is given for performing badly. In fact, the countries that perform the worst often get the cheapest money for the next loan. Some of our incentives are strange.

Multilateral development banks and countries have different incentives. Multilateral development banks have to get the money out, and governments have to please their major stakeholders. What we have to work on is getting governments and the people they represent committed to improving health systems. The challenge for evaluators is learning how to motivate commitment.

We should begin by evaluating changes in power relationships and in the direction power is flowing—toward the poor or away from them. To do this, we can use the following indicators:

- We can begin to measure political campaign debates. Has health care become a national issue? Who is participating in the debates? Are the

debates taking place where the poor can hear them?
- We can review newspaper articles, television discussions—even barroom conversations. We really have to learn how the poor learn and how to get information into the political arena. It is not enough to say that a project needs to be fixed. We need to see whether information about projects that citizens are paying for is getting to the citizens.
- We should identify which interests are represented by civil society and which are not. Our programs are only as sustainable as the beneficiaries who support them. Without public support, these programs can be altered overnight, after the last disbursement is made.
- We should monitor the effects of decentralization, because so many social services are decentralizing. Although decentralization is supposed to create more opportunities for the poor, it may simply exchange one oligarchy for another more locally entrenched, one.

In other words, as we evaluate formal Bank programs, we should also discuss who is in control, who is making decisions, and which groups are organized. We should be aware that our evaluations cannot change things much without our clients' committment to change. This means, of course, that we must engage in both a technical and a political discussion with opinionmakers when we do our evaluations. That way, evaluations can become agents for change instead of mere records of events.

Floor Discussion: Delivering Social Services: Lessons on Health, Nutrition, and Population

Sawang Hong thanked Stout for sharing practical suggestions.

Lawrence Haddad of the International Food Policy Research Institute said his organization was involved in major monitoring and evaluation activities in Mozambique and Mexico, which he thought overcame some of the problems Stout had discussed. The only way his institute had been effective in getting government agencies to buy into evaluation was to develop a survey that addressed questions institute employees wanted answered three years down the road and to have institute employees sit with government employees in their government offices for two or three years. But this approach did not really work if one wanted to have a real impact at the country level. It worked better with academic audiences or Washington-based or European-based organizations.

Haddad wanted to know three things. First, if everything were tied to outcomes, did one not run the risk of going where it was easiest to get a major increase in outcome? If one were using poverty headcount or poverty incidence as an outcome measure, for example, it would be quite easy to target people just below the poverty line. But if one wanted to reach people who were far below the poverty line, one had to use different outcome indicators.

Second, if the Bank kept getting into institutional analysis, which he thought was crucial, what was the Bank's comparative advantage? Government agencies might perceive the Bank as meddling in internal affairs and be very nervous about this.

Third, did OED have the skills needed to do institutional evaluations?

Haddad's first point (the problem of embedding monitoring and evaluation) and third question were related, said Stout, and the answer was that the Bank had not had enough experience trying to build evaluation capacity. Most experience she was aware of was in the agriculture sector. For Stout, the basic problem was not the technical assistance, but the interest. It was easier to have an academic and Washington-based focus because somebody sitting in a research institute getting paid to produce lessons on how to make early childhood development project more effective would find a way to do that. Somebody sitting in a ministry of health with a budget 10 percent lower than last year's budget, regardless of performance, would not be especially interested. When Stout had worked for a state government in the United States, the federal government made funding for maternal and child health programs contingent on changing outcomes, so the staff got remarkably good at measuring outcomes quickly. The place to start was creating the right incentives. Worrying about the relative effectiveness of different kinds of technical assistance could come later.

Sawong Hong of the United Nations Children's Fund moderated the discussion.

In response to Haddad's question about choice of outcome indicators, Stout agreed that such indicators would always embody donors' norms and the achievements they valued, so the outcome should not automatically be prevalence or total fertility. An important example of this was the eradication of smallpox. For many years, vaccination prevalence was the output measure donors were interested in, although during that time the actual prevalence of the disease did not change much. When for operational reasons donors changed the definition of outcome to the actual number of cases, which villagers could recognize, they found quick and profound changes in behavior. Both consumers and providers could recognize a smallpox case and say, "This is here. I know the government, the NGOs, and the whole provision network do not want this here. They should come get rid of this smallpox case and vaccinate all my friends and neighbors." The challenge was to find outcome measures that were as meaningful to the very poorest as they were to evaluators. In other words, accountability and demand and the definition of outcomes must be considered together. Focus first on who the poor are and how they define an outcome, not on the technically best definition.

Did the Bank have a comparative advantage in institutional analysis? This was not a strong area for the Bank, said Stout. She believed the Bank had to find ways to discuss these issues without embarrassing both its partners and clients. The Bank needed to get people talking about these issues as a factor in performance.

Tim Frankenberger agreed on the problem of incentives within the Bank. The Bank's culture was, "We are all terribly sophisticated analysts of something disciplinary." The staff wrote papers and produced gems called project appraisal documents. Bank staff were responsible for judging the quality of the Bank's intentions; the borrowers really bore the risk. Maybe the Bank should share some of that risk. If the Bank did that, the incentives for doing evaluations would change remarkably. Stout's point was that the Bank should start by discussing incentives, both internally and externally. As part of its own internal budgeting process, OED was looking increasingly at its internal incentive system.

Sometimes designs were so complex, given institutional capacity, that a project failed simply because the institution could not do it, said Frankenberger. That problem might stem partly from using sophisticated consultants to design programs and to respond to the Bank's demands for reviews without really considering the operating environment. He wondered how the Bank would approach that problem.

Returning to a point Haddad had made, Frankenberger observed that different places in a country could have more or less achievable outcome measures simply because some environments were more favorable than others. How did the Bank weigh outcome changes in different operating environments so that it did not penalize a place with little infrastructure that showed less change than a place with quite a bit of infrastructure? One problem was that much of the poverty in the poorest areas would probably not be targeted because it was harder to get results in those places. Did the Bank have some kind of weighting formula for project design?

This was a critical issue, Stout responded, and the Bank was a long way from having a procedure for weighting for fairness in performance allocation or for linking performance to resource management.

Had Stout seen any encouraging signs in the past few years? She saw positive signs in the general trend toward more participatory approaches combined with more field-based staff. It would be a good sign if the Bank could link those to a genuine commitment to working with the participants to define outcomes. As for complexity, Bank and government resources had become increasingly constrained, so the Bank's ambitions were increasingly unattainable. The risks in the current environment were that those same factors would encourage the Bank toward more programmable lending, which could become focused much more on simple resource transfers than on indicators of effectiveness.

On the complexities of evaluation and accountability, Stout thought that there was a good risk of overwhelming the people who actually could do things, such as NGOs on the ground. Between requiring no evaluation in the Bank's approval process and overwhelming NGOs with requests for information, there was surely a happy medium. The Bank would be better off focusing on a few outcomes than having NGOs measure their procurement rates.

Crisis Prevention

16

Tackling Horizontal Inequalities

Frances Stewart

Civil wars are a major source of poverty. Eight of the ten countries with the worst human development indicators and eight of the ten countries with the lowest gross national product per capita have had major civil wars in the recent past.[1] About half of all low-income countries have experienced major political violence. Causality works both ways, because low incomes lead to conditions that are conducive to violence (see, for example, the statistical evidence produced by Auvinen and Nafziger 1999). The evidence suggests, however, that major civil wars are associated with markedly worse performance in economic growth, food production per capita, and human indicators such as infant mortality and school enrollment (Stewart and Fitzgerald forthcoming). Hence prevention of conflict must be put at the center of any comprehensive strategy to tackle poverty. Conflict prevention has been regarded as a desirable political objective, but it has not been part of the poverty reduction or human development agenda. For example, the Bank's poverty reduction strategy documents deal little, if at all, with this issue, nor does UNDP's Human Development Report treat it as central to human development. Partly for this reason, development strategies in general and antipoverty policies in particular have tended to neglect issues related to conflict. Yet recognizing the prevention of conflict as central for poor societies may substantially alter the design of policies. The aim of this paper is to explore how economic and social policymaking would be affected by focusing on the prevention of conflict in low-income countries.

Crisis prevention is essential for poverty reduction, and policies aimed at reducing political violence are needed for all low-income countries, given their propensity for violence. Similar policies are also needed for particularly vulnerable middle-income countries, though the incidence of civil war is substantially lower among these countries, partly reflecting the fact that they have succeeded in becoming middle income by avoiding conflict.

The aim of this paper is to identify how introducing crisis prevention into policymaking would alter the design of policy for low-income countries. It does so, first, by some general analysis of conflicts, drawn from the findings of a recent research program on the economic and social causes of conflict; second, by an explanation of the concept of horizontal inequalities as a key element in understanding and preventing conflict; and third, by an overview of the policy recommendations emerging from the analysis.

Motivation, Mobilization, and Conflict

The human motivation of the actors involved is clearly at the heart of any conflict. If a conflict is to be avoided or stopped, this motivation must be understood, and the political, cultural, and economic conditions predisposing the actors to engage in conflict must be reduced or eliminated.

This paper is concerned with the conflicts among organized groups, not with the random violence committed by individuals. Group organization may be quite informal, but the purpose of the violence is usually, and often implicitly, agreed upon. Some members of the group, the leaders, instigate or orchestrate the conflict by, among other things, enhancing the perception of group identity. Other members, the followers, actively carry out or support the fighting. The group element differentiates such violence from crime, although in extreme cases where fighting parties disintegrate into gangs (see Keen [forthcoming] on Sierra Leone, for example), the distinction between crime and conflict becomes blurred.

Groups have been differentiated and mobilized in different ways. For example, in central Africa, ethnic identity is the major source of group definition and mobilization; in Central America, group identification and organization are along class lines but with some overlapping ethnic dimensions; in Somalia, the cultural source of group differentiation and mobilization is clans (different lineages within broadly the same ethnic group); in Northern Ireland and the Balkans, religion is the major factor. Another source of differentiation is regional location, which can, but does not always, coincide with ethnic or language divisions as, for example, in Biafra, East Pakistan (Bangladesh), and Eritrea.

The view of this paper is that political leaders construct group identity. Numerous examples have shown how "ethnicity was used by political and intellectual elites prior to, or in the course of, wars" (Alexander, McGregor, and Ranger forthcoming). Some shared circumstances are needed for group construction, such as speaking the same language, sharing cultural traditions, living in the same place, or facing similar sources of hardship or exploitation.

Similarity of circumstance among potential group members, however, is not by itself enough to bring about group mobilization. Several other conditions must be present. Leaders must see the creation or enhancement of group identity as a way to realize their political ambitions and must work actively to achieve it through education, propaganda, and other means. Government policies, particularly toward education, frequently play a role by discriminating in favor of some group and against others. The enhancement, or maybe even creation, of differences between the Hutu and Tutsi by colonial and postcolonial governments is a powerful example (Gaffney forthcoming, Uvin forthcoming).

Economic and political differentiation among groups is of fundamental importance. If an entire society is impoverished, there may be despair, but there is no motivation for group organization. Even if political leaders hope to use group mobilization as a source of power, they would find it difficult to secure sufficient response among followers without some underlying economic differences among the people they hope to mobilize. We define differences in group conditions as horizontal inequalities.

Relevant economic differences vary according to the nature of the economy. For example, land may be irrelevant in modern urban societies and employment relevant, but the converse could be true in rural-based economies. Although the prime cause of group conflict is relative inequality, the absolute situation may also be relevant because an absolute deterioration in conditions may focus attention on the relative situation. For example, people may fight about water if it becomes scarce but not when it is plentiful. Conversely, when incomes and resources are increasing, people may be expected to care less about their relative positions. The latter situation occurred in Kenya in the 1960s and 1970s and is thought to be one reason why, despite persistent relative inequality among tribes, large-scale conflict did not result (see Klugman forthcoming). In some contexts, though, improvements can lead to conflict if they are unfairly distributed, as in Nigeria in the late 1960s (see Nafziger 1983).

> We define differences in group conditions as horizontal inequalities.

It is not necessarily the relatively deprived who instigate violence. The privileged may do so, fearing loss of position. For example, the prospect of loss of political power can be a powerful motive for state-sponsored violence against opposition groups. State terrorism is an important cause of humanitarian emergencies. This was the case, for example, in most of the major episodes of violence in Haiti, in Iraq's suppression of the Kurds, and in Uganda (Holsti forthcoming).

In many societies, some level of organized violence persists for long periods. If underlying conditions are conducive to conflict, low-level conflict may exist for certain periods, followed by periods of violence on a greater scale (civil war), which sometimes culminate in major catastrophes. The history of violence then contributes to group identification, animosities, and the likelihood of future conflict. This has been shown statistically by Auvinen and Nafziger (1999). Many countries—for example, Burundi, Rwanda, and Somalia—appear to have had a long history of fluctuating levels of violence.

Dimensions of Differentiation in the Political, Economic, and Social Position of Groups

Leaders often seize on, change, and exaggerate cultural or religious differences as a means of group mobilization. Making these symbolic systems (the values, myths, rituals, and ceremonies used to organize and unite groups [see Cohen 1974]) effective in mobilizing for violence requires political or economic differences. These can be categorized into four areas: political participation, economic assets, incomes and employment, and social aspects. Each of these categories contains a number of elements. For example, political participation can occur at the level of the cabinet, the bureaucracy, the army, and so forth. Economic assets include land, livestock, machinery, and so on. The relevance of a particular element varies according to whether it is an important source of income or well-being in a particular society. The allocation of housing, for example, is generally more relevant in industrial countries. Land is of enormous importance where agriculture accounts for most output and employment but becomes less important as development proceeds. Water is extremely important in parts of the world where rainwater is inadequate. Access to minerals can be a source of great wealth, and gaining such access can be an important source of conflict in countries with mineral resources (see Fairhead forthcoming, Reno forthcoming).

Other Elements That Contribute to Conflict

In addition to the horizontal inequalities described above, four other elements play a role in group violence: perceptions, private costs and benefits, constraints, and resources.

First, we have already noted the important role of perceptions. People are not born with a sense of which group they belong to and who friends and enemies are; the family, the community, and the state construct this sense.

Second, while social influences are especially important in conflict, group members also experience conflict's private benefits and costs.

Individual action is taken partly (the extreme neoclassical position would argue entirely) as a result of the individual's calculation of the private costs and benefits of action. Of course, especially at times of high tension, group gains or losses also affect individual welfare. In some situations, people have been observed to take actions completely counter to their private interests. For example, rioters in Sri Lanka have burned down factories where they themselves work, thereby destroying their own place of employment (Stewart andO'Sullivan 1999).

Individuals and groups may gain from conflict, for example, through the act of looting, the use of forced labor, the creation of changes in the terms of trade, the creation of new economic opportunities, and the control of emergency aid. Keen (1994, 1998) has analyzed such gains in Sudan and elsewhere. However, many people lose from the physical violence, disrupted markets, reduced state benefits, theft, and looting. The private calculation of costs and benefits also depends on the potential gains from avoiding conflict, including the economic rewards of development in a peaceful environment. The cost-benefit calculation may be different for leaders and followers. If followers are strongly supportive of conflict, against the views of their existing leaders, new leaders may emerge.

Any long-run solution to the problem of group violence must try to change the calculations of both leaders and followers with respect to individual and group costs and benefits. Bribes can be offered to stop fighting—for example, power and status for leaders and finance and jobs for followers. Unless the underlying causes of the conflict are addressed, though, new leaders and followers are likely to emerge.

Third, conflicts can be prevented by strong constraints, normally in the form of a strong state (or other authority) that suppresses violence, even when individuals and groups have a strong motivation for conflict. Some of the conflicts in the former Soviet Union can be attributed to the weakening of the state. In Sierra Leone and Somalia, as well, the weakening of the state has permitted conflicts to erupt and enlarge, while in Kenya, by contrast, a relatively strong state has kept violent conflict at a fairly low level (Klugman forthcoming). As noted earlier, the state can also deliberately foster violence to undermine opposition groups, often provoking violent reactions by its actions (as in Burundi, Haiti, Rwanda, and Uganda).

Fourth, conflicts need resources, including arms, soldiers, and food. Fighting groups can survive without foreign resources, but the availability of support, credit, food, technical advice, and arms helps feed the conflict. Resources supplied by governments helped finance the wars in Afghanistan, Cambodia, Central America, and Sudan, for example. Private finance from companies seeking mineral resources, from the sale of drugs, and from international crime have been important in Angola, Afghanistan, the Balkans, Congo, and Guatemala.[2] Finance is rarely an effective constraint, partly because wars do not always cost much (a low-level conflict, like the one in Somalia, does not use expensive weapons), partly because they create opportunities for making money (through theft, black markets, and other crimes), and partly because generous sources of credit seem to be available for those at war.[3]

Trigger Events

Where there is a high potential for conflict, a trigger event may cause it to erupt. A trigger can be a change in relative access to an important resource; a political event, such as the Russian invasion of Afghanistan; a policy change; or an endogenous or international development. Endogenous or semiendogenous developments include growing population or land pressures; environmental changes, such as desertification; or changes brought about by the success or failure of a development model, which results in changes in absolute and relative access to employment and income. For example, some have argued that tensions arising from growing land pressures contributed to the recent eruption of the Rwanda conflict (André and Platteau 1995).

Policy changes that may lead to conflict include the following:

- **Adjustment and stabilization policies.** Sharp changes in the terms of trade resulting from devaluation, price deregulation, the removal of consumer subsidies, reduced employment and incomes, or changes in state benefits associated with adjustment policies have been suggested as causes of conflict. Yet careful empirical evidence shows that while these often lead to violent protests, the violence tends to be of relatively modest proportions (see Morrisson forthcoming).
- **Political or patronage policies.** These include changes in the distribution of state benefits for political reasons.

International developments can also lead to changes in the relative access of different groups to markets, international terms of trade, debt and interest payments, capital flows, and foreign aid. Reduced aid after the Cold War was arguably one of the causes of the conflicts in Liberia and Sierra Leone, because the governments no longer had the resources to secure allegiance from potential rivals.

Horizontal Versus Vertical Inequality

Unequal societies are not invariably ridden by major conflict. For example, great inequality in Brazil, Kenya, Pakistan, and Thailand has not led to large-scale conflict. Economists' normal way of measuring inequality is a vertical measure—that is, they take everyone in society from top to bottom, measure their incomes, and determine the inequality. What is needed for our analysis is a horizontal measure of inequality between groups, where groups are defined by region, ethnicity, class, or religion—whatever to the most appropriate type of group identification is for a particular society. Sharp vertical inequality with no horizontal inequality is possible, for example, if the average income of all groups is the same but the distribution within each group is highly unequal. It is also possible to have considerable intergroup inequality but little vertical inequality overall because there is little intragroup inequality.

Strong intragroup vertical inequality may actually reduce the potential for intergroup conflict because it may make it more difficult to achieve group cohesion and because elite members of a group may identify more with members of the elite from other groups than with lower-income members of their own group. That may broadly describe the situation in Kenya, but is not always the case. Strong vertical inequality within groups can lead to intragroup resentments, which group leaders exploit by directing animosity against other groups (this crudely summarizes the situation in Rwanda).

It is possible to use the same measures for horizontal inequality as for vertical inequality, such as the Gini coefficient or Theil index, where the population consists of groups rather than individuals. A simpler summary measure is the coefficient of variation. The ratio of the worst-performing group to the average performance and to the best performance are other useful measures. From the perspective of causing resentment and ultimately conflict, consistent relative deprivation across a number of dimensions may be as relevant as the actual coefficient of variation with respect to any one dimension. This may be measured by looking at (and averaging) rankings in performance on different dimensions (elements). Persistence in the same horizontal inequalities across time is another relevant factor. If gaps between groups narrow or reverse, their potential to cause conflict is reduced. Conversely, widening gaps are more likely to provoke conflict. Whether high levels of horizontal inequality are likely to cause serious conflict also depends on the importance of the various groups. Where groups are very small, even if they are discriminated against consistently, their potential to cause conflict on a substantial scale—that is, enough to constitute a complex humanitarian emergency—is limited.

> Economists' normal way of measuring inequality is a vertical measure—that is, they take everyone in society from top to bottom, measure their incomes, and determine the inequality. What is needed for our analysis is a horizontal measure of inequality between groups, where groups are defined by region, ethnicity, class, or religion—whatever the most appropriate type of group identification is for a particular society.

In practice, data may not be available to measure horizontal inequality because most of the focus to date has been on vertical inequality, and even measures of that are often lacking. Moreover, in politically tense societies, governments do not want to publicize horizontal inequalities. However, it is important to collect such data, which are essential for identifying potential problems and possible solutions. Measurement may be relatively easy for some elements, including some aspects of political participation. Rough estimates may be made for others, or proxies may be used—for example, using regional data to represent differences among ethnic groups or using distribution of land as a proxy for distribution of agricultural income.

Identifying the appropriate groups for measuring horizontal inequality presents some fundamental difficulties. In most conflicts, group differentiation is constructed rather than based on objective differences between people. Group construction is dynamic and fluid, changing with circumstances. In some situations, group identification may be obvious, as when a conflict has gone on for many years and the lines of differentiation are clearly drawn. In others, groups may split or new groups may emerge in response to the developing situation. Not only may it be difficult to identify, but doing so may actually change the situation, either by reinforcing distinctions or by creating perceived political advantages in new alliances and groupings. Moreover, announceing the existence of a large degree of horizontal inequality may itself be conflict provoking. It is clearly important that the act of measurement, and subsequent policies, avoid making a conflict situation worse.

Policy Conclusions

Analysis of the sources of conflict has strong implications for policy formulation aimed at preventing or ending conflict. Policy needs to address the underlying causes systematically. As a priority, policy formulation needs to consider both horizontal inequality among groups and private incentives to leaders and followers; the two sets of issues overlap but are not the same. Policy change is particularly difficult to achieve in a country that has experienced violence, because of inherited memories and grievances, entrenched group identity, and intergroup animosities. The government is rarely broadly based. In some cases, it is even questionable whether the government wants peace, given the prevalence of state-instigated violence. The same may be true of the international community, which has also taken actions that are conflict provoking.

Group (or Horizontal) Inequality

Policy must strive to reduce group inequalities. To achieve this, it is essential that government be inclusive politically, economically, and socially. Political inclusiveness means that all major groups in a society share political power and participate in the administration, the army, and the police. Economic inclusiveness implies moderate horizontal inequality in such economic factors as assets, employment, and incomes. Social inclusiveness means that horizontal inequality in social participation and well-being is also moderate.

Political Inclusiveness

The universal requirement for preventing conflict is political inclusiveness, which is one of the most difficult changes to institute. It is not just a matter of democracy, defined as rule with the support of the majority, because majority rule can be consistent with the abuse of minorities, as in Cambodia, Rwanda, and Zimbabwe. In a politically inclusive democratic system, particular types of proportional representation are needed to ensure participation by all major groups. Representation of all such groups is essential not only at the cabinet level but also in other areas of government, including the civil service, the army, and the police.

Every case of conflict observed lacks such inclusiveness. Thus the requirement for political inclusiveness can be regarded as a universal prescription for conflict-prone societies. Politically inclusive policies have been adopted by well-known peacemaking regimes—for example, the post-Pinochet Chilean government, South Africa under Mandela, and Uganda under Museveni.

These political requirements for conflict-prone countries do not currently form part of the dialogue of political conditionality. The usual political conditionality includes rule with the consent of the majority, multiparty democracy, and respect for human rights. Political conditions for avoiding conflict certainly include respect for human rights. The requirement for majority rule, however, is not sufficient for conflict avoidance, as noted above, while multiparty democracy may not be consistent with conflict prevention because political parties are often formed along ethnic or other group lines and can encourage group animosity (see Stewart and O'Sullivan 1999).

Economic and Social Inclusiveness

Appropriate economic and social recommendations are likely to differ among countries, but those that concern government expenditure and jobs are universal:
- Balanced in-group benefits from government expenditure, investment, and aid
- Balanced in-group access to education (at all levels), health services, water and sanitation, housing, and consumer subsidies (if relevant). Equality of access to education is particularly important, because it contributes to equity in income-earning potential, while its absence perpetuates inequality in incomes
- The private sector as an important source of group differentiation. It is generally a less explosive source of conflict than an inequitable state sector because it is under less direct political control. Still, in societies

such as South Africa, where the private sector is a major source of group inequality in jobs, incomes, and assets, horizontal inequality in the private sector could be conducive to conflict. In such a situation, policies are necessary to reduce the horizontal inequalities in the private sector. Depending on country circumstances, there could be policies to address the following:
- Land reform, to ensure fair access to land by different groups in countries such as El Salvador, where differential access to land is an important aspect of horizontal inequality.
- Balanced participation in education and the acquisition of skills at all levels.
- Balanced access to industrial assets and employment. This need be attempted only where the private sector is a major source of group inequality, which is rarely the case in conflicts in developing economies. Where the private sector is a major source of horizontal inequality, regulations need to be introduced to address the inequality. For example, private firms may be required to have an equal opportunity policy and to provide a certain proportion of jobs at every level to members of the main groups. Similarly, banks may be required to spread their lending across groups. Asset redistribution across groups can be achieved by government purchase of assets and redistribution to disadvantaged groups. Policies of this sort were introduced by the Malaysian government in its New Economic Policy, which effectively narrowed the gap in income, employment, and assets among the major groups.

Policy requirements differ for every country. The important recommendation is that inclusive policies be established to offset major elements of horizontal inequality.

Many governments are pursuing precisely the opposite policies. It is critically important that the international community require such policies in dealing with conflict-prone countries. They do not do this at present, but distribute aid according to efficiency or poverty considerations, which may not coincide with the need to reduce horizontal inequality. IMF and Bank policy conditionality is blind to these issues—taking no account of horizontal equity in policy prescriptions. As lead institutions, the Bank and IMF must incorporate such considerations into conditionality, not only in project allocation but also in policy conditionality applied to government economic interventions and expenditures. This would require a marked change in programs for conflict-prone countries.

Private Incentives

Policies addressing the need for inclusiveness and group equity might be sufficient to eliminate the underlying causes of conflict. When conflict is already ongoing, however, policies to tackle the root causes may need to be accompanied by policies to encourage particular individuals to stop fighting—that is, to change private incentives. Leaders can be offered positions in government, and lower-level leaders can be offered jobs in the army or civil service or money, as was the case in South Africa and Uganda. Followers need employment, so jobs, land, or agricultural credit can be offered in exchange for arms. The offer of a lump sum upon demobilization appears to have been quite effective after the Mozambique and Uganda wars. Such policies can be expensive and need international support. Moreover, they are difficult to apply in less-organized conflicts, where large numbers of people move in and out of the conflict and no clear demarcation is made between those who fought and those who did not.

General Development Policies

Both general analysis and some econometric evidence suggest a connection between the predisposition to conflict and levels and growth of per capita incomes, although the correlation is not strong (see Auvinen and Nafziger 1999). Equitable and poverty-reducing growth is likely to reduce the propensity to conflict and might make persisting inequalities more tolerable. Hence, policies that succeed in promoting such growth should form part of any pro-peace policy package. Again, however, growth must be widely shared. Inequitably distributed growth can reinforce horizontal inequality and thus promote conflict, as happened in Rwanda.

Conclusion

Conflicts occur in a wide range of countries and situations, and the search for country-specific causes continues. One conclusion stands out. In every major conflict, economic, political, and cultural factors interact with group perceptions and identity, normally historically formed, enhanced by sharp differentiation between groups in political participation, economic assets, income, social access, and well-being. Action on any one front alone—for example, addressing economic but not political inequalities or vice versa, or attempting to change people's views about their identity without changing the underlying inequalities among groups—is unlikely to work.

Notes

This paper draws heavily on a research program conducted by WIDER and Queen Elizabeth House, Oxford, United Kingdom, directed by E. W. Nafziger, F. Stewart, and R. Väyrynen (see Nafziger, Stewart, and Väyrynen forthcoming (a) and (b); Nafziger and Väyrynen 1999).

1. Among the ten countries with the lowest human development indicators, Burundi, Eritrea, Ethiopia, Guinea, Mali, Niger, Mozambique, and Sierra Leone have all suffered civil conflict at some time during the past 20 years.

2. In Angola, for example, the impoverished government is acquiring financing to fight the rebels by selling licenses for oil drilling.

3. A seven-country study of countries at war showed debt rising more rapidly in countries at war than in countries not at war (see Stewart and Fitzgerald forthcoming).

References

Alexander, J., J. McGregor, and T. Ranger. Forthcoming. "Ethnicity and the Politics of Conflict: The Case of Matabeleland." In E. W. Nafziger, F. Stewart, and R. Väyrynen, eds., forthcoming. *The Origin of Humanitarian Emergencies: War and Displacement in Developing Countries.* Oxford, U.K.: Oxford University Press.

André, C., and J-P. Platteau. 1995. "Land Tenure and Unendurable Stress: Rwanda Caught in the Malthusian Trap." Namur, Belgium: Centre de Recherche en Economie du Développement, Faculty of Economics.

Auvinen, J., and E. W. Nafziger. 1999. "The Sources of Humanitarian Emergencies." *Journal of Conflict Resolution* 43(3): 267-90.

Cohen, A. 1974. *Two-dimensional Man: An Essay on the Anthropology of Power and Symbolism in Complex Society.* Berkeley, CA: University of California Press.

Fairhead, J. Forthcoming. "The Conflict over Natural and Environmental Resources." In E. W. Nafziger, F. Stewart, and R. Väyrynen, eds., forthcoming. *The Origin of Humanitarian Emergencies: War and Displacement in Developing Countries.* Oxford, U.K.: Oxford University Press.

Gaffney, P. Forthcoming. "Burundi: The Long Sombre Shadow of Ethnic Instability." In E. W. Nafziger, F. Stewart, and R. Väyrynen, eds., forthcoming. *Weak States and Vulnerable Economies: Humanitarian Emergencies in the Third World.* Oxford, U.K.: Oxford University Press.

Holsti, Halevi K. Forthcoming. "The Political Sources of Humanitarian Disasters." In E. W. Nafziger, F. Stewart, and R. Väyrynen, eds., forthcoming. *The Origin of Humanitarian Emergencies: War and Displacement in Developing Countries.* Oxford, U.K.: Oxford University Press.

Keen, D. 1994. *The Benefits of Famine: A Political Economy of Famine Relief in Southwestern Sudan, 1983-1989.* Princeton, NJ: Princeton University Press.

_____. 1998. "The Economic Functions of Civil Wars." Adelphi Paper 320. International Institute of Strategic Studies, London, U.K.

_____. Forthcoming. "The Political Economy of Civil War." In F. Stewart and E. K. V. Fitzgerald, eds., forthcoming. *The Economic and Social Consequences of Conflict.* Oxford, U.K.: Oxford University Press.

Klugman, J. Forthcoming. "Kenya: Economic Decline and Ethnic Politics." In E. W. Nafziger, F. Stewart, and R. Väyrynen, eds., forthcoming. *Weak States and Vulnerable Economies: Humanitarian Emergencies in the Third World.* Oxford, U.K.: Oxford University Press.

Morrison, C. Forthcoming. "Economic Adjustment." In E. W. Nafziger, F. Stewart, and R. Väyrynen, eds., forthcoming. *The Origin of Humanitarian Emergencies: War and Displacement in Developing Countries.* Oxford, U.K.: Oxford University Press.

Nafziger, E. W. 1983. *The Economics of Political Instability: The Nigerian-Biafran War.* Boulder, CO: Westview.

Nafziger, E. W., F. Stewart, and R. Väyrynen, eds. Forthcoming (a). *The Origin of Humanitarian Emergencies: War and Displacement in Developing Countries.* Oxford, U.K.: Oxford University Press.

_____, eds. forthcoming b. *Weak States and Vulnerable Economies: Humanitarian Emergencies in the Third World.* Oxford, U.K.: Oxford University Press.

Reno, W. Forthcoming. "Liberia and Sierra Leone: The Competition for Patronage in Resource-Rich Economies." In E. W. Nafziger, F. Stewart, and R. Väyrynen, eds. Forthcoming (b). *Weak States and Vulnerable Economies: Humanitarian Emergencies in the Third World.* Oxford, U.K.: Oxford University Press.

Stewart, F., and E. K. V. Fitzgerald. Forthcoming. *The Economic and Social Consequences of Conflict.* Oxford, U.K.: Oxford University Press.

Stewart, F., and M. O'Sullivan. 1999. "Democracy, Conflict and Development: Three Cases." In G. Ranis and others, eds., 1999. *The Political Economy of Comparative Developments into the 21st Century: Essays in Memory of John C. H. Fei.* Cheltenham, U.K.: Edward Elgar Publishing.

Uvin, P. Forthcoming. "Rwanda: The Social Roots of Genocide." In E. W. Nafziger, F. Stewart, and R. Väyrynen, eds., forthcoming. *Weak States and Vulnerable Economies: Humanitarian Emergencies in the Third World.* Oxford, U.K.: Oxford University Press.

Comments: Tackling Horizontal Inequalities

Lawrence Haddad

Stewart's paper argues that differences in groups' economic, political, or social circumstances—horizontal inequalities—are strong contributing factors to civil war. And civil wars not only generate human suffering but undermine economic growth and poverty reduction efforts. Stewart recommends that development policy should pay attention to these horizontal inequalities as well as to the more traditional concerns of efficiency and vertical inequality, such as income distribution by income class.

In my view, the paper might have (1) provided a few data-based examples of horizontal inequalities and explained to what degree they corresponded to vertical inequalities, (2) supplemented the policy conclusions with more concrete recommendations, and (3) assessed the international community's efforts to address horizontal inequalities and discussed what is keeping the international community from doing more. Let me offer comments section by section.

The Causes of Conflict

In the section on motivation, mobilization, and conflict, Stewart analyzes the causes of conflict, contending that they are a function of the interaction among (1) structural conditions, including large relative differences among groups, or horizontal inequality; (2) means, including political leadership, to mobilize the group as well as opportunities for finance; and (3) triggers, including land pressures, changes in aid flows, and political realignments. This section is interesting, but Stewart does not make it clear why horizontal inequality predisposes a society to conflict any more than, say, a diminishing level of welfare throughout the population.

Horizontal and Vertical Inequality

In the section on the differences between horizontal and vertical inequality, Stewart poses two hypotheses: that horizontal and vertical inequality do not necessarily go hand in hand and that intragroup equality may promote intergroup conflict, all other things being equal. He also describes some of the problems in measuring horizontal inequality. I have several comments on this section.

- Identifying the groups on which politicians focus will bring the long-ignored dimension of political economy into the economic analysis of economic growth and poverty reduction efforts. Why do governments behave as they do? In this regard, a reference to the work of Besley and Case (1995) might be useful. If some of these groups can be identified, the difficulties of constructing measures of horizontal inequality may prove to be overstated, given the availability of data from World Bank household surveys, DHS surveys, IFPRI surveys, and others.

- It would then be possible to begin testing Stewart's hypotheses, perhaps within a cross-country or time-series regression framework. Perhaps it would even be possible to establish some kind of early warning system about conflict. Perhaps USAID's FEWS initiative, for example, could assemble information of value to diplomatic missions throughout the developing world.
- The literature on microcredit deals with the subject of social cohesion within informal, joint liability types of organizations. In general, these studies find that increased social cohesion leads to higher repayment rates and that with greater economic heterogeneity, enterprises become more sustainable. In other words, horizontal and vertical inequality combine to form effective institutions (see Zeller 1998).
- The literature on social capital (for example, Grootaert 1998; Maluccio, Haddad, and May 1999) is also relevant. The crude measure of one's social capital is typically the number of groups to which one belongs, the strength of those groups, and their heterogeneity (more being better). Assumptions about social capital could well be tested by breaking out group heterogeneity along economic and sociocultural lines.

Conflict and Policy Change

As Stewart notes in his policy conclusions, there is a good deal of consensus about the policies needed for poverty-reducing growth, and reductions in poverty do much to reduce the propensity for conflict. But Stewart stresses that a conflict-prone environment makes it much less likely that these policies will be adopted or, if adopted, will be effective. He also asserts that (1) conflict-prone countries are often unable or unwilling to make the type of policy changes recommended here, (2) international policy conditionality is blind to these issues, and (3) the international community may be unwilling to adopt the types of policy changes recommended. I have several comments on this section.

- It would be interesting to test the lack of correspondence between democracy and political inclusion. One could do so by using the country indexes of political and civil liberties assembled by organizations such as Freedom House (1997).
- International conditionality is probably blind to these issues because donors do not know the country context well enough or perceive that paying attention to such issues would be resented as meddling. Stewart himself warns that attention to horizontal inequalities could make matters worse.
- Transaction costs could limit countries' ability to reduce persistent horizontal inequalities. I draw on three examples from recent work:
  - In Mozambique IFPRI undertook the first poverty profile ever conducted. There it found poverty to be greatest in opposition-held areas. You can imagine how sensitive this was for the government. They

argued—correctly, we felt—that these areas were the poorest because they were hardest hit by war and that it was in these areas that the infrastructure so crucial to development was most lacking. One must look not simply at the differences in welfare between groups but also at the trends in those differences (Datt and others 1999).
- In the western Cape in South Africa, IFPRI found 1997 public works expenditures to be skewed away from black and colored neighborhoods and skewed toward the white neighborhoods. The government was disappointed with this allocation outcome, a legacy of apartheid. The better-connected communities were able to put together better proposals for government funding (Adato and others 1999).
- In Ethiopia, a recent study found food aid to be skewed toward government-supported areas. In the early 1990s these were indeed the poorest areas, but in the late 1990s they no longer were. Given the difficulty of constructing new infrastructure, it is not surprising that the new food aid followed the old infrastructure (Jayne, Strauss, and Yamano 1999).

Gender Inequality

Finally, gender inequality is a form of horizontal inequality that governments and international institutions often examine. Gender inequalities do not lead to civil war at the national level. They might at the household level, but it is an unequal fight. Women tend to have fewer fallback positions in the event of noncooperation, as well as less ability to bargain at a given fallback position (Haddad, Hoddinott, and Alderman 1997). Lessons may be available from the literature on gender inequality to include in broad policy on horizontal inequalities. The bargaining model might also be a useful economic tool for helping to conceptualize the actions of different groups. Groups that initiate conflict tend to think that nonconflict (cooperation) will lead to welfare outcomes worse what they could expect from conflict (noncooperation). Depending on the bargaining perspective, these groups think either that they have nothing to lose from conflict or that they have everything to gain.

I look forward to seeing Stewart's hypotheses supplemented by links to other literature and then put to the test with quantitative data. Following Kanbur and Lustig's (1999) recent arguments, this paper gives one more reason why inequality is back on the agenda.

References

Adato, M., and others. 1999. "The Performance of Labor-intensive Public Works in South Africa." Washington, D.C.: IFPRI.

Besley, T., and A. Case. 1995. "Incumbent Behavior: Vote Seeking, Tax Setting, and Yardstick Competition." *American Economic Review* 85(1): 25-45.

Datt, G., and others. 1999. "Poverty Levels and Determinants in Mozambique." Washington, D.C.: IFPRI.

Freedom House. 1997.

Grootaert, C. 1998. "Social Capital and Household Welfare in Indonesia." World Bank, Washington, D.C.

Haddad, L., J. Hoddinott, and H. Alderman. 1997. *Intrahousehold Resource Allocation: Methods, Models and Policy.* Baltimore, Maryland: The Johns Hopkins University Press.

Jayne, T., J. Strauss, and T. Yamano. 1999. "Targeting of Food Aid in Rural Ethiopia: Chronic Need or Inertia?" Michigan State University, Lansing, Michigan.

Kanbur, R., and N. Lustig. 1999. "Why Is Inequality Back on the Agenda?" Eleventh Annual Bank Conference on Development Economics, April 28-30, World Bank, Washington, D.C.

Maluccio, J., L. Haddad, and J. May. Forthcoming. "Social Capital and Income Generation in South Africa, 1993-1998." *Journal of Development Studies.*

Zeller, M. 1998. "Determinants of Repayment Performance in Credit Groups: The Role of Program Design, Intragroup Risk Pooling and Social Cohesion." *Economic Development and Cultural Change* 46(3): 599-620.

Floor Discussion: Tackling Horizontal Inequalities

Several participants said they were beginning to see safety nets in a different light, because Stewart's paper made them aware that policy changes or shocks to the system could lead to a complicated pattern of distributional change, including inequality. By protecting people generally, safety nets could prevent political or economic changes from causing dangerous ethnic or regional realignments. Conflict is a normal dynamic in every society, but it is important to manage that conflict peacefully. Although the aim is to prevent an acute or violent crisis, conflict has led to many positive social changes and to poverty reduction efforts.

The problem was donors did not see conflict as an issue unless it became acute or violent, so they did not engage in risk management when they operated in an environment of relatively peaceful conflict. Even now there are groups in Ethiopia and Somalia, for example, that are trying to maintain an "us versus them" approach to political, social, and economic problems. These are the groups donors should be targeting.

Lessons about risk management can be learned from societies that have moved or are moving out of conflict. Such societies are very careful. In South Africa's new constitution, for example, or the Northern Ireland peace agreement, the aim is to avoid situations in which the majority, often poor or politically disenfranchised for many years, could harm the elite minority.

In addition to managing tensions arising from such vertical inequalities, donors need to study how to bridge horizontal inequalities within groups. They also need to consider how they might have created some of those inequalities by giving more resources to certain populations. This reallocation of resources itself could trigger conflict.

One major problem in conflict prevention is knowing how to measure and collect data. We need to learn how to define the needs of different groups, especially groups that are fluid, that form and then reform themselves. We also need to learn how to better measure inequality between groups. Measuring vertical inequality is important for poverty reduction; measuring horizontal inequality is better for conflict prevention. Indonesia is a case in point. It did well in reducing vertical inequality and poverty, but left many horizontal inequalities, of which we are now seeing the results.

The development community does not yet accept the idea of studying the causes of conflict or learning from the literature on conflict. Preventing conflict in low-income societies is an exciting new field, one in which much work remains to be done.

Sawong Hong of the United Nation's Children's Fund chaired the discussion.

17

Governance and Anticorruption: New Insights and Challenges

Daniel Kaufmann

A recent survey of African government officials and high-level representatives of civil society during a Bank seminar revealed their opinion that the highest cost of corruption was increased poverty and reduced access by the poor to public services. This is a major change. Corruption is no longer seen primarily in moral or ethical terms but in terms of its impact on poverty. We cannot alleviate poverty in a sustainable way without combatting corruption and without evaluating the relevance, effectiveness, and efficiency of anticorruption programs.

The fight against corruption includes three major components: institutional reforms; collective action and leadership of governments, civil society, and private sector institutions; and, most important, data, information, and knowledge.

The work that the Bank is planning to do on governance and anticorruption emphasizes both process and substance. In the past few years, the Bank has collected an extensive databank on governance and institutional indicators. Staff are collecting more data in several African countries, particularly on the importance of the leadership of public, civil society, and financial institutions. They are finding important differences in the nature and magnitude of corruption. Clearly, one must differentiate within regions and be careful about generalizations. The claim that Africa is totally corrupt is a myth. Botswana, for example, rates better on corruption and bribery than most other developing countries; Angola, Cameroon, and Nigeria rate worse on corruption and bribery; and a number of other African countries fall in the middle.

Another consideration is the multidimensional nature of corruption with its many different manifestations. Judiciary bribery may be more prevalent in Latin America. In transition economies, bureaucratic bribery may be more common because the bureaucracy is the main locus of decisionmaking. Russia and Ukraine are rated as extremely corrupt in the banking sector.

The notion that corruption never changes or changes extremely slowly is a myth, as some data suggest. For instance, El Salvador and Poland have both shown major improvements in governance. These countries initiated institutional economic reforms without touting major anticorruption campaigns. Instead, they tackled economic and social fundamentals.

Let us review some of the challenges we face in fighting corruption and improving governance, starting with a story from Ukraine.

The Challenges

It is a Thursday in October 1994 at the Kiev World Bank resident mission's weekly roundtable debate with the media, public officials, and civil society. The topic this afternoon is the ever latent potential for economic reform and recovery. The newly appointed vice premier in charge of the economy, a reformist, is engaged in a heated discussion about the government's intention to reform, arguing that this time the intention is in earnest. The skepticism of many of the roundtable participants is palpable, and one participant reminds the group of the country's poor record in implementing reforms.

One of the most prominent journalists in the country challenges the vice premier by pointing out that, no matter what macroeconomic reforms the new cabinet manages to implement, growth prospects remain dim. The journalist eloquently states that growth derives only from a thriving private sector, yet such prospects do not exist, he says, because of the private mafia, which extracts a high toll from any private enterprise.

The new vice premier calmly concurs about the need to focus on small enterprises in the emerging private sector. Furthermore, he agrees that a private mafia does exist and does extract a "tax" from private businesses. His back-of-the-envelope calculations suggest that, on average, such a tax amounts to about 10 percent of a firm's revenues. While this is far from negligible, he continues, it pales in comparison with the predatory behavior of the government mafia. His quick calculations indicate that this private sector tax exceeds 50 percent.

Four years have since elapsed. Recent accounts suggest little has changed, and not only in Ukraine. The challenge of addressing government predation is not universal, but it is ubiquitous. It is worth considering the subtle wisdom conveyed by the vice premier during that Thursday roundtable to ask whether his advice has been heeded or whether a major challenge still remains.

The vice premier showed a basic understanding of the power of transparency in a participatory public forum, given his admission of government fallibility so early in the post-Soviet era. He also exhibited unusual foresight in conceptualizing corruption as a public sector development challenge and not merely a private criminal activity. He implicitly challenged the Bank to quantify the problem, indicating that generalized pronouncements about the harm inflicted by different factors was not enough. He indicated that blaming the private mafia instead of predatory politicians and bureaucrats only diverted attention from the true problem. He hinted at the desirability of anchoring the understanding of corruption in the discipline of public finance, unwittingly challenging the prevailing views of institutional and legal fixes and myriad soft ethical exhortations. He implicitly suggested that the Bank examine taxation, bribery, dwindling public revenues, and the absence of the rule of law in an integrated fashion by framing the problem in terms of the tax burden. He challenged those at the conference to address corruption on a sound analytical basis.

Global Progress

The struggle to combat corruption has made progress in many corners of the world, but most of the challenge posed by the Ukrainian vice premier four years ago remains. Participatory approaches still require more rigorous integration with concrete reforms of incentives, systems, and institutions; the role of detailed, in-depth empirical work needs to be expanded; and bribery and corruption need to be examined within a broader analytical framework, either through public finance or other disciplines or through an interdisciplinary approach.

Because the field of empirical investigation into the causes of, consequences of, and "cures" for corruption is still in its infancy, I intend here not to present definitive answers but to raise questions and issues about coming challenges in the field. I'll discuss four broad challenges emerging from recent collaborative work.

Participation by Civil Society

The growing involvement of civil society and NGOs in the fight against corruption is an undisputed fact, as is their role in increasing awareness and mobilizing support. Progress in the fight against corruption requires at least a minimum level of organization in civil society and an environment in which civil liberties are safeguarded. In many countries, these conditions do not exist, although the importance of civil liberties is clear. Current empirical research indicates that countries with improved civil liberties are significantly more successful at addressing corruption, even after controlling for other determinants.

Promoting a more effective civil society in a country with no tradition of doing so is a major challenge. First, the Bank must make full use of the power of data and technology to mobilize civil society and to apply pressure on political structures. The use of survey data, public workshops, and in-country focus groups, combined with the involvement of the media and other stakeholders, builds momentum and spearheads new activities by civil society and NGOs.[1]

Second, although it may seem paradoxical, many in the public sector can become significant allies—however silently at first—in fighting corruption. Collaboration between reform-minded public officials and NGOs may be particularly productive when civil society is not fully developed. Survey results from more than 60 countries reveal a remarkable degree of consensus between civil society and the public sector on the severity of the corruption challenge.

Third, the empowerment of women to mobilize civil society, particularly against corruption, needs further attention. Research suggests that corruption is more prevalent when women's rights are restricted.

Fourth, new tools and insights are emerging regarding participatory approaches to fighting corruption. National chapters of Transparency International and NGOs in India have explored these approaches, using the citizens' scorecard approach.

Fifth, the intricate links between politics and civil liberties need to be better understood to deepen our understanding of the roots of corruption. The extent of political liberties (that is, democracy) has a positive correlation with improved control of corruption, but may be less potent than that of civil liberties. Where executive political will exists, NGOs and civil society may act as partners with the government in implementing anticorruption programs. Where such political will is absent, civil society needs to foster a willingness to reform among the political leadership.

Finally, how relevant is the government's political ideology in addressing corruption? Evidence shows that a government's ideology is irrelevant. On average, the extent of corruption is the same whether the government is left-wing or right-wing. The challenges lie elsewhere.

Integrating Participatory Processes with Institutional Reforms

For too long, economists have underestimated the importance of participation in development. The evidence is now clear that participation is the key to development. In the context of anticorruption efforts, major strides are taking place in developing and applying a well-structured technology to grassroots participation. Parallel strides have been made in understanding how economic and institutional reforms help control corruption. These two approaches are complements to each other, not substitutes. Any participatory process should lead to concrete results beyond enhanced participation and heightened awareness. Equally important, the implementation of institutional reform benefits from the participatory process developed for anticorruption activities.

Toward Methodological Rigor

Serious anticorruption action programs are in their infancy and rife with misconceptions about strategies and policy implications, often for lack of in-depth analytical and empirical underpinnings for the proposed anticorruption actions. Research on corruption must probe data from not only an economic but a multidisciplinary standpoint. A better understanding of the causes and costs of corruption will probably reveal that improved measurement of corruption indicators is also necessary.

A challenge not yet addressed is the best approach to corruption as a field of inquiry. Should it be a freestanding field of investigation and academic training, consistent with its belated, yet acknowledged, importance for development and social welfare? Or because corruption is increasingly recognized as a symptom of institutional weakness, should it be integrated within existing fields of inquiry that until now have not paid sufficient attention to corruption? If so, which fields of inquiry?

> A better understanding of the causes and costs of corruption will probably reveal that improved measurement of corruption indicators is also necessary.

As the Ukrainian vice premier's remarks suggested, a strong case exists for expanding the treatment of corruption within a public finance framework. This would make it easier to determine (a) the costliest types of corruption, (b) the costs and benefits of different government interventions, (c) the losses to public finance resulting from corruption, (d) the role and costs of regulatory intervention, and (e) the correct incentives to discourage bribery by foreign investors.

The Empirical Challenge

Not long ago it was a truism that corruption by its intrinsic nature was impossible to measure. The advent of new surveys and other data gathering techniques helped dispel this belief. A rich empirical body of data is emerging on governance variables and government performance in general, and on corruption in particular. The challenge is to improve the gathering, analyzing, and disseminating of these new data.

Increasingly, the media and opposition politicians are using and interpreting indexes such as those of Transparency International as if they provided an accurate picture of a worldwide corruption ranking, although most indexes typically cover only fifty or so countries and the margin of error in the ranking of a particular country can be large. Sounder survey data and methodologies are needed to help make responsible choices about programs to control corruption.

The Challenge of Concrete and Informed Action

The challenges discussed here are by no means exhaustive. We still need to understand the reasons for the paucity of successful public sector reform in developing countries. In the countries where reforms have succeeded, we need to identify the particular measures and institutions that account for that success. Poland might be an interesting case study because its governance and economic performance have been remarkable, particularly in contrast to many other countries in the region. What produced these remarkable results? Indeed, what actually accounts for Poland's superior governance performance compared with its neighbors to the east, including the Ukraine?

This presentation has made a case for significantly expanding the empirical approach to controlling corruption and improving governance. We need to continue to probe, explore, and innovate, recognizing that we are in the midst of a fast-paced learning process. What we do know is that working in partnership with local institutions and experts is essential. Citizens—in or out of government—know their country better than outsiders.

At the same time, the data and lessons garnered from experience worldwide are beginning to provide clear insights that need to be disseminated confidently and widely. These insights, if effectively adapted to country conditions and if complemented by political will, could yield concrete results. The challenge for political leadership, civil society, and the donor community is to capitalize on the insights and momentum generated by the diagnostics, move from diagnostics to action, and make meaningful progress on institutional reforms.

Note

1. Data are far more than a passive research tool. When well gathered, analyzed, and presented, survey data complemented by hard financial information is virtually impossible for authorities to ignore.

Comments: Governance and Anticorruption: New Insights and Challenges

Anwar Shah

Assuming that current anticorruption strategies have been pursued successfully, Kaufmann tries to persuade the Bank to move on to the next steps in anticorruption efforts, which in Kaufmann's view are as follows:
- Mobilize civil society by using the power of data gathered through surveys, workshops, and focus groups.
- Support collaboration among reform-minded public officials and NGOs.
- Empower women to mobilize civil society.
- Use new tools such as those used by national chapters of Transparency International.
- Understand the intricate links between politics and civil liberties.
- Do not worry about the political ideology of the ruling party.
- Use participatory processes to implement institutional reforms.
- Use analytical rigor and improved data.

His message is to do more of what is being done now. No systematic evaluation is available, but neither data nor perceptions about corruption support the rosy picture Kaufmann's paper paints on progress in fighting corruption.

Kaufmann's perspective on corruption implicitly recognizes that public officials cannot be trusted to manage the public purse, because the temptations are too great for poorly paid civil servants to steal for their personal enrichment. One can broadly characterize Kaufmann's views as flowing from Aristotle's tradition of advocating transparency in government so money flows can be traced. The Athenian city council adopted an opposing view, requiring all elected officials to swear they would leave the city better and more beautiful than it was when they took office. Kaufmann's (Aristotelian) approach emphasizes accountability for misdeeds; the Athenian approach emphasizes accountability for results, with evaluation.

The Aristotelian approach—emphasizing transparency in government and mechanisms for pursuing corrupt officials—is universally embraced by the development community, including the Bank and the IMF. Aristotle argued that to protect the Treasury from being defrauded, all government business should be conducted openly and multiple copies of all monetary transactions should be deposited in various wards. Transparency in government has formed the cornerstone of the anticorruption strategies advocated by the IMF, the Bank, the UNDP, and Transparency International. The usefulness of such a strategy is beyond question, but its effectiveness in curtailing corruption is unclear.

The results-oriented management and evaluation approach, which the council of the city of Athens pursued, is the one most Western countries tend to follow. In Athens, the focus of this strategy was to gain public trust through improved public performance. Such an improvement in public performance was to be brought about not by controlling inputs (an emphasis for which transparency is important) but through a sense of public duty and accountability for results. This is the commitment elected leaders in the Western world make to their electorates. In moving from a corrupt to a responsive, accountable public service, the Western world has always focused more on improving public sector performance than on catching the big fish and frying it. Introducing the results-based approach to curtailing corruption in developing countries would require creating an incentive structure that transforms the culture and values of the civil service. The anticorruption approaches discussed in international forums do not yet recognize such an emphasis on accountability for results. Citizens in developing countries yearn for this approach but have no voice in changing policy responses.

Let us review and comment on some of Kaufman's stylized facts:

Corruption is pervasive in many developing countries. One can hardly disagree with Kaufmann's highlighting of the pervasiveness of corruption in the developing world. But development finance officials' perceptions about corruption differ greatly from those of citizens in corrupt societies, as do their needs and proposed solutions for corruption.

Awareness about corruption is strong in the developing world, but its explicit recognition in the development assistance community is relatively weak. A few years ago, as Kaufmann notes, Bank staff could not even use the word "corruption." Now the Bank is launching major efforts to raise awareness about the incidence and consequences of corruption. This laudable effort, attuned to the needs of the development assistance community, is of little benefit to ordinary citizens in developing countries. Average citizens on the streets of Brunei, Nigeria, Pakistan, or Rwanda know exactly what they have to pay to get access to various public services. Although the development community's awareness-raising efforts are wasted on these citizens, they are valuable to the development finance community and to public officials in the developing countries.

Anticorruption programs are in vogue but appear to be having little impact. The incidence of corruption appears to be on the rise. Indeed, the more corrupt the country becomes, the more institutional arrangements to deal with corruption it seems to have. Pakistan, for example, has the Office of the Auditor General, the Anticorruption Agency, the Ethics Office, the Ehtisab (Accountability) Bureau, the Criminal Investigations Agency, and special courts dealing with corruption. But corruption remains pervasive because, although the punishment for malfeasance could be severe, the probability of being caught is slight. This is especially true when internal controls require that the loot be shared by all, including the audit and anticorruption agencies. What is missing is an incentive framework to ensure accountability for results. Corruption is a symptom of a broader disease. Before we can curtail corruption, we must first deal with the disease, which includes the bureaucratic command-and-control culture and the lack of concern about, and responsiveness to, citizens and service delivery issues.

Despite many advances, the measurement of corruption is still in its infancy and is subject to major limitations. The measurements that exist are overly focused on the needs of the development community rather than on the needs of people in the developing world. Transparency International's extremely useful corruption perceptions index, for example, is a composite of seven or eight components, only one of which (introduced in 1997) measures citizens' perceptions about corruption. The other components measure foreign investors' and business executives' perceptions about corruption, reflecting its focus on the development community's needs.

Globalization, localization, the information revolution, and a tendency toward more contractual arrangements are having a restraining influence on corruption. Two factors that are having a major impact on corruption—globalization and localization—have little to do with corruption. Globalization has substantially reduced the influence of central governments, in terms of state activities. The nation state is becoming too small to tackle large issues and too large to tackle small issues. Corruption declines and governance improves with the greater citizen empowerment that has come with both localization and consumer access to global markets (Huther and Shah 1998).

> The nation state is becoming too small to tackle large issues and too large to tackle small issues.

Moreover, we are moving from a public sector in which jobs are permanent to a public sector that is performance oriented. Contractualism, which is increasingly significant in the industrial world, is happening only piecemeal in the developing world. Still, the ideas are influencing policy thinking in developing countries. The new model requires a cultural change: from controlling inputs to accountability for results, from top-down accountability to bottom-up accountability, from a focus on low wages with high perks to competitive wages with little else, from lifelong rotating appointments to a stay-with-it culture, and from intolerance for risk to freedom to succeed or fail. In this new culture it may be easier to deal more effectively with corruption.

Evaluation literature on corruption is limited. Those involved in developing an anticorruption strategy must recognize that external perspectives differ from those of local citizens, both on the causes of corruption and on what should be done about it. The perspectives of developing country officials and citizens also differ. Officials have more affinity for external policy prescriptions than do most countries' residents. In analyzing the causes of corruption through assistance programs, many external entities tend to focus on such issues as low awareness of corruption, low wages and wage compression, heavy public employment, and the size of the public sector. Citizens place more emphasis on bottom-up accountability, the rule of law, the lack of a citizen's charter, and similar factors. In terms of action plans, external entities are more interested in carrying out surveys, holding workshops, running anticorruption programs, strengthening top-down accountability, and raising public sector wages. Citizens seek reform of the public sector, including changes in the bureaucratic culture and stronger accountability from the bottom up.

To get the strategy right and to encourage sustainable local ownership of efforts to get at both the causes and consequences of corruption, evaluation needs to be done in a more participatory way, taking all stakeholders' viewpoints into account.

References

Huther, Jeff, and Anwar Shah. 1998. "Applying a Simple Measure of Good Governance to the Debate on Fiscal Decentralization." Policy Research Working Paper 1894. Washington, D.C.: World Bank.

Floor Discussion: Governance and Anticorruption

The discussion began with a question about whether Kaufmann thought the anticorruption strategies sponsored by multilateral donor organizations could build sustainability into the programs so that those efforts were not just temporary, but part of each country's institutional framework.

Kaufmann said the key was to institutionalize the programs. He described a recent fascinating interview he had had with the Colombia head of police, a maverick in the midst of chaos and corruption. The man had managed to reform the police department in ways Kaufmann thought virtually no other Latin American country could have done. Kaufmann asked the man what would happen when someone else succeeded him. Would the reform be sustainable? The man replied that he was certain his successor would not revert to corrupt practices, for three reasons. First, they had reformed institutional incentives in such a way that it would be difficult to reverse them. Second, they were using the power of information. They conducted constant surveys and the information from those surveys was transparent at every level. Third, they had created a board of overseers composed of the most respected members of civil society in Colombia. That board kept the police honest by overseeing independent surveys of what was going on within the police department and by surveying the police officers themselves. These were the police chief's hope for the future.

A member of the audience asked what topics the Bank was addressing to combat corruption.

Kaufmann replied that to fight corruption, one had to analyze its fundamental causes. As Shah had suggested, this was an important learning period for the Bank, which had just completed the first stage of increasing awareness of the problem. The Bank would have to learn considerably more before it knew what action programs might work. It did not have the answers yet.

Without question, institutional reform was essential for combatting corruption. The first task was to analyze which institutional reforms made sense — and these might be very different in different countries. The Bank was facing a multidimensional, multidisciplinary task, which would probably require attention to at least five different types of issues: 1) taxes, deregulation, budgetary reform, and how to minimize rent-seeking; 2) public sector reform, especially the training of civil service professionals; 3) law enforcement, which might require legal and judicial reform; 4) financial management, with procurement procedures as the first reform target; and 5) better oversight by civil society. Different issues would be more or less important in different countries.

Asked about changing the bureaucratic culture, Kaufmann said he thought bureaucratic culture could change, perhaps not within weeks, but relatively

---

Gabriel Karissa of the African Development Bank chaired the discussion.

fast when the whole incentive structure changed. The question was how to to make changes, which was something everyone involved was trying to grasp.

A participant from Finland said that corruption could add considerably to the costs of any program, crippling donor efforts, so it had to be mainstreamed into evaluation the way gender or environmental issues were now being mainstreamed. Anyone carrying out evaluation should look at corruption. In Finland, politicians had been paying considerable attention to corruption and foreign assistance, and the parliament wanted to know what his organization was going to do about it, how it was going to implement guidelines to fight corruption. Because of rampant corruption, Finland had cut back on foreign assistance in many activities that were otherwise possible. The dilemma of rampant corruption causing so many cutbacks made the participant's organization feel helpless. In the end the corruption and cutbacks would most hurt the very poor, so it was important how the conferees saw evaluation addressing the problem of corruption. He wanted to know what came out of the evaluation studies and how his organization could reprogram its efforts to continue cooperation.

Another participant asked if the Finnish participant's organization had already built the issue of corruption into its evaluations. He was told it had, although most donors probably had not. There was no question, said the participant from Finland, that donors' evaluations must address the issue of corruption. They needed to have a response when citizens asked, "Where is our money going? If we give a dollar to save a baby and 50 cents of it goes to corruption, our dollar could have saved two babies."

Another participant asked to comment on the need for transparency and gave an example from Argentina. The local NGO partners of Transparency International went to Buenos Aires, collected information on the cost of a school lunch, and found that it was on average US$5 per child for a school lunch. In the province of Mendoza, however, it was only US$1. This broke as a major scandal in the local newspaper and heads were rolling within a week. So transparency could be simply an issue of getting the information out to the public. Sometimes donors needed to be innovative at working around government. The notion that an anticorruption campaign could be run from a government office was a fantasy. Engaging NGOs more in corrupt countries could help.

Building on that point, a participant concluded that one conference objective was to look at partnerships in evaluation. Addressing corruption, more than any other development issue, should be at the heart of participatory and partnership approaches to evaluation. One could not learn effective lessons from evaluations of corruption and anticorruption measures without involving all of the different partners. One could achieve objectivity in evaluations only by hearing the voices of all the relevant stakeholders and thereby getting a balance of perspectives.

18

Panel Discussion: Combatting Public Corruption

Jack Titsworth, Navin Girishankar, El Sayed Zaki

Jack Titsworth

Corruption is the abuse of public office for private gain. Therefore, corruption could be financial, nepotism in public appointments, or orientation of a policy to favor somebody. Data from the Bank show that several areas of the world have a high rate of corrupt practices.

The word corruption has existed in African languages for a long time, *barushwa* in Swahili and *seraven* in languages of West Africa. *Seraven* means a gift given at night that you cannot see. Someone spoke about corruption being like mushrooms, which can be poisonous and grow in the dark.

Corruption has always existed, but it has increased over the years. Poor people have usually had to pay bribes, but now they have to pay bribes almost every time they have encounters with the government. A Ugandan journalist described a child carried on its mother's back learning the routine of corrupt practice. The child's mother has to pay something every time she meets a public servant, and the child thinks this is normal.

The level of corruption in a country fluctuates. In 1992, when I was living in Kenya, estimates indicated that about 8 percent of GDP was siphoned off, mainly through the Goldenberg scandal, which involved fictitious exports of gold, with the government paying something along the way.

However, the pervasiveness of corruption varies a great deal in Africa. Nigeria represents the global median for corrupt practices, but surprisingly, Cameroon, Congo, and Guinea rank much higher than Nigeria for corruption. These data are based not on just one measure but on several. South Africa ranks the lowest.

Robert Klitgaard came up with the formula that corruption is equal to monopoly plus discretion minus accountability and transparency. If you are importing a car and you have to pay somewhere between 10 and 20 percent, you negotiate because the customs officer has the power of discretion. People often choose a fee that is mutually advantageous to both the customs officer and the importer.

We have done a survey of the supreme audit institutions in Africa, and the only one in the whole continent that meets all the criteria was one in South Africa that reports to parliament and that has its budget voted on by parliament. The institution has a professional staff, and it does not report to the president or any other individual. In addition, its budget does not come through the finance minister, who also has to be audited.

Surveys and other tools have shown us that corruption in Africa is driven by the quality and strength of institutions, beginning with the political ones, where the Bank has no particular comparative advantage. We do not even have a mandate to deal with them, but they are very important.

More than 50 percent of the income investment budget of African states comes from donors, and much of that budget does not pass through the parliament.

We recommend integrated reforms. We must assess where the greatest weaknesses are and focus programs accordingly; these assessments are important challenges for evaluators. In some areas the Bank cannot help, but others can.

Navin Girishankar

I would like to begin with a theme from OED's civil service reform study. In the past two decades, the Bank has had some experience with the reform of governance institutions that affect the civil service. While this type of activity has only started taking off, some of the lessons from OED's evaluation could be useful as the Bank prepares for much more intensive efforts to fight corruption.

In the mid- to late 1990s, the Bank did break from the type of downsizing and capacity-building initiatives it supported for much of the 1980s and early 1990s. It began supporting intrapublic sector regulatory reform as well as the establishment of external checks and balances to change the rules of the game that affect civil service performance. These institutional reforms included imposing external watchdogs, revising internal codes of ethics and civil service statutes, or introducing other procedures. Most of these reforms were actually designed to limit corruption and other types of arbitrary actions by civil servants and politicians. Even though these institutional reforms represented a break from the past, they were done in a technocratic way. A group of consultants flew in to revise the civil service statutes or other regulations on the books and then left. There was no process whereby civil servants could actually come to own these rules or understand the rules so as to change behavior.

Some implicit lessons in this story about institutional reform are worth highlighting. First, if the Bank and its clients are to affect changes in behavior, they must focus on the informal and formal rules of the game. Informal and formal rule systems provide the context within which capacity-building, civil service reform, service delivery, and a whole range of activities can be undertaken and sustained. More important than the rules themselves are the ways in which the rules are interpreted. Very much at issue in changing the rules of the game is whether the rules are credible or legitimate, whether civil servants interpret them in similar ways, and whether public sector leaders can resolve competing interpretations of the same rules. We know that it is easy to codify what looks like a good set of codes on the books. The degree to which they are understood and followed is quite another issue, subject in part to social and political context. The civil service reform portfolio includes cases of the Bank helping set up auditor general offices and other watchdogs only to find them infected by the same types of political interference and patronage they were designed to combat. Agencies designed to protect became tools for abuse. This is something for the Bank to watch for as it undertakes this next generation of public sector activities that Titsworth spoke about.

The second important issue that came out in our study was the problem of path dependence. With any type of strategy of directed institutional change, the ends preexist in the means. The path and the processes that donors and governments use to affect institutional change themselves shape the types of institutions that emerge. Unfortunately, we as donors are often guilty of a certain degree of self-effacement with regard to the impact of our own processes on the evolution of institutions in countries. For example, the use of enclaves or project implementation units (PIUs) clearly affects the credibility of rules within the civil service and the ethos of civil servants who do not work in PIUs. What does the use of PIUs to disburse development assistance imply for our contemporary concerns with the predictability, stability, and legitimacy of governance institutions? Are we undermining our own efforts?

A third and related thought I had after listening to Titsworth and reflecting on my most recent trip to Africa was the question of entry points for reform. If the Bank were to focus on the formal and informal rules of the game as well as on the processes used to affect changes in rules, what would this imply for reform strategy or entry points for public sector reform efforts? Countries can adopt one of two broad strategies. The first strategy derives from the traditional public management literature: get the basics right, and you can then move to results. This includes having a pay policy, a hard budget constraint to prevent overstaffing, tight controls on resource flows and other inputs, a simple and clear code of ethics, and so forth. This results in a reputable bureaucracy that is relatively free of corruption and capable of carrying out economic management, delivery, and regulatory functions. Only after this is achieved can the question of moving to an output or outcomes focus be seriously considered. This is the approach that donors would use to support formal checks and balances, such as the judiciary, even if the civil service were rightsized and core public management systems were strengthened. From the point of view of reform strategy, this is not very different from what the Bank has done in the past.

An alternative point of entry is not to commit a priori to downsizing or comprehensive reforms of core public management but to start with frontline performance in service delivery—that is, at the bottom rather than the top. I think some of the comments that Stiglitz made in this conference alluded to this. You can start from the bottom and slowly work your way back up to the core. In Africa today there is a lot of support for this. Speaking to people in Ethiopia, Senegal, and Tanzania, I found that the notion of locating constraints on frontline delivery performance in core management systems resonated. A great deal of frustration existed with technocratic, top-down approaches because the purported benefits of reform (in terms of efficiency) often failed to trickle down to the level of service delivery.

This goes to the heart of the issue with which we began: changing the rules of the game. You can create demonstration effects so that the poor and service providers see the new rules of the game at work—for example, demand-driven delivery using a social fund—and then make your way up to change the larger systems needed to sustain those new rules. In many countries undergoing decentralization, such as Ethiopia, reformers are struggling to identify workable, informal relationships that are producing results, formalize or mainstream them, and then sustain them with appropriate reforms in the core management and regulatory framework for delivery. According to this approach, core systems and regulations are evaluated on their ability to sustain or promote results on the ground.

The problems of the bottom-up approach should be acknowledged. If demonstration effects are localized, how do you embed them and then scale them up so that they are not simply novelties in a particular district or small town? How do you make them standard practice if they work? How do you get bureaucrats within the core, in either regional or federal government, to support these innovations? It is not unrealistic to face resistance from these very people. In the bottom-up approach, what is required to leverage systemic change?

This is a difficult and complex question. I would like to highlight one piece of the puzzle—information, particularly evaluative information. The availability of relevant and timely information is critical for leveraging systemic change. Evaluative information on frontline performance is the basis for transferring elements of good practice. More important, though, the development and use of evaluative information about service delivery is political and therefore has an important impact on whether state institutions come to be legitimized in the eyes of the poor. More literature is becoming available about how the use of indicators in performance management systems can act not only as incentives but also as metaphors for public discourse. It is crucial that information on performance be collected in a participatory way so that the basis for evaluation is broad-based and ultimately credible in the eyes of users, providers, and regulators. These new forms of information can set in motion new forms of accountability from below. Once internalized by users and providers, evaluative information can also spark learning.

What types of information are relevant to do this? Under decentralized, pluralistic delivery, beneficiaries will need specific types of evaluative information to fulfill three more or less new roles, as follows:

- They will have to be much more informed consumers; therefore, performance data should help people make better choices. For example, data on the performance of schools is the type of information consumers might need to make a better choice.
- Users will need to be better coproducers, which is something that has already been done by the Bank and many countries. For example, water users associations need a certain minimum amount of technical knowledge and skill to manage irrigation systems. They will also need information on better practice in irrigation from other associations, communicated in accessible ways.
- The users in pluralistic and decentralized systems will increasingly find opportunities to deliberate either in planning or in standard-setting activities. Participatory evaluation, especially when it dovetails with local planning activities, provides one venue for interactive learning, debate, and deliberation.

Much well-known work has been done on evaluation techniques that can support this participatory evaluation, benchmarking, and so forth. I would say two things about this. First, transaction costs are lowered when participatory approaches to generating information on performance are matched to local capacity and cultural context. For example, evaluation exercises should be conducted in the appropriate language and metaphors of the population concerned. The second point is really a question. How do we lock in participatory evaluation at the local level so that it can be supported rather than crowded out by more formal evaluation systems at higher levels?

El Sayed Zaki

It is heartening that all stakeholders in the development and poverty reduction processes by now consider the fight against corruption a symbol of good governance. The negative effects and impacts of corruption on economic development, efficient resource use, appropriation of funds, distribution of benefits, social peace and order, and environment are widely recognized. The tremendous progress in the study of, analysis of, and recommended measures to combat corruption is fascinating. Even though scholars, donors, and civil society institutions have an important role to play, particularly in awareness creation, national governments' responsibility and commitment are the dominant factors in curbing corruption. Accountability (moral, political, and financial) is critical for national governments' effectiveness in this endeavor.

As a reminder, the impacts of corruption are lower-quality services provided at a higher noncompetitive cost. Also, project services may not reach the intended target groups. On both accounts, considerable economic and social losses occur.

To understand corruption processes and to recommend appropriate prescriptions, a classification scheme is essential. We can identify four types of corruption, as follows:

- Corruption by proxy, which is associated with the misuse of political powers
- Extortion, or rent seeking by public service officers, which is equivalent to indirect taxation and is unjust
- Bribery, which could be divided into business bribery linked to contract awards and service facilitation
- Embezzlement of funds, whose main outcome is low salaries and lack of incentives.

These types of corruption are not mutually exclusive. For example, corruption payments could be viewed as a tax, but if corruption payments are perceived as essential, changing the decision in favor of the business firm making the payment is then bribery. However, in both cases, it is part of the cost of the service.

Moreover, corruption is vicious and comprehensive in the sense that one corrupt practice leads to another. In many developing countries weak, unqualified personnel are selected for important positions because of their political association or because of kinship (nepotism). In addition, civil servant salaries that are too low to cover household basic needs—especially within the context of the extended family—combined with weak qualifications, inappropriate and noncompetitive methods of selection, and low incomes, become a recipe for corruption. At higher levels of government, this represents the link with international procurement corruption in the implementation of donor-financed projects and programs. This is a major concern because of the nature and size of funds involved, in addition to the negative impacts.

The following factors and situations facilitate corruption at various levels:
- A social order that is conducive or receptive to rent seekers
- A lack of transparency in management and procurement decisions
- Complex financing arrangements that help rent seekers hide and that are missed by auditors
- The selection of managers—that is, project or financial managers—based on considerations other than merit. This is particularly the case when the system misuses special incentive packages designed to attract competent management to select seemingly competent managers
- The fungibility of funds and unwarranted flexibility in budget allocation, which release national resources for nonpermissible goods and services under the terms of financial agreements
- The lack of, and delays in conducting, both internal and independent audits.
- The introduction of decentralization, which may enhance accountability and reduce corruption but may also result in more corruption in certain situations, such as a top-down or a centrally controlled political apparatus and poorly qualified staff.

Social Inclusion and Civil Society

19

Nongovernmental Organizations and Evaluation: The BRAC Experience

Salehuddin Ahmed and Mohammad Rafi

Bangladesh is one of the poorer countries in the world. Because of the multitude of problems, both natural and manmade, that Bangladesh has had to face since its inception, we may have lost sight of the fact that Bangladesh has also achieved significant results. Its people have managed to survive on a land mass and with resources that would have been depleted overnight by almost anybody else. Despite its rapid growth in population, from 75 million at independence to 120 million in 1997, the country has in 25 years become nearly self-sufficient in food grains. Seventy percent of newborn children are now immunized, and fertility rates have fallen sharply. Infrastructure has been set in place, and the country has reaffirmed its commitment to democracy.

The country's development needs at independence, and the willingness of outsiders to help, generated a large community of NGOs. Bangladesh has become renowned for the effectiveness of its development community in alleviating poverty. This paper discusses the evaluation work of the Bangledesh Rural Advancement Committee (BRAC), which has significantly contributed to poverty reduction in Bangladesh in recent years.

The Bangladesh Rural Advancement Committee (BRAC)

BRAC, one of the larger NGOs in Bangladesh, has the twin objectives of poverty alleviation and empowerment of the poor. It works mainly with women whose lives are dominated by extreme poverty, illiteracy, disease, and malnutrition. Since its inception, BRAC has evolved into one of the larger NGOs in the country.

BRAC started in 1972, just after liberation, by helping the refugees returning from India to Shalla, a remote, war-torn village near the northeastern border. BRAC provided the villagers with materials for house construction and tools to use in earning a livelihood. Within a short time, however, BRAC realized that relief and reconstruction activities were only stopgap measures (Lovell 1992) and could not meet people's longer-term needs. In 1993, therefore, BRAC launched an integrated community development program in 200 villages in the northeast. The program offered a package of services, including agriculture, horticulture, fisheries, adult education, health care, family planning, and vocational training.

This approach was based on two sets of assumptions: (a) that the rural poor would become less passive and more conscious of their situation through education and training; (b) that villagers would work cooperatively and pool their resources (Chen 1991); and (c) that the extension of essential services and demonstration of their use would motivate people to use the services, which in turn would stimulate development. However, adult education programs failed to attract villagers, vocational training was found to be out of context in the village, the level of community spirit was disappointing (Chen 1991, Lovell 1992), and no progress was made toward development.

The failure of the integrated community development approach led BRAC to adopt the alternative approach of participatory development, in which people actively take part in planning and implementing development programs. The failure of the villagers to work together also led BRAC to realize that a village is a mix of groups with different interests (Lovell 1992). Thus, in 1974 BRAC launched a cooperative credit program for some of the poorer subgroups—namely, the landless, fishermen, and women. The credit program worked in the villages in conjunction with the participatory development program.

It soon became apparent, however, that because of the nature of the rural power structure, the distribution of resources was benefiting the rich rather than the poor in the villages. BRAC therefore became convinced that (a) the programs designed for the poor must address the rural power structure and (b) the capacities and the institutions of the poor must be developed in order to address the rural power structure. Consequently, in 1978 BRAC shifted from the notion of credit cooperatives for the poor to the concept of organizing groups of the poor, or the target group approach (Chen 1991).

This approach focused on mobilizing the poor into village organizations (VOs). Villagers who owned less than half an acre of land and with at least one family member selling manual labor for one hundred days a year were eligible to join. A VO would be organized in a village as soon as an adequate number of poor were interested. VOs plan and manage group activities, both social and economic. BRAC supports the activities by providing training, credit, and logistical assistance.

The evolution of the current BRAC model for poverty alleviation was based on several important principles:

- **Learning.** BRAC is a learning organization and continuously uses the lessons of experience to redefine its development strategy.
- **Holistic approach.** BRAC believes that poverty is a complex syndrome that goes beyond the lack of financial resources. Therefore, along with income and employment generation, BRAC works for empowerment of the poor through raising awareness, mobilizing savings, helping with access to primary education and health care, promoting gender equality, and providing training.
- **Social mobilization.** Social mobilization is the basis of empowerment. The process starts with the identification of the poor. Through the awareness program, they start to understand the socioeconomic and political system and find ways to change it in their favor.
- **Participation of women in the development process.** BRAC has been promoting a new culture in the development field, with women in the forefront of all activities. Women make up 96 percent of credit recipients, 70 percent of students, 80 percent of the teachers in BRAC schools, and 100 percent of the health workers and poultry workers.
- **Scaling up.** BRAC believes that involving as many people as possible in its programs will lead to greater impact.
- **Sustainability.** BRAC looks at sustainability from two angles: sustainability of the impact of BRAC interventions and sustainability of BRAC itself.

Relations with the Bangladesh Government, External Donors, and Other NGOs

BRAC, like other NGOs operating in Bangladesh, must have permission from the government to conduct its development activities. Most NGOs also collaborate with government organizations, receive funding from donors, and share experiences with other NGOs. So far, poverty alleviation NGOs have rarely entered into partnerships with the private sector.

The relationship between NGOs and the government has changed over time. In the 1970s the two sectors coexisted but had little interaction, the 1980s were characterized by polarization, and the 1990s saw an increase in understanding and in cooperative projects. These projects can take three forms: (a) subcontracts, with the government selecting an NGO to carry out a project on the basis of competitive bidding; (b) joint implementation, with the government as cofinancier or joint executor of a project; and (c) government as financier of an NGO project (World Bank 1996).

BRAC has learned through its collaboration with the government that the details of cooperative ventures should be finalized before a program is launched. The failure to do so could lead to difficulties that might adversely affect the program.

BRAC's relations with its donors have been based on the mutual understanding that development is a long-term process and on the sharing of failures and problems as well as successes. Its relations with other NGOs have been based on the sharing of assets and skills, which has enabled BRAC to diversify and scale up its poverty alleviation efforts. BRAC jointly implements programs with other NGOs and helps more than 230 small local NGOs run informal primary schools. These interactions provide the small NGOs with experience and learning, which contribute to their development efforts.

Major Development Programs

BRAC's integrated development program is actually a package of programs, the most significant of which are in human development, health, and education.

Human Development

BRAC's core human development package comprises (a) group-based microcredit, (b) essential health care, and (c) human development training. All VO members participate in this package. VO members also have access to another package of programs in seven sectors: agriculture, poultry, livestock, sericulture, fisheries, social forestry, and rural enterprises. Members participate in these on a selective basis. The core human development package and sector programs together are known as the Rural Development Program (RDP) package, which is BRAC's major poverty alleviation program. RDP operates in 60 percent of the villages in the country and covers 3 million households.

Health

Health has been an important component of BRAC interventions since the early days. The program received a major boost in 1980 with the introduction of the nationwide oral rehydration therapy program for the treatment of diarrhea, a major killer in Bangladesh. Since 1990 BRAC has carried out a women's health program that focuses on reproductive health. Other important elements of BRAC's health program are family planning and nutrition. Currently the program covers about 3 million people in rural areas of the country.

Children's Education

BRAC started an informal primary education program in 1985 with 22 schools. Two important features of the program are that it promotes female education (70 percent of the students are girls) and enrolls children from poorer families. Currently more than 34,000 such BRAC schools are functioning throughout the country.

Audits, Monitoring, Training, Research, and Evaluation

BRAC also audits, monitors, trains, and carries out research to enhance the effectiveness of its poverty alleviation programs.

Audits. BRAC's Audit Department routinely evaluates its monetary transactions and ensures the validity of the accounting and financial reports produced by BRAC's departments and programs. By detecting errors and financial corruption, the Audit Department gives BRAC the opportunity to recover from such losses and take corrective measures. The department also investigates the effectiveness of internal controls and of the management and resource distribution system and makes recommendations for improving these functions. Such evaluations are essential for the effective functioning of BRAC programs and departments.

> Evaluations are essential for the effective functioning of BRAC programs.

Monitoring. The Monitoring Department contributes to the effectiveness and efficiency of programs and departments by ensuring that procedures are followed.

Training. The goal of the Training Division is to improve the management capacities of development practitioners, both within and outside BRAC, and to enhance the human and operational skills of the group members and program participants. These efforts are kept consistent with BRAC's poverty alleviation and empowerment goals.

Research and Evaluation. BRAC set up its Research and Evaluation Division (RED) in 1975 to gain a better understanding of rural society and to design more effective programs. RED holds a unique position in the organization. To avoid any influence that might distort its research findings, RED reports directly to the executive director. At the same time, it maintains close, regular contact with the programs and evaluates their effectiveness. Evaluation to improve programs is one of RED's main functions.

Evaluation of BRAC Programs

BRAC's RED evaluates both BRAC programs and those of other NGOs, sometimes with the assistance of outside experts and sometimes in collaboration with other organizations. RED recently conducted four impact studies of BRAC programs in rural development, human rights and legal education, and informal primary education, as well as its two most significant evaluations to date, which were major impact assessment studies (IAS I and II) of the RDPs completed in 1996 and 1998. The objectives of these studies were to measure the success of the program in raising the socioeconomic status of RDP participants, identify the program's shortcomings, and assess its sustainability.

The learning from IAS I was immensely helpful in conducting IAS II more efficiently. For example, income data were collected in IAS I to determine the economic condition of respondents. The income was underreported, so IAS II collected expenditure data, which more accurately depicted the economic condition of respondents.

Lessons Learned from the Second Impact Assessment Study of Rural Development

The second study, IAS II, carried out in 1996-97, observed 1,250 BRAC participant households and 250 comparison households. IAS II found that the RDP had a significantly positive impact on the social and material well-being of its participants. BRAC households had 380 percent more assets, 50 percent higher net worth (assets plus savings minus outstanding loans), and 200 percent more savings than comparison households. However, even though member households owned more assets, the rate of growth had been higher for the comparison group during 1993-96.

In addition, calorie consumption and food and nonfood expenditures were higher for member households, as were the value of housing and the amount of per capita floor space. A higher percentage of member households also used tubewell water for washing utensils and clothes and for bathing, and 24 percent used sanitary latrines, as opposed to 9 percent of comparison households. The rate of contraceptive use among eligible couples was 40 percent for BRAC households and 27 percent for comparison households.

Although the dependence of BRAC households on noninstitutional loans was reduced, households with self-employed heads increased their borrowing from noninstitutional sources. Newer BRAC members showed comparatively better performance than older ones in terms of the rate of increase in the value of their houses, the amount of per capita floor space, the level of savings and assets, and so forth. These newer members had higher initial endowment than older ones, but older members enjoyed better health and sanitation facilities. Households headed by men had better socioeconomic indicators than those headed by women.

Both the incidence and severity of poverty declined for BRAC households as length of membership increased, and BRAC households were not as poor as nonmember households. BRAC households also faced relatively fewer food deficiencies and used more positive mechanisms to cope with crises.

The direct involvement of women in income-generating activities increased from 28 percent before joining BRAC to 45 percent as length of membership increased. The income from such activities was usually spent on household and personal needs. The majority of women (53 percent) gave their loan money to male household members because of social norms.

More than 90 percent of the members owned some assets, productive or unproductive, but their ownership was partial and their control of assets was limited before joining BRAC. After joining, their status in the family improved significantly in most cases.

Issues Evaluation

Program evaluation should be a routine activity for NGOs. Evaluations can focus on (a) progress toward achieving the program's goals, (b) the impact of unexpected events (for example, BRAC evaluated losses to RDP participants caused by the flood of 1998), and (c) new issues arising as a result of program or policy changes such as those in response to study recommendations.

A number of new evaluation issues have arisen following recommendations made in IAS II. To begin with, IAS II indicated that BRAC programs still do not cover a large proportion of the hard-core poor. Family crises such as chronic illness or disability of the male income earner often discourage villagers from becoming VO members. In response to this finding, RDP has taken measures to bring these people into its poverty alleviation initiatives. The next evaluation of the RDP may investigate the success of these measures.

> Program evaluation should be a routine activity for NGOs. Evaluations can focus on (a) progress toward achieving the program's goals, (b) the impact of unexpected events and (c) new issues arising as a result of program or policy changes such as those in response to study recommendations.

The study also proposed that the selection criteria for VO membership needed reassessment, as follows:

- The land ceiling seems to be an inappropriate criterion, because the effective use of land depends not on size but on quality and location and because many rural households have other sources of livelihood.
- The recent selection of better-off members for the VOs has had some adverse consequences for coverage of the poorest, but the selection of VO members with the help of rapid rural appraisal and participatory rural appraisal techniques was observed to be a check against this bias and against the land ceiling bias as well. The next evaluation may look at the effectiveness of member selection techniques.
- BRAC requires VO members to deposit regular savings but imposes restrictions on withdrawal. The study indicated that members were interested in saving more so they could use their savings to cope with crises. The restriction on withdrawal of savings acted as a disincentive for increased savings and was one of the reasons found for the discontinuation of membership. Recognizing the importance of a provision for savings withdrawal, BRAC has been conducting a pilot program in selected areas to devise an appropriate mechanism. The preliminary recommendation from the pilot program is that BRAC needs to introduce a flexible savings withdrawal system as soon as possible. The next evaluation may also assess the effectiveness of this policy.

Methods for Evaluating Poverty Alleviation Programs

The following tools and methods should be taken into account when evaluating poverty alleviation programs:

- **Indicators.** The evaluation of a program should be based on selected indicators. The objectives of the program will determine which indicators should be observed. The indicators should be limited and should remain relevant to the program for a period of time. This is particularly important when the findings from one evaluation are compared with others. The indicators can be both quantitative and qualitative. The data on qualitative indicators can be collected easily and within a short period, but quantitative data need a longer time. The skills required to collect and analyze these data are also different.
- **Assessment of the impact.** To identify and measure the impact of a program, statistical tools may be needed to separate the contribution of external effects. IAS II attempted to determine BRAC's contribution to the upward mobility of program participants by comparing the changes in different socioeconomic indicators for program and nonprogram households over time. Maintaining a true comparison group was difficult, however, because of the involvement of many comparison households in other development programs.
- **Use of quantitative and qualitative methods.** Quantitative and qualitative methods serve different purposes. The quantitative approach is used to estimate levels of poverty, construct summary poverty measures, and assess impacts on material and social well-being. Quantitative data are amenable to statistical analysis, especially when data need to be decomposed to isolate the effect of a single variable from the composite effects of multiple variables. The qualitative or participatory method, in contrast, is used to deal with subjective issues such as perceptions, attitudes, and motivations or to provide explanations of facts derived from the quantitative approach. In some cases, both methods may be necessary to serve the purposes of an impact study.

Program Sustainability

As noted earlier, sustainability is one of the main features of the BRAC model. To reduce its dependence on donors, BRAC has set up a number of commercial ventures and obtained ownership of assets such as office blocks, cold storage, printing presses, and retail stores. More than 40 percent of BRAC's expenditures are now funded from its own sources. The RDP will shortly be completely independent of donors.

The sustainability of the impact of BRAC interventions is also of concern and is inherent to the nature of the interventions. The comprehensive approach of raising awareness, extending credit, using the credit in productive sectors, monitoring credit use, creating employment, and providing training ensure the sustainability of program impacts.

Lessons Learned from Evaluations Conducted at BRAC

Objectivity
An evaluation must be objective. Distorted findings from a nonobjective evaluation can do more harm than good to the program. The objectivity of the evaluation can be ensured to a great extent by creating an environment where evaluators are independent of any outside influence and by selecting an evaluation team with a strong commitment to carrying out its responsibilities.

Timing and Number of Evaluations
Timing and scheduling of evaluations must be carefully thought out.
- The timing of an evaluation should be planned to minimize the effects of seasonal variations.
- Evaluations should not be conducted at a time when the findings are likely to be influenced by a crisis, unless the objective of the study is to determine the effects of the crisis.
- Evaluations should not be too frequent. Evaluations tax the program financially and distract from its routine activities. During the data collection phase, program staff often have to give time to the evaluation team at the expense of their daily activities.

Evaluation Team
The composition of the evaluation team should be based on needs.
- Consultants are not always available for evaluations. Therefore, organizations should develop in-house expertise, while keeping in mind that developing such expertise is a long-term process.
- Team members should include those who participated in previous evaluations and newer members with needed expertise. The integration of both groups is likely to make the evaluation process more effective.

Indicators
Indicators should be selected to achieve the objectives of the evaluation, keeping the following in mind:
- Indicators should be chosen in consultation with program staff and participants.
- Too many indicators raise the cost and can unnecessarily complicate the process.
- Both qualitative and quantitative indicators should be used, where appropriate.
- Qualitative indicators (in most cases dealing with social aspects of development) are difficult to monitor. Although case studies can be used for this purpose, they are a time-consuming technique. In contrast, data on quantitative indicators can easily be collected within a short period and with a minimum level of expertise.

- The indicators selected should have relevance to the program for a considerable length of time so that the findings from a number of similar evaluations can be compared.

Data and Sample

A balance of qualitative and quantitative data is needed and sampling may be complicated by the difficulty of selecting a comparison group.
- A tendency exists to question the validity of any findings based on qualitative data because such data allow for only a limited number of observations.
- Qualitative data can best be used for in-depth analysis. The researchers themselves should collect these data. Researchers with a thorough knowledge of evaluation are likely to be in the best position to collect usable qualitative information.
- Qualitative data should not be transformed into quantitative data. For example, information on the state of women's empowerment derived from case studies should not be presented in a table, which might lead to the distortion of reality. In cases where data are transformed, extra care should be taken so that the exact meaning of the findings is not distorted.
- Selection of a comparison group is always a problem, particularly when several development organizations are operating in the society. In the case of a longitudinal study using panel data, the problem is complicated by the attrition of the respondents.

Method of Analysis

Methods must be found to show the relationship between variables and the direct impact of the program.
- The evaluation often has to show the relationship between variables and explain its causes. The presence of the relationship can best be shown by the quantitative method, while its causes can best be explained by the qualitative method.
- An IAS should distinguish the effect of the program, or any part of it, from the effect caused by the confounding factor. For example, an impact assessment of training, in the case of a program that provides both training and fertilizer (the confounding factor), should calculate the yield contributed by the training after separating it from the one caused by the fertilizer. This is not possible in all impact assessments, particularly those concerned with social impact.

Results

Program staff and program participants should validate the evaluation report before it is finalized. This validation process is likely to enhance acceptance of the report.

Conclusion

Evaluation is an expensive, but necessary, cost that should be part of the program budget. If it uses appropriate methodology, it can help improve the effectiveness of poverty alleviation efforts and can make the program more credible to both donors and recipients.

References

Chen, Martha Alter. 1991. *A Quiet Revolution: Women in Transition in Rural Bangladesh.* Dhaka: BRAC Prokashana.

Lovell, Catherine H. 1992. *Breaking the Cycle of Poverty: The BRAC Strategy.* Dhaka: University Press.

World Bank. 1996. P*ursuing Common Goals: Strengthening Relations Between Government and Development NGOs in Bangladesh.* Dhaka: University Press.

Comments: NGOs and Evaluation: The BRAC Experience

Ariel Fiszbein

The paper by Ahmed and Rafi provides a welcome opportunity to review some of the critical challenges in poverty reduction.

The name BRAC commands respect among development practitioners, and this story about the BRAC experience is a good vehicle for talking about what works and what does not work in poverty reduction, about the role of evaluation as a learning tool, and about the need to build learning organizations.

Empowerment

One of the paper's central messages is that poverty reduction is at least partly about power relations. The authors say BRAC's original approach failed because it did not recognize this fact. Lately, many mainstream economists have started to understand this and are paying more attention to political economy in analyzing poverty reduction strategies and programs.

The BRAC experience illustrates that to address these power structures, the poor must be organized and their organizations must be strong. BRAC's success has as much to do with organizing and mobilizing the poor as with having strong service delivery capabilities. This is an important lesson for those of us trained in an intellectual tradition that focuses more on individuals and on invisible hands than on group behavior and social movements.

By highlighting the importance of building organizations of the poor, the paper emphasizes empowerment. What it does not mention is how the process of social mobilization goes on within the broader political story. The authors do not discuss the links between the organizations promoted by BRAC and other political and social institutions, such as political parties and labor unions, or whether the degree of state decentralization and other characteristics of national or local governance help or hinder those organizations' growth.

Another aspect of empowerment one wonders about is the link between economic and political empowerment. Is it possible to address the rural power structure, as the authors suggest, without altering the distribution of economic power? This brings up such public policy issues as land or tax reform. In other words, it would be helpful to see the impact of efforts to build the organizations of the poor within the broader context of political and economic reform.

Partnerships

The authors contend that BRAC's approach to poverty reduction was successful at least partly because of partnerships with the government, communities, donors, and other NGOs.

We can all benefit a great deal from good, systematic assessments of successful experiences such as BRAC's. It would be useful to examine two things further. First, the authors imply that by working with others BRAC enhances its own capacity to implement poverty reduction programs. Is that because its partners bring to the partnership assets and skills that BRAC lacks or are partnerships mostly about adding more of the same? BRAC's extensive experience could provide rich material for an analysis of the ecology of partnerships.

Second, we could also learn from hearing about the difficulties and barriers—formal (legal) and informal (attitudinal)—BRAC has experienced in building partnerships with government, donors, and so on.

Finally, based on my own experience in Latin America and the Caribbean (see Fiszbein and Lowden 1999), I found it surprising that the discussion referred only briefly to the fact that Bangladesh's business community was not involved in BRAC's partnerships.

Evaluation as Learning

As an evaluation of the BRAC experience and a discussion of evaluation by BRAC, the paper makes interesting, valuable points about how BRAC has handled the evaluation of its programs and strategies.

Most important, it shows BRAC as a learning organization—that is, an organization that reflects intelligently on what it does, learns from that reflection, and adapts. The historical perspective with which the paper starts shows how BRAC learned from its own mistakes, including the failure of the integrated community development approach, which led BRAC to adopt participatory development. Evaluation in this context is seen not as an almost academic exercise but as part of operational work. This is as much a matter of organizational culture as one of institutional policy.

> BRAC is a learning organization—that is, it reflects intelligently on what it does, learns from that reflection, and adapts.

It is also important that BRAC has developed the capacity to conduct evaluations in-house. Knowing more about how BRAC did this would be useful. How is BRAC organized, how long did it take BRAC to set up this capacity, and how does BRAC sustain it? This has important implications for the NGO world, particularly for NGOs that are not as large as BRAC (which is true of most of them). It is another area in which partnerships could play an important role.

The Business of Poverty Reduction

An interesting subtext in the paper is what I would call, without any negative connotation, the business of poverty reduction. BRAC, we are told, has a core service package (the human development package) that it provides to all its clients (the member VOs). It has training and research and evaluation divisions with well-defined functions central to the organization's core business and with clear organizational links with its operational groups. It has set up commercial ventures. Furthermore, it seeks to generate on its own the funds needed to finance the services offered to clients (a goal BRAC expects to achieve soon). The message: Poverty reduction is a serious business and BRAC is taking a businesslike approach.

This is an interesting aspect of the BRAC experience and one that I, though not an expert on NGOs, have noticed increasingly among NGOs in other regions.

Reference

Fiszbein, Ariel, and Pamela Lowden. 1999. *Working Together for a Change: Government, Civic, and Business Partnerships for Poverty Reduction in Latin America and the Caribbean.* Learning Resources Series. Washington, D.C.: World Bank Institute.

Floor Discussion: NGOs and Evaluation: The BRAC Experience

The theme emerged that various stakeholders had different views of evaluation and its relationship to sustainability and governance emerged. Having all stakeholders—poor people, NGOs, and CBOs—involved in an evaluation creates a balance of power so that the dominant institution cannot steer the evaluation in a particular way.

In response to several comments, Ahmed explained that BRAC knew its programs had to be both economically and socially sustainable. To make institutions created at the village level economically sustainable was not difficult; to make them sustainable as institutions was a complex task. They had to relate to other institutions in the central and local government, to the power structure, and to the elite. This was where BRAC's capacity building was important. For example, the women in a BRAC village went through paralegal training to help them understand their legal rights. One of the biggest instruments of exploitation was the isolation of the poor, so giving them information allowed them to empower themselves. Looking at both the economic and the social sustainability of programs was the point of development, and BRAC had taken this as a serious business, not just for poverty alleviation. That was also why BRAC had gone into business itself: so the country could reduce its dependence on foreign aid. Out of US$104 million, BRAC was now generating more than 50 percent of its income internally, which gave it a lot of power in society.

What made BRAC so successful, said one participant, was that, organizationally speaking, it had been able to achieve clarity on the complexity of evaluation. Essentially, it had a three-layered system. At one layer were the management information systems that kept management aware of how the programs were doing. The next layer was an independent monitoring system that helped identify potential problems immediately and formulated them for discussion. The final layer was the high-level, equally independent layer of the powerful overseas and local research organizations. Having these three levels had worked well for BRAC. In other NGOs, including the one for which the participant was working, the local structure, the history, and the labor market for the kinds of manpower needed to do these things were simply unavailable.

Another theme of the paper was whether individual well-being or social well-being was being evaluated. Would increasing individual endowments reduce social exclusion and other social dimensions of poverty? One conferee said that this heavy focus on individuals excluded many social externalities and often excluded looking at things in terms of group function. Maybe there was something about the well-functioning family, well-function-

---

Michael Edwards of the World Bank chaired the discussion.

ing village, and well-functioning society that was slightly different and that was more than the sum of individuals.

According to Michael Edwards and others, this depended on the level of the evaluation: individual, society, national political economy, and international political economy. As one participant said, it is probably not very useful when people who had to go to a country and do an evaluation in five days were told, "Look at everything under the sun." Some guidelines were warranted. One did not do everything every time, said another participant, pointing out the danger of evaluating at the micro level and not noticing what was happening at the macro level. For example, Bangladesh had achieved success at the micro level, but still had a lot of poverty at the macro level.

> There is a danger of evaluating at the micro level and not noticing what is happening in the macro level.

Perhaps there was a need for different kinds of data collection by local governments, national governments, and donors. The Bank was currently moving toward bringing information from one place to many other places, said one participant. However, information was not generally derived from one point in time, or even from different points in time when different issues became involved. In examining the impact of structural adjustment on indigenous populations in Southeast Asia, for example, one would want to use a range of qualitative methods to find out how different groups in the community were affected. After a year or so, one would start aggregating information one had gathered at different levels. It was not an either-or situation. There was a need to build in-house capacity, so countries themselves could get information analyzed. Donors should be doing more such capacity building.

Another theme of the paper was partnerships between governments and NGOs and between NGOs and the communities they were trying to serve. These relationships could be complicated, depending on the relative power of the actors. Fiszbein said he was still thinking about Frances Stewart's question about the paradox of NGO effectiveness. He tended to agree that it was not always a question of substitution, since a wealth of potential complementarities also existed. Possibly partnerships would not do simply more of the same, but would help create social wealth. It would be interesting to know what in the government structure of Bangladesh was creating this divergence between performance in public and private organizations and at the same time creating an enabling environment. Many other countries had equally ineffective governments, but were effective in restricting the NGOs' capacity to bloom.

Relating the above to the question of evaluation, Ahmed said BRAC had implementation at the grassroots level and the people doing project monitoring collected the data. Researchers who worked at a higher level also collected data. Both were internal to BRAC. BRAC also collaborated with other research institutions and donors, who also collected data. Donors came in and evaluated all the programs from the top down. So poverty reduction was evaluated in several different ways, all stemming from three decades of BRAC history. In the first decade, BRAC was slow and the government was disorganized. In the second decade, the 1980s, BRAC grew and became more capable. It also became more arrogant and the government grew more suspicious. Now BRAC had a relationship in which the government felt it needed the NGOs to cover the poor people. The real danger now was that the government would try to co-opt the NGOs. If that happened, BRAC would have real problems. The challenge lay in maintaining the NGOs' flexibility and funding base. If one were able to create a funding base and show that it can work, one could become more involved with the political economy of the country.

A member of the evaluation staff at Norway's Ministry of Foreign Affairs said she had just realized that BRAC employed about 50 times as many people as her ministry. That gave her a perspective on NGOs in relation to government organizations. Norway was known for having the densest NGO population per capita, and its government was not known to be particularly bad. Therefore a correlation did not necessarily exist between government and the number of NGOs. Commenting on the remark that BRAC was a learning institution, she said that her ministry worked hard to learn from evaluations, which turned out to be extremely difficult.

What one learned from these evaluations, said one participant, depended on what one wanted to learn and on what one targeted. If one wanted to learn how to do a project in agriculture, for example, one did a microlevel assessment of the impact of one project. If one wanted to learn about the cross-cutting impacts of that project on a wider scale, one did a different level of evaluation. It was a question of which discussion in the organization one wanted to inform through the evaluation. If the intent was to push further in project design, one did a very different kind of evaluation than one did if the intent was to push further in policy analysis. Evaluations at the project level were done for very different reasons from evaluations at the organizational level.

Ahmed added that donors had different questions about results from poverty alleviation efforts than did BRAC donors and were trying to learn different things and inform a different decision. Not only were levels of analysis different, but also levels of learning—including learning at the level of policy, project design, and organizational management.

Social Exclusion and Rural Underdevelopment

Adolfo Figueroa

This paper develops an approach that focuses on social inequality in the developing world and introduces the concept of social exclusion. In so doing, it asks whether inequality is a result of peculiar forms of social integration or a result of some exclusion taking place in the social process.

As a fact of life, a group of people who participate in some social relationships may, at the same time, be excluded from others. Hence, to say that a person is excluded from something is a purely descriptive statement with no analytical value. An analytical statement would have to reveal whether some exclusions have important effects on social equality. It would have to answer several questions. What are these exclusions in a capitalist society? Who is excluded and from what? Why do exclusions take place? Social exclusion theory is a logical construction aimed at answering these questions.

Social Exclusion Defined

Consider a society that is heterogeneous, organized as a capitalist democracy, and overpopulated in the sense that it has significant surplus labor.[1] In this capitalist democracy individuals participate in economic and social exchange endowed with three types of assets: economic, political, and cultural. Economic assets refer to productive resources, such as land, physical capital, financial capital, and human capital. Political assets refer to the capability of exercising the rights established by the society. Cultural assets refer to the characteristics of language, race, gender, kinship, education, occupation, religion, and geographical origin belonging to different social groups that society places in a hierarchy of values. At any point in time, individuals are endowed with different amounts of these assets.

Economic assets indicate what a person has; political and cultural assets indicate who a person is. Citizenship is a political asset, and an individual's personal characteristics are his or her cultural assets and give the individual either social prestige or social stigma, discrimination, and segregation. Clearly, an individual with a given set of personal characteristics would have a different mix of cultural assets if the system of cultural values changed. Political and cultural assets are intangible. They cannot be traded, so they do not have market value. However, they do play a significant role in the economic process.

Economic inequality is inequality in economic assets, while social inequality is a combination of inequality in economic, political, and cultural assets. A society in which the only source of inequality is economic assets could be called a liberal society. Political and cultural assets are evenly distributed. In this society, "the only difference between the rich and the poor is that the rich have more money," as the famous dialogue between Fitzgerald and Hemingway goes.

Democratic capitalism functions with a system of rights that, among other things, sets limits on the inequalities generated by the market system and thus makes society viable. Various factors determine what the rights are in a particular capitalist democracy. On the demand side, the main factors include the degree of democracy, social pressure, tolerance for inequality, the culture of inequality, and the level of income that the poor have. On the supply side are the production capacity of the economy, the preference of the ruling classes to allocate scarce resources to the production of rights in the form of public goods, and international agreements.

Exclusion from the political process means that some individuals do not have access to rights. When rights are not universal, or when formally universal rights are not effective in practice, some people may be excluded from participation in the administration of political power (the right to elect and be elected), property ownership, judicial and social protection, and basic services such as education and health care. Different categories of citizenship are then created.

Exclusion from the cultural process means that some individuals cannot participate in particular social networks. Some people may be segregated from residential areas, schools, and club memberships created by and for the wealthy. This places limits on social mobility.

Exclusion from the economic process means exclusion from market exchange. Conventional economic theory assumes that all markets are Walrasian, in that individuals can realize the exchange of goods in the quantities they desire at the prevailing market price. In Walrasian markets, rationing operates through prices, because prices keep changing until all individuals can realize the exchange they are willing to make. In these markets, some people can buy only small amounts because their real income, or productive capacity, is too low to exchange larger quantities.

In social exclusion theory, some markets are assumed to be non-Walrasian, implying that some people may not be able to realize the exchange they are willing to make because they are excluded from market exchange, despite having sufficient real income or productive capacity. Quantitative rationing is used. In non-Walrasian markets, goods or services are exchanged under conditions of imperfect information. The expected quality of a commodity or service demanded or supplied is a function of its price. The economic literature suggests that the labor, credit, and insurance markets may be non-Walrasian. This is significant because these markets are basic markets. They play the most important role in the generation of income and its distribution, and they are fundamental for the reproduction of income inequality.

Because exchange in non-Walrasian markets is carried out under conditions of imperfect information and uncertainty, it is based on promises, such as promises to repay a loan or to work hard. Asset endowments provide signals for the rationing process. Exclusions from non-Walrasian markets are not random; they depend upon the asset endowment of individuals. Individuals who are poorly endowed with assets are more likely than others to be excluded from basic markets. Asset endowment determines the markets (labor, credit, or insurance) in which individuals can participate. Governments have no incentive to change asset endowments. Governing through clientelistic relations is politically more profitable than simply establishing and securing economic rights.

In the heterogeneous capitalist democracy we started with, the labor market (a non-Walrasian market) operates as the primary mechanism of social exclusion. This market determines the quantity of wage employment, real wages, profits, and, given the labor supply, the total quantity of surplus labor. In an overpopulated economy, surplus labor takes the form of unemployment and self-employment. The incomes from self-employment must be lower than wages. This income difference creates an incentive for workers to prefer and seek wage employment. The logical consequence is that those who are excluded from the labor market become the poorest. Most of the surplus labor is also excluded from the credit and insurance markets. Banks and insurance firms do not expect to make much profit by doing business with individuals excluded from the labor market—that is, rural residents or the urban self-employed. Surplus workers thus cannot escape from becoming the poorest.

What other assets do those excluded from the labor market have? For a given type of labor, workers with the fewest cultural assets are the most likely to be excluded. Employers view social groups that belong to different subcultures inside the society as the least reliable. Employers may also expect language and cultural barriers to raise the cost of extracting economic surplus. Thus, through the workings of the labor market, people who bear a social stigma among the capitalist class are placed at the bottom income level.

An empirical prediction of exclusion theory is that a country's inequality today will depend on its initial conditions. Its historical origin and foundational shocks, such as having a colonial heritage or having imported certain ethnic groups as slaves, are important. Countries that were born freer will have become in the long run more homogeneous and more equal today than those that were born more heterogeneous and hierarchical. Inequality in the short run is explained by other factors, such as external shocks to the country and macroeconomic policies.

Rural Underdevelopment as a Test of Exclusion Theory

Because rural incomes can explain a significant part of the overall income inequality in developing countries, explaining rural underdevelopment is a way to test exclusion theory. Assume that part of the surplus labor takes the form of a peasant economy. Also assume that peasant households are endowed with the lowest amounts of economic, political, and cultural assets in society.

The peasant household is defined as a unit that operates with family labor. It is relatively well endowed with labor. It has small endowments of land, physical capital, and working capital in relation to its labor force. Its human capital endowment is low relative to what is found in the capitalist economy. With these resource endowments, it does not have enough savings for capital accumulation. The assumed economic logic of peasant households is the maximization of total family income. Theodore Schultz has said that peasants are poor but efficient, but this is a proposition that holds true only within the context of a traditional and static economy (Figueroa 1984).

While the peasant economy constitutes the poorest segment of this society, it could grow. Because the peasant economy operates within a dynamic capitalist sector where technological change and new goods and new markets appear, much room is available for the peasantry to adopt these innovations. Innovations are new production methods and new goods that give rise to new markets. Actually, the productive capacity of the peasant economy should expand with the adoption of innovations. Its economy should grow faster than the capitalist sector does and should generate innovations at a higher speed, but this is not what we observe in the developing world, where the peasantry is stagnant and rurally underdeveloped.

The literature contains various hypotheses about what factors hinder the economic growth of peasant households. The principal factors mentioned include little education, lack of profitability, inappropriate supply of innovations, and cultural factors. Instead, I would like to suggest that the main factor is social exclusion.

Assume that technology in the peasant economy is such that land, physical capital, labor, and working capital must be combined in fixed proportions. They cannot be substituted one for the other. They are limitational factors. Physical capital and labor could be assumed to be substitutes, although imperfect substitutes, but still the capital-labor mix cannot be substituted for the other factors.

Given its factor endowments, economic logic, and technological constraints, the peasant household will seek to maintain a balance between the limitational factors, which constitute its relatively scarce production factors, to eliminate any excess supply or underuse.

Because the peasant household carefully balances its use of resources over time, its current equilibrium will be efficient. It is a low-level equilibrium, however, and breaking out of it would be difficult, because the peasant household would need to increase all its limitational factors. At low-level equilibrium, the peasant household does not demand credit to obtain working capital because it has nothing to gain if only credit increases, nor does it demand credit to accumulate physical capital for the same reason. Even its demand for land is not significant. Observed peasant movements for land either seek to seize additional assets or try to recuperate previously confiscated land. As agrarian reform programs have demonstrated, land redistribution is not a sufficient condition for raising the labor productivity of peasants.

Another assumption is that peasants have a level of human capital that is sufficient to manage current technology. They have neither an excess nor a deficient supply of human capital. Increased human capital permits individuals to adopt innovations faster and more cheaply. They can understand better the knowledge, new practices, and organizations implicit in innovations. However, if no innovations are available to adopt, high levels of human capital may have little economic value, and if innovations exist, individuals may not adopt them if they lack human capital. Human capital operates as a restriction solely in a dynamic world. In a static world, it plays no role. In any case, the accumulation of human capital requires financing.

Given an exogenous supply of innovations, financing sets limits on development of the productive capacity of the peasant economy. Its development is limited by lack of financing for the various types of capital expansion needed to adopt innovations: working capital, physical capital, and human capital. The peasant economy is not restricted in its development by one sole "limitative factor."[2] Various limitative factors exist, but all of them can be reduced to one—the lack of financing.

With the adoption of innovations, the peasant economy would be able to increase its productivity. As a consequence, it would have the capability to take out and pay back loans. Peasant households could become recipients of credit. Under current conditions, though, they cannot obtain credit in the credit market and therefore cannot increase their productivity. Thus, a vicious cycle of poverty is created. A key question is why the market mechanism has not resolved this problem.

Start-Up Costs

An answer is offered by start-up costs, expressed in the following way. The introduction of an innovation in a rural area generates new markets for the products used by the innovation, called primary goods. For example, the introduction of innovations such as fertilizers, pesticides, and herbicides creates markets for those goods, which in turn requires the development of complementary goods such as credit and technical assistance. The markets and industries for the primary and complementary goods may not get established, however. This is because the prices at which firms can offer these primary and complementary goods are high because of the small scale of initial demand. Supply and demand curves will not meet. These high prices constitute the start-up costs of rural development (Ciccone and Matsuyama 1996).

If these markets do not get established, innovations will not take place, and peasants will remain in the trap of underdevelopment. The peasant economy is poor because markets are underdeveloped, and the markets are underdeveloped because the peasant economy is poor. This is another way of saying that supply and demand curves do not intersect.

In developed markets, capitalist development generates positive externalities for the adoption of innovations such as information, demonstration, and expansion of the primary and complementary markets. It is possible for the peasantry to adopt innovations and gain access to all markets, including the credit market. The peasant household could become a capitalist enterprise. Nevertheless, the credit market excludes peasant households because they are small. At their scale of operation, it is not profitable for banks to do business with them. The credit market is non-Walrasian. Other sources of credit that include capitalist agroindustrial firms may be available, but these loans are usually tied, short term, and rationed.

In underdeveloped markets, with little market penetration, positive externalities do not exist. The costs of information and learning are high, and the markets associated with innovations do not exist. Financial capital can come from the small savers in rural areas but only for short-term loans in small amounts. The peasant economy will thus remain deprived of the ability to adopt innovations.

In both cases, the peasant economy will not achieve development, despite the existence of innovations. This constitutes a market failure.

Linking Start-Up Costs and Social Exclusion

Peasant households can escape this trap of both developed and underdeveloped markets if they receive exogenous financing to accumulate physical and human capital. This intervention will set into motion the development process. Peasant households will be able to increase their productivity, will become recipients of credit, and will be integrated into new markets. They will transform themselves into capitalist firms. Thus, the limitative factor in the development of the peasant economy is financing. In the first stage of development, the financing must be exogenous. Later financing will be endogenous, through the development of credit markets, and will proceed in an accumulative manner.

The quantity of public goods and their financing are likewise exogenous variables in the production function. Building up human capital through public education and health services is one of the principal mechanisms that connect public goods to an increase in productivity. Public goods also have a positive effect on the development of markets. Building up the transportation and communications infrastructure reduces transaction costs. Public goods come not from private investment but, rather, principally from state investment. Because the state must finance the start-up costs, rural underdevelopment is the result of state failure.

The sequence of development is first public financing and later market-based financing. Productivity and private profitability are established, in the initial phases, with public financing. Banks come later, once viable recipients of credit have emerged. In the economics literature, as reviewed by Levine (1997), diverse points of view are seen concerning the relationship between financing and growth. For some, such as Joseph Schumpeter, the development of banks precedes growth. For others, such as Joan Robinson, banks follow growth. For modern economists, such as Robert Lucas, financing does not have any importance to growth and only real factors matter. Development economists have simply ignored the issue. According to social exclusion theory, in the initial and take-off stage, exogenous financing outside the financial markets, or state financing, is crucial, and banks come after the initial growth take-off.

Empirical Predictions

The theory of start-up costs predicts that the rural areas where incomes are higher have a larger stock of public goods than those where incomes are lower. This empirical prediction seems to be consistent with the data from developing countries. We observe that when rural areas are heterogeneous in their levels of income, public goods are unevenly distributed, and these variables tend to be positively correlated. The link between start-up costs and exclusion theory in this context is that the lack of public goods in peasant areas is a reflection of political exclusion.

Several studies on small farming have found that the adoption of technological innovations depends on the level of the education of the farmers. If this level is beyond a threshold number of years of schooling, farmers will adopt and adapt innovations, but the proportion of farmers having this level of schooling is small (Figueroa 1986). This is consistent with one of the predictions of exclusion theory. Not only is the supply of public education services in rural areas limited, but also cultural segregation makes learning at school more costly for peasants.

Bank credit excludes most of the peasantry. Banks set thresholds of land size to select farmers for eligibility for credit, and most peasants do not meet those thresholds. Peasants are financed through informal credit markets and through social networks. This is consistent with another prediction of the theory of social exclusion.

The general observation is that backward rural areas are relatively poor in public goods. These are also areas where markets in general, and the credit market in particular, are less developed, education levels are lower, technology is more traditional, and income levels are lower. This general observation fits the theory's empirical predictions well. Backward rural areas can be seen as cases of low-level equilibrium with high start-up costs.

Hence, rural backwardness is the result of both market and state failures. The peasantry in general is excluded from the market and from state policies. Why is it that the state does not finance the start-up costs needed for rural development? Why is it that markets leave peasants out? At the bottom of these failures lies the problem of social exclusion. If it were not for social exclusion theory, it would be difficult to explain productivity stagnation in a peasant economy that operates within a dynamic capitalist economy. Social exclusion theory attempts to explain inequality by looking at the performance of institutions.

According to social exclusion theory, the rural poor are not only people whose incomes are low but are also different people. They are poorly endowed with the economic, political, and cultural assets of a capitalist society. They are excluded from basic markets. Thus, the peasantry makes up the hard core of exclusion, and therefore poverty, in a heterogeneous society.

Policies and Project Evaluation

Given the empirical consistency of the theory of social exclusion, it can be used to discuss economic policies and evaluation. Rural development can be achieved if the mechanisms of social exclusion are eliminated or weakened, but this is a massive endeavor. It is not a question of reaching the pockets of poor peasants. For a massive action, the market and the state must not continue to operate under the same logic. The expansion of so-called civil society, or the third sector, seems to be the result of market and state failures, but the scope of this sector is limited. The policy principle would be to resolve market and state failures. This implies the generation of innovations directed toward altering the mechanisms of social exclusion. These are innovations that change the technology of the production of new goods and new institutions. Without innovations, economic development is not viable.

Innovations are not free goods, however. They must be produced. Therefore, they also have a technology of production and costs of production. This technology needs improvements as well. Technologies to produce innovations—technologies to produce technologies, the metatechnology—need to go through a process of innovation themselves. In short, innovations also need financing.

> Given the empirical consistency of the theory of social exclusion, it can be used to discuss economic policies and evaluation.

What type of innovations should be financed if the objective is to resolve institutional failures? This is a problem that project designers and project evaluators must help resolve. This problem is quite different from the standard one, in which the institutional context is taken as given, institutional failures are ignored, and social exclusion does not exist.

References

Ciccone, Antonio, and Kiminori Matsuyama, 1996. "Start-up Costs and Pecuniary Externalities as Barriers to Economic Development." *Journal of Development Economics*: 33-59.

Figueroa, Adolfo. 1984. *Capitalist Development and the Peasant Economy in Peru.* Cambridge, U.K.: Cambridge University Press.

_____. 1986. *Educación y Productividad en la Agricultura Campesina de América Latina.* Rio de Janeiro: Publicaciones ECIEL.

_____. 1999. "Social Exclusion as a Distribution Theory." Paper prepared for the Social Exclusion and Poverty Reduction in Latin America workshop, May 26-27, World Bank, Washington, D.C.

Georgescu-Roegen, Nicholas. 1967. *Analytical Economics.* Cambridge, MA: Harvard University Press.

Levine, Ross. 1997. "Financial Development and Economic Growth." *Journal of Economic Literature* 35: 688-726.

Comments: Social Exclusion and Rural Underdevelopment

Aloysius Fernandes

Figueroa said that the expansion of so-called civil society, or the third sector, seemed to be the result of market and state failures. I would like to comment on this in the context of operations—namely, exclusion theory's relevance to relationships in projects where NGOs, as the third sector, work with governments and with multilateral and bilateral agencies. This might show how the theory can be put into practice

First, the third sector is not just NGOs. It is NGOs, community-based organizations (CBOs), and various other types of groups. I will consider just NGOs and CBOs to make things easier.

Second, within the group that relates to or recognizes government in terms of development strategy are (a) those (mostly NGOs) who challenge government and are seldom included in any government programs; (b) those (also basically NGOs) who use the resources of government or the official system and risk being caught between the pressure to be co-opted and the need to preserve their identity; and (c) the CBOs set up by government, or even by NGOs, to implement their programs. In other words, a program or a project exists, and these CBOs are regarded as implementers or as institutions that manage assets—the last link in the delivery chain but very much part of the system. This is where the whole issue of participation originally started. When I ran the Bank's first participation workshop in 1989, we asked, "How do we get people to participate in these programs?"

With another type of group, which does not relate to government, the issue of social inclusion or exclusion comes up. Within this group are (a) those who go their own way, including church organizations, and (b) the CBOs in heterogeneous societies. These groups exist before an intervenor enters the picture, unified by something we have begun to call affinity. We try to identify this affinity but often lack the sensitivity to do so. We try to build on affinity and find that these groups usually develop self-reliance and build up their own resources. We conducted a referendum among 5,000 such affinity groups, telling them they could get money from the government if they were registered and asking them if they would like to register. Their answer was unanimous: They did not want to be part of the system. They believed the moment they showed interest in the government the government would impose rules and regulations and they would become vulnerable to petty officials.

Having opted for exclusion from the system, the affinity groups started credit, savings, and lending organizations, empowering themselves to manage credit and to use it to educate themselves and to learn management skills. But they remained far more like what we call creditless groups. In India, we had to tell banks in the formal banking system, "These groups are not in your system. They have savings and they are lending at their own rates of interest. Are you willing to lend them money?" The banks said, "Oh, no, we have to cover unit costs, we have to cover all the rules of viability, and we have to lend to individuals who will create assets."

"What about consumption?" we asked. "What about lending to the group?" To cut a long story short, the banks accepted the principle but had to be trained in how to assess an institution by learning how to assess a project. The issue we need to examine is, how do you assess an institution from various points of view?

There are groups now that can convince some part of the official institution to relate to them on their terms. These groups may be sustainable but they need space to grow, which brings up another set of problems about our basic development models. For example, should the dominant growth model include a safety net? After all, these groups are structurally exclusive. A related model coming out of India now is export-led growth. We also have a strategy based on growth with social justice and a similar model one can describe roughly as growth first and export as a consequence. This strategy recognizes the role of self-reliant strategies and the causal link between self-reliance and equity. Growth with social justice is what India stood for in the early years. Do we give up social justice or do we act on the assumption that growth will lead to greater equity in due course? I submit that we cannot give up equity and that growth must be inclusive.

Floor Discussion: Social Exclusion and Rural Underdevelopment

One participant wondered if social exclusion theory defined a binary system and was all or nothing—either one was excluded or one was not. Normally, the conferees didn't work with binary systems. One gained quite a lot using a binary system but probably lost a real picture of society. He would have made education a much more central source of exclusion.

Figueroa said that one hypothesis about education he had not yet tested was whether it was much more costly to get the same type of education for the nonexcluded. Was there an economic incentive not to go too far? He did not think targeting created any redistribution in terms of the trends he was talking about.

Tim Frankenberger had trouble with Figueroa's approach because it was structural but not dynamic. Many households that were not excluded initially might be excluded later because of recurrent shocks and their inability to reciprocate, so that they no longer belonged to networks. A growing number of people could eventually become excluded simply because they were unable to participate.

A good starting point for safety nets, said Frankenberger, might be a clear understanding of how traditional safety nets operated so that donors could ensure consistency between what local populations were accustomed to supporting and what made sense in their particular context. Donors externally imposed safety nets. Many populations were totally unaware of informal social safety nets and often displaced them, making the poor more vulnerable, rather than less. Many were totally unaware of informal social safety nets; displacing them would make the poor more vulnerable, rather than less.]

The communities CARE worked with were dynamic institutions in the sense that inequality was always present. CARE always faced the problem of knowing which level of targeting would not threathen the long-term security of community households. Targeting that was too precise could make people worse off in the long run than no targeting. What was needed was a negotiated process in which donors came in with interventions that were appropriate for all the people in the community, but that allowed the donor also to work with the people who were more vulnerable. In their zeal for dealing with problems of exclusion, donors must be careful not to worsen the situation.

A good example of targeting too precisely and not taking a broader perspective occurred with a project in Nepal that tried to allocate state-owned common property resources to landless people in some of the hill areas. The land was divided, demarcated, and allocated to the very poor villagers without taking into account that villagers with animals had been using those common property resources for grazing. By taking away those

---

Aloysius Fernandes of Myrada, India, moderated the discussion.

grazing resources, the project created a huge conflict within the community. By trying to distribute resources equally, the project made the people who owned animals dependent on others in the community for loans, employment opportunities, and a number of other resources. Over time, their livelihood and security deteriorated.

Focusing on the structural, long-term aspects of exclusion as influenced by income and economic policy, Figueroa responded that one way to test the theory would be to ascertain whether it could explain the persistent increase in income inequality in Latin America over the past 15 or 20 years, especially in some of the more homogeneous countries. He added that in Latin America the facts tended to coincide with the theory's predictions. Exclusion could be taken as a long-term income distribution theory. Countries with very low income inequality had ups and downs, but at the same level. Short-term income distributions changed but long-term distributions did not seem to change much. Something structural was keeping income inequality in place and it was hard to dislodge. That was the idea of social exclusion theory.

Another participant wondered how a larger system reproduced itself and what one could actually do on the margin to improve access, as opposed to exclusion and distribution. For evaluation and program design, one had to understand the process before jumping in and saying, "We need a safety net here, an NGO there, or a community-based organization of one kind or another there." He suggested that donors be more explicit about the theoretical framework they use and signal when they were making the transition to applied social science.

Three years ago, said another participant, nobody thought about social capital. One had no exclusion problems with the social capital approach.

Figueroa asked what prevented traditional agriculture from adopting the innovations being adopted elsewhere in the system. What negative factors impeded the adoption of innovations? Financing was a limiting factor because markets had to be financed from outside the market system, and the government did not do that.

Notes

1. This section summarizes my theoretical construction. For a more complete view see Figueroa (1999).

2. Following Georgescu-Roegen (1967), we may say that a factor is "limitative" when its increase is a necessary and sufficient condition for increasing production. This indicates that the other factors are redundant; they are in excess supply relative to the limitative factor. A factor is "limitational" when its increase is a necessary but not a sufficient condition for increasing the quantity produced. This indicates that this factor cannot be substituted for the other factors of production. While the limitational character of a factor of production reflects the nature of technology, the limitative characteristic reflects the firm's factor endowments.

Conclusions

Panel Discussion: Final Roundtable

Frances Stewart, Ravi Kanbur, Joachim von Braun, Nora Lustig

Frances Stewart

This conference is important because evaluation determines what policies are adopted next. However, the questions that were asked earlier—Are we doing the right thing? Are we doing it right?—imply a single correct solution, whereas a number of alternative solutions are generally available and a unique right solution is impossible.

From the point of view of how evaluation influences what we do, let me give you an example. If we define poverty as the lack of private income, we automatically think of the solution of raising people's private incomes—that is, increasing their earnings. If, by contrast, we define and evaluate poverty in terms of what I call human development failures, which is a much broader concept, then the possible solutions of course include private income, but also many other things, such as public sector support for social services.

Another way evaluation determines policy is in the area of targeting. Targeting suffers from at least three important errors, while evaluators tend to focus on just one. The first targeting error is to include people who should not be in the target group—for instance, the rich or well nourished—this is the error most people focus on. The second targeting error, which is much more serious than the first, is to fail to reach those who ought to be reached—namely, the poor. The third targeting error is to fail to reach people in time, even though you may reach the right people. For example, in the Indonesian financial crisis, the benefits from social safety net schemes reached people one year after the onset of the crisis.

How you focus on these targeting errors actually determines both the evaluation and design of interventions. If the only concern is excess coverage, then things like social funds and demand-driven schemes may work extremely well. However, if the concern is to cover everybody and cover them quickly, they work extremely poorly. Much of the debate about social funds is concerned with this problem.

The second issue I would like to consider is what unit to use when conducting an evaluation. In general, we seem to use units at two different levels, either at the level of the individual, or perhaps the household, or at the national level, and we ignore the levels in between. Yet we know that individuals function well only if their families are functioning well, families function well only if their communities are functioning well, communities function well only when their regions are functioning well, and regions function well only when their country is functioning well. Thus, an evaluation should look at all these levels and not only the level of the individual or the nation. Similarly, the design of any intervention would depend on whether communities were functioning well or poorly and so on.

One level addressed in my paper for this conference was the level of the group, as defined in terms of ethnicity and religion. To avoid conflict, ensuring that large inequalities do not exist between groups is particularly important. This should inform much of our work, even the work concerned mainly with poverty reduction, because the worst thing for poverty is the outbreak of conflict.

Finally, I want to consider the macroeconomic level, the penultimate level before the global level. This conference has not dealt sufficiently with the macroeconomic level, although Eric Thorbecke's paper did discuss some macroeconomic issues. Most of the conference was concerned with particular interventions; however, one should not underestimate the importance of the macroeconomic level for poverty reduction.

This question has received considerable attention in the Bank's own *Assessing Aid* (World Bank 1998), which points to the importance of appropriate policies at the macroeconomic level. Even more important is the question of macroeconomic fluctuations and how they can cause tremendous poverty and set back progress in poverty reduction. This is where a country's achievement of growth comes in, and this is particularly relevant to Africa. If African countries could achieve sustained per capita income growth, that growth would do far more for poverty than many of the microinterventions we are undertaking.

> Evaluation should look at all levels, not just the level of the individual or of the nation.

The final factor at the national level is the government's attitude toward poverty, which is obviously critically important. Governments that are poverty minded have much better records on poverty reduction than governments that are not.

The next level is the international level, which, again, can present a fundamental problem for poverty reduction. We have omitted many of the units of analysis we should consider when looking at poverty reduction. We have focused too much on the individual unit with insufficient focus on the bigger units.

Ravi Kanbur

Four things trigger my comments. The first is a sense that perhaps the conference has underplayed the issue of evaluation by governments or by countries themselves. We talked a good deal about donors carrying out evaluation and the kinds of techniques they might use, but we did not focus on the countries' capacity to carry out evaluation, how they might evaluate their own projects, and the effectiveness with which they use the funds they borrow. The second is a sense that the conference may also have underplayed the systemic evaluation of the mechanisms of aid delivery in and of themselves. The third is my experience in the operational part of the Bank when I was working here. The fourth is a study that I have just completed for the Overseas Development Council on the development assistance system.

What I want to focus on is the mechanisms of aid delivery. We have heard considerable discussion of the evaluation of specific projects and of policies overall, but little about myriad donors and about such things as the links between, say, a country's forestry department and the relevant department in the aid agencies. In other words, we have not paid enough attention to the way things actually work on the ground.

Therefore I want to contrast that reality with the conclusion of the Bank's *Assessing Aid*, that if a country has the right policies in place, increasing the volume of aid to that country by even a small amount would have positive effects in terms of growth and similar outcomes. What I want to talk about is how an increase in volume is actually delivered in that context, and my contention is that with the current delivery mechanisms, even if the policies were right, the increment in the volume of aid might not have the desired effect. In addition, institutional mechanisms of aid delivery have an influence on a country's institutions, and sometimes that influence might be strongly negative. In this connection, all of us who work or worked in operations are aware that many of a country's key policymakers spend much of their time interacting with donors rather than convincing their populations that the projects and programs planned are the correct ones. Thus, we need to reform the mechanisms of aid delivery to alleviate this problem.

We are in this position for several reasons. First, people hold different views about what works and what does not work in development. *Assess-*

ing Aid indicates that we now have consensus on certain things. We may agree on some of the broad macroeconomic issues, and on the need for extension, although perhaps not the method of implementing it, but an overall consensus does not exist. Different countries use different mechanisms for resolving this lack of consensus. For example, the United Kingdom provides aid through its direct bilateral aid programs. It contributes to IDA and to the European Union. Thus the current mechanism reflects the variety of perspectives, giving rise to the reality of a complicated mess on the ground.

The second issue concerns verification and monitoring. Northern taxpayers do not fully appreciate the concept of fungibility. They want to see the receipt for the dollars they gave to build a primary school. A lot of our mechanisms respond to this attitude. What if a question were asked in Congress about where this dollar went? Explaining the concept of fungibility at this juncture would be a lost cause, even though the receipt for building a primary school might be completely meaningless because the money was actually spent to buy jets. This mindset is what leads us to require impossible monitoring requirements from recipient countries, with each donor having its own criteria.

Finally, the donor agencies also suffer from bureaucratic inertia.

Therefore, in a way, we are actually too close to our clients. The relationship is too symbiotic and too closely related, and it is dysfunctional. It is not so much aid dependence, but codependence. While countries and their bureaucrats certainly need the aid agencies, aid agencies need them just as much. Paradoxically, my line of argument is essentially that we should try to introduce more of an arm's-length relationship to get around the particular institutional failure that I see in current aid delivery mechanisms.

Let me put forward a simple, naive, ideal sort of approach, and you will see that many elements of this are already happening. A country develops its program, its government sells it to its own people first, this program is presented to the donor community, and each donor assesses the program. Here is where we come to an important question. How do we do an assessment? How do we evaluate this particular program as opposed to another project? However, in this ideal system, the donor has only one decision to make—namely, how big a check to put into a common pool that finances the program. This is the approach we should strive toward to break the unhealthily close relationship between donors and recipients.

> Evaluation under a CDF approach is tougher than evaluation of a particular project or sector. It truly calls for comprehensive evaluation.

While this approach may appear to be new and radical, it really is not. We have gradually been moving in that direction, for instance, by means of the sector investment programs and the CDF. Note, however, that donors still pick their projects for the CDF. Funding does not go into a common pool.

What is the role of evaluation in this type of setting? I suggest that evaluation under such an approach is tougher than evaluation of a particular project or sector. It truly calls for comprehensive evaluation.

Joachim von Braun

Let me start by addressing James Wolfensohn's question of what a poverty project is. We heard that anything can be a poverty project: roads, water supply, or the legal system. Note, however, that you can do all these things in an antipoor way rather than a pro-poor way. This is a key issue for evaluation experts to address. You can build a road, for example, in a labor-intensive way or in a capital-intensive way. You can build a highway, or you can expand the feeder road system.

My first point is the effect of evaluation on poverty reduction. The accepted approach is to take a careful look at policies, programs, projects, and their direct and indirect impacts on the poor. You learn, and as a result, you may adjust programs. The problem with this approach is that you learn only from what you already have on your agenda—that is, from what is already in your project, program, or policy portfolio.

Let us now consider one portfolio item that tends not to be evaluated because it is typically missing from the agendas of most donors—that is, comprehensive social security systems. The history of poverty reduction policies among OECD countries is mixed. Some comprehensive social security policies that have included universal coverage at low cost have worked successfully for a century or longer. If the state was efficient, it managed without resorting to NGOs. Yet other states have not accomplished this. We need to reopen this agenda because social security and insurance for the poor against major risks is an issue that goes beyond the investment portfolio, which is mostly what we have discussed here.

My second point is that the 1990s were full of approaches to reduce poverty through international initiatives: the Children's Summit, the Social Summit of the United Nations, *World Development Report 1990* (World Bank 1990) and the resulting Bank strategy, the CGAP initiative, and now the CDF. While these initiatives are useful, they also need to be evaluated to ensure that they do not quickly draw attention and then become forgotten. However, we lack an international evaluation mechanism to do this. I suggest that the Bank play a role here, but not alone. We need to establish criteria for judging such international initiatives.

> What is missing in evaluation is a focus on the efficiency of the evaluation process itself.

My third point is that, while it is good that the Bank is looking back to 1990 and its experience since *World Development Report 1990*, we must ask what have we learned since then, not just the Bank but collectively as a development community. Do we have better understanding of where aid and nonaid resources go in low-income countries? Do they reach those living on less than a dollar a day more effectively and, if so, with what effect? We know more than we did in 1990, but not enough.

My fourth point is that what is missing in evaluation is a focus on the efficiency of the evaluation process itself. Three major evaluation reports have just come out on the European Union's development programs—the Atlantic, Caribbean, and Pacific Countries program, the Mediterranean program, and the Latin American program. These are huge aid programs, yet the reports show considerable deficiencies in relation to where the aid resources went and with what effect. Donors can learn a great deal from each other, as can agencies in recipient countries. The Bank can play an even bigger role in facilitating this kind of learning.

Nora Lustig

An evaluation of the impact on poverty reduction of institutions such as the Bank should start by assessing the impact of the development strategy and macroeconomic policy recommendations. The development strategy in the 1980s and 1990s was based on three tenets: market liberalization, privatization, and decentralization. It is rather surprising that we do not know more about the impact of these three elements on poverty reduction. We have some notions about the impact of trade liberalization on income inequality, particularly among wage earners, but not about the impact on the poor of the whole market-oriented reform package, which is forcefully supported by institutions like the Bank. It thus seems obvious that the Bank's OED should address this question in a systematic way.

The second area where a systematic evaluation is needed is the relationship of macroeconomic policy and poverty. This is particularly important in the realm of crisis prevention and crisis response. We have evidence that macroeconomic crises, apart from wars, are the single most important cause of poverty increases. The paper I presented at this conference with Arianna Legovini illustrates this.

One important issue to address is an evaluation of what policies work best to prevent crises and whether they would differ if their impact on poverty were considered. Specifically, what exchange rate regime makes countries more resilient to adverse shocks, how should financial liberalization be implemented to avoid banking crises, and so on. The recommendations may be different if their impact on the poor is taken into account. For example, although currency boards may be a good shield against irresponsible policymaking, defending them when countries face external shocks may be quite costly in terms of loss of output and unemployment, as in Argentina in 1995 and 1999.

Likewise, we need to know more about the impact on the poor of alternative crisis response policies. For example, if a country has a choice, is it better for the poor that it stabilizes by relying more heavily on fiscal austerity or on restrictive monetary policy? The answer will depend on the impact of alternative policies on gross domestic product performance. From the perspective of the poor, it is generally better to avoid sharp contractions in the short run, even if this means a slower recovery. It will also depend on the impact of alternative policy responses on GDP performance of the sectors where the poor are concentrated, such as agriculture and construction.

The relationship between policies designed for crisis prevention, crisis response, and poverty is one of the main themes addressed by a forthcoming report of our unit at IADB. It remains a major challenge, however, to develop adequate analytical tools that at the same time are sufficiently practical to enlighten policy recommendations when they are needed. Despite their limitations, the techniques to assess the impact of projects on poverty reduction are more readily available and their rigor and robustness have been tested. The same cannot be said of the assessment of policies on the poor. For one thing, it is difficult to put in practice controlled experiments in crisis response.

> One important issue to address is what policies work best to prevent crises and would they differ if their impact on poverty were considered.

Counting with the appropriate methodological framework is essential to evaluate the impact of macropolicies, and OED should encourage the development of such a framework. My colleague Kanbur developed a partial equilibrium approach several years ago that can give some answers. Thorbecke and his colleagues from Cornell University have recently been working on a new version of the social accounting matrixes and have linked them to macroeconomic modeling. New developments in the field of macroeconometric modeling of the type that Victor Rios Rull from the University of Pennsylvania and others have worked on could be applied to evaluate the impact of macropolicy on the poor.

With the appropriate tools, we will be able to evaluate the impact of alternative macroeconomic policy combinations on the poor and to reduce the prevalence of egregious mistakes, such as engaging in counterproductive restrictive fiscal policies in the initial response to the crisis in Asia.

Floor Discussion: Final Roundtable

Kanbur recognized that fungibility could be a serious issue, said Anwar Shah, and that countries needed greater autonomy so that decisionmaking, flexibility, and program design would be consistent with local needs, alleviating the need for conditionality. What Shah missed in Kanbur's presentation was accountability for results. Accountability for results required that the money be available conditionally, with the conditions being what objectives would be achieved, not how the money would be used.

Stewart thought Kanbur's aid solution was attractive. One of its great merits was that countries could buy technical assistance if they thought it worthwhile rather than have it thrust upon them. And competition for technical assistance would be good.

Another participant said that what donors do in the name of accountability is not currently working. A donor might say, for example, that if this Canadian firm or that German firm monitors what goes on in a particular ministry of health, the amount of money going to health will increase by US$5 million. This kind of deeply corrosive "accountability" is one of the major problems in the current system. Genuine accountability is needed in terms of outcomes, not in terms of whether specific funds will be spent on this or that.

Niels Dabelstein said one key problem is that donors work with governments, most of which are not democratically elected, are elitist, and do not care at all about the poor. How should donors address the problem of their day-to-day partners being part of the problem?

This is why evaluation has such a central role to play, von Braun responded. Members of the general public in the donor countries want aid to help the poor and do not trust the governments in many of the countries where donors work. That is why the aid community absolutely must be accountable.

In this context, von Braun continued, we should address the problem that the supply of evaluation is currently governed essentially by effective demand and not by the latent demand of the poor. Are donor agencies' boards and those who request evaluations really demanding evaluation that fosters approaches that work and prevents those that do not? Donors must seriously rethink the demand side of evaluation and get the poor more involved.

On the issue of how donors work with so-called bad governments, Stewart emphasized that donors must always be sensitive to the situation, understanding that situations vary both politically and economically. A good government that needs a bit of balance of payments support might not need poverty projects at all. By contrast, with a bad government that has no intention whatsoever of doing anything about poverty, donors might try poverty conditionality, which is different from the sort of macroeconomic

---

Ray Rist of the World Bank Institute chaired the discussion.

policy conditionality they normally impose. Or they could try to support nongovernmental organizations or local governments or, as a last resort, simply go away and work with countries they think will use the money for poverty reduction. The important thing is not to assume there is a single correct solution. Solutions will vary by context.

22

Concluding Remarks

Robert Picciotto

This has been a successful conference. From my perspective, the main performance indicator is qualitative; it is the "feel" of the event. I liked the feel of this conference. The mood was curious, messy, and contrarian; it was a bustling market of ideas. This is a far cry from the intellectual certainty, economic parsimony, and spare elegance of what would have taken place, for instance, in an "assessing aid" conference. Let me reflect on the last couple of days.

Jim Wolfensohn made clear why the topic of poverty reduction is crucial to the future of the planet. To have 1.3 billion people or more living at the periphery of the global economy in abject poverty while industrial countries prosper is simply not acceptable. To see inequality rise precipitously, to witness the marginalization of entire societies, and to observe rising ethnic dislocation and environmental destruction can only lead to disillusionment about the development enterprise. Therefore, the topic of this conference is timely. How can evaluation help improve development effectiveness and alleviate poverty?

Evaluation: Moving from a Capital to an Institutional Model of Development

No need exists to debate at length what evaluation is about. Each of us may hold distinct views about methods and processes, but these are not fundamental differences. We can all agree that evaluation is about helping decisionmakers do the right things and do them right. The iron triangle of relevance, efficacy, and efficiency is how OED measures development outcomes.

Joseph Stiglitz and others talked at length about the importance of focusing evaluation on ultimate outcomes. In addition to outcomes, Partha

Dasgupta, in his compelling intellectual framework, highlighted the need to take account of how development interventions affect the capital stock of the nations we serve. This is why evaluators must learn to assess institutional development and sustainability. True development leaves a legacy. Therefore, relevance, efficacy, efficiency, institutional development, and sustainability are the five key evaluation criteria on which we can all agree.

> How can evaluation help improve development effectiveness and alleviate poverty?

This still leaves many methodological issues on the table. Evaluation resources are limited, so it is not easy to agree even in specific cases about how comprehensive the evaluation framework should be. It is also not easy to agree on how we can reach accurate judgments while moving evaluation to the higher plane of the country program, let alone the global development arena that we are increasingly called upon to evaluate.

This is not because the evaluation questions have changed. They have not. Going beyond projects does not raise fundamental questions of evaluation doctrine. As Dasgupta pointed out, a project is a privileged particle of policy or a small, manageable element of policy. What has changed is our concept of development. We used to focus exclusively on physical capital. This is no longer the case. The development community shifted toward human capital and then natural capital, and we recognized in the 1990s that we are social beings and that inclusion is a key instrument of poverty reduction. This is why it has become urgent to learn how to define and evaluate social capital.

In parallel, we have come to realize that poverty reduction requires holistic development. In the new development agenda, governance is at the top. This explains why the first four columns of the CDF focus on good and clean government, a resilient judiciary, a good enabling environment for the private sector, and a sound system of financial intermediation. Hence, the relevance of the excellent contributions by Daniel Kaufmann, Anwar Shah, Jack Titsworth, Navin Girishankar, and El Sayed Zaki.

The philosophy of the CDF also requires the involvement of the voluntary sector and the poor themselves as privileged partners, for the reasons articulated so eloquently throughout the conference by Salahuddin Ahmed of BRAC.

The *World Development Report 1990* Poverty Reduction Strategy in Retrospective

Let me now turn to the question of the poverty reduction policy pursued by the World Bank and its development partners since the *World Development Report 1990* (World Bank 1990). Alison Evans has been struggling with this topic during the past year in OED's evaluation of the Bank's poverty reduction strategy. The Bank's policy had three pillars: (a) labor-intensive growth, (b) equitable access to social services, and (c) social safety nets.

As Frances Stewart reminded us, the idea of the policy was not to have a blueprint but to adapt to the circumstances of individual countries. This is what most development assistance agencies tried to do. The *World Development Report 1990* triad was the broad consensus of the development community.

The first leg of the strategy did not fare well. As noted by Thorbecke and others, not enough growth has occurred to reduce poverty. In particular, between 1980 and 1996, average per capita incomes did not improve in many countries in Africa and declined in most transition economies of Eastern Europe and Central Asia. In the Middle East and North Africa and in South Asia, growth has been sluggish, while in East Asia and in Latin America and the Caribbean it has been a stop-and-go affair, a positive trend interrupted by crises that have been most cruel to the poor, as we heard from Nora Lustig.

Significant progress has occurred, however. We have seen macroeconomic distortions vanish. We have seen many economies open up and grow out of their debt crises. The labor-intensive aspect of the strategy did not work as well as we expected, though, for the simple reason that land, capital, and labor are no longer the only foundations of development. In the new global economy, information, institutions, and incentives are the engines of development. Thus, labor-intensive growth did not constitute an appropriately broad-based development strategy for the goal of poverty reduction. Rural development is critical, and it is labor intensive, but we have not sufficiently addressed the institutional and technological obstacles needed to trigger sustainable rural development in the poorest developing countries.

The second leg of the strategy, equitable access to social services, has fared somewhat better, despite the inefficiencies highlighted by Susan Stout in her evaluation of Bank-financed health programs. A child born in a developing country today can expect to live 16 years longer than 35 years ago, child malnutrition has declined by a quarter, school enrollment has gone up substantially, and access to safe water has improved remarkably. Looking ahead, however, the focus of social service delivery has got to shift to improved institutions and better connectivity across sectors, and it has got to tap the energies and resources of nongovernmental actors.

The third leg of the strategy, social safety nets, has been the weakest. This is the major lesson of the 1990s and of the 1997 financial crisis. The rising economic tide left a lot of boats stranded on the beach when it receded. Social protection was poorly articulated. It was, in a way, almost an afterthought when *World Development Report 1990* was written. This is confirmed by what happened afterward. We have had a lot of symbolic social fund projects, but they have not addressed the issue of vulnerability and risk in a fundamental way for the reasons that Judith Tendler and Soniya Carvalho identified. Genuine social protection is going to require a great deal more policy attention and far more evaluation resources than we have allocated.

In brief, we did not fully live up to the 1990 paradigm, and the paradigm itself was flawed, if only because it conceived development in terms of a capital model. Adding social capital to the model helps, but we still need to break away from this linear mode of thinking and adopt a totally different perspective grounded in the new institutionalism.

The New Institutionalism and Implications for Evaluation

Basically, according to Douglass North, standard development theory draws its inspiration from physics and the input-output thinking of capital growth models. This should be replaced by a model of change based in evolutionary biology, with an important difference being that selection mechanisms should be informed by beliefs about the potential consequences of alternative actions in a world of pervasive uncertainty.

North is talking about a radically different model of social learning that starts with beliefs and values, leading to institutions—that is, both formal and informal rules of the game—and organizations—that is, the actors that play the game. The social change process is path dependent because beliefs and values take a lot of time to change, and they change only on interpretations of what has happened. Thus, the adaptation of individual and organizational behavior to perceptions and interpretations of economic and social change is critical to development.

Hence, the relevance of evaluation and of this conference. We have been talking here about evaluation, about learning, and about knowledge. We have also been talking about evaluation as a feedback mechanism that links values, roles, players, and outcomes. If you look at development in this way, then you can see that evaluation is beneficial only if it accelerates social learning by affecting the perceptions of individual decisionmakers, the design of the rules of the game, and the behavior of the players. Furthermore, confirming Ahmed's remarks, this development model also recognizes the importance of advocacy as a crucial determinant of social change through changing beliefs and values. Thus, you can see why evaluating advocacy, as well as other development interventions, is important.

> Evaluation is beneficial only if it accelerates social learning by affecting the perceptions of individual decisionmakers, the design of the rules of the game, and the behavior of the players.

So, again, as you move from a capital model to an institutional model, you can also see why theory-based evaluation, as articulated by Carol Weiss, makes sense.

What we need to measure is not only the return on new capital assets but also how people are behaving, what rules they are setting for themselves, what policies they are creating, and what is happening as a result.

Institutions and Cultural Values Matter

Therefore, development is not a quick-fix business of getting the prices right. We must also get the institutions right, and this is bound to take time, if only because beliefs are slow to change. One silver lining of economic crises is that they can help to accelerate social learning. Surprise and risk make individuals receptive to learning. This also applies to organizations. Of course, it is cheaper to learn from the crises experienced by others, and this is the fundamental role of evaluation.

What lessons did we draw from the recent crisis in South Asia and the lingering ones in many transition economies? OED's *Annual Review of Development Effectiveness* (World Bank 1998) drew the following lessons. First, sound macroeconomic management is a necessary, but not a sufficient, development prerequisite. Second, institutions matter, particularly economic governance and also the financial sector, which proved to be the "hole in the boat" in both Indonesia and Thailand. Third, the lack of social safety nets has been extraordinarily evident in the East Asia crisis, but even more so in the transition economies, where the number of poor people has escalated enormously.

Consider these numbers. Inequality worsened in 49 countries after 1974. During the 1990s, only ten countries reduced inequality. In this whole debate about growth and distribution, Richard Gerster highlighted that growth really is a pretty blunt instrument of poverty reduction and that we have certainly neglected the importance of the politics of inclusion and lack of equitable access.

Crisis-affected countries suffered major shocks because globalization has a dark side. Not everything is policy and not everything can be controlled at the country level through macropolicies. In particular, the significance of institutional problems in finance was neglected, in part because policymakers and private traders were just looking at macroeconomic indicators. The result was that developing countries were vulnerable to buffeting by global forces, which led to a five-year setback in the global poverty reduction campaign.

Look at the transition economies if you need to be convinced about the importance of institutions. The number of people in poverty has increased there from 14 million to 168 million. The programs that Jeffrey Sachs and others were pushing at the time neglected institutional constraints, and so poverty became a far bigger problem than we expected for the transition economies.

Changing beliefs and values bring up a number of dilemmas. Should we look for universal values or a diversity of cultures, as in biodiversity? How should one balance cultural transformation versus cultural preservation or competition versus cooperation in terms of the rules of the game? In a crowded world, has the time not come to place more emphasis on cooperation in the nonmarket areas without losing the hard edge of competition in the market areas? How can one make use of the low transaction costs of social capital in an African tribe or a local community without paying the cost of social exclusion and fragmentation?

These are evaluation questions. They are also part of the new poverty reduction strategy that we need to design if we wish to have better results. We need to make full use of the current economic crises to accelerate social learning. We had the food crisis, which put rural development on the map. We had the energy crisis, which triggered the environmental revolution. We had the debt crisis, which created the neoclassical resurgence. The current crisis should help inaugurate a new approach to sustainable and equitable development.

Economic history teaches that a high probability of error exists and that effective feedback mechanisms are crucial. Yet, while evaluation has limits, institutional evaluation still urgently needs to be strengthened, because if you look at the ratings of completed projects, institutional development is the weakest of all the criteria we rate. The question is how to assess the institutional balance between the state, the market, and the voluntary sector.

We have moved from the state to the market, and the time has now come to give more emphasis to the voluntary sector in order to produce more civil goods and to deal with environmental destruction, which is the dark side of growth. Vinod Thomas is going to produce an important reconsideration of *World Development Report 1989*. His work will show that much of the recent growth has not been environmentally friendly. Unless we create institutions that ensure sustainability, which means institutions that are not simply focused on competition but that include a sense of restraint and cooperation, we will not have sustainability in poverty reduction.

In addition, tensions exist between security, empowerment, and opportunity, and these tensions need to be mediated through policies. Globalization has increased those tensions significantly, and the problem with the right approach to poverty reduction is that no enforcement mechanism exists at the global level for economic rights. The state has become weaker, so a capacity gap exists at the state level. Political rights need to be protected and, of course, all the dilemmas of collective action for social rights at the local level need to be considered.

Conclusions

In conclusion, to achieve poverty reduction, we need new concepts that are holistic, results based, and participatory. This is what I heard throughout the conference.

We must design more effective systems for keeping score. Because what gets measured gets done, Jim Wolfensohn is absolutely right when he seeks evaluation parity between economic management and finance factors and structural and social and human factors. We must focus on public expenditures with special attention to results.

> What gets measured gets done.

Many of you have highlighted the problem of not monitoring and evaluating the results of our development efforts. The BRAC approach of building evaluation into the fabric of management is helpful for this purpose. This is why building capacity for M&E is a key poverty reduction investment. We must give priority to capacity building.

Finally, we need better instruments to do the important work of development assistance. Among others, we need to move from the country assistance strategies of individual donors to country partnership strategies that involve not only government but also civil society and the private sector. We will have to build trilateral alliances among the public, private, and voluntary sectors to do our work as development professionals and to try to alleviate the enormous burden that the poor people of the world have to carry.

Thank you for coming and for your participation. We have much to do together. I hope we will meet again at the next conference on evaluation and development.

References

World Bank. 1998. *Assessing Aid: What Works, What Doesn't, and Why*. New York: Oxford University Press.

World Bank. 1998. *Annual Review of Development Effectiveness*. Operations Evaluation Department. Washington, D.C.

_____. 1990. *World Development Report 1990*. New York: Oxford University Press.

List of Authors and Discussants

Salehuddin Ahmed
Deputy Executive Director, BRAC Bangladesh

M. Nurul Alam
Evaluation Advisor, UNDP

Mona Bishay
Senior Evaluation Officer, IFAD

Soniya Carvalho
Evaluation Officer, The World Bank

Monique Cohen
Senior Evaluator, USAID

Thomas Cook
Professor, Northwestern University

Niels Dabelstein
Head of Evaluation Secretariat, DANIDA and Chair of the Working Party on Aid Evaluation, DAC

Octavio Damiani
Consultant, MIT

Partha Dasgupta
Professor of Economics, University of Cambridge

Michael Edwards
Social Scientist, The World Bank

John Eriksson
Consultant, The World Bank

Alison Evans
former Senior Evaluation Officer, The World Bank

Osvaldo Feinstein
Manager, OED, The World Bank

Aloysius, Fernandez
Executive Director, Myrada, India

Adolfo Figueroa
Professor Pontificia Universidad Catolica del Peru

Ariel Fiszbein
Sr. Economist, The World Bank

Raghav Gaiha
Professor of Public Policy, University of Delhi

Sarah Gavian
Evaluation Officer, USAID/FEWS

Richard Gerster
SDC/OED Consultant, Switzerland

Navin Girishankar
Evaluation Officer, The World Bank

Margaret Goodman
Principal Evaluator, IADB

Lawrence Haddad
Director, IFPRI

James Heckman
Professor, University of Chicago

Johan Helland
Senior Researcher, Christian Michelsen Institute, Norway

Sawon Hong
Evaluator, UNICEF

Edward Jackson
Director, CSTIER, Carleton University

Ravi Kanbur
Professor, Cornell University

Gabriel Kariisa
Director, Operations Evaluation Department, African Development Bank

Daniel Kaufmann
Manager, WBI, The World Bank

Arianna Legovini
Inter-American Development Bank

Marc Lindenberg
Dean and Professor, Univ. of Washington

Nora Lustig
Chief of Poverty Unit, IADB

Mohini Malhotra
former CGAP Manager, Principal Private Sector Development Specialist, The World Bank

Sohail Malik
Sr. Evaluation Officer, The World Bank

Timothy Marchant
Sr. Statistician, The World Bank

David Marsden
Sr. Anthropologist, The World Bank

Elizabeth McAllister
former OED Director, The World Bank

Moise Mensah
former Finance Minister, Benin

Robert Picciotto
Director General, Operations Evaluation Department, The World Bank

Jan Piercy
Executive Director, Chair of the Committee for Developoment Effectiveness, The World Bank

Detlev Puetz
Consultant

Ray Rist
Evaluation Adviser, WBI, The World Bank

Rolf Sartorius
President, Social Impact

Anwar Shah
Principal Evaluation Officer, The World Bank

Andrew Shepherd
Senior Lecturer, University of Birmingham

Niccoletta Stame
President, Italian Evaluation Association

Frances Stewart
Director, Queen Elizabeth House, Queen Elizabeth House

Joseph Stiglitz
former Chief Economist, The World Bank

Susan Stout
former Evaluation Adviser, The World Bank

Kalanidhi Subbarao
Principal Economist, The World Bank

Judith Tendler
Professor of Political Economy, Massachusetts Institute of Technology

Jack Titsworth
Consultant

Vinod Thomas
Vice President, World Bank Institute, The World Bank

Erik Thorbecke
Professor, Cornell University

Joachim von Braun
Director, ZEF, Bonn

Michael Walton
Director, The World Bank

Carol Weiss
Professor, Harvard University

James Wolfensohn
President, The World Bank

El Sayed Zaki
former Finance Minister, Sudan

Index

Accountability, 8, 16, 70, 273, 278, 280, 317-19, 364
  bottom-up, 309
  top-down, 309, 339
Acquired immunodeficiency syndrome (AIDS), 53, 78, 81, 89-90
Advocacy, 17, 70-71, 370
Afghanistan, 287-88
Africa 19, 89, 99, 102, 104, 106, 163-81; 301, 313-16, 358, 369
  agriculture, 165-68, 175
  central, 285
  collectivization, 167
  compared to Asia, 163-69, 175, 178
  cost of living, 165-66
  exploitation of, 175
  governance, 178
  industrialization, 167, 175
  land distribution, 166
  population density, 265
  poverty reduction in, 163
  roads, 165
  South, 291-93, 298-99, 313-14, 369
  taxation, 166, 175
  trade, 165
  villagization, 167, 175
  West, 269
Agencies
  bilateral, 16, 61, 350
  development aid, 71
  intermediary, 241
  multilateral, 16, 61, 65, 68, 350
  traditional, 243
Agriculture, 169, 197-98, 222, 230, 286, 326, 339, 353
Aid coordination. *See* coordination
Analysis
  content, 82, 267
  cost-benefit, 31, 35-36, 50, 60, 131
  cost-effectiveness (CE), 125, 132
  cost-results, 132-33, 138
  data, 113, 159, 209
  econometric, 206
  holistic, 6, 70-71
  institutional, 268, 270, 278-79
  microlevel. *See* microlevel
  multivariate, 79
  regression, 79
  sectoral, 267, 272
  units of, 13

Angola, 287, 295n. 2, 301
Annual Review of Development Effectiveness, 20, 371
Anticorruption, 9, 23, 301-12. *See also* corruption programs
Approaches
  best-practice, 186
  bottom-up, 316
  demand-driven, 236
  informal, 149
  interpretative, 184
  logframe, 101, 104, 110n. 1
  low-cost, 206, 208
  middle-range, 205-6, 208, 212
  multilayered, 190
  multisectoral, 190
  participatory, 83-84, 224, 280, 303-5, 307, 310, 312
  quantum, 63
  survey-based, 84
  "Swiss Army Knife," 99-100, 103
  top-down, 316, 319
Argentina, 78, 94, 197, 312, 363
  Buenos Aires, 312
  decline in incomes, 247
  financial crisis, 247
  fiscal adjustments, 252
  poverty, 247, 249
  Trabajar (Work) program, 252, 254
  unemployment, 247, 252
  wages, 248
Asia, 20, 163-81, 363
  agriculture, 165-68
  Central, 19, 227, 369
  conditions, 163-64
  compared to Africa, 163-69, 175, 178
  cost of living, 165-66
  development, 164, 169, 178
  East, 163, 165, 167, 169, 178, 197, 248, 369, 371
  financial crisis, 163, 235, 247-48
  human capital, 261
  industrialization, 167, 197
  land distribution, 166
  population density, 163
  poverty reduction in, 163
  road network, 165

  South, 163, 165, 167, 369, 371
  Southeast, 163, 169, 338
  taxation, 166
  technological environment of, 165-66
  trade, 165
Assessment
  client-level, 217
  environmental, 155
  field, 253
  impact. *See* impact
  institutional, 217
  large-scale, 206
  qualitative, 253
  subjective, 100
Assets
  cultural, 341-42, 344
  economic, 341-42, 344
Assistance
  bilateral, 22-23
  multilateral, 22-23

Balkans, 67, 284, 287
Bangladesh, 7, 10, 25, 51, 57, 94-95, 152, 156, 201, 206, 208, 210-12, 284, 323-39
Bangladesh Rural Advancement Committee (BRAC), 10, 57, 323-39, 373
  history, 323-25, 335, 339
  lessons learned, 331-32, 334-35, 337, 339
  program
    development, 326-27
    evaluation, 327-29, 337
    sustainability, 330, 337
  services, 324, 339
Barriers
  formal (legal), 335
  informal (attitudinal), 335
Benchmarking, 112, 317
Beneficiaries
  eligible, 223
  ineligible, 223
  intended, 224
Benefits
  compensation, 80
  downstream, 125-42

Benin, 63-65
Biafra, 284
Biodiversity, 372
Bilateral aid programs. *See* programs
Birth control, 53, 328
Black market, 170, 288
Bolivia, 211
  decree powers, 261n. 1
  fiscal adjustments, 252
  poverty, 249
Bolivian Fund, 238-39
Botswana, 301
Brazil, 197, 235, 240, 244, 267, 388
Bribery, 287, 301-3, 305, 313, 318
Brunei, 308
Burkina Faso, 200
Burundi, 286, 287, 295n. 1

Cambodia, 20, 287, 291
Cameroon, 171, 175
Capacity building, 15, 68, 70, 338
Capital
  financial, 47, 341, 346
  growth, 370
  human, 47, 164, 341, 344, 347, 368
  intellectual, 133-34, 138
  natural, 368
  physical, 47, 341, 344-45, 347, 368
  political, 188
  social, 9, 12, 47, 129, 139, 164, 188, 193, 255, 297, 353, 368, 370
  working, 344-45
CARD, 212
CARE, 352-53
Caribbean, 247, 335, 369
  financial crisis, 247, 250, 258
  insurance, 252
  systemic shocks, 252
  social investment funds, 252
Case studies. *See* studies
Causal inference, 89, 92
Centers for excellence, 130, 142. *See also* Regional Centers for Excellence
Central America, 284, 287. *See also* Latin America
Centralization

reversing, 149
vs. decentralization, 120
Children's Summit, 361
Chile, 197, 291
  decline in incomes, 247
  malnutrition, 248
  poverty, 249
  wages, 247-48
Chilean Fonds de Solidaridad e Inversion Social (FOSIS), 238
Chilean Fund, 238
China, 19, 95, 166
Citizens
  benefits and costs for, 131-32, 132t, 138, 141
  return on investment, 134, 138
Civil liberties, 303-4, 307
Civil war. *See* war
Columbia, 311
Comprehensive community initiatives, 113-16, 118f
Committee on Development Effectiveness (CODE), 21, 126
Community-based organizations (CBOs). *See* organizations
Comprehensive Development Framework (CDF), 11, 20, 24, 51, 65-66, 126, 130, 361, 368
Conflict, 9, 283-90, 293 296-98, 300
  vs. nonconflict, 298
Congo, 177, 287, 313
Consensus, 112, 155-56, 208-9, 237, 255
Constituents, 30, 32-33, 45n. 1
Constraints
  fiscal, 252
  and group violence, 286-87
  institutional, 371
  technological, 69, 345
Consultative Group for International Agricultural Research (CGIAR), 222
Consultative Group to Assist the Poorest (CGAP), 208-9, 211, 216-17, 361
Control groups. *See* groups
Controls. *See also* methods
  constructed, 78, 81
  establishing, 78-79, 96

experimental, 78
nonexperimental, 78
  generic, 78, 81
  shadow, 78, 81
  statistical, 78
randomized, 78, 81
quasi-experimental, 78
Coordination
  of aid, 106-7, 108-9t, 110-11
  service, 114, 117
Corruption, 10, 138, 175, 255, 268, 301-12. See also anticorruption
  challenges of, 302-3, 305-6
  classification of, 318
  combating, 303-4, 311, 313-19
  definition of, 313
    in African, 313
  formula for, 314
Costa Rica, 37, 197
Costs
  administrative, 225-26, 244
  front-end, 128-42
  indirect, 225
  recovery, 237, 244
  social, 248-50
  start-up, 11, 346-48
Counterfactuals, 4, 29, 76-77, 85-87, 90-91, 95, 155, 168-69, 171-72, 179, 200
Countries
  conflict-prone, 291-92
  host, 66
  low-income, 283-84
  middle-income, 284
  partner, 66
  recipient, 65
Credit, 64, 68, 197-98, 207, 214, 224, 287, 330, 346-48
Crime, 284, 288
Crisis
  debt, 369, 372
  financial, 24
  food, 372
  energy, 372
  macroeconomic, 247-61, 362
    responses to, 253-57
  management, 9
  prevention 4, 9, 284, 362-63

  response, 362-63
  social, 253
Criteria
  appraisal, 241
  community-relevant, 70
  eligibility, 219n. 2, 241
  financial, 205
  normative, 70
  performance, 207
  standard, 62

Danish International Development Agency (DANIDA), 68, 71
Data
  baseline, 231
  collection, 96, 104-6, 113, 120, 126, 159, 224
  cross-sectional, 80, 176
  longitudinal, 80
  panel, 80-81, 83, 96, 331
  performance, 317
  primary, 104
  qualitative, 212, 331
  quantitative, 212, 331
  reliability of, 81
  satellite, 104, 106
  secondary, 104
  sources, 80-82
  time-series, 81, 126
  validity of, 81
Debates
  political, 276-77
Decentralization, 35, 99, 111-12, 119, 126, 155, 186, 191, 196, 235-38, 255, 269, 277, 316, 319, 334, 362
  vs. centralization, 120
Degradation
  of institutional capacity, 106
  of resources, 37
Delivery
  community-based, 56
  mechanisms. See mechanisms
  service, 7, 10, 59, 235, 316
    social, 265-80
Democracy, 291, 297, 304, 323
  capitalist, 341-42
Denmark, 68, 71

Department for International Development (DFID), 19, 150-51, 183-202, 211
  chronicle of, 187b
  evaluation
    approaches, 184
    department of, 199
    synthesis, 188-91
  lessons, 187-94, 199-200
  methodological changes, 185-86
  preliminary findings, 185b
Determinants, 30, 32-22, 45n. 1
Devaluation, 250-51
Development
  agricultural, 164, 223
  capitalist, 346
  early childhood, 254
  global, 368
  holistic, 12, 20, 368
  impact, 4, 107
  institutional, 6, 256
  Policy. *See* policy
  rural, 164, 224, 369, 372
  social, 5, 9
  studies, 70, 107
  strategies. *See* strategies
  top-down, 149
Development Assistance Committee (DAC), 20, 60, 67, 200
Direct measurement, 100
Discount
  social rates of, 39, 45n. 3
Disease, 63
Donor
  assistance, 11
  bilateral, 65, 142
  collective, 66
  community, 360
  evaluations, 206, 236, 244
  individual, 66, 373
  norms, 279
  multilateral, 69, 142, 311
Drugs, 10, 53

The East Asian Miracle, 168
East Pakistan. See Bangladesh

Economics
  environmental, 43
  resource, 43
Economy
  capitalist, 344, 348
  peasant, 344, 346-47
  political 16, 179, 230, 254, 296
  static, 344
  traditional, 344
  transition, 371
Ecosystems, 30, 34, 36, 38. *See also* systems
  Catskill watershed, 38
Ecuador
  decree powers, 261n. 1
  financial crisis, 247
Education, 10, 25, 34, 36, 45n.1, 53-54, 55f, 56-57, 59, 64, 68-69, 87, 102-3, 103f, 164, 170, 178, 194, 205, 254, 267, 285, 291-92, 326-27, 341-42, 344, 347-48, 352
Effects
  indirect, 232
  intersectoral, 223
  microlevel. *See* microlevel
  multiplier, 62, 142, 231
  of projects, 75-77, 76f
  spillover, 13, 62
  unplanned, 118
Elite, 231, 289, 300
  intellectual, 285
  political, 191, 194
El Salvador, 292, 302
Embezzlement, 318
Employment
  public, 76
  seasonal, 217
  self, 211, 217, 343
  and violence, 285
  wage, 343
Empowerment, 334, 337, 372
Environment
  global, 71, 199
  institutional, 241, 272
  operating, 279
  organizational, 272
  socioeconomic, 241

Eritrea, 284, 295n. 1
Errors
  type one, 221
  type two, 221-22
Ethiopia, 167, 180, 295n. 1, 298-99, 316
Ethnicity, 13, 284, 291, 358
Europe
  Eastern, 19, 227, 369
European Union (EU), 71, 360, 362
Evaluation
  client-focused, 180
  criteria, 368
  defined, 29, 75
  demand-led, 17, 364
  design, 4, 22, 192-94
    facilitator, 148, 150
  impact, 75-97, 99, 101-2, 168, 206-7
    independent, 180
  individual, 15
    joint, 15-17, 65-68, 70, 192
    participatory(PE). *See* participatory evaluation
  partnerships. *See* partnerships
  policy and techniques, 42-43
  priorities, 17
  problem, 76, 76
  project, 34-36, 64-65, 95
  roles in, 96
    steps for good, 76
  self, 128, 180
  subjective, 112
    techniques, 8, 178
  theory-based, 13, 86, 113-121, 180, 240, 370
  theory of change, 116, 118
    training, 15
    unit of, 358
  vs. monitoring, 75
Expenditures
  household, 214
  per capita, 65
  public, 65
  social, 244
Experiments
  ideal, 93
  randomized, 92
  social, 93
Externalities, 4, 13, 346
Failure
  information, 55-58
  institutional, 10, 360
  market, 346, 349-50
  state, 349-50
Family planning, 266, 272-73
Famine Early Warning System (FEWS), 104-6, 297
Field work, 158
Financing
  exogenous, 347
  market-based, 347
  private, 347
  public, 347
  state, 347
Finland, 312
Fiscal adjustments, 8, 250
Fiscal deficit, 250
Fiscal targets. *See* targeting
Follow-up studies. *See* studies
Food, 63-64, 231, 287, 328. *See also* nutrition
  security, 104-6
  insecurity, 105
  production, 283
Forced savings, 260, 329
Formula weighting, 280
Framework
  cross-country, 297
  evaluative, 7, 368
  general equilibrium, 232
  health care, 266-67
  institutional, 311
  methodological, 363
  regulatory, 316
  time-series regression, 297
Freedom from Hunger (US), 210
Freedom from Hunger International (France), 210
Freedom House, 297
Frontline performance, 316-17
Funds
  community development, 120
  demand-driven investment, 120
  misuse of, 175
  municipal development, 120

public sector, 217
social capital, 4, 7, 24, 62, 197, 235-45 255, 358. *See also* capital
  effect of, 236
  evaluation of, 119-121, 119f, 121f
  strengths of, 236
  supply/demand-driven, 237-38, 241-44
Fungibility, 360

Gambia, 171
Gangs, 284
Gender, 155, 253, 298, 311, 341
Ghana, 67, 102, 103f, 243
Gini coefficient, 249, 289
Global distribution, 66
Globalization, 197, 309, 371-72
Goldenberg scandal, 313
Goods
  complementary, 346
  pleasure, 12
  primary, 346
  public, 347-48
  and services, 32, 35, 40, 46-47, 63, 65, 69, 101, 155
    nonmarket, 141
  valuing, 34-36
Government
  "bad," 364
  colonial, 285
  "good," 364, 368
  postcolonial, 285
  reform. *See* reform
  traditional, 236-37, 241, 243-44
Governance, 9-10, 12, 23, 45n. 6, 155, 270, 301-12, 314, 318, 334, 337, 371
Grameen Telecom, 222
Green revolution, 7, 166
Grenadines, 151
Gross domestic product (GDP), 38-39, 51, 65, 170, 248-51, 313, 363
Gross national product (GNP), 32, 37, 283. *See also* net national product
Group
  affinity, 350

comparisons, 77, 79, 96, 331
  methods of identifying, 79
  control, 76-79, 85-86, 89, 95, 112, 208
  baseline, 78, 83
  defined, 76
  demobilization, 293
  experimental, 77-78
  identity, 284-85
  mobilization, 285-86
Guatemala, 197, 249, 287
Guinea, 167, 295n.1, 313

Haiti, 286-87
Health care, 6, 8, 10, 12 36, 49, 51-60, 62, 68-69, 80, 114, 164, 175, 190, 194, 222, 230, 240, 254, 265-280, 291, 326, 328, 342, 347
  accessibility of poor to, 266
  consumer satisfaction, 266
  economic efficiency, 266
  salaries in, 269
  service quality, 266
  training, 272
  work force, 269, 274
Health, nutrition, and population (HNP), 265, 267-68, 270, 272-73, 275
  project performance, 267-68, 268f
Healthy Homes, 151
Heavily Indebted Poor Countries Initiative (HIPC), 46, 175-76
Holistic development. *See* development
Holistic programs. *See* programs
Honduras, 143, 210
  poverty, 249
  Program of Family Assistance, 254
Horizontal inequalities. *See* inequalities
Hospitals, 271
Households
  community, 352
  nonpoor, 172
  peasant, 344-45, 347
  rural nonpoor, 172
  rural poor, 172, 348
  urban poor, 172

Housing, 86, 206, 267, 286, 291, 329
Human Development Network, 60
Human Development Report of the United Nations Development Programme (UNDP), 30-31, 33, 283, 307
Hygiene, 151

IDA, 151, 360
Illegality, 138
Illiteracy, 15
Immunization, 266
Impact
  assessments, 12, 14, 63-65, 93, 94, 104, 184, 192, 200, 330
    lower-cost, 208-9
    in microfinance, 205-19
  indicators, 64, 102
  institutional, 272
Impact Assessment Studies (IAS I and II), 327-30, 332
Incentives, 55, 58-59, 164, 201, 276, 278, 293, 319
Inclusion, 290-91, 293, 368, 371
  economic, 290-92
  political, 290-92, 297
  social, 24, 290-91, 350
Income
  base, 214, 339
  distribution, 250, 257, 296
  evaluation 104
  generation, 69
  household, 82, 213
  per capita, 389
  rural, 344
Indexes
  political flexibility, 258
  Theil, 288
  transparency, 305-6, 309
India, 19, 84, 151, 183-84, 188, 189, 193, 201, 266-67, 304, 350-51
  employment, 261
  Kerala, 84
  Panchayats, 8, 256-57
  Uttar Pradesh, 84, 151
Indicators
  baseline, 96, 107, 111
  choosing, 96

  performance, 76
  qualitative, 106, 330-31
  quantitative, 330-31
Industrialization
  state-sponsored, 169
Inequality, 300, 371. *See also* social exclusion
  economic, 342
  gender, 298
  horizontal, 9, 283-300
    defined, 285
  income, 353
  land, 170
  social, 342
  vertical, 288-89, 296-97, 300
Infant
  mortality. *See* mortality
  survival, 37
Informal systems. *See* systems
Infrastructure
  physical, 164, 194
  socioeconomic, 194
Innovations, 344-46, 348-49, 353
Inter-American Development Bank (IADB), 235, 252, 276, 363
Interlocutors, 191-93
Institute of Development Studies (IDS), 127-28
Institutional capacity, 106, 236, 255, 271
Institutional development. *See* development
Institutional performance, 42
Institutional pressure, 59
Institutions
  civil society, 4, 110, 193
  grassroots, 69, 224
  inefficient, 138
  informal, 12
  multilateral, 71
    financial, 249
  nonmarket, 40, 42-43
  private sector, 4, 24
  structure of, 57-58
Instrumental variables. *See* variables
Insurance, 50, 59, 210, 214
  unemployment, 243, 260
Internet, 129-30

Index

International Development Research
  Center (IRDC), 127-28
International Economic Association,
  178-79
International Finance Corporation, 25
International Food Policy Research
  Institute, 105, 217
International Fund for Agricultural
  Development (IFAD), 223-26, 231
International Monetary Fund (IMF),
  24, 250, 252, 292, 307
Intervention
  black-box, 93
  civic, 179
  collective, 67
  development, 22-23, 106, 190
  health program, 266, 266f
  outcome, 76-77
  quality of, 8
  targeted. *See* targeting
Interviews, 81,100
Investment
  aggregate, 170
  foreign, 253
  private, 347
  state, 347
Iraq, 286
Ireland. *See* Northern Ireland
Italy, 139

Job Training and Partnership Act
  (JPTA), 93
Joint evaluations. *See* evaluations
Joint planning, 117
Joint and several liability, 50

Kenya, 169, 176, 285, 287-89, 313
Korea, 163, 166, 169
Kosovo, 67

Labor, 8, 345
Labor unions, 10, 334
Land, 285-86, 344-45
  ceiling, 329
  inequality. *See* inequality
  irrigated, 166
  rainfed, 166
  reform. *See* reforms

tenure, 197
Latin America, 167, 196-97, 244,
  247-61, 284, 302, 311, 335, 353,
  369. *See also* Central America
  employment, 260
  financial crisis, 247-48, 250, 258
  food assistance, 251
  education, 252
  health care, 251-52
  human capital, 261
  infant mortality, 248
  insurance, 251-52
  living standards, 247
  poverty, 249
  schooling, 248, 251
  social funds, 251-54
  shocks, 252
  training, 251
Leakage, 224-25, 231
Liberalization
  financial, 362
  market, 362
  trade, 254, 362
Liberia, 288
Life expectancy, 27
Links
  causal, 240-41
  cross-sectoral, 58
  institutional, 209, 243
Literacy, 158
Localization, 309
Logframe matrix , 13
"Lost decade," 247

Macroeconomic
  context, 270
  crisis. *See* crisis
  environment, 272
  intervention, 191
  management, 178, 184, 371
  model. *See* models
  policy, 250-51, 362-64, 371
Macrolevel, 126, 137, 157, 338
Macropolicy. *See* macroeconomic
  policy
Madagascar, 171
Mafia
  government, 302

private, 302-3
Malaria, 81
Malawi, 167
Malaysia, 250, 292
Mali, 200, 210, 267, 295n. 1
Management
  activity-based, 126
  results-based (RBM), 126-27, 308
  risk, 211-14, 256-57, 268, 300
Manpower Demonstration Research Corporation (MDRC), 88
Market research, 102, 104, 180, 210
Markets
  complementary, 346
  credit, 343, 346
  developed, 347
  insurance, 343
  labor, 8, 227, 343-44
  non-Walrasian, 343, 346
  undeveloped, 347
Mauritius, 175
Means testing, 221, 225
Mechanisms
  coping, 224
    household, 253
  delivery, 4, 52, 60, 267, 359-60
  feedback, 272
  group-based, 223, 256
  individual assessment, 223
  institutional, 359
  targeting. *See* targeting
  traditional, 9
Mesolevel, 126, 129, 137, 157
Methodological rigor, 305, 307
Methods
  collection, 80-82
  evaluation of, 4, 11-17, 56, 82
  experimental, 77, 91-92
  nonexperimental, 77, 79-80, 92
  participatory, 77, 200, 330
  qualitative, 77, 92, 95, 99-112, 130, 184, 202, 209, 253, 330, 332, 338
  quantitative, 99-112, 130, 184, 200, 202, 209, 330, 332
  quasi-experimental, 77, 91

Mexico, 278
  education, 248
  financial crisis, 247, 251-52
  food stamps, 248
  health, 248
  infant growth, 248
  malnutrition, 248
  poverty, 247, 249
  Programa de Empleo Temporal (Temporary Employment Program), 252
  Progresa, 254
  social spending, 248
  unemployment, 247
  wages, 248-49
Microcredit, 57, 297, 326
Microfinance, 6, 25, 62, 205-219, 230
Microfinance institutions (MFI), 205-8, 210, 213-14, 216-17
Microlevel, 8, 69, 71, 79, 86, 126, 137, 157, 270, 338
Minerals, 286
Ministries. *See* government
Mobilization, 10, 57, 284-86, 296, 307, 325
Models
  alternative, 94
  bargaining, 298
  computable general equilibrium (CGE), 14, 171-72, 175, 179
  delivery, 236
  development, 379
  econometric, 96
  evaluation. *See* evaluation
  experimental, 93
  household, 211
  institutional, 239, 367-68, 370
  macroeconomic, 171-72, 175, 363
  social learning, 370
Monitoring
  community, 8, 16, 56-57, 253
  defined, 75
  and evaluation (M&E), 99-101, 102f, 110n. 1, 130, 134, 144-45, 148, 150-51, 159, 159n. 1, 270, 272-74, 373
  outcomes, 101-4, 111

and participatory evaluation (PME).
See Participatory Monitoring and
Evaluation
portfolios, 274
results-based, 68-69, 155
social, 8, 253
vs. evaluation, 75
Mortality, 33, 51, 52f, 53-54, 55f,
57, 298
Mozambique, 6, 20, 71, 167, 176,
128, 183-84, 188, 193, 278, 293,
295n. 1, 297
Multiplier effects. See effects

National Rural Water Supply and
Sanitation Program, 151-52
Nepal, 40, 141, 151, 352
Sahel, 41
Nepotism, 313, 318
Net national product (NNP), 31-35,
4. See also gross national product
Networks
migration, 253
support, 253
social, 45n. 6, 47, 242
Net worth, 46
New Economic Policy, 292
New Zealand, 46
Nigeria, 14, 171, 175, 285, 295n. 1,
301, 308, 313
Nongovernmental organizations
(NGOs). See organizations
Nonmarket channels, 12
North America, 197
Northern Ireland, 284, 300
Nutrition, 8, 60, 76, 222, 230, 265-
80, 326. See also food

Observation, 81
OECD Development Centre, 167, 171,
200, 361
Ombudsman, 159
Operations Evaluation Department
(OED), 3, 6, 14, 20, 21, 106, 113,
180, 226-228, 227, 228, 265-67,
278-79, 314, 362-63, 367-68

Organizations
community-based (CBO)
defined, 11
nongovernmental (NGO)
defined, 10-11
and evaluation, 323-39
Outcome
indicators, 80, 279
measures of, 8, 60, 75-76, 79, 95,
279
monitoring. See monitoring
Overseas Development
Administration, 186, 195n.1, 199
Overseas Development Council, 358

Pakistan, 288, 308
Panama, 249
Participation
resident, 117
second-generation, 156-57
Participatory evaluation (PE), 4, 14-
17, 24, 125-42, 145, 146, 149,
151, 156, 317
approaches to, 145
benefits of, 128-29
conducting, 147-49
mainstreaming, 141
moderating costs for, 129-32, 141
transformative (intrinsic), 126-27,
145
pragmatic (instrumental), 126-27,
145
Participatory monitoring and
evaluation (PME), 143-59
examples of, 150-53
key lessons, 144t
rationale for, 143-44
self-assessments for, 147
tips for, 147-49
written plan for, 146
Participatory poverty assessment
(PPA). See poverty
Participatory rural appraisal (PRA),
146, 149, 150-52
Partnership
donor. See donor
development, 17

evaluation of, 15, 20, 68, 71
joint, 15d
local, 106
long-term, 24
mutual, 15, 156
Payment
    severance, 254
    third-party, 55
People
    displaced, 193
    far-sighted, 41-42
    international vs. local, 148, 152
Performance improvement planning (PIP), 147, 149, 150-51
Perturbations
    institutional responses to, 39-42
Peru, 245, 261n. 1
Pharmaceuticals, 269
Philippines, 54, 179, 211-12
Poland, 10, 302, 306
Polarization, 241
Policy
    choices, 250-53
    development, 30, 70
    pro-growth, 4
    public
        defined, 29-30
        targeted. *See* targeting
Political correctness, 178
Political economy. *See* economy
Political interference, 243
Political leadership, 296
Political parties, 10, 258
Political power, 276, 285
Population, 265-80
    programs. *See* programs
Portfolio
    economic, 214
    policy, 361
Poverty
    alleviation
        BRAC model, 325
        effects, 169
        mechanisms, 231
        methods for evaluating, 330
        strategies. *See* strategies
    causes of, 63-64
    chronic, 164, 225

definition of, 66, 68, 357
dimensions of, 66, 68
incidence of, 193-94, 278, 367, 371
measures of, 104
ongoing studies of, 210-11
participatory assessment of (PPA), 129, 192-93
perceptions of, 6
profiles, 8, 179-80, 252-53, 297
reduction
    business of, 335-36
    challenges in, 334-36
    lessons in, 187-92
    motives for, 120-121, 121f
    priorities in, 63
    strategy. *See* strategies
    rural, 196-98, 224
    transient, 164

Price distortions, 252
Priorities
    bilateral, 24
    individual, 24
    multilateral, 24
    strategic, 71
Privatization, 196, 253, 362
    partial, 236, 238
Productivity, 59, 63, 344-48
Program of Targeted Interventions (PTI), 227-30
Programs. *See also* projects
    bilateral aid, 183-202, 360
    broad-based, 6
    and consequences
        negative,117-19, 118f
        positive, 118-19
    financial adjustment, 65
    holistic, 6, 70
    impact of, 78
    population, 8, 60
    pro-poor, 252, 254-55
    public works, 7
    structural adjustment, 41-42, 105, 235, 243
Project appraisal documents, 279
Project implementation units (PIUs), 315

Projects. *See also* programs
  alternative investment, 38
  effects of. *See* effects
  design of, 8, 96, 202, 225, 238, 270, 274, 339
    complexity of, 270-71, 271
  implementation, 225, 267, 270
  infrastructure of, 6, 24, 58, 60, 62
  public employment, 76
  public works, 235
  rural development, 197
  soft-sector, 229
Propaganda, 285
Provisioning, 222
  pro-poor, 222
  universal, 6, 221
Public health care. *See* health care

Quality assurance, 8, 274
Quality Assurance Group, 21
Quality of life. *See* social well-being

Random assignment, 87-92
Randomization, 13-14, 93, 95-96
Recession, 249
Reciprocity, 42
Recovery, 191, 193, 302
Reforms
  anticorruption, 301-3
  budgetary, 311
  finance, 271
  government, 190-91, 196, 235, 243
  institutional, 304-6, 311, 314-15
  labor market, 253
  land, 292
  legal and judicial, 311
  public sector, 260, 311
  price, 253
Refugees, 221
Regional Centers of Excellence, 16-17
  See also centers for Excellence
Regionalization, 99
Regression equation, 77
  multiple, 169-70
Rehabilitation, 193
Religion, 284, 288, 341, 358
Replication, 201
Reproduction, 267

Research and Evaluation Division (RED), 326
Resettlement, 191
Resource
  aid/nonaid, 362
  allocation, 41-43, 71, 201
  bases, 42
  distribution, 111
Retrospective historical comparisons, 168-69, 176
Roads, 36, 62, 68-69, 90, 159, 361
Rights
  economic, 372
  human, 12, 291, 326
  intellectual property, 176-77
  political, 372
  property, 164
  labor, 255
Royal Ministry of Foreign Affairs of Norway, 19
Rural Development Program (RDP), 326-28, 330
Rural poor, 258-59
Rural rich, 258
Rural underdevelopment, 341-54
Russia, 45n. 6, 247-48, 288, 302. *See also* Soviet Union
Rwanda, 67, 286-89, 291, 293, 308

Safety nets, 4, 7-8, 24, 42, 65, 164, 168, 189-90, 201, 235, 244, 249-54, 257, 259-60, 300, 351-53, 358, 369, 371
St. Vincent, 151
  Rose Place, 151
Samples
  large probability, 100
  quota, 100
  random, 200
  self-selecting, 230
  small probability, 100
Sanitation, 20, 52-53, 53f, 54f, 151-52, 194, 241, 254, 267, 291, 328. *See also* water
SARAR, 151-52
  defined, 159n. 2
Save the Children, 105
School enrollment, 283, 369

Screening tests, 224
Sectors
  agricultural, 278
  evaluation of, 67
  export, 197
  private, 37, 110, 291-92, 302, 368
  public, 37, 269
  productive, 188-190
  social, 65, 188-90
  rural, 175
  third, 348, 350
  transportation, 65
Selectivity
  bias, 79-80
  strategic, 9, 274
Senegal, 316
Services
  and adolescents, 114-17
  coordination. *See* coordination
  extension, 197-98
  gaps in, 117
  infrastructure, 227
  lending, 274
  nonlending, 274
  redundant, 117
  social, 25, 54, 190, 227, 369
Shocks, 212, 219n. 3, 252-53, 256-57, 300, 344, 352, 363
Sierra Leone, 287-88, 295n. 1
Slaves, 344
Slum upgrading, 254
Small Enterprise Foundation, 210
Smallpox, 274, 279
Social costs. *See* costs
Social capital. *See* capital
Social development. *See* development
Social exclusion, 11, 24, 341-54, 372. *See also* inequality
  defined, 341-44
Social funds. *See* funds
Social monitoring. *See* monitoring
Social Monitoring and Early Response Unit, 255
Social norms, 42
Social profitability, 35-37, 39
Social protection, 247-61, 370
Social security systems. *See* systems
Social services. *See* services

Social Summit of the United Nations, 361
Social well-being, 30-35, 37, 293, 337
Society for Participatory Research in Asia, 127
Soldiers, 287
Somalia, 284, 286-88, 300
South Africa. *See* Africa
Southeast Asia. *See* Asia
Soviet Union, 287. *See also* Russia
Special Programme for Africa, 186, 190
Spillover effects. *See* effects
Sri Lanka, 150, 287
Stabilization, 252
Statistical adjustment techniques, 90, 92
Statistical inferences
  cross-sectional, 169-70
  time series, 169-70
Statistical matching, 80
Strategies
  alternative, 14
  development 9, 51, 176-78, 256, 350, 362
  growth, 5, 23
  partnership, 373
  poverty
    alleviation, 164
    reduction, 368-69
  targeting, 268
Studies
  case, 100, 187-88, 196, 209, 331
  follow-up, 110
Sub-Sahara Africa (SSA). *See* Africa
Subsistence, 249
Substitution bias, 93
Subtargeting, 260. *See also* targeting
Sudan, 287
Sugar Protocol of the European Union, 175
Sustainability, 12, 142, 237, 243-44, 325, 337, 368, 372
Survey instruments, 93, 112
Surveys
  cross-sectional, 80-81
  DHS, 296
  household, 99-100, 103, 105, 296

IFRPI, 296
sample, 83, 105
selecting, 100-101, 101f
types of, 100
Swedish International Development Authority (SIDA), 186
Swiss Agency for Development and Cooperation, 19
Switzerland, 141, 176
Systems
  canal. *See* systems, managed irrigation
  community-based information, 111-12
  early warning, 9, 297
  ecological, 42-43. *See also* ecosystems
  economic, 29-30, 34
  informal, 9
  insurance, 9
  legal, 361
  judicial, 164
  managed irrigation, 40, 317
  social security, 9, 243, 361
  socioeconomic, 42-43, 96
  test measurement, 219n.2

Taiwan, 166, 169
Tanzania, 51, 150, 167, 169, 171, 176, 316
Targeting. *See also* subtargeting
  areas, 95
  before-and-after, 224
  costs, 7, 222
  countries, 111
  deficits, 250, 252
  depth vs. width, 225
  design, 224-25, 232
  errors, 357-58
  groups, 5, 83, 97, 179, 230, 324
  growth, 6
  indicators, 221
  interventions, 6, 54, 69, 221-32, 228t
    institutional development impact, 228, 228t, 229
    outcome, 227, 227t, 229
    riskiness of, 228, 228t, 229
    sustainability of, 227, 228t, 229
  mechanisms, 224, 241, 261
  operational, 7
  optimal, 222
  outcomes, 14
  poor, 275
  populations, 111
  policies, 4
  self, 221, 223
  strategies. *See* strategies
  two-stage, 245
  universal, 225
  vs. nontargeting, 221-32
Taxation
  direct, 166-67
  indirect, 166-67
Technical assistance, 69, 278, 287, 364
Technology
  advanced, 139
  communications, 222
  information, 222
  pro-poor development, 222
Terrorism, 285
Thailand, 288, 371
Theft, 288
Theory
  exclusion, 344-46, 348
  income distribution, 353
  program, 113, 114f, 120, 240
Theory-based evaluation. *See* evaluation
Tobacco use, 267
Togo, 175
Tools. *See* surveys
Toxic waste, 50
Transparency, 307-8, 312, 319
Transparency International, 304-5, 307, 309, 312
Transportation, 59
Triangulation, 82, 82b, 184
Trigger event, 288, 296
Tuberculosis, 78, 81
Turkey, 94

Uganda, 51, 141, 183-84, 188, 211-13, 286-87, 291, 293, 313

Ukraine, 302, 306
United Kingdom (UK), 19, 105, 183-84, 191, 194, 199, 273, 360
United Nations Capital Development Fund (UNCDF), 150
United States, 19, 22-23, 25, 80, 88, 113, 278
United States Agency for International Development (USAID), 59, 95, 104, 209-12, 214-15, 218n. 1, 273
Urban poor, 258
Urbanization, 64

Valuation
  compared with evaluation, 29
  defined, 29
  techniques, 36
Variables
  geographic, 80
  individual, 80
  instrumental, 79
  multiple, 330
  political, 80
Venezuela, 247-48, 252
Village Organizations (VOs), 324, 326, 329, 335
Violence, 284-87, 290
Virtual meetings, 209-10
Vulnerability, 212, 218n. 1

War, 283-84, 286, 288, 296, 298, 362
Watchdogs, 314-15
Water, 20, 32-33, 36, 40, 52-53, 53f, 54f, 58, 62, 68-69, 90, 151-52, 194, 241, 243-44, 254, 267, 286, 291, 317, 328, 361, 369. *See also* sanitation
Welfare, 75, 86
Women
  empowering, 54, 218n. 1, 213 304, 307, 325, 331
  and education, 326
  equal opportunities for, 36, 255
  and income generation, 328
  and health care, 269, 326
Women's groups, 201
Workfare, 251, 254, 260

Worksheet planning, 145-46, 146t
Workshops, 147, 150
World Development Report 1990, 6, 31, 33, 49, 61, 184, 206, 361-62, 368-70, 371
World Development Report (WDR) 2001, 211, 215
World Food Fund, 105
World Health Organization (WHO), 274

Zambia, 6, 183-84, 188, 189t, 193, 201
Zimbabwe, 68, 269, 291